Microsoft Power Automate
Cookbook

Automating Business Processes Easily,
Intuitively, and Quickly

Ahmad Najjar

O'REILLY®

Microsoft Power Automate Cookbook

by Ahmad Najjar

Published by O'Reilly Media, Inc., 1005 Gravenstein Highway North, Sebastopol, CA 95472.

O'Reilly books may be purchased for educational, business, or sales promotional use. Online editions are also available for most titles (*http://oreilly.com*). For more information, contact our corporate/institutional sales department: 800-998-9938 or *corporate@oreilly.com*.

Acquisition Editor: Andy Kwan	**Indexer:** WordCo Indexing Services, Inc.
Development Editor: Angela Rufino	**Cover Designer:** Karen Montgomery
Production Editor: Gregory Hyman	**Cover Illustrator:** José Marzan Jr.
Copyeditor: Stephanie English	**Interior Designer:** David Futato
Proofreader: Piper Content Partners	**Interior Illustrator:** Kate Dullea

June 2025:   First Edition

Revision History for the First Edition

2025-05-29:   First Release

See *http://oreilly.com/catalog/errata.csp?isbn=9781098142766* for release details.

978-1-098-14276-6

[LSI]

Table of Contents

Preface

Microsoft Power Automate has transformed the way businesses approach automation. As a low-code platform, it has redefined how organizations create, customize, and automate business processes. Originally launched as Microsoft Flow under the Office 365 umbrella, Power Automate has since evolved into a comprehensive, all-in-one automation solution.

Microsoft's strategy with Power Automate—and the Power Platform as a whole—has centered around empowering business users, or citizen developers. By providing a high level of abstraction and ease of use, Power Automate allows nontechnical users to create custom workflows and business applications without relying on professional developers. This shift has significantly reduced bottlenecks in IT departments, enabling organizations to be more self-sufficient and cost-efficient, saving millions of dollars by redistributing automation tasks from developers to business users.

While Power Automate is built for business users, it also caters to professional developers, offering a highly customizable and scalable platform for building advanced solutions tailored to specific needs. This balance between simplicity and power is crucial in today's fast-changing business landscape, allowing organizations to remain agile, innovative, and responsive.

Over the years, Power Automate has expanded its capabilities, integrating seamlessly with Microsoft 365, Dynamics 365, and a wide range of external data sources. Its deep integration with Azure services offers even greater flexibility for advanced automation and intelligent workflows. Furthermore, Power Automate's AI capabilities through AI Builder empower users to create AI models without extensive programming knowledge, bringing machine learning–driven automation within reach of business users.

Power Automate has grown from a simple automation tool into a comprehensive business solution platform. Its ability to streamline operations, reduce dependency on IT, and provide powerful automation capabilities makes it an essential tool for organizations looking to enhance efficiency, improve workflows, and stay competitive in a rapidly evolving digital world.

This *Microsoft Power Automate Cookbook* is designed to provide hands-on recipes to help you simplify workflows and unlock the basic automation potentials using Power Automate, putting you on track to unlock even more possibilities for your business application and personal productivity.

Why I Wrote This Book

Honestly, I didn't plan to write a book at this stage in my career, despite being approached by many publishing houses. However, when O'Reilly reached out, I felt compelled to take on the challenge! O'Reilly was one of the first and finest publishers I turned to and read in the early 2000s, and I deeply admired their content and authors. When the opportunity arose, I couldn't say no.

This book project presented many challenges. The biggest challenge was deciding how to structure the book. Initially, I wanted to write a more advanced book, incorporating my 20-plus years of experience and perspectives on low-code automation. However, I decided that this book should serve beginners, an often-overlooked audience.

I love automation, and my goal with this book is to demonstrate how anyone can create simple to intermediate-level automation with Power Automate. I hope with this book to create a go-to resource that simplifies Power Automate through practical recipes, helping individuals and organizations build powerful, scalable automation solutions with confidence.

I hope you enjoy it! Happy automating!

Who This Book Is For

The beauty of Power Automate is that you don't need to be highly technical to start using it. This book is designed for a broad audience, including the following:

- Newcomers to Power Automate—and Power Platform—who want to understand automation from the ground up
- Slightly more experienced makers looking for practical, step-by-step guides to enhance their workflows
- Business decision-makers seeking to grasp Power Automate's capabilities in a business context
- Junior developers interested in a jump start into Power Automate

Anyone with an interest in automation should be able to pick up this book and start learning. While experienced Power Automate users might find fewer new insights, the structured recipes provide a valuable reference for solving specific automation challenges.

How This Book Is Organized

This book is structured into 12 chapters. The first two chapters provide an introduction, covering the history of automation and getting started with Power Automate. From Chapter 3 on, the book consists of hands-on recipes, each presented in the standard O'Reilly format: Problem, Solution, Discussion, and See Also.

Readers have the flexibility to either read the book sequentially or jump directly to specific chapters or recipes. Each recipe is self-contained, ensuring that concepts are easy to grasp independently. Where cross-references are needed, appropriate pointers are provided to enhance understanding and continuity.

Conventions Used in This Book

The following typographical conventions are used in this book:

Italic
> Indicates new terms, URLs, email addresses, filenames, and file extensions.

`Constant width`
> Used for program listings, as well as within paragraphs to refer to program elements such as variable or function names, databases, data types, environment variables, statements, and keywords. Also indicates commands or other text that should be typed literally by the user.

> This element signifies a general note.

O'Reilly Online Learning

For more than 40 years, *O'Reilly Media* has provided technology and business training, knowledge, and insight to help companies succeed.

Our unique network of experts and innovators share their knowledge and expertise through books, articles, and our online learning platform. O'Reilly's online learning platform gives you on-demand access to live training courses, in-depth learning paths, interactive coding environments, and a vast collection of text and video from O'Reilly and 200+ other publishers. For more information, visit *https://oreilly.com*.

How to Contact Us

Please address comments and questions concerning this book to the publisher:

O'Reilly Media, Inc.
1005 Gravenstein Highway North
Sebastopol, CA 95472
800-889-8969 (in the United States or Canada)
707-827-7019 (international or local)
707-829-0104 (fax)
support@oreilly.com
https://oreilly.com/about/contact.html

We have a web page for this book, where we list errata, examples, and any additional information. You can access this page at *https://oreil.ly/power-automate-cookbook*.

For news and information about our books and courses, visit *https://oreilly.com*.

Find us on LinkedIn: *https://linkedin.com/company/oreilly-media*.

Watch us on YouTube: *https://youtube.com/oreillymedia*.

Acknowledgments

In the name of Allah, the Most Gracious, the Most Merciful...
"And say, My Lord, increase me in knowledge."

—*Surah Ta-Ha 20:114*

The Prophet Muhammad (PBUH) said:
"Seeking knowledge is an obligation upon every Muslim."

—*Narrated by Ibn Majah*

In the light of these teachings, I'm always motivated and inspired to seek knowledge, not just for worldly success but as a means of fulfilling faith and responsibilities. The empowerment of individuals through knowledge is a core principle of my beliefs, as it enables informed and ethical decision-making that enhances the well-being of communities. I firmly hold that a society rooted in knowledge drives scientific and intellectual progress, paving the way for advancements in technology, medicine, and governance, just like many Islamic scholars and scientists have flourished based on these principles. The pursuit of knowledge is fundamental to upholding justice and fostering ethical leadership, ensuring that institutions are built on wisdom, integrity, and fairness. I strongly believe that continuous learning nurtures critical thinking, empowering individuals to discern truth from misinformation and make sound, ethical decisions in both their personal and professional lives. The pursuit of both religious and practical knowledge is essential in shaping well-rounded individuals who contribute meaningfully to all societies. Ultimately, a knowledge-based culture is the foundation for progress, moral integrity, and an unwavering commitment to truth and wisdom. Seeking knowledge is a fundamental pillar in life! It plays a vital role in spiritual development, serving as a form of worship that strengthens faith and deepens one's connection with the All-Knowing Creator. These are some of the principles that I hold at the core of my values.

> *May the knowledge and experience I share in this book serve as a light for those who seek knowledge and benefit all who come across it.*
>
> *—Ahmad Najjar*

Writing this book has been an incredible journey, and this book wouldn't have been possible without the guidance, blessings, and assistance of Allah, all praise and gratitude belong to Him!

I owe my deepest gratitude to many incredible people for their support, encouragement, and guidance.

First and foremost, my heartfelt thanks go to my parents, whose unwavering prayers, endless encouragement, and belief in me have been a guiding force, a source of motivation and blessings, not just with this book but in every step of my life. To my family, my loving wife and my two amazing sons, the best two men in my life, your endless love, patience, and support have made this journey worthwhile. Your encouragement and care have kept me grounded and inspired. To my brother and sister, thank you for your love and support. Your presence in my life has always been a source of strength and reassurance.

A special thanks to Jussi Roine, who offered his help at the very beginning of this project and later took on the role of a reviewer, providing invaluable feedback that helped shape this book. I am equally grateful to Nick Brattoli, my second reviewer, whose thoughtful insights and encouraging words made me feel incredibly proud of this work.

To Claire Edgson, your mentorship, guidance, and support have been instrumental throughout this journey. Your belief in my abilities and willingness to share your wisdom mean more than words can express.

I am deeply grateful to everyone at O'Reilly who played a role in making this book possible. The confidence, dedication, patience, and expertise of the entire team have been invaluable throughout this journey. From refining content to shaping its presentation, each contribution has enriched the final product.

A special thank-you to those who ensured clarity, precision, and structure, making this book the best it could be: Andy, Angela, Gregory, Stephanie, David, José, and Kate. I'm truly fortunate to have worked with such a talented and dedicated team—this project would not have been possible without each and every one of you!

I also extend my gratitude to the tech community, whose insights, discussions, and challenges continue to inspire and push me forward. The collective knowledge and camaraderie within this community have been a driving force in my professional and personal growth.

Finally, to everyone who has contributed, encouraged, or inspired me along the way, thank you! This book is not just a reflection of my experiences but a testament to the incredible people who have supported me throughout this journey.

My Tribute

The Prophet Muhammad (PBUH) said:

"Indeed, Allah, His angels, the inhabitants of the heavens and the earth, even the ant in its nest and the fish in the sea, send prayers upon the one who teaches people goodness."

—Narrated by At-Tirmidhi

I dedicate this work to the Master and the best of those who taught people goodness, our Prophet Muhammad (peace and blessings be upon him).

To the great Islamic scholars whose knowledge and inventions paved the way for the advancements and technologies we rely on today: Al-Khwarizmi, the father of algebra, whose mathematical foundations shape our modern world; Al-Jazari, the father of robotics, whose ingenuity in mechanics and automation laid the groundwork for modern engineering; Ibn al-Haytham, the visionary who gave the world the science of optics, unlocking the mysteries of light and vision; Abbas ibn Firnas, the dreamer who dared to challenge the skies, inspiring generations to reach for the impossible; and many others whose brilliance shaped civilizations yet whose names are often forgotten in history's pages.

Their work was not just knowledge, their inventions were not just ideas; they were the seeds of progress! And though ideological erasers have tried to remove their names, their impact remains woven into the very fabric of the world we live in today.

To the resilient souls who endure hardship, to those who fight for justice and freedom, and to the countless voices that were silenced under the weight of oppression. To the brave hearts who stand against injustice, refusing to surrender their dignity. To those who suffer in silence yet carry the unshakable spirit of hope. And to those who have perished, beneath rubble, behind bars, in tyranny's dungeons where nightmares became reality, and in the forgotten corners of the world where their cries went unheard, your struggles are not in vain, and your stories will not be erased.

To those who have been starved to death, to those who have lost the souls of their souls, for every child who died before they were born, and for every child who lost a mother, a father, or both, your absence is a wound on the conscience of humanity, and your stolen futures will not be forgotten.

To those who have lost their limbs, to those who shake in pain, who tremble in the cold and the darkness, and to those who bid their last farewells to their loved ones, I grieve with you, I will never forget you, and I dedicate these words to you.

To the children who wake up to the sound of destruction instead of laughter, to the mothers who carry both grief and resilience in their hearts, and to the fathers who fight battles unseen to provide safety and dignity for their families, I see you, the world must see you, and history must never forget you.

To those who endure, to those who fight for a better tomorrow, and to those who refuse to let the light of humanity fade, I dedicate this to you. May we never lose faith in a future where justice prevails, where knowledge illuminates the path forward, and where no one is forgotten.

To the dreamers, the seekers of truth, and those who refuse to accept silence as an answer, may knowledge be your light, may words be your shield, and may your courage echo beyond borders.

With all the sorrow that weighs upon this world, I still believe in hope—hope that one day, suffering will no longer be your resident pain. That the echoes of injustice will be drowned out by the voices of those who refuse to be silenced. That knowledge, wisdom, and unity will lead us toward a world where dignity is not a privilege but a right. That one day, we will come together in joy and prosperity.

This book is for you!

CHAPTER 1

History of Automation

In this chapter, I'll briefly explain how automation became mainstream in every aspect of our lives. I'll review the correlation between people and automation and how it impacts us. Then I'll define Power Automate and the platform it belongs to. Finally, I'll discuss what makes up a flow in Power Automate, the different automation types Power Automate provides, its correlation with Microsoft 365, and when and why to use Power Automate.

Life Before Automation

I reckon that a long list of things might cross your mind if someone said, "life before automation," such as how life used to look before computers, cell phones, cars, or any modern technology, but what I'd like to highlight here are a couple of humanity's milestones that were vital and relevant to automation.

In 1206, Ismail Al-Jazari invented the first crankshaft (Figures 1-1 and 1-2), a piece of machinery (technology) that transforms continuous rotary motion into a linear reciprocating motion. It was fundamental to modern machinery such as the internal combustion engine, automatic controls, and the steam engine, which was an essential stepping stone in the Industrial Revolution in the 1700s.

Figure 1-1. Ismail Al-Jazari's crankshaft

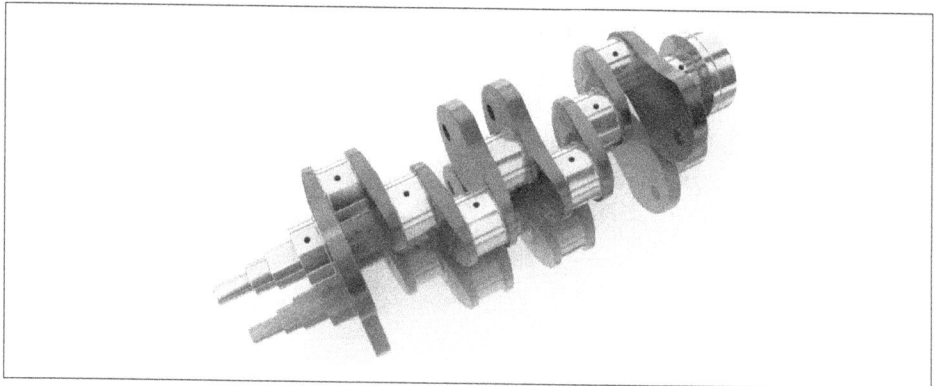

Figure 1-2. Modern crankshaft

The Father of Robotics

Ismail Al-Jazari (1136–1206) was a prominent Muslim polymath, inventor, and engineer. Renowned as the "father of robotics," Al-Jazari made significant contributions to the fields of mechanical engineering and automation. His most influential work, *The Book of Knowledge of Ingenious Mechanical Devices* (1206), documents over 100 mechanical inventions and is considered a masterpiece in engineering history. Among his notable inventions are the first programmable humanoid robot, a water-powered automaton used to serve drinks, and sophisticated water-raising devices like the crankshaft-driven pump. He also designed intricate clocks, such as the famous Elephant Clock, which combined mechanics and cultural symbolism, and created automated mechanisms like self-filling lamps and musical fountains. Al-Jazari's innovations laid foundational principles for modern robotics and engineering.

Humans tried to harness the power of steam long before the Industrial Revolution. The first recorded primitive steam engine, the aeolipile, was developed between 30 and 15 BCE. However, it wasn't until 1712 that Thomas Newcomen's steam engine became the first commercially successful design, primarily used to pump water out of coal mines. This type of steam engine remained the dominant technology until the early 20th century. Another significant breakthrough came in the 1770s when James Watt improved steam engine efficiency, making it viable for powering textile machinery and driving industrial advancements.

From 1900 through the 1920s, relay logic was introduced with factory electrification, which is a type of control system that uses relays, switches, and other simple components to create a logical sequence of operations. It works by creating a series of circuits that are connected to relays and switches in a way that creates a specific sequence of events. With relay logic, central control rooms became common. However, most process controls were only on-off. Operators' typical daily job was to monitor charts drawn by recorders that plotted data from instruments. They needed to manually turn switches on or off to make any corrections. Color-coded lights were also used in control rooms to send signals to workers in a plant to make certain changes manually. Automatic controllers were introduced in the 1930s and were able to make calculated automatic changes in response to deviations from a set point rather than manual on-off control.

Reading through this brief history, you'll notice that humans used "automation" by harnessing the available "technologies and mechanisms" to reduce human intervention in their daily routines. They wanted to be "productive" by finding a better use for their physical and mental powers. Life before automation seemed tiresome and time-consuming and needed a lot of workforce and effort.

Even though circumstances, technologies, and mechanisms were different back then—versus what we have harnessed today—the motives for automation are very much the same. While steam engines powered the Industrial Revolution, the next great leap came with electronic computing. In the 1960s, the first modern computers emerged, marking the transition from mechanical power to digital processing. Powered by silicon chips and transistors, these computers revolutionized industries, paving the way for today's advanced computing technologies.

Fast-forward to today, where everything has become or is becoming digitally transformed, where automation is at the heart of digitization. Automation covers a wide range of applications ranging from a household thermostat controlling the temperature of an underground heating system to a modern mega-factory control system with tens of thousands of input measurements and output control signals. Automation has been achieved by various means, including mechanical, hydraulic, pneumatic, electrical, and electronic devices (including computers). Complicated systems, such as modern robotic factories, airplanes, and ships, typically use all these combined techniques. Modern automation, aided by AI and now generative AI, has dimensions beyond reducing human intervention. One example includes adding a cushion of safety, like the autopilot in airplanes and self-driving capabilities in vehicles.

Automation has become so mainstream that it's embedded in every aspect, device, system, and process we use in our lives. Therefore, if you mention automation today in its absolute form, it might be contextually and lyrically lacking, meaning that you need to specify what type of automation you're discussing.

Life Before BPA

Business process automation (BPA) is the automation of simple to complex business processes and functions beyond conventional data manipulation and record-keeping activities using an automation-enabler toolkit. BPA enables organizations to achieve work simplicity, productivity, and efficiency, in addition to digital transformation, cost containment, and more.

So, what did life look like before BPA? Or at least before you automated your daily routines with a BPA toolkit? In a world swarming with data, you constantly move information from one device to another and from one "data system" to another. You receive inputs or notifications on your devices and cascade them into another routine action. You're also using many systems, apps, and services to collaborate and organize your work and the way you work. Nevertheless, you might still remember tasks across pen and paper, Excel sheets, or even by flagging emails. Like many people, you might have become a great systems integrator; however, humans aren't especially efficient system integrators. Most of these "data systems" are not designed to integrate with one another. Integration among these systems will instantly become a sophisticated

IT project that could take a long time to accomplish, require extensive integration expertise, and cost a lot from your company's budget.

This is where most BPA toolkits come to the rescue. You can automate routine tasks to be more efficient as a business user and use your brain cycles on real work instead of wasting it on mundane tasks. By focusing on real work, you might also find new ways to accomplish things using BPA.

People and Automation

Interestingly enough, the sole purpose of automation is to reduce—or sometimes eliminate—human intervention, not to marginalize people but to reduce the time and effort spent on repetitive routine tasks. As a result, human error reduction and quality would increase, and productivity and consistency would increase too.

Relieving humans from repetitive work means more time spent on core work and less on routines. In some industries, it means reduced direct human labor costs and expenses. In other industries, automation has relieved people of dangerous work stresses and occupational injuries. Automation has also helped remove people from dangerous working environments like nuclear facilities, chemical facilities, outer space, fire, etc.

Implementing automation also has its cons. It often comes with an initial high cost, whether it's factory automation (production lines), BPA, the cost of licenses, or even home automation where smart home appliances (automation-enabled) are much pricier than standard ones.

Reducing or eliminating human intervention also comes with a cost, especially when automated processes are defective. Automated production lines can rapidly propagate mistakes if the systems in place aren't perfect. In the context of BPA, defective workflows could mean the loss of valuable data, documents, or files.

Implementing preplanned automated responses for every situation is often difficult because it's hard to anticipate every contingency. Therefore, unanticipated costs and delays may occur due to unanticipated interventions and changes.

Again, let's take automated production lines as an example; an unanticipated input in a factory's automated production line could result in defective products, which in turn means production has to stop for hours or days to figure out the cause of the issue. Additionally, recollecting defective products can produce unanticipated costs if they reach the market. The same applies to BPA, a workflow with certain business logic; an unanticipated input can cause delays or even the birth of a new unnecessary project to fix the issue(s) with that business logic.

Automation deployment may seriously disrupt people, especially when no similar jobs are readily available. In most mass production factories, human-powered production lines have been replaced by automated production lines requiring less human supervision. For instance, some production lines have been replaced with robotic arms requiring even less human supervision than automated ones. Though BPA doesn't have the same immediate impact on jobs, the cumulative impact of continuous BPA deployment can affect some traditional roles in some businesses.

Now, this is where the idea of automation is seriously misunderstood by many, who think it is putting people out of their jobs. While automation deployment could contribute to putting some workers out of their jobs, there is evidence that new industries and jobs in the technology sector outweigh the economic effect of people being displaced by automation, according to the World Bank's world development reports (*https://oreil.ly/ER-NT*).

Implementing automation also folds into using a power source, whether electricity or fuel, contributing to the CO_2 emission problem. Ironically, automation is being used to help with sustainability, where automation-enabled machines are put into standby mode when idle for a certain period to reduce the amount of power used. Most BPA services run in cloud data centers with their own sustainability plans to reduce power usage.

We evolved from the crankshaft to the robotic arm, from pen and paper to BPA workflows! This evolution is more of a necessity and less of a facility because we live in a fast-paced world where we demand things immediately. Traditional human-powered production lines can no longer accommodate high demand, whether it's for food, cars, or even devices. As a result, automated production lines must replace traditional ones. The same applies to the way we work, where business processes must move at a high pace in all workplaces and there is no room for inefficient activities like pen and paper or conventional Excel sheets; as a result, BPA must replace traditional time-consuming ways of work.

And this is where BPA toolkits, like Microsoft Power Automate, come in handy!

What Is Microsoft Power Automate?

Microsoft Power Automate (formerly known as Microsoft Flow) is a *low-code* cloud-based automation service and toolkit by Microsoft for building automated workflows and business process automation to streamline businesses for simplicity. Power Automate is one of Microsoft's Power Platform services. Low code is not a new programming approach; it has been around for over a decade. However, the definition could slightly change if you define pro developers' low-code platforms versus business users' (nondevelopers'). We'll define *low-code* in the latter context, the one meant for Power Automate.

A *low-code toolkit* is a platform to facilitate self-service programming for business users and nondevelopers, enabling them to build useful functional automation (workflows), apps, or reports. You could think of some of Excel's features as low code. For example, you can connect to various databases and data sources in Excel without writing code. Similarly, you can connect to databases and data sources with Power Automate without writing code, allowing you to embed data in your automation (workflows).

Does that mean you are limited? No, although low-code platforms have a high amount of abstraction—making it easier for nondevelopers to create applications—most low-code platforms allow big room for expansion in case programmers are required to step in to add more complexity to whatever nondevelopers have built. This facility also applies to Power Automate.

A cloud-based toolkit implies the service runs on another computer/server on the web, which indicates it's not taking processing resources out of your computer. It also might mean that you don't need to download special software to build your automation (workflows) or apps, whereas the design authoring experience is browser-based. Similarly, this applies to Power Automate, where the design authoring experience is browser-based. However, one of the recent additions to Power Automate (Power Automate Desktop [PAD]) requires you to install a desktop app on your machine. Nevertheless, the desktop app saves your PAD automation in the cloud.

Microsoft Power Platform

The Microsoft Power Platform has a rich history marked by its evolution as a suite of business applications designed to empower organizations through low-code and no-code solutions. Microsoft recognized the increasing demand for tools that allow users with varying technical backgrounds to create custom applications and automate processes without extensive coding expertise. This realization led to the formation of the Power Platform in 2016, combining Power BI, Power Apps, and Microsoft Flow (now Power Automate) into an integrated suite.

The Power Platform's historical journey includes continuous enhancements and expansions, marked by the introduction of new capabilities and services. The platform's transformative power lies in its ability to democratize app development, data analytics, and workflow automation across organizations, fostering a culture of innovation and agility. As Microsoft embraced the paradigm of the citizen developer, the Power Platform became instrumental in enabling individuals with diverse skill sets to contribute actively to digital transformation initiatives within their respective domains. This ongoing commitment to accessibility and innovation has positioned the Power Platform as a dynamic force in the realm of business application development and process automation.

Microsoft Power Platform includes the following products:

Power BI
A service for visualizing data and building reports.

Power Apps
A service for building custom business applications.

Power Automate
A service for building automated workflows and business process automation.

Copilot Studio (formerly Power Virtual Agents)
A service for building chatbots.

Power Pages (formerly Power Apps Portals)
A service for building, hosting, and managing external-facing websites.

Power Fx
A low-code syntax for implementing logic in Power Apps, Dataverse calculated columns, and Power Automate Dataverse triggers.

AI Builder
A service for building, customizing, and training AI models that can be consumed across the Power Platform. It also includes prebuilt AI models that can be used right out of the gate!

Dataverse (formerly Common Data Service)
A storage and data management service that can be used across the Power Platform.

The Power Platform is a one-stop-shop for all your development needs, from business intelligence, reporting, app development, and connectivity to business process automation, storage and data, and chatbots (Figure 1-3).

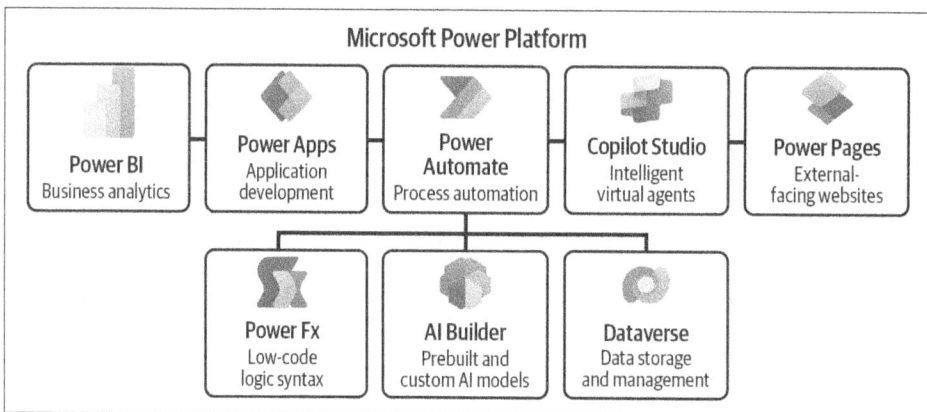

Figure 1-3. Power Platform overview

The Power Platform is under continuous development, enhancement, and expansion to accommodate the different business and technical exponential needs for building business apps. That said, the Power Platform is subject to change at any time. Therefore, some of the information and knowledge provided in this book is subject to change.

Connectors

In the dynamic landscape of modern business processes, *connectors* serve as the linchpin for effective communication and data flow between different components of the Power Platform, including Power Automate, Power Apps, and Power BI. Connectors are essentially prebuilt interfaces that facilitate the interaction between the Power Platform and external systems, databases, or cloud services, eliminating the need for extensive custom coding. The robust catalog of connectors empowers users to effortlessly link their applications to a myriad of third-party services, enabling a streamlined and interconnected approach to automating workflows, building applications, and extracting valuable insights from data sources across the enterprise.

Connectors play a fundamental role in the Microsoft Power Platform, acting as the bridge that seamlessly integrates various data sources, applications, and services into a unified ecosystem. A connector allows you to connect to an underlying service in the context of your credentials. For example, you can use the Outlook.com connector to connect to the Outlook.com service, in the context of your *@outlook.com* email and password, to send emails on your behalf from a Power Automate flow.

The connector concept is viable because almost every service has an API or multiple APIs. An API is a piece of code or program that allows two applications to talk to each other. A good example is mobile apps, where almost every app uses an API. So, when you check the weather on your cell phone, the weather app connects to the weather service provider through an API to get the weather forecast information.

A connector is a wrapper around an API that allows the underlying service to talk to Power Automate. Each connector provides a set of operations classified as triggers and actions. Once you have connected to the underlying service by creating a connection using your credentials on that service, you can leverage the different operations in your flows that the connector provides.

Microsoft categorizes connectors based on their licensing scheme:

Standard connectors
> Included in your standard Microsoft 365 subscription.

Premium connectors
> Not part of your standard Microsoft 365 subscription and require an additional license through standalone or seeded plans. Standalone plans are dedicated plans

purchased individually based on what you plan to build with Power Automate, while seeded plans are rights gained to use Power Automate seeded from other purchased plans or subscriptions.

> Microsoft 365 includes a suite of productivity tools such as Outlook, Teams, and SharePoint, and it also provides access to automation—and low-code development—through the Power Platform. More on Microsoft 365 later in this chapter.

Any other grouping of connectors will fall under these two categories—in most cases, under the latter category, premium connectors.

> To learn more about Power Automate plans and licensing, refer to Microsoft's documentation (*https://oreil.ly/0DvF0*).

What Makes a Flow?

Workflows built using Power Automate are called *flows*. From this point forward, we'll call any automation or workflow in Power Automate a flow.

Let's illustrate the main components that make up a flow in Power Automate.

Triggers

A *trigger* initiates a flow, which activates the sequence of steps (actions) that comes after. The type of trigger you choose for your flow will decide the type of automation. We'll discuss this in detail in the next section.

Some flow trigger scenarios are connector-based, meaning that the flow will initiate based on an event on the service side. For example, we may want to begin a flow when we get an email from x, or initiate a flow when an item is created on some data source. However, some other trigger scenarios are not connector-based—for example, initiating a weekly flow on Mondays at 10:00 A.M.

Power Automate allows you to define only one trigger for each flow you build; however, some triggers can be initiated based on combined conditions, such as when an item in a data source is created or modified. A few other triggers allow you to choose when to initiate the trigger.

You can add trigger conditions for any given trigger in Power Automate by adding expressions (Excel-like formulas) in the trigger settings section.

Actions

A Power Automate flow can have only one trigger step defined. Therefore, any step(s) after the trigger step is an *action* (Figure 1-4).

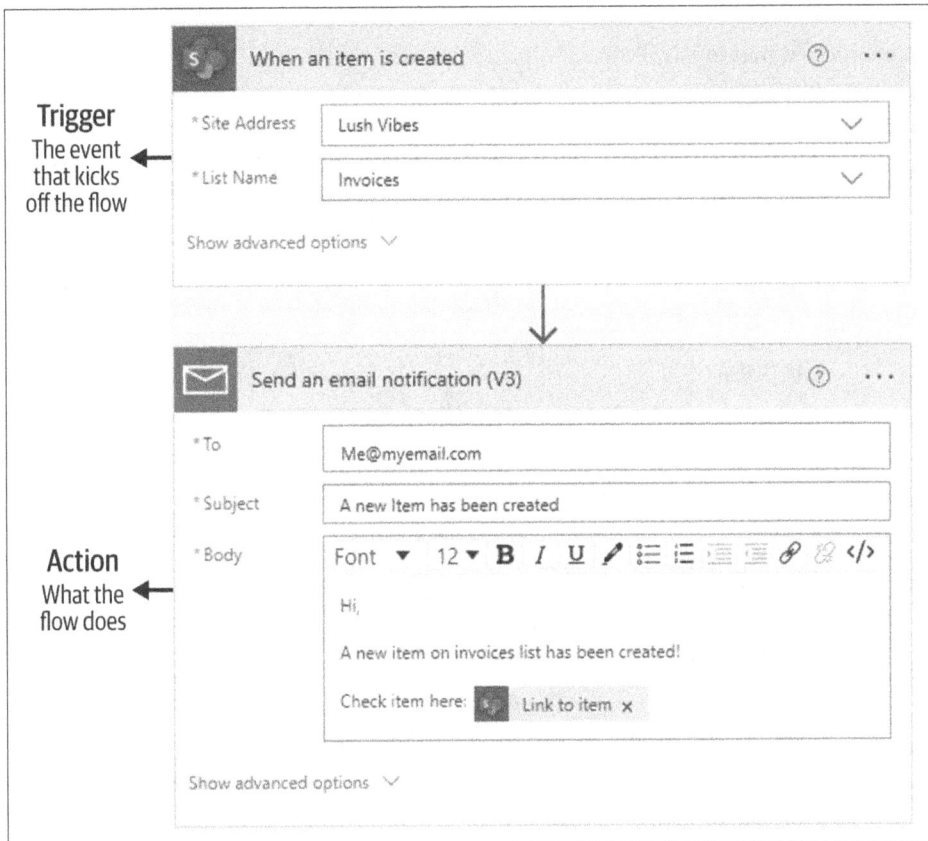

Figure 1-4. Trigger and action

Just like triggers, actions are classified as connector-based and nonconnector-based. A connector-based action executes an operation against the underlying service, such as getting items from a data source or sending an email from your Outlook.com account. A nonconnector-based action doesn't need any connection, as it executes data operations locally (on the flow level, not on the service level), such as initiating or setting a variable, filtering a collection of items, or using a scope action that bundles multiple actions together.

Finally, an action has its own settings section, just like triggers. One of the most important settings is the "configure run after."

Flow of Data

Flow of data is how triggers and actions output stream in a flow, from one step to the other. An output from a trigger can be used as an input in any of the actions that follow. Trigger or action outputs are called *dynamic content* in Power Automate.

As mentioned previously, Power Automate allows you to define one trigger per flow. A trigger may have one input, multiple inputs, or not have any inputs at all, and because a trigger is the first step you need to define, no outputs are coming from a previous step. A trigger usually has multiple outputs, which will be available as inputs for the following action(s). The same applies to the first action you define (after the trigger), as its outputs will be available for the following actions (Figure 1-5).

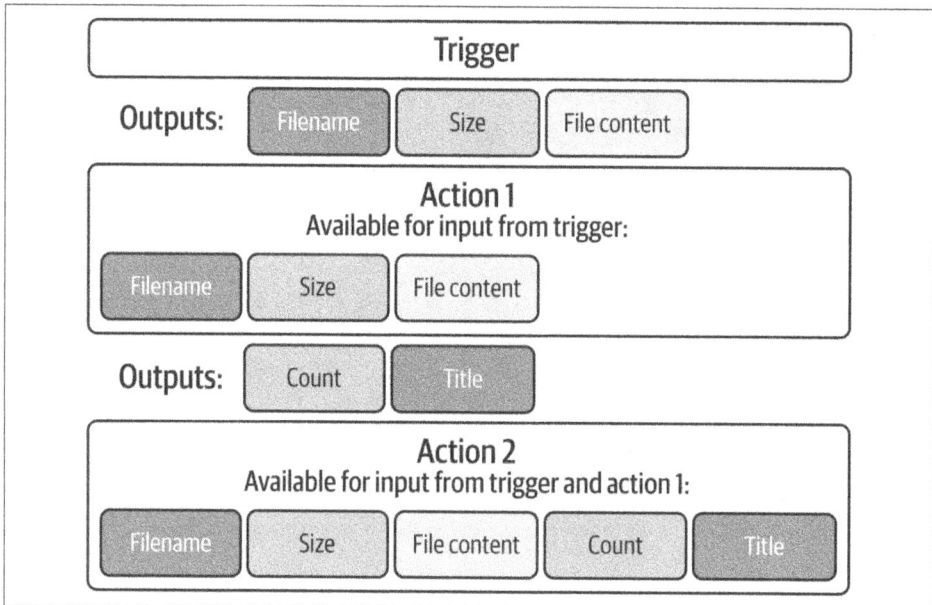

Figure 1-5. Flow of data

Another aspect of the "flow of data" is how actions' executions stream in a flow. Generally, actions in a Power Automate flow are executed sequentially (waterfall style). However, that doesn't mean you're limited, as there are actions, features, and workarounds that enable you to do more than one-lined sequential flows.

Power Automate flows allow you to define parallel branches, which means that you can run several streams of actions simultaneously. This facility will impact action outputs, as the actions' outputs will not be accessible in the other simultaneous branch(es); nevertheless, once these branches converge, all outputs from all actions will be accessible in the converging step/action onward (Figure 1-6).

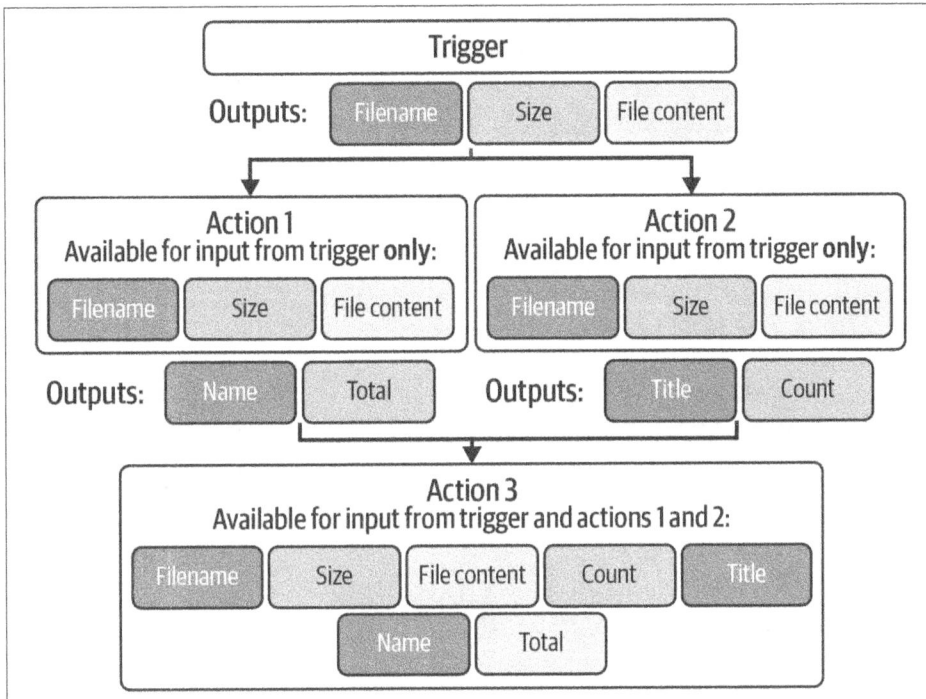

Figure 1-6. Parallel branch flow of data

It's important to mention that sometimes outputs are not visible. Each output has a datatype; similarly, each action input expects a specific datatype, therefore, the outputs won't be visible if datatypes don't match. In such a case, you need an expression to convert the output to match the action input.

Expressions

Expressions are simplified functions/formulas that perform inline data manipulations, calculations, conversions, comparisons, and more in your flow. The flow designer has a built-in help experience that shows you how to use each expression as you build your flow (Figure 1-7).

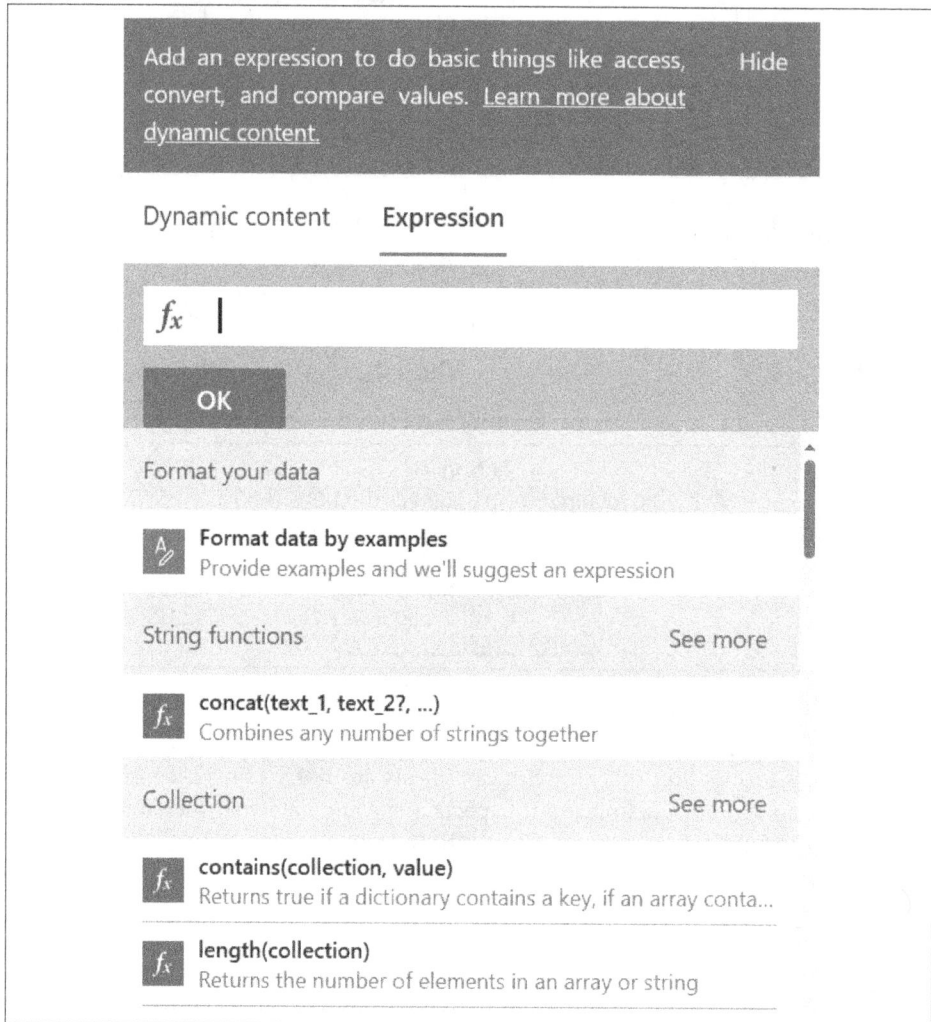

Add an expression to do basic things like access, convert, and compare values. Learn more about dynamic content.   Hide

Dynamic content   **Expression**

f_x |

OK

Format your data

Format data by examples
Provide examples and we'll suggest an expression

String functions   See more

concat(text_1, text_2?, ...)
Combines any number of strings together

Collection   See more

contains(collection, value)
Returns true if a dictionary contains a key, if an array conta...

length(collection)
Returns the number of elements in an array or string

Figure 1-7. Expressions

Expressions are an essential component of most flows. It's sometimes necessary to reformat or convert a trigger/action output before passing it into the following action as input.

In Power Automate, expressions are categorized by their general purpose:

String
> Used to perform operations on string datatypes only, like concatenation, string replacement, substring, and more.

Collection
> Used to perform operations on collections, generally arrays, strings, and, sometimes, dictionaries (`first`, `last`, `contains`, and more).

Logical
> Used to work with conditions, compare values and expression results, or evaluate various kinds of logic (`if`, `and`, `or`, and more).

Conversion
> Used to change a value's datatype or format; you can use these conversion functions. For example, you can change a value from a Boolean to an integer (`bool`, `int`, `string`, and more).

Math
> Used to perform math operations on integers and floats (`add`, `div`, `sub`, and more).

Date and time
> Used to perform date and time operations on date/time datatypes (`addDays`, `addMinutes`, `dateDifference`, and more).

Referencing and workflow
> Used to perform workflow-related operations, such as getting details about a workflow instance at runtime, working with the inputs for instantiating flows, or referencing the outputs from triggers and actions. For example, you can reference the outputs from one action and use that data in a later action (`action`, `body`, `item`, and more).

URI parsing
> Used to perform operations against uniform resource identifiers (URIs) and get various property values for these URIs (`uriHost`, `uriQuery`, `uriPath`, and more).

Manipulation
> Used to perform operations with JSON objects and XML nodes (`addProperty`, `removeProperty`, `xpath`, and more).

Power Automate has an abundance of expressions you can pick and choose from; we're not going to discuss each one individually. Nevertheless, we'll explain the ones used in the flow recipes in this book. For more about expressions, take a look at the workflow expressions documentation (*https://oreil.ly/6IA43*).

Power Automate expressions and Power Fx are separate languages, but Power Fx is increasingly being integrated into Power Platform automation scenarios. Power Fx is generally easier to use and more readable, while Power Automate expressions are better suited for data manipulation in flows.

Power Automate Automation Types

Automation needs differ from one case to another, so you need to have the flexibility to trigger flows based on your use case(s). This variation of needs demands that the automation tool you choose must provide different ways to initiate automation/flows, which Power Automated does offer. So, in short, the type of trigger you require to start your flow determines the type of flow you need to create.

Cloud Flows

Cloud flows represent automated workflows that are designed to connect and automate tasks across different cloud-based services and applications. These cloud-based workflows enable users to create, manage, and automate processes that span multiple platforms without the need for intricate coding or with minimal technical experience. Cloud flows are highly versatile, allowing users to integrate services like Microsoft 365, SharePoint, Dynamics 365, and various third-party applications.

Users can trigger cloud flows based on specific events or conditions, such as receiving an email, updating a database record, or posting on social media. The flexibility and scalability of cloud flows make them a powerful tool for enhancing productivity and efficiency by automating routine tasks and orchestrating complex business processes in the cloud environment.

There are three types of cloud flows in Power Automate:

Automated
> Triggered by an event (usually on the service side). Similar to when you create a file, receive an email in your inbox, or an item is added to a data source that you use.

Instant
> Manually (on-demand) triggered flows. An example is when you push a button in your Power Automate mobile app or run the flow for a selected file.

Scheduled
> Triggered on a preplanned date and time schedule you decide beforehand, such as daily, weekly, monthly, etc. An example is sending a weekly reminder to your team members to submit their timesheets.

Desktop Flows

Cloud flows require that you create the trigger and the sequence of actions to automate a certain task. In contrast, *desktop flows*, built using PAD, are UI-based automation, which produces the sequence of actions by recording the user conducting a task on a Windows desktop. These automations are then executed by replicating the recorded actions directly on that desktop, allowing you to turn manual desktop tasks into automated workflows.

This type of automation is also known as *robotic process automation* (RPA), leveraging software robots (bots) and AI to interact with applications just like a human would. PAD enables businesses to automate repetitive, rule-based processes across modern and legacy systems.

Here are two examples of what you can do with desktop flows (PAD):

- Organize your files and documents in a dedicated folder.
- Move data from a legacy system (desktop app) that doesn't have an API to a cloud data source, or vice versa.

Business Process Flows

Business process flows (BPFs) allow you to build tailored stage-based flows aided by a visual user experience to lead users through the predefined desired business process. That way, you can define the logic, conditions, interactions, and activities required to complete the business process. In each stage, you can define a set of steps to be fulfilled to complete that stage. The visual indicator tells people where they are in the business process. BPFs reduce the need for training because users, especially new ones, don't have to focus on what to do because they can let the process guide them.

A good example of when to use BPFs is the onboarding process. An onboarding process is typically established and predefined in most organizations. HR personnel are familiar with its required stages and steps. This allows all business process participants to collaborate and complete the onboarding process by fulfilling the necessary steps and stages.

While BPFs are not traditional workflows, some people have informally referred to them as workflows within model-driven apps. However, BPFs are primarily used for process guidance, while automation is now handled through Power Automate.

Power Automate and Microsoft 365

Microsoft 365 is a productivity and cloud-based service suite containing online services such as Outlook, OneDrive, and Teams. It also includes programs formerly marketed as Microsoft Office, such as Word, Excel, and PowerPoint. Microsoft 365 also has enterprise products and services associated with these products, such as Share-Point and Yammer. Power Automate is part of these cloud-based services under the Microsoft 365 umbrella, which gives a powerful message about the strong correlation between Power Automate and the rest of the services under Microsoft 365. (During the writing of this book, Microsoft rebranded Office 365 to Microsoft 365. So, to save you the confusion, some articles, blogs, books, and even Power Automate connectors still refer to Microsoft 365 as Office 365.)

One of the heavily used cloud-based services in Microsoft 365 is *SharePoint*. Share-Point is a web-based collaboration workspace that facilitates storing, managing, and sharing content, data, and information using lists and libraries. According to Micro-soft, SharePoint has over two hundred million users (*https://oreil.ly/g3AKA*).

Previously, workflows in SharePoint were created using either SharePoint Designer (SPD) for low-code workflows or Windows Workflow Foundation (WWF) and .NET for custom-coded workflows. While SPD provided a low-code solution, it was often limited and cumbersome, requiring workarounds for more complex scenarios. On the other hand, custom-coded workflows demanded significant development effort, making even simple automation tasks complex and time-consuming. In conjunction with the announcement of the deprecation of SPD, Microsoft introduced Power Automate (then Microsoft Flow) as the successor to replace SPD workflows. Unlike its predecessors, Power Automate became a universal automation tool, not only for SharePoint but for all Microsoft 365 applications and beyond.

The SharePoint connector in Power Automate was one of the first to be introduced in the first batch of connectors. There were fewer than 100 connectors when Microsoft Flow was still in beta in 2016. This introduction sent SharePoint users on an adoption bonanza. As the SharePoint connector persisted in getting better and better with new actions and triggers introduced periodically, adoption exploded exponentially, mak-ing the SharePoint connector one of the most used connectors in Power Automate. (Note that there has been no official report from Microsoft until now, though based on all the organizations and companies I have worked with since 2017, observations and reports always showed that the SharePoint connector is the top-used connector among all the other connectors.)

Another heavily used service in Microsoft 365 is *Teams*, which launched in 2017 as a successor to Skype for Business, a chat and video conferencing workspace, file stor-age, and application integration offering from Microsoft. Throughout the COVID-19 pandemic, Teams gained heavy traction as collaboration and meetings moved to vir-tual platforms. According to Microsoft, Teams now has over three hundred million monthly active users (*https://oreil.ly/Hi9yK*).

By design, Teams abstracts some SharePoint functionalities in its folds. For instance, every "team" you create in Teams is a Microsoft 365 group (a SharePoint site, basi-cally), meaning that you can leverage SharePoint libraries (file storage) and lists (data and information storage) in Teams. This correlation between Teams and SharePoint—among other factors—turned Teams into the "new collaboration workspace" for almost every organization, as organizations now prefer to surface their apps, documents, data, and information through Teams (instead of SharePoint). Nevertheless, that doesn't mean that SharePoint is going anywhere; it is still being used heavily and has its own unique direct and indirect applications.

This shift to the new collaborative workspace imposed its necessities, as organizations needed to implement automation as part of this "new collaboration workspace," Teams. Microsoft Teams has its own connector under Power Automate to answer those automation needs.

Almost every service under Microsoft 365 has its unique story and use case. However, what makes things even more interesting from an automation perspective is that each of these services has its unique connector in Power Automate to accommodate all your automation needs for Microsoft 365.

Power Automate: When and Why?

Power Automate is a powerful automation service indeed! It covers a vast area of automation use cases. Moreover, because of its native nature of integration-ability with other services and systems, it gained a reputation for integration, but whether to use it as an integration service is a different question. In this section, we'll go through use cases and when and why (and why not) to use Power Automate to automate routines and/or integrate with data and services.

Let me start by stating the obvious: Power Automate is one of the strongest tools for personal productivity and business applications. Due to its ease of use, low code, and intuitive nature, Power Automate is an easy pick for anyone to start automating daily routines, like setting reminders or even creating a to-do list based on items created in a SharePoint list or library.

Another example could be saving email attachments to OneDrive; your work email might be your daily workspace, and you might get hundreds of emails daily, making it hard to keep track of some attachments. Therefore, organizing your email attachments in OneDrive would definitely make things easier.

Moving data between systems and data sources is another use case for Power Automate. As mentioned, you can keep your system's data and data sources in sync due to Power Automate's integration-ability with systems, services, and data sources. For example, you might use Outlook Calendar to organize your day at work, while you use Google Calendar (with your family) to organize your personal events. Using two calendars to organize your day can be challenging, as events can easily conflict, especially when you have personal appointments during working hours. Power Automate can help in such cases, as you can create a flow that triggers when an event is created in your Outlook calendar and copy that event to your Google calendar; this way, you can keep your day in sync between two calendars. Another example could be keeping your data in sync between different sources. Say you have a tasks list in SharePoint that you collaborate on with other team members, but you want to keep track of your tasks in another list or on a to-do list. You can create a Power Automate flow to create an item on your list (SharePoint or to-do) whenever a new task item is assigned to you.

Another use case where Power Automate can come in handy is automating (digitizing) business processes. Whether you automate processes with cloud flows, a BPF, or both, that's up to you. A good example is automating the onboarding process, where you already know the required stages and the steps to fulfill each stage. This way, all business process participants can collaborate—in a guided manner—to complete the onboarding process by fulfilling the required steps and stages using a BPF. Another example is automating the "customer leads" process, usually an established and predefined process with multiple stages and steps to fulfill.

Automating desktop routines on your local machine is yet another use case for Power Automate. For instance, say you have a folder in which you store all your documents and files; this folder might have grown over time and become a repository of hundreds of files, and sorting those documents and files is indeed time-consuming. This is where PAD can help, by sorting those files with a couple of clicks without writing code. Another example where PAD can be useful is integrating with old legacy systems and apps. Such systems and apps don't have APIs to integrate with, and keeping your data in sync between new cloud apps and old legacy apps becomes manual and subject to human error when moving data back and forth between those systems. You can automate those repetitive manual chores of moving data back and forth using PAD by recording your desktop activities (mouse clicks, keystrokes, copying, and pasting) from your local machine. The workflow, once triggered, will repeat and mimic your desktop activities.

Now let's discuss why we should *not* use Power Automate in some cases. But, before going into details, note that when I recommend not using Power Automate in some cases, it is absolutely not an attempt to undermine Power Automate—it's a recommendation to drive value and to use the right tool(s) for the right job. Accordingly, my golden rule is "Let the Requirements Drive the Decision!"

Let's start by addressing the elephant in the room. Integration is a controversial topic when it comes to Power Automate, and this controversy comes from the different backgrounds and opinions around integration. Some perceive the definition of integration differently, believing a sequence of actions connecting through APIs to apps, data sources, and databases is not integration. They believe instead that integration is connecting completely heterogeneous apps or systems through a queued messaging mechanism that ensures sync or async data flow between two (or more) systems, with full data tracking. The latter (for me) is the definition of advanced integration that is usually implemented in business-to-business (B2B) or business-to-consumer (B2C) integration scenarios. In such cases, organizations often leverage iPaaS (integration platform as a service) solutions, such as Azure Logic Apps, Azure Service Bus, or API Management, which are designed for low-latency, high-throughput integrations that require minimal human intervention. In contrast, Power Automate excels in automation within a productivity context, where human interaction, approvals, and business processes are the focus. While Power Automate can connect apps and data sources via APIs, it is not optimized for enterprise-grade, large-scale integrations that require message queuing, event-driven architecture, or guaranteed delivery mechanisms.

Understanding B2B/B2C

One of the most extensive implementations of B2B/B2C integrations is Amazon.com. On the B2B side, Amazon integrates with retailers and merchants, allowing them to list and sell their products on the platform. This enables businesses to reach a vast customer base while Amazon facilitates product visibility and transactions. On the B2C side, Amazon manages the entire consumer experience, from presenting products to handling orders, payments, logistics, and fulfillment. Once a transaction is completed, Amazon integrates back with retailers and merchants, ensuring seamless processing and coordination of inventory, shipping, and financial settlements.

Power Automate has integration aspects in its folds, though you can't use them for advanced integration scenarios because you cannot control its execution consumption and capacity plans. Nevertheless, developers can use Power Automate for simple integration scenarios where the requirement is to keep data in sync between different apps and services. However, there are two things you must keep in mind. First, you shouldn't implement simple integration using Power Automate for enterprise-scale or large data volumes. Second, you shouldn't implement simple integration using Power Automate if data is time critical. Note that some of these limitations are not a spin-off of Power Automate, though they are a by-product of the underlying APIs (connectors). On the other hand, Power Automate does stand out when integrating with old legacy systems that have no APIs through their UIs using PAD. It even has big leverage for its simplicity and capability over many advanced tools out there.

One of the foundational goals of the Power Platform is to enable and empower business users (citizen developers), and Power Automate aligns with this goal. Needless to say, Power Automate is the perfect tool for automation when it comes to personal productivity and self-service scenarios. These citizen developers usually spend their day working in Microsoft 365. Therefore, Power Automate should be your first pick if you're automating business processes in Microsoft 365.

Finally, approvals are a fundamental part of many BPA scenarios. Power Automate has four approval types you can choose from to create and manage approvals, enabling you to get things approved in your organization with a few clicks. I'll talk more about approvals in Chapter 8.

Conclusion

Microsoft Power Automate stands out as a low-code, cloud-based automation service provided by Microsoft, designed to construct automated workflows and streamline business processes for simplicity. Functioning as a low-code platform, it empowers business users and nondevelopers to engage in self-service programming, allowing them to create functional automation (workflows).

Power Automate offers various automation types, including cloud flows, desktop flows, and BPFs covering a vast area of countless automation scenarios in a dynamic digital landscape. Unsurprisingly, this puts Power Automate on the top as an automation and transformation accelerator.

Power Automate signifies a robust connection between its automation capabilities and the broader array of services within Microsoft 365, SharePoint, Dynamics 365, and other Microsoft and non-Microsoft services. As a versatile and powerful automation service, Power Automate offers an easy-to-use, low-code service with an intuitive nature that makes it accessible for anyone looking to begin automating their daily routines.

CHAPTER 2

Getting Started with Power Automate

In this chapter, I'll start with an introduction to what the prerequisites are to begin automating with Power Automate. In addition, we'll explain a fundamental concept in Power Automate: environments. Then, we'll illustrate how you can create your first automation using templates, starting from blank. Finally, we'll end this chapter by explaining the Power Automate mobile app and its use cases.

Know Before You Start

Before creating your first Power Automate flow, there are two prerequisites. First, since Power Automate is a Microsoft 365 service, you must have a Microsoft 365 (formerly Office 365) account before using Power Automate. Second, you must have a license/plan assigned to you. If you don't have a Power Automate license/plan given to you and you are part of an organization, I recommend you ask your IT administrator(s) for a license.

How would you know if you have a Power Automate license? Well, that's simple. Go to the Microsoft Office home page (*https://oreil.ly/kT2zX*). Log in with your Microsoft 365 account credentials. On the Microsoft 365 landing page (home), open the waffle menu (top-left corner):

If you don't see Power Automate under the apps section:

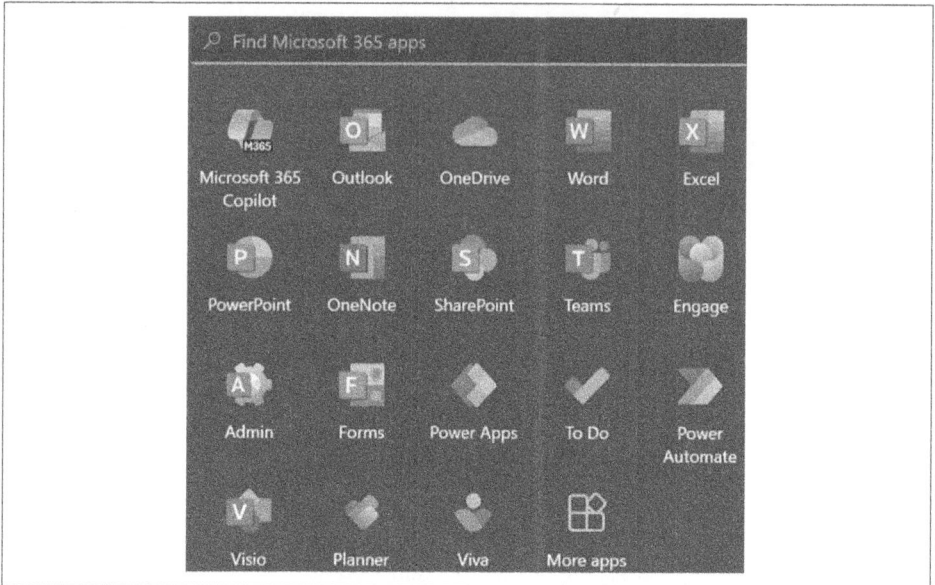

In the search field, search for "Power Automate":

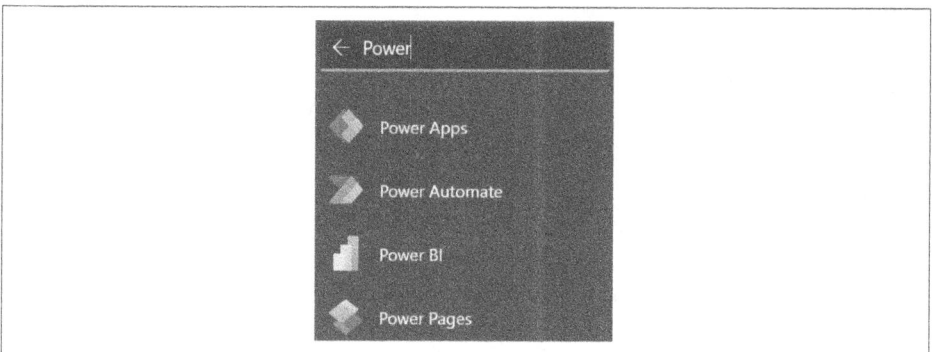

If you didn't find Power Automate there either, then you don't have a license. You can still try Power Automate for free by going to the Power Automate home page (*https://oreil.ly/bPdrg*). Then, from the top-right, click "Try for free":

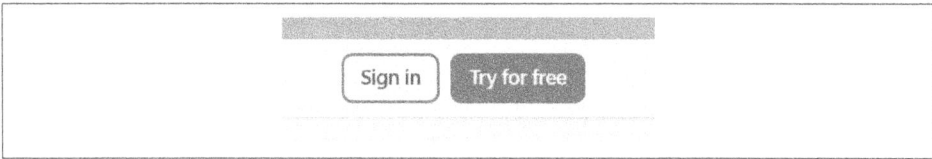

| Sign in | **Try for free** |

Follow the instructions on the next page, and you should be able to use Power Automate for a trial period:

You've selected Microsoft Power Automate Free

(1) Let's get you started

Please solve the puzzle so we know you're not a robot.

Next

Audio

(2) Create your account

(3) Confirmation details

Note that your organization (IT administrator) might have a policy that disallows users to sign up for a Power Automate free trial. In that case, you need to ask your IT administrator for a license.

Once you have sorted out your Microsoft 365 account and Power Automate license, you are ready to make your first flow with Power Automate!

Creating Your First Flow

The first fundamental concept you should learn upon building flows in Power Automate (Power Platform generally) is *environments*. An environment is a space or medium to build something.

To know which environment you're about to build flows in, check the top right corner where it says "Environments":

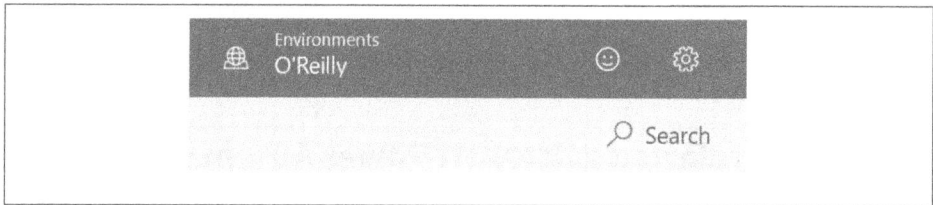

Click on the currently selected environment to change the environment or see the available environments list:

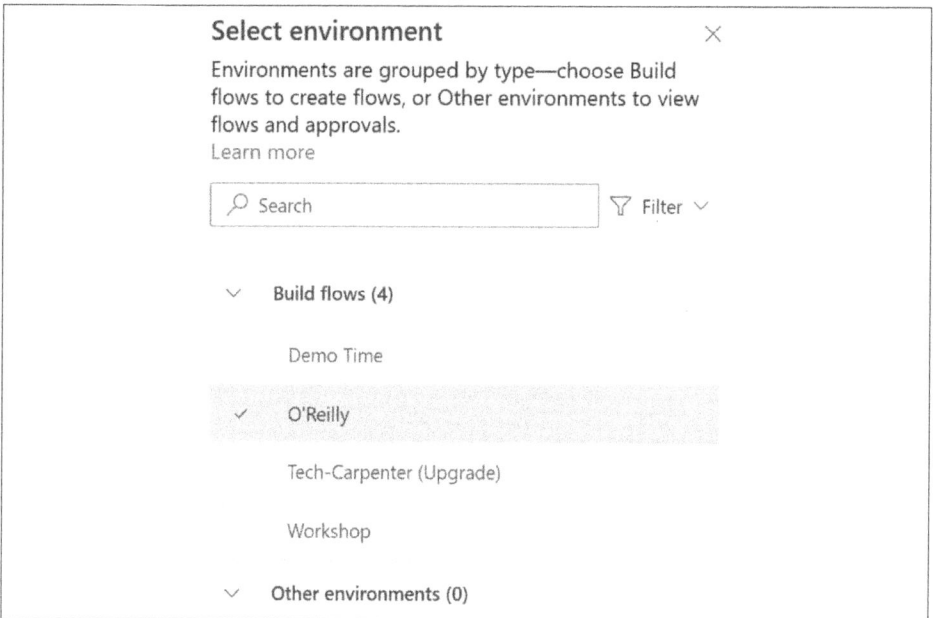

It's essential to know which environment you are building flows in, especially if you're part of a team collaborating on building flows. However, it's not that important if you build flows for your own personal productivity.

Understanding Environments in Power Platform

In Power Platform, an environment is a container for your apps, data, and flows, providing a structured way to manage resources and access within your organization. Environments help separate development, testing, and production workloads, ensuring that changes and updates don't disrupt live business processes. Each environment has its own data source, security settings, and user permissions, making it easier to control access, governance, and compliance. By default, every Power Platform user gets access to a default environment, but you can create multiple environments for better organization and security.

Using separate environments is crucial for maintaining a stable and scalable setup. For example, an organization might use a Development environment for building and testing new Power Automate flows before moving them to a production environment where real users interact with them. This setup minimizes errors and allows for safe testing and innovation.

Starting from Templates

Templates are predefined flows for common and useful automation scenarios. You can create a flow instance from any listed template with minimum configuration to get you up and running in no time. Templates are created by Microsoft or the Power Automate community (approved by Microsoft).

Templates are a good starting point for Power Automate beginners, not only for building the first automation but also as a good stepping stone for expanding a flow and taking it to the next level. Therefore, before you start building any flow from scratch, make sure there is no template for it.

To explore the available templates, go to the Power Automate site (*https://oreil.ly/O-MRf*). Sign in with your Microsoft 365 account credentials. Then click on Templates in the left-side menu:

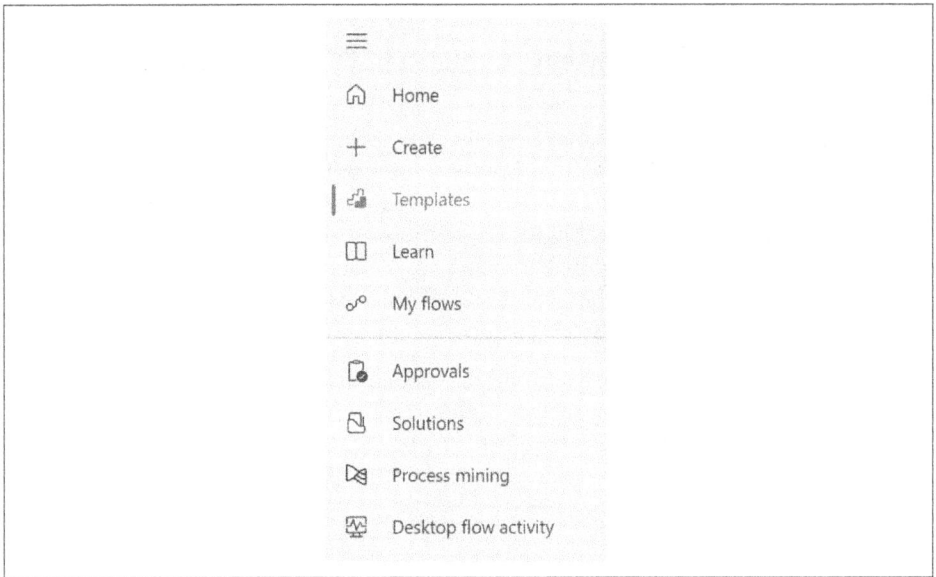

On the Templates page, you are welcomed with the list of all templates sorted by popularity. However, Microsoft has classified templates into several categories to make it easy to find what you're looking for. There is also a search text field and a drop-down list you can sort by:

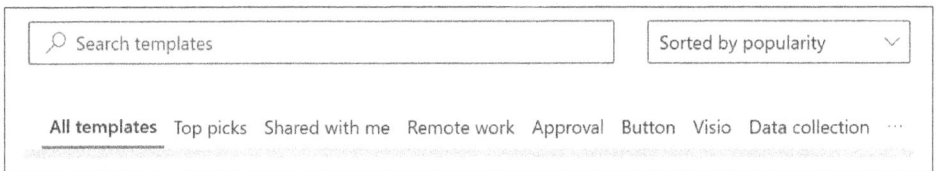

You can sort results by popularity, name, and published time:

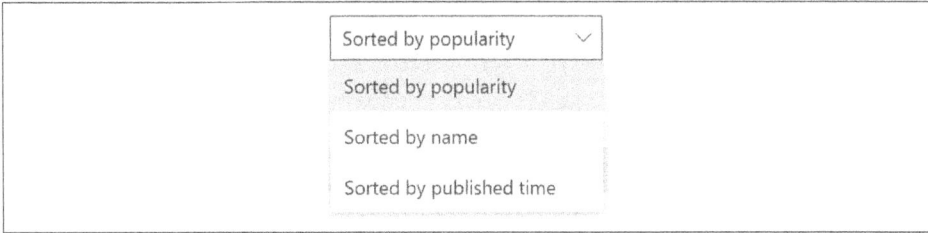

Sorted by popularity ⌄
Sorted by popularity
Sorted by name
Sorted by published time

Templates are categorized as follows:

- All templates (default)
- Top picks
- Shared with me
- Remote work
- Approval
- Button
- Visio
- Data collection
- Email
- Calendar
- Mobile
- Notifications
- Productivity
- Social media
- Sync

Categories are pretty self-explanatory. To show the full categories list, you can simply click on the ellipses (on the top, to the right side of the categories):

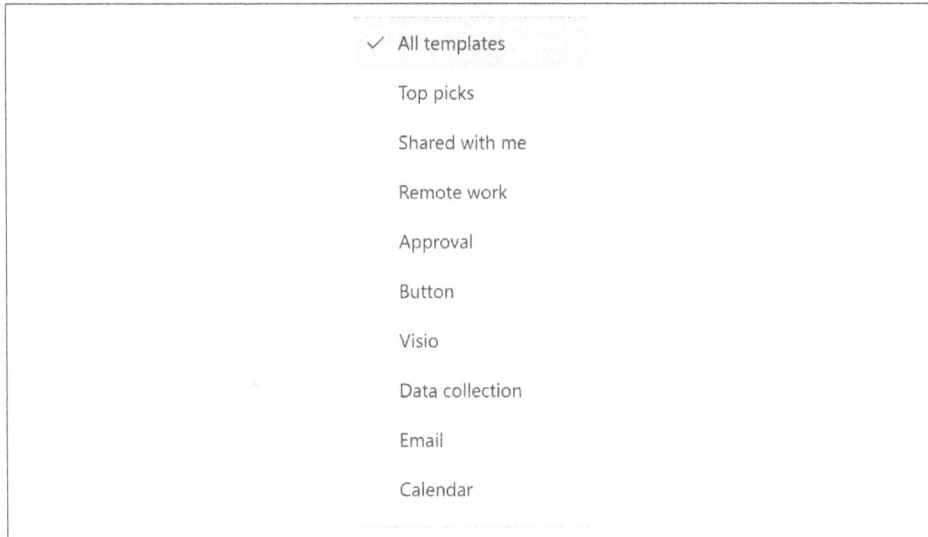

✓ All templates
Top picks
Shared with me
Remote work
Approval
Button
Visio
Data collection
Email
Calendar

You can use the search text field to search through templates based on the selected category. You can narrow your search for a selected category by searching on template name, product, or service. Remember that you can combine categories, the sorting drop-down, and the search text field to filter your search. Currently, the search text field doesn't provide live search (search as you type). Therefore, remember to hit the Enter key each time you type in or change your search text:

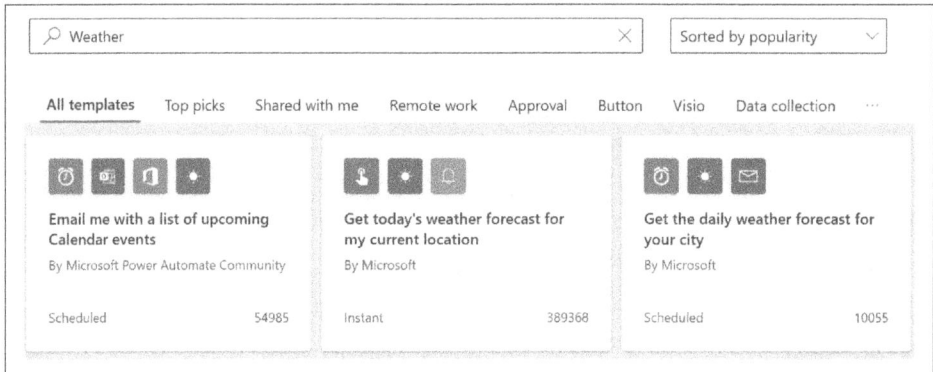

Microsoft is continuously adding (and removing) templates to the list; anyone can submit their own flow as a template if they think it's useful to share, thus becoming part of the Power Automate community by contributing to the templates list.

Now that you know how to find what you're looking for in the templates list, let's explore how you can create a flow from a template. Go to the Templates page (*https://oreil.ly/mhX0a*). Make sure that you're in the correct environment:

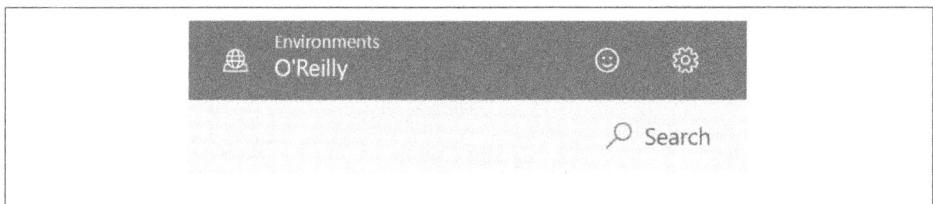

In the search text field, type `Get the daily weather forecast` and hit the Enter key. From the search results, choose the template "Get the daily weather forecast for your city":

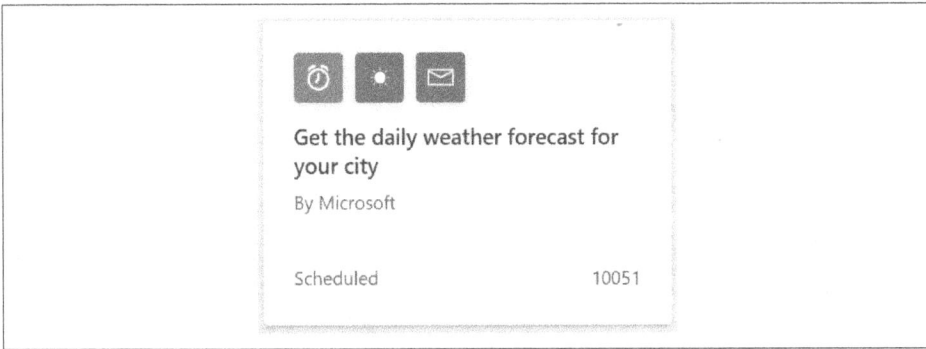

Get the daily weather forecast for your city

By Microsoft

Scheduled   10051

On the next page, you'll find a brief description of what this template does. Note that the box on the left is the trigger (Recurrence), whereas the box on the right holds all or some of the connectors used in this template:

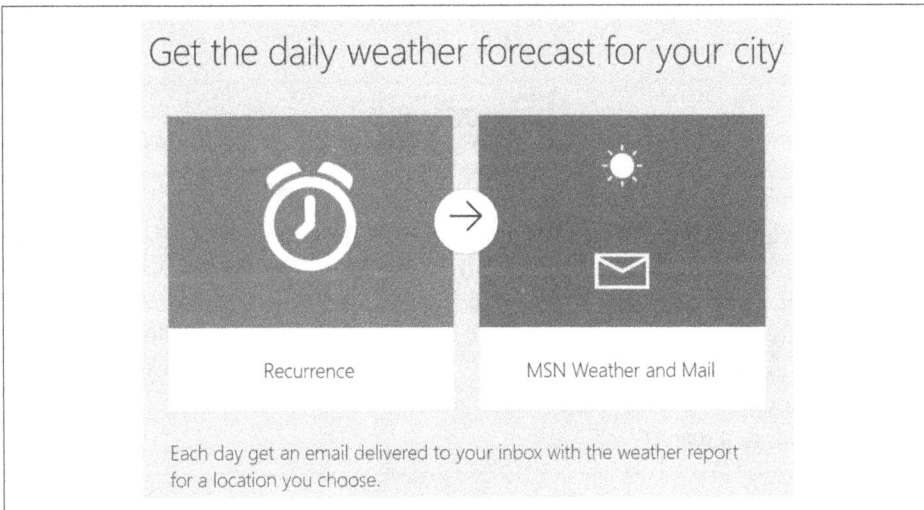

Get the daily weather forecast for your city

Recurrence   MSN Weather and Mail

Each day get an email delivered to your inbox with the weather report for a location you choose.

On the bottom, the page will show which connectors you must create connections for (with your credentials):

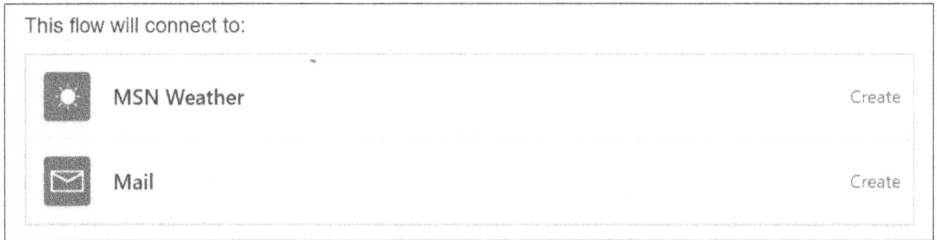

This flow will connect to:

◉	MSN Weather	Create
✉	Mail	Create

Create and sign in to the necessary services. The connections you create against the different services are stored securely and safely within Power Automate. Once you have created and signed in to the required services (green ticks), click Continue:

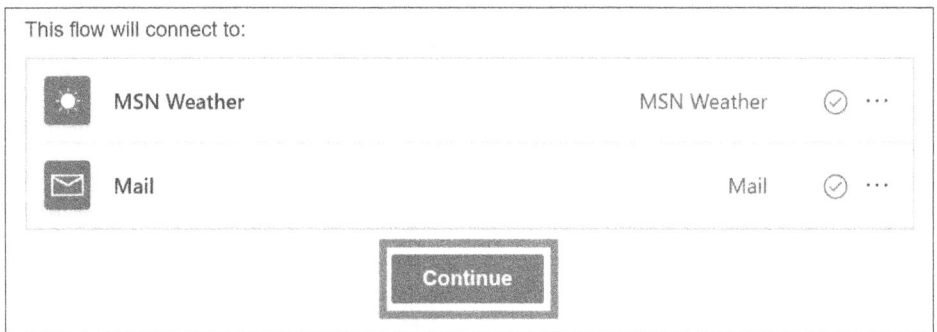

This flow will connect to:

◉	MSN Weather	MSN Weather	✓	⋯
✉	Mail	Mail	✓	⋯

Continue

After you click Continue, Power Automate will create a flow instance based on the selected template, and you'll automatically navigate to the Power Automate flow designer. This designer is where you build your cloud flow(s) in Power Automate. The created flow is almost ready to use; it needs only a few inputs. Before punching in these inputs, let me illustrate how this flow works from the trigger to the last action. The trigger is a recurrence trigger, meaning it runs on a schedule. By default, it's set to run once a day:

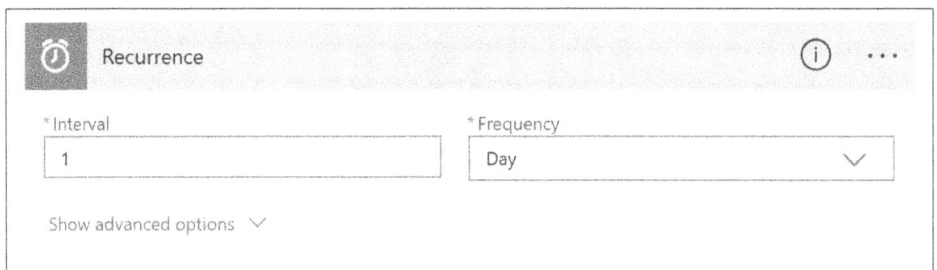

⏰ Recurrence		ⓘ ⋯
*Interval	*Frequency	
1	Day	∨
Show advanced options ∨		

The first action after the trigger is the "Get forecast for today" action from the MSN Weather connectors. Now you need to add inputs for this action. First, type your location; this can range from your city to a specific longitude and latitude (check the tooltip by hovering on the input field to learn about the possible inputs for the location). Second, select the measurement unit for the weather forecast:

The final action sends you an email with the weather forecast day summary. Now, type your email address in the To field. Notice that the forecast details are taken from the "Get forecast for today" action outputs:

You're all set at this point to save your flow. Click Save either at the bottom of the flow designer under the last action:

+ New step   Save

or at the top right of the flow designer:

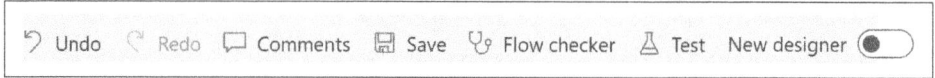

↺ Undo   ↻ Redo   💬 Comments   💾 Save   🩺 Flow checker   ⚗ Test   New designer   ⬤

Make sure that your flow is saved successfully and that there are no error messages. The green notification on the top confirms that:

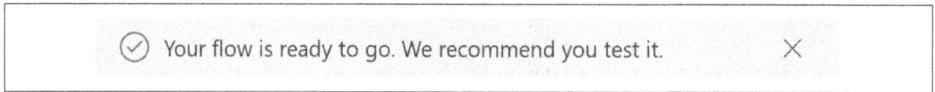

⊘ Your flow is ready to go. We recommend you test it.   ✕

Once your flow is saved, you can test it immediately by clicking Test in the top right of the flow designer:

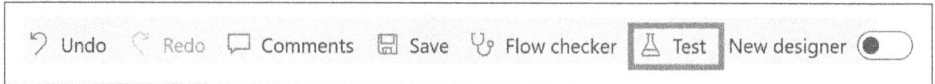

↺ Undo   ↻ Redo   💬 Comments   💾 Save   🩺 Flow checker   ⚗ Test   New designer   ⬤

From the right pane, under Test Flow, choose Manually:

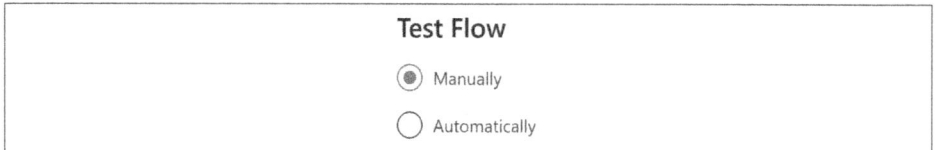

Test Flow

◉ Manually

◯ Automatically

Then click Test at the bottom of the right pane:

Test   Cancel

Next, click "Run flow" at the bottom of the right pane:

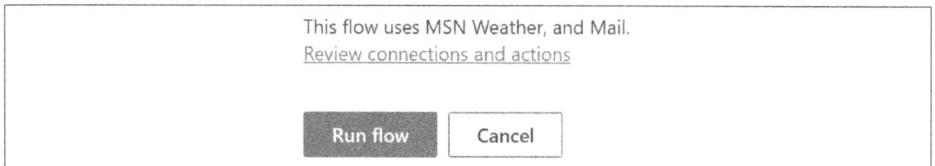

This flow uses MSN Weather, and Mail.
Review connections and actions

Run flow   Cancel

You'll get a confirmation that your flow has started successfully:

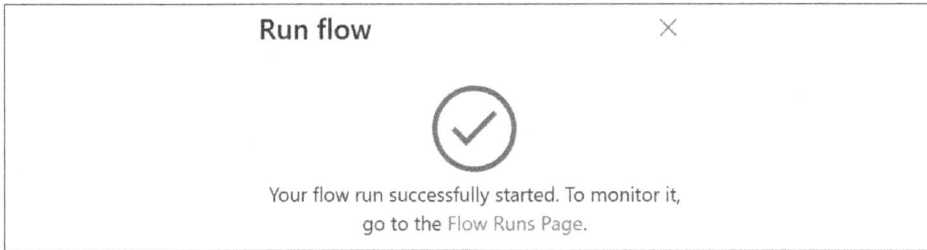

Run flow ✕

Your flow run successfully started. To monitor it,
go to the Flow Runs Page.

Click Done at the bottom of the right pane and make sure that your flow ran successfully. The green notification on the top confirms it:

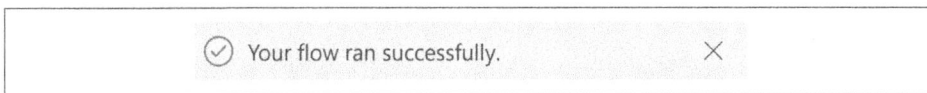

Your flow ran successfully. ✕

Finally, check your email. The email you'll receive should look like the following:

Weather for Oslo, Norway today is Partly sunny

Ahmad Najjar

To: ⊗ Ahmad Najjar   Wed 5/14/2025 10:25 PM

Today: Partly sunny.

There is a 11% chance of precipitation. The
high will be **60F** and the low will be 39F.

Humidity will range from 29 to 54, and the
maximum wind speed is 17 mph.

At this point, you have created a fully functional flow from a template. The recurrence trigger is set to run once daily at a random time. To make it more practical, you might set the trigger to run an hour before you leave home for your office in the morning, at 7:00 A.M, for instance. To do so, go back to your browser, and click Edit in the top right of the flow designer. Expand the trigger by clicking on it. Then click Show advanced options. Select your time zone so your flow runs in your local timezone. Then set the "At these hours" to 7:00 by checking 7 from the checkbox drop-down:

Finally, save your flow.

Starting Your Flow from Scratch

This is where most beginners (especially business users) flounder. It's something that I've witnessed over and over with my clients, where they struggle to identify where to begin or which trigger to choose to start their flow(s).

The following simple guidelines will help you choose your triggers correctly every time:

- The first question you must ask yourself is, Where does the flow start? Does it start on the service side? For example, does it start in OneDrive, SharePoint, or Outlook.com? Typically, a flow starts (triggers) where data initially resides.
- If yes, look for the corresponding service connector and the trigger you want the flow to initiate when it happens. For example, the trigger could be when a new file is created/added to OneDrive or when a new item is added to a specific list in SharePoint (automated cloud flow).
- If you can't find the trigger that satisfies your business needs, you might want to consider checking the service's data/files periodically, meaning that you need to pull the data to check for changes (through action[s] after the trigger). Then you need to run this flow on a schedule (scheduled cloud flow).
- Now, if the flow doesn't start when something happens on the service side, then you can skip looking into automated cloud flow triggers and ask yourself, Does it run on a regular basis (periodically)? If so, then it's a scheduled cloud flow.
- Otherwise, you want to run the flow on your own terms (on-demand). Then it's an instant cloud flow. For example, run the flow for a selected file or item in SharePoint, for a selected message in Teams, or manually from a physical button or a flow button (mobile app).

All the scenarios mentioned will be elaborated on in the upcoming chapters. Let's begin by creating the first flow from scratch, aiming to receive an email notification for every new top news story from CNN. If you search the list of connectors, you won't find a connector for CNN, although they may have a public API that can be used to build a connector. However, all sites that deliver content to their users, such as news sites and blogs, usually provide a Really Simple Syndication (RSS) feed. RSS is a web feed that allows users and applications to access website updates in a standardized, computer-readable format. Subscribing to an RSS feed allows you to keep track of the website's updates, which constantly monitor the site for new content, eliminating the need for you to check them manually. Websites with frequently updated information usually use RSS feeds to publish their information, such as blog entries, news headlines, audio and video series episodes, or podcast distribution. Interestingly, this can be automated with Power Automate using an RSS trigger.

To create this flow, go to the Power Automate home page (*https://oreil.ly/O-MRf*). Again, ensure that you're in the correct environment:

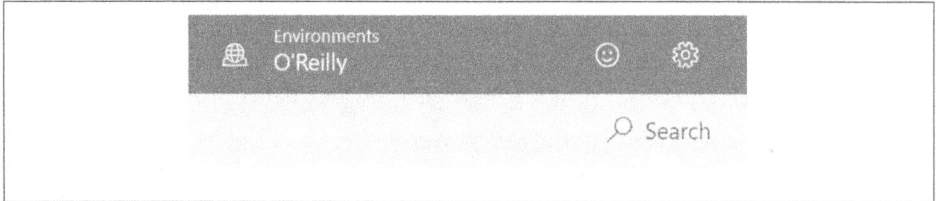

Click on Create from the left menu:

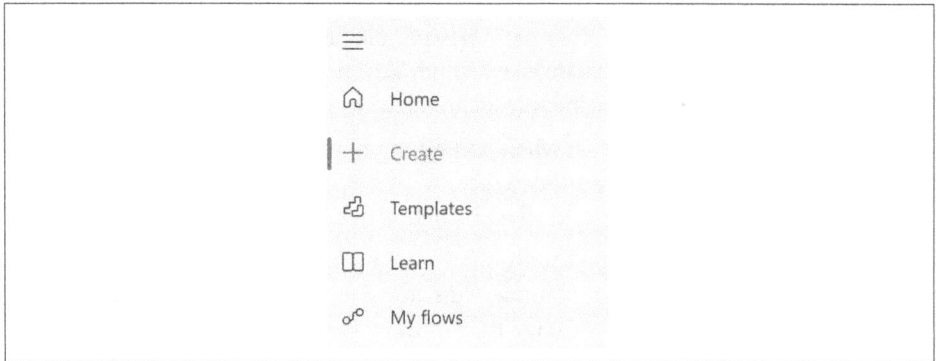

Choose "Automated cloud flow" from the available choices on the top:

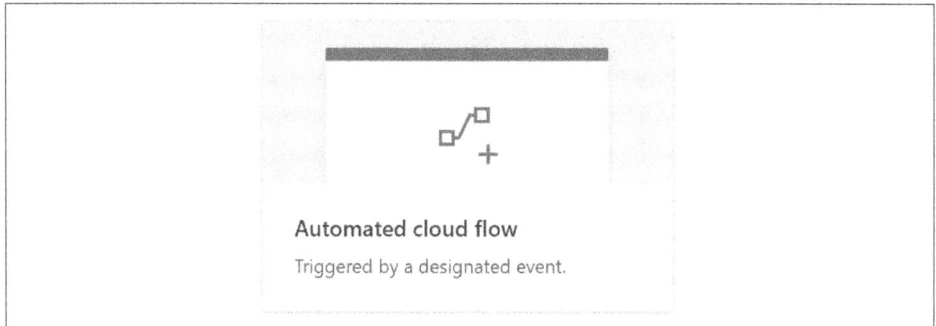

In the pop-up window, name your flow "Get CNN top stories." Then search for the RSS trigger by typing RSS in the search field. Choose the "When a feed item is published" trigger, then click Create:

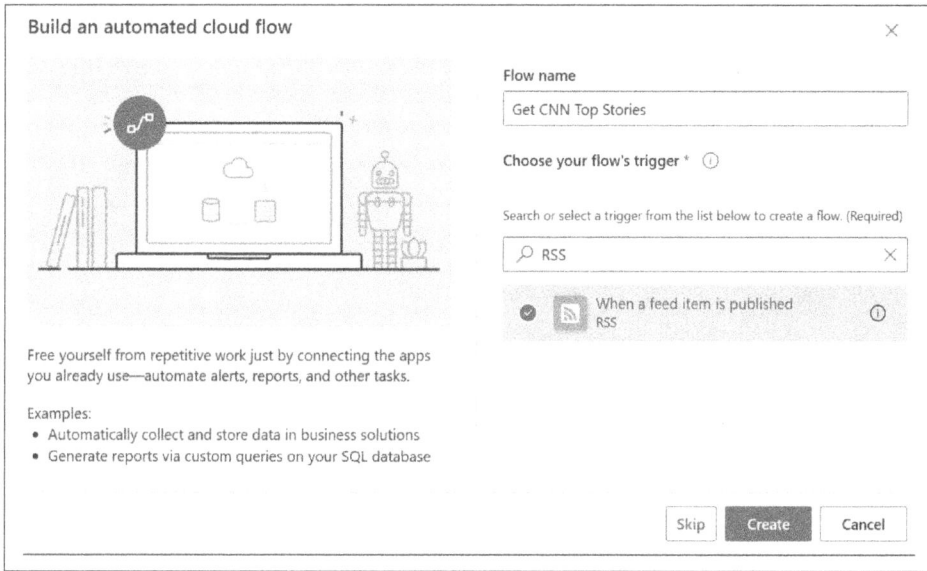

Build an automated cloud flow   ✕

Flow name

Get CNN Top Stories

Choose your flow's trigger * ⓘ

Search or select a trigger from the list below to create a flow. (Required)

🔍 RSS   ✕

✓   When a feed item is published   ⓘ
    RSS

Free yourself from repetitive work just by connecting the apps you already use—automate alerts, reports, and other tasks.

Examples:
- Automatically collect and store data in business solutions
- Generate reports via custom queries on your SQL database

Skip   **Create**   Cancel

Once you click Create, you'll automatically navigate to the flow designer. In the trigger, fill the "The RSS feed URL" field with `http://rss.cnn.com/rss/cnn_top stories.rss`. Note that you can use any RSS feed URL in this step. For this example, I'm using the RSS feed from CNN. Keep the second property, "Chosen property will be used to determine which items are new," as PublishDate:

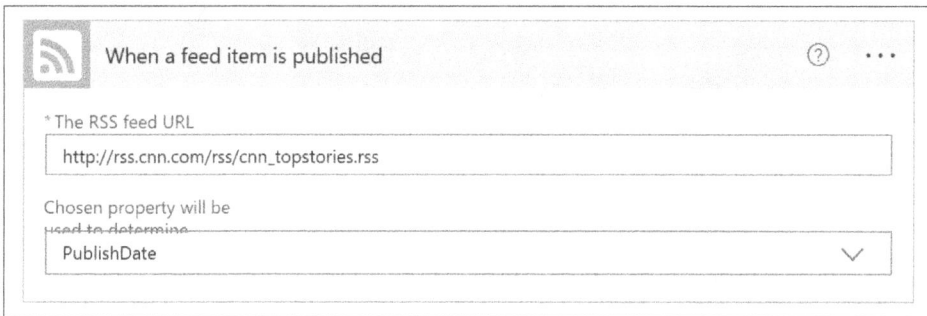

When a feed item is published   ⑦   • • •

* The RSS feed URL

http://rss.cnn.com/rss/cnn_topstories.rss

Chosen property will be
used to determine

PublishDate   ⌄

At this point, you're done setting up your trigger. Click "+ New step":

In the search field, type office. Then, choose the Office 365 Outlook connector:

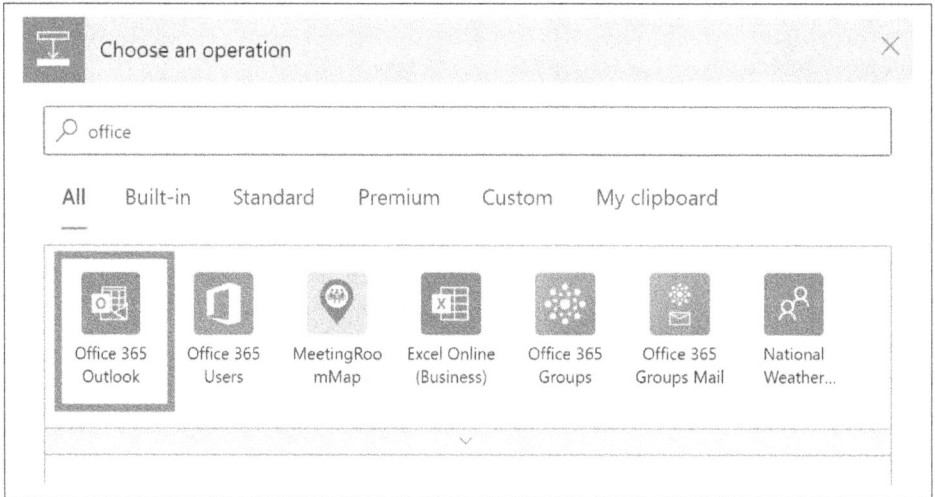

Again, in the connectors search field, type send, then choose "Send an email (V2)":

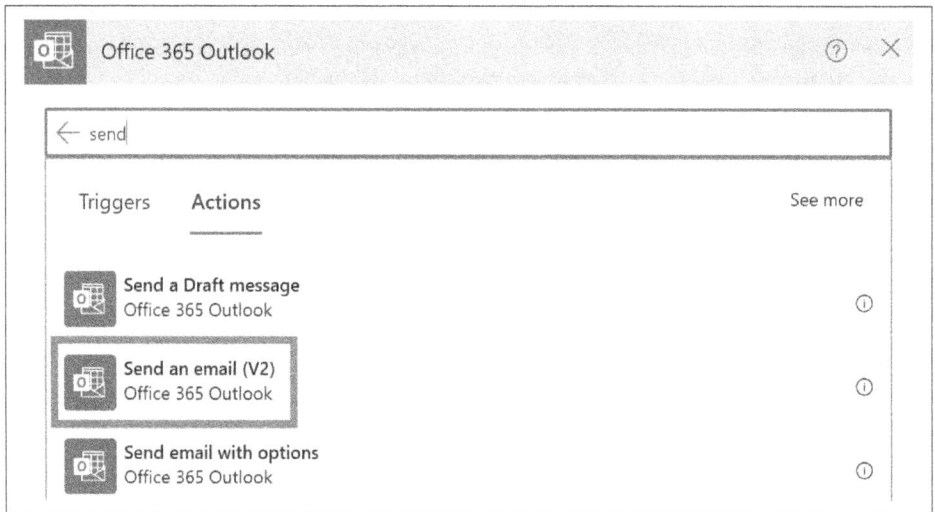

In the To field, type your name and then choose your user account. Note that this field can work as a "people picker" from your organization's accounts. You can type in emails instead of picking accounts by switching to Advanced Mode:

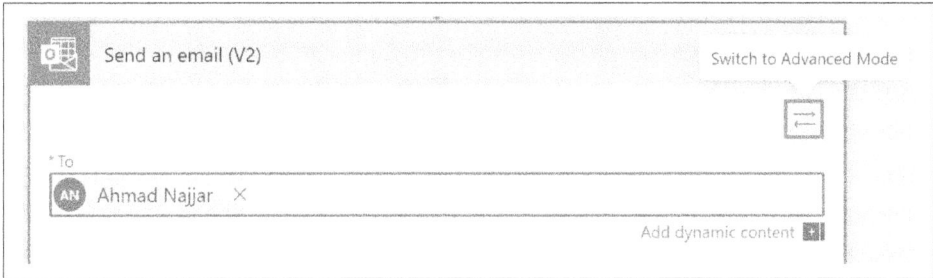

In the Subject text field, type A new CNN top story published on, then at the end, add/choose "Feed published on" from the dynamic content provided, which is automatically parsed from the output data of the trigger:

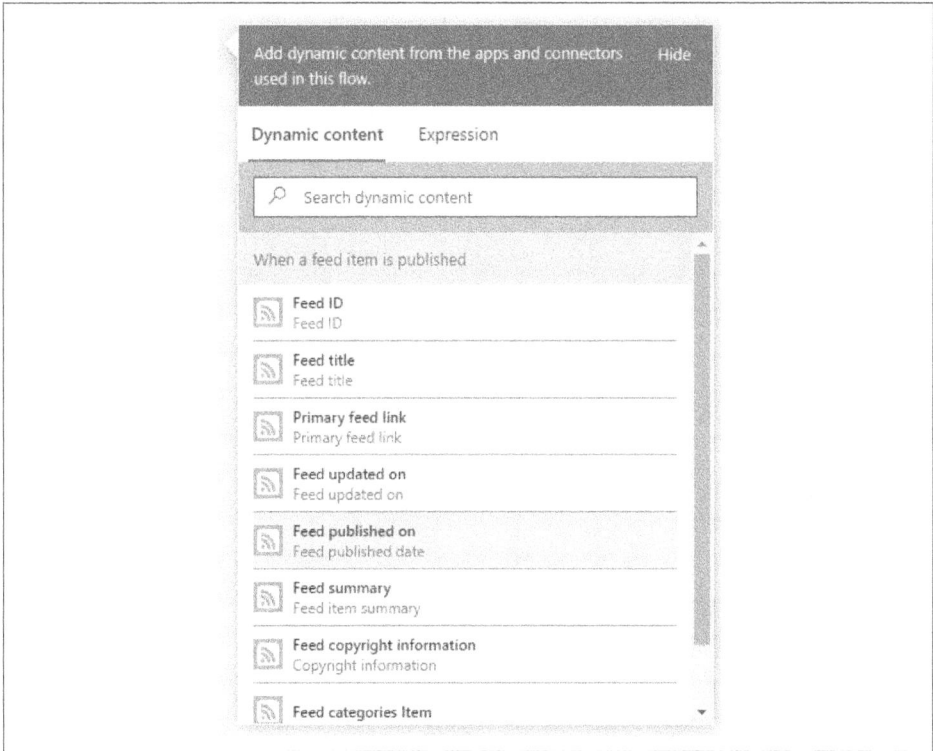

In the Body rich-text field, type in something like the following:

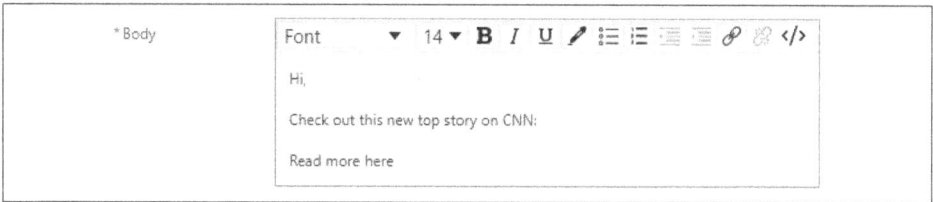

Now, you must add some dynamic content to make this notification meaningful. So, after the "…on CNN:" add a new line and pick the "Feed title" from the dynamic content. Then, on a new line, pick the "Feed summary." Finally, under the "Read more here" line, pick the "Primary feed link" from the dynamic content. Then save your flow:

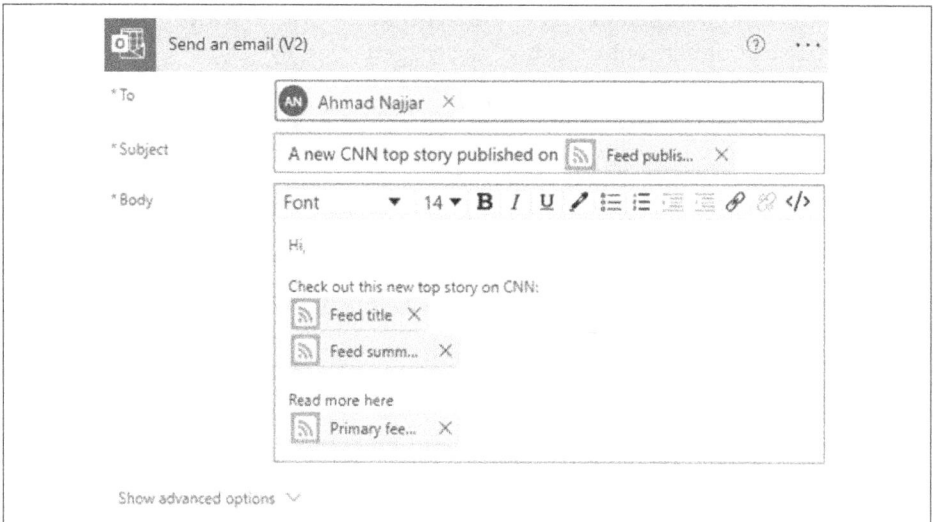

At this point, all you have to do is wait until the RSS feed you chose publishes new content, so keep checking your email. Choosing a news website RSS feed is your best bet to test this because news is published at a high frequency on such websites. The notification (email) you'll receive should look like the following image:

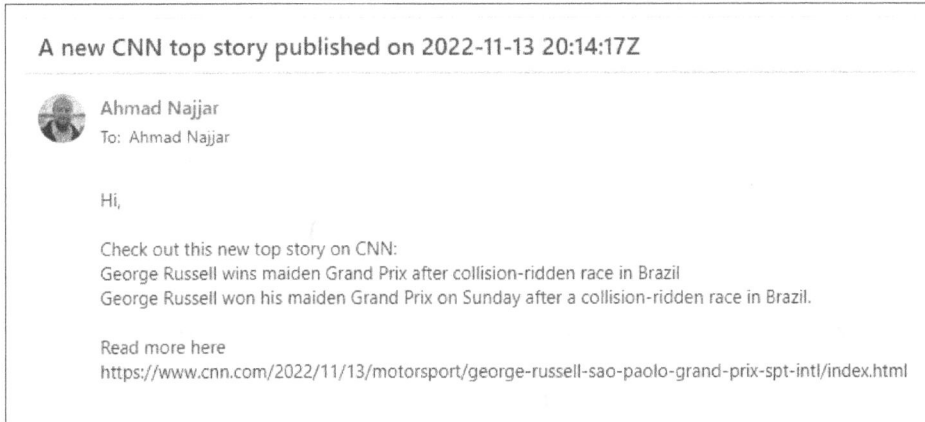

You can use this flow as it is now, though there is room for improvement. Making the feed URL clickable from the email can improve your experience. To do so, remove "Primary feed link" from the email body by clicking on the "x" to the right of "Primary feed link":

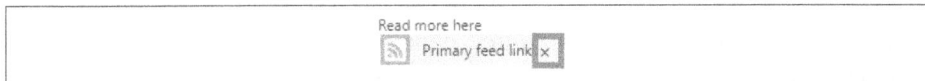

Now, highlight the word "here" and click on the chain icon in the Body rich-text field. Clicking on the chain icon creates a link with "here" as the Link Title:

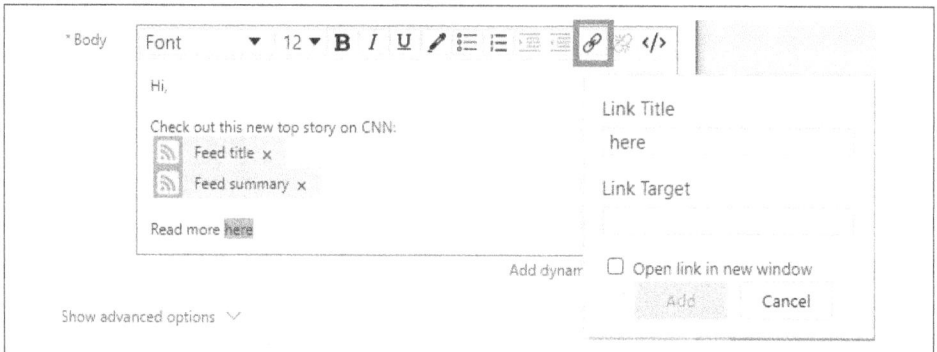

However, the Link Target (URL) cannot be set as a dynamic value from here. Therefore, type in Test in the Link Target for now, and click Add. To set the link as dynamic content, you need to edit the email body in code view. Click on the HTML tag icon at the top to the right of the chain icon:

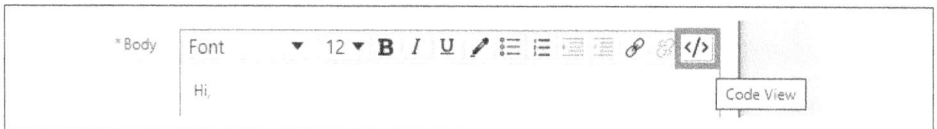

After you have opened the Body field in code view, locate `<a href="">` (this should be at the very bottom), then place the text cursor between the double quotations and select "Primary feed link" from the dynamic content:

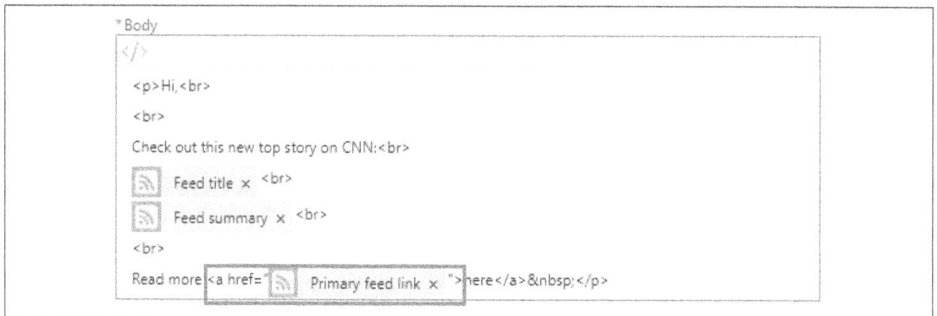

Finally, save your flow and wait for the next RSS feed update. The email notification will look like the following:

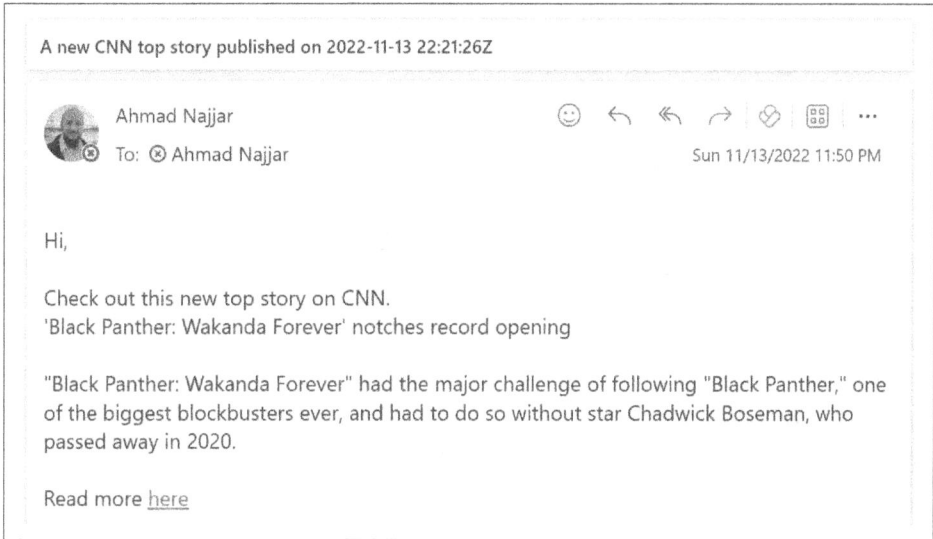

A new CNN top story published on 2022-11-13 22:21:26Z

Ahmad Najjar

To: ⊗ Ahmad Najjar

Sun 11/13/2022 11:50 PM

Hi,

Check out this new top story on CNN.
'Black Panther: Wakanda Forever' notches record opening

"Black Panther: Wakanda Forever" had the major challenge of following "Black Panther," one of the biggest blockbusters ever, and had to do so without star Chadwick Boseman, who passed away in 2020.

Read more here

One final note you should take into account is that once you add dynamic content into HTML properties (like you did in the previous step), you can't go back to the HTML view again unless you remove any dynamic content from HTML tags properties.

Mobile App

Power Automate has a native mobile app that you can download on your mobile (for both iOS and Android) to manage and explore your flows. Before heading on with this section, I want to state that the UX on the iOS version is different from the Android version. However, in this book, I will focus on the shared experience, which you can have on iOS and Android. Additionally, I wouldn't recommend creating flows on the go using your mobile app (despite being possible only on iOS).

To install the Power Automate mobile app, you can simply scan one of the following corresponding QR codes:

Android   iOS

Go to the corresponding app store based on your mobile: Google Play for Android devices and the App Store for iOS devices. Then search for the Power Automate app and ensure the publisher is Microsoft Corporation. Then, install the app. Once the app is installed, open the app and sign in with either Azure Active Directory or your Microsoft account (Microsoft 365).

You can view flow properties and definitions, turn flows on or off, or review run history on the different environments by selecting the environment icon:

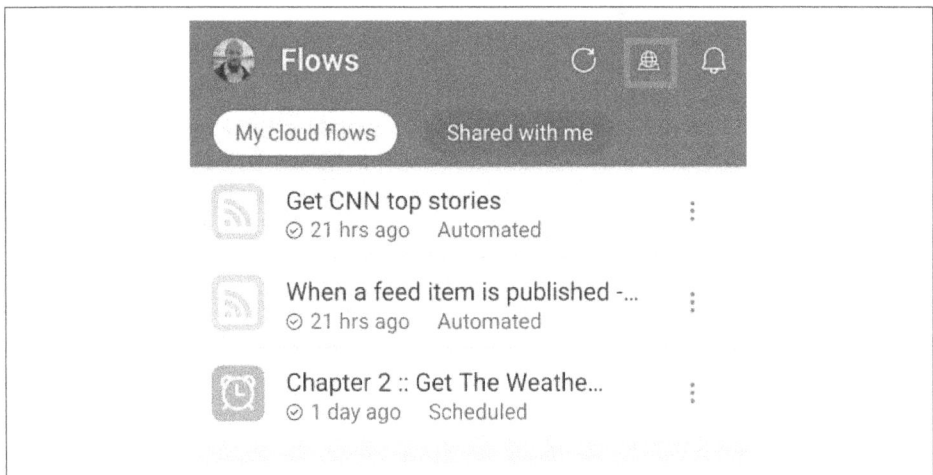

Select the environment you want to access:

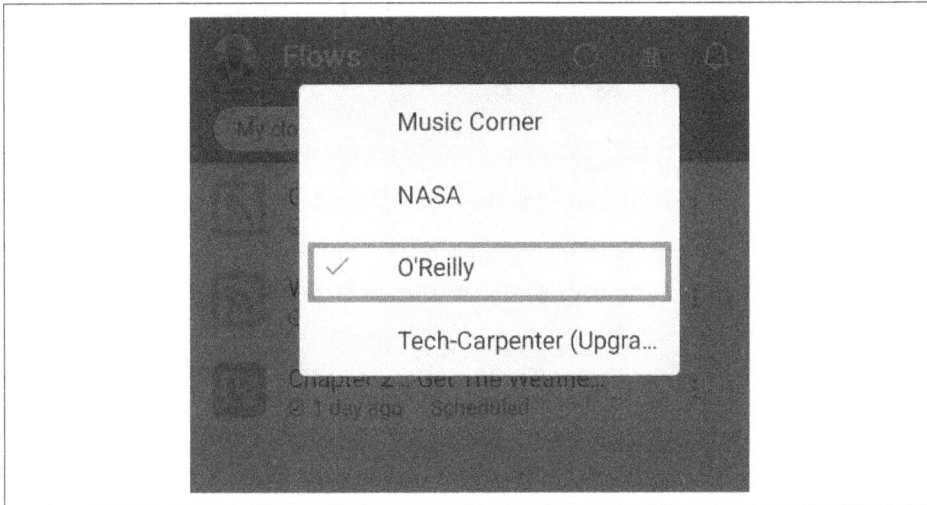

You can view your flows in a selected environment:

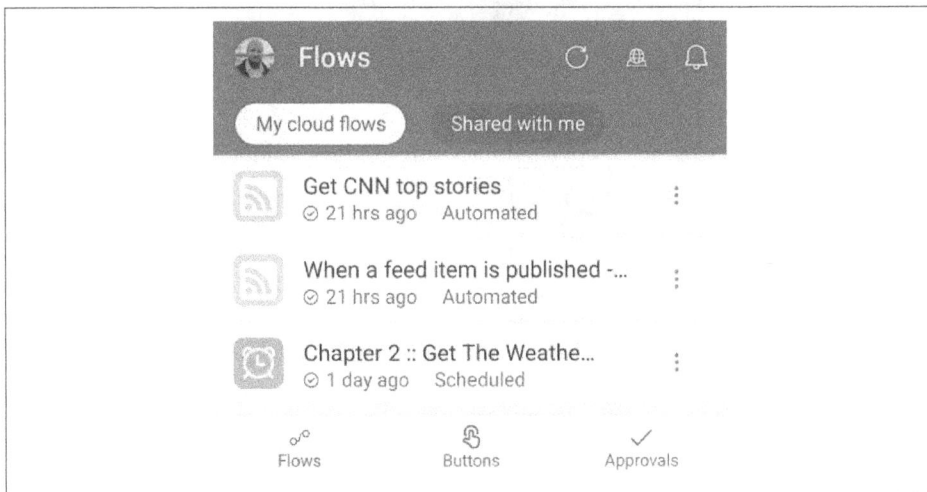

Click on the three dots (to the right of each flow):

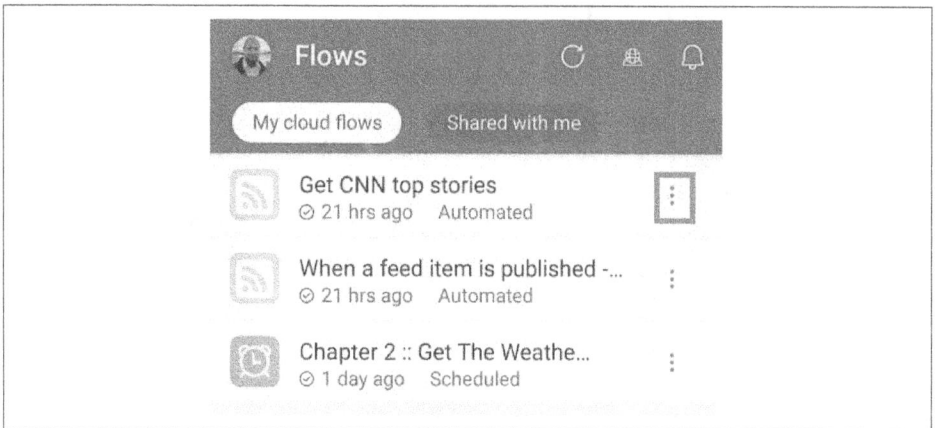

The pop-up menu will appear so that you can manage your flow:

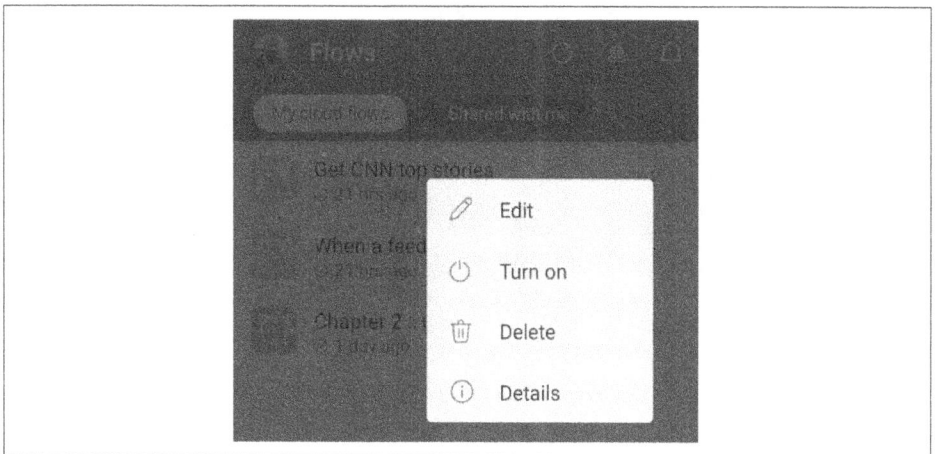

You can edit:

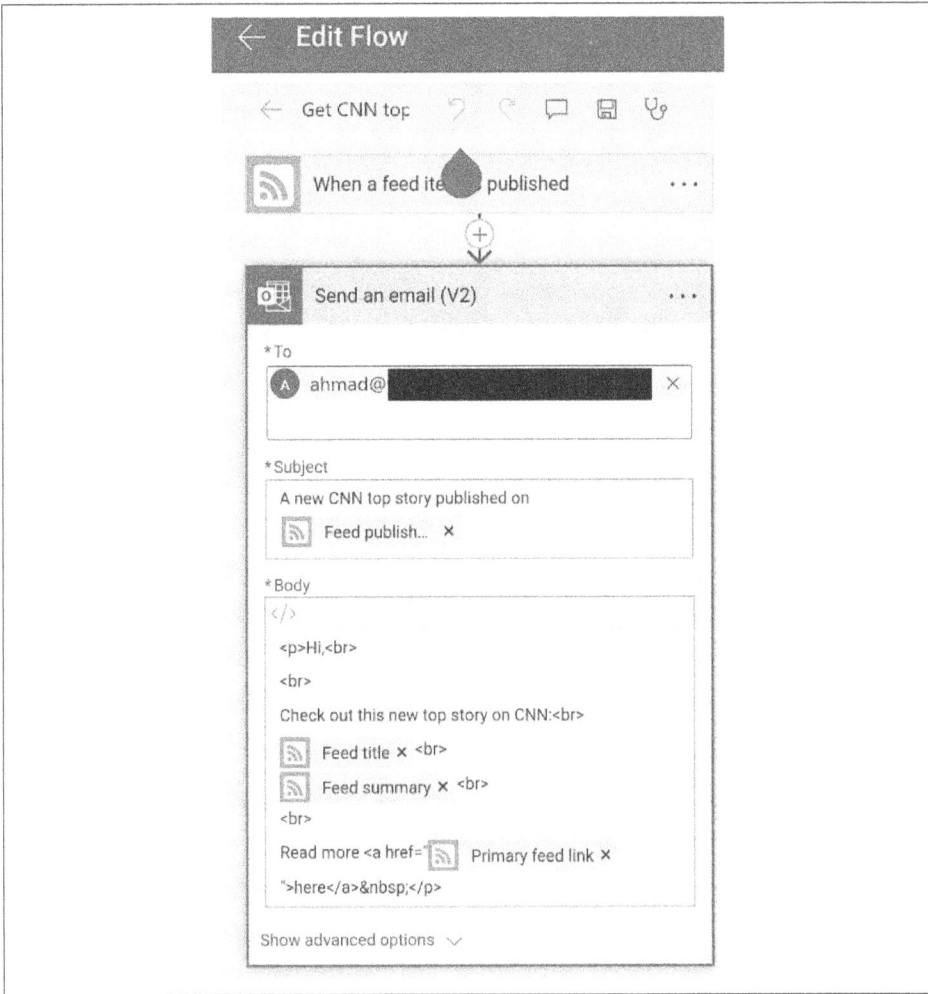

You can also turn on or off, delete, or show details:

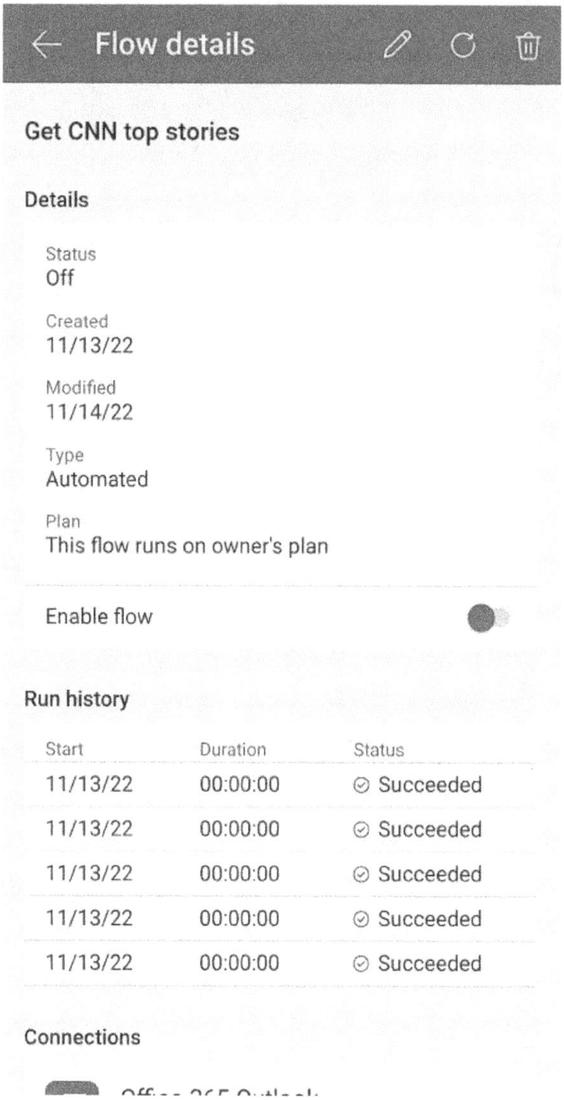

You can get push notifications from your flow that include details and a customized link. To check the received push notification, you can click on the pop-up notification on your cell phone:

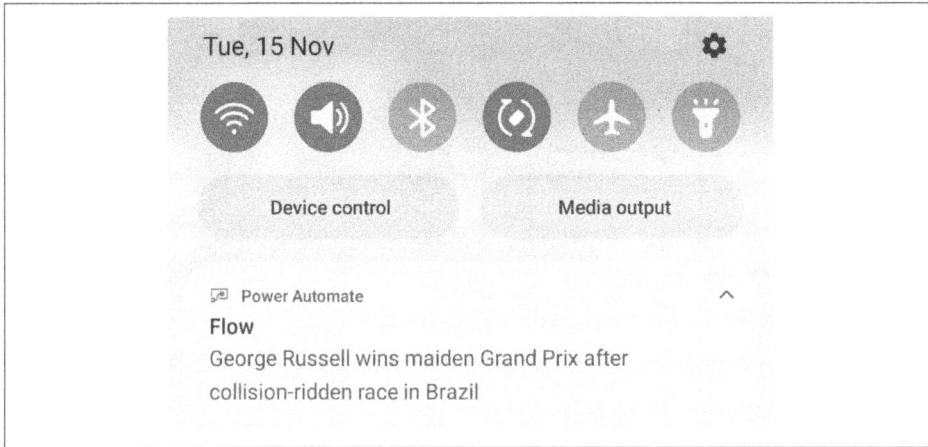

Get notifications from the Power Automate mobile app by clicking on the bell icon on the top:

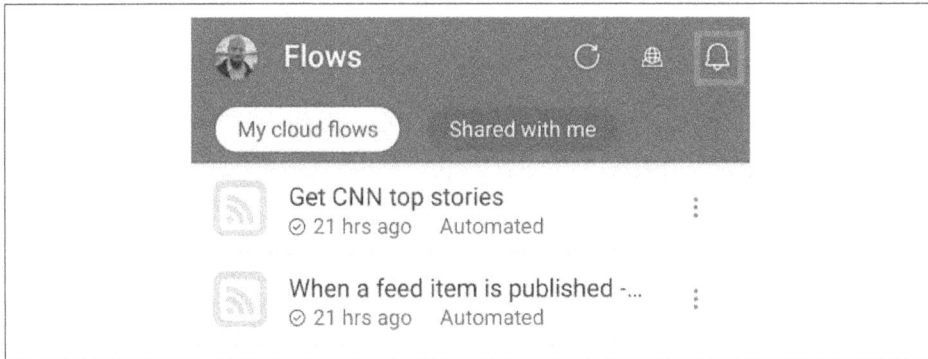

and then check new and old notifications:

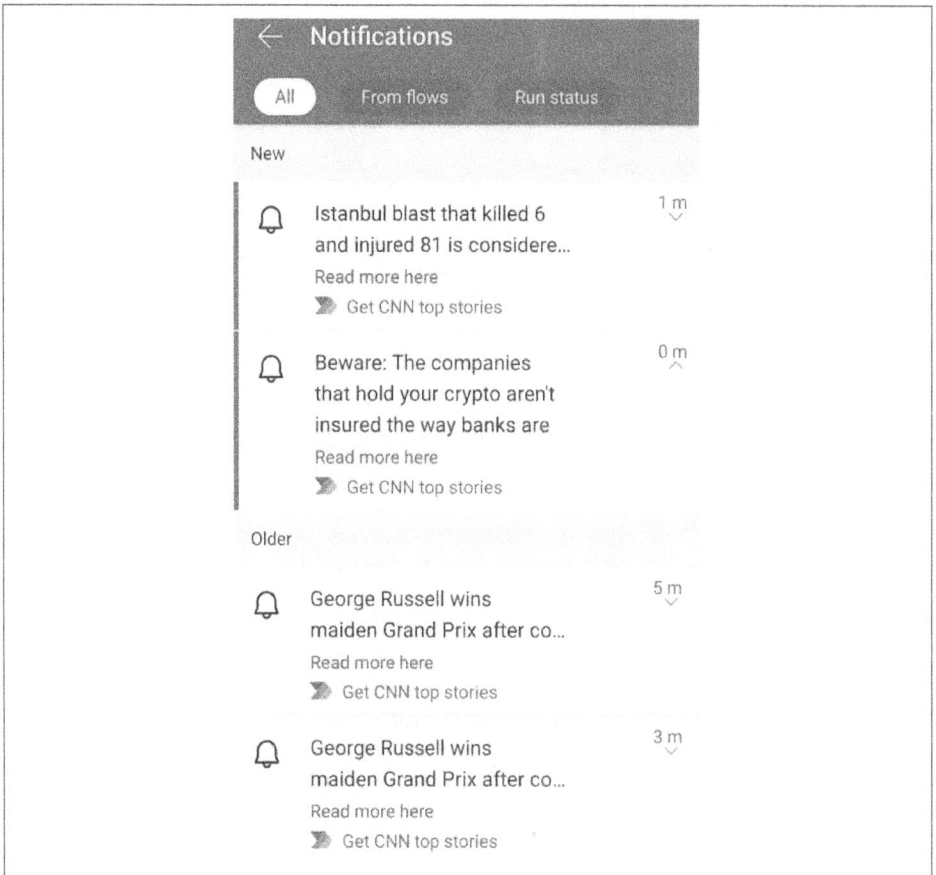

Additionally, you can instantly respond to approval requests through the mobile app. As with notifications, you can check approval requests from the mobile pop-up notification or by opening the app and from the bottom menu in the app choosing Approvals:

There you can respond instantly to approval requests assigned to you:

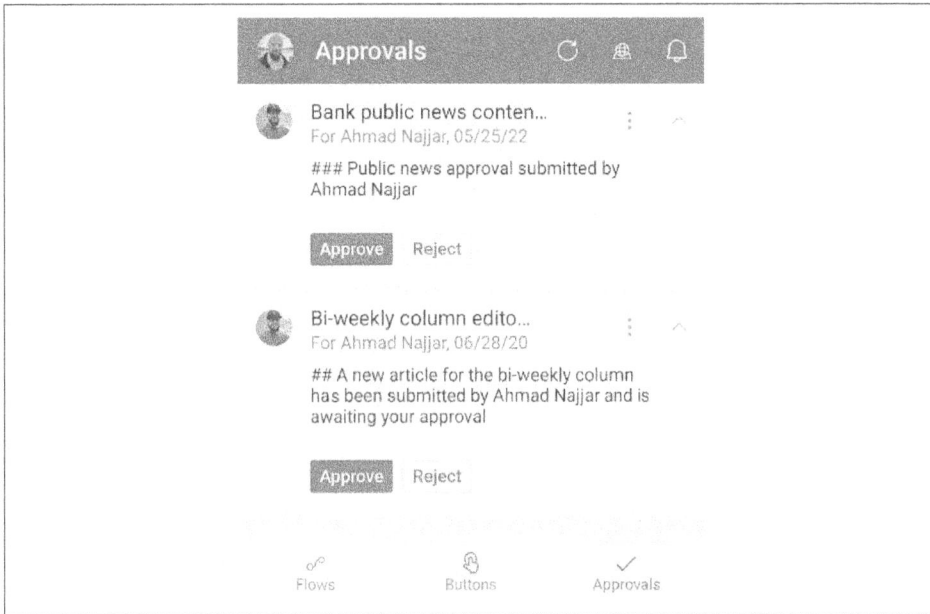

Finally, you have the power to run flows instantly under your fingertips by using mobile buttons. These will be covered in detail in Chapter 9. To list available instant flow buttons, choose the Buttons item from the bottom menu in the app:

On the next screen you find a list of available instant flows that you can run from the mobile app:

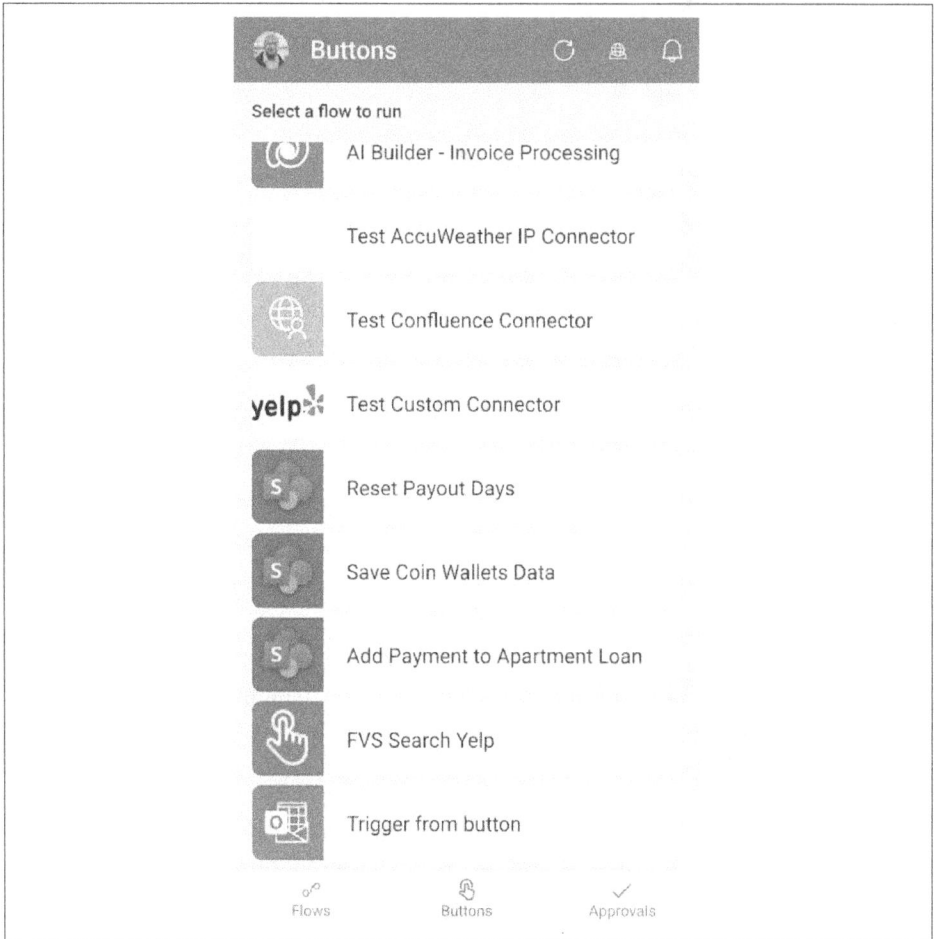

Conclusion

You have now gained proficiency in navigating Power Automate. This includes understanding the necessary licenses and accounts, selecting your preferred environment(s), crafting flows from predesigned templates or starting from scratch, accessing previously created flows with their specific details, and becoming familiar with the Power Automate mobile application.

CHAPTER 3

Working with Notifications

Notifications in Power Automate allow you to receive email, push, or other notifications when certain events occur in your flows or other connected applications, keeping you informed about important events and tasks in your work. In most real-world situations, notifications play a crucial role within processes. Whether to stay informed about specific events and connected applications or to confirm the successful execution of critical actions or workflows, notifications are an integral component. They serve the dual purpose of keeping users in the loop about significant developments and ensuring the reliable completion of essential tasks.

Email Notifications

Email notifications are one of the most common types of notifications used in Power Automate. They allow you to keep track and stay on top of important tasks in your inbox. They also enable you to notify your team members of issues that must be addressed.

The possibilities for email notifications are nearly limitless, depending on your specific needs and scenarios. I will, however, present some common recipes to help you build a foundational understanding of the diverse possibilities.

3.1 Sending Recurring Reminders

Problem

You want to send a scheduled (recurring) email notification to remind your team member to submit their timesheets.

Solution

Create a scheduled cloud flow, setting the required frequency, that then emails the targeted recipients in the desired format.

Discussion

There are several apps and tools available that can help you set up reminders. However, our attention is often absorbed by active tasks, with a primary focus on scheduled meetings in our calendars, causing us to overlook smaller yet crucial matters, such as submitting timesheets. Nevertheless, a simple reminder email in your inbox can always help to refresh your mind and give you a little extra push to action.

As a team leader, you should send weekly—or bi-weekly—reminders to your team members to submit their timesheets and expenses on time so that you stay up-to-date with your team's billable hours. To do this, navigate to the Power Automate home page (*https://oreil.ly/O-MRf*). Then click on Create from the left navigation menu:

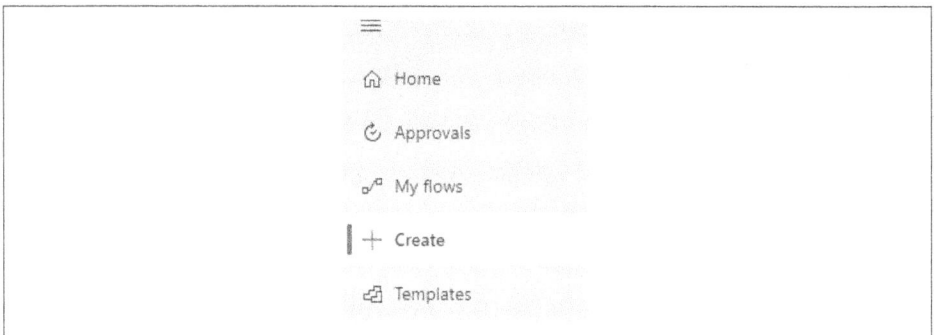

Select "Scheduled cloud flow":

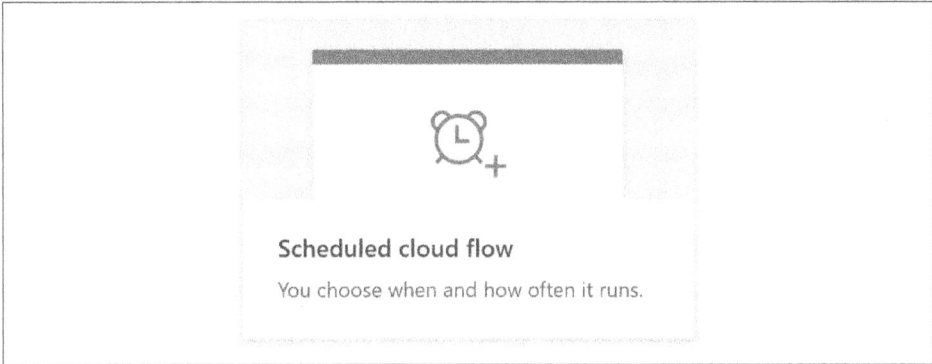

In the pop-up window, under "Flow name," provide a name for the flow, such as "Team Timesheet Weekly Reminder":

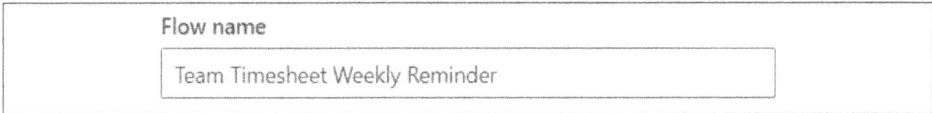

Under "Run this flow," set the starting date and time. Starting date is the effective starting date for this flow, while starting time is the effective start time for the first and future runs:

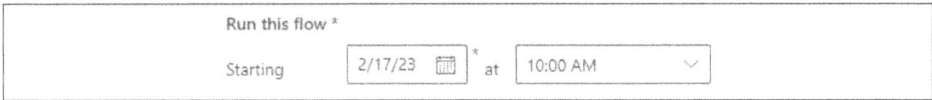

Set the frequency by setting the input fields beside "Repeat every." For this flow scenario, we are scheduling the flow to run once every week, so select Week from the frequency drop-down and leave the repetition as 1:

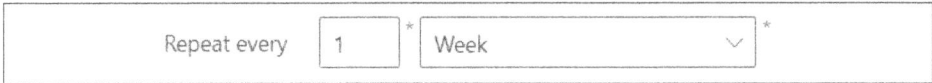

Setting the flow to run weekly will present us with an additional input, "On these days," which stages which days this flow would run. By default, all weekdays are selected; however, for this recipe, we want the reminders to be sent on Fridays, so we check Friday (F) and unselect all other weekdays:

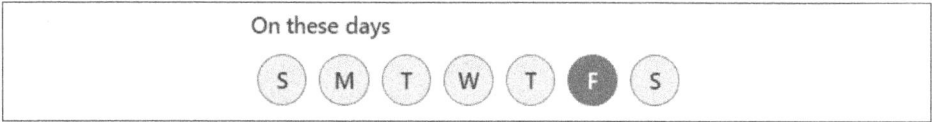

At this point, our scheduled trigger is ready. Remember that we can always change this schedule after the flow designer creates the flow. Click Create. This will take us to the flow designer page. Next, click "New step." Then, in the search field, type office. Choose the Office 365 Outlook connector:

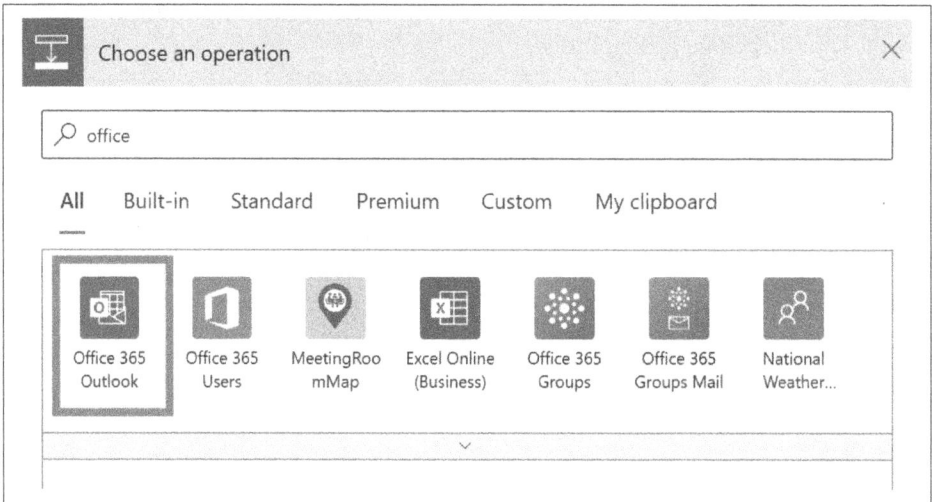

Again, in the connectors search field, type send and then choose "Send an email (V2)":

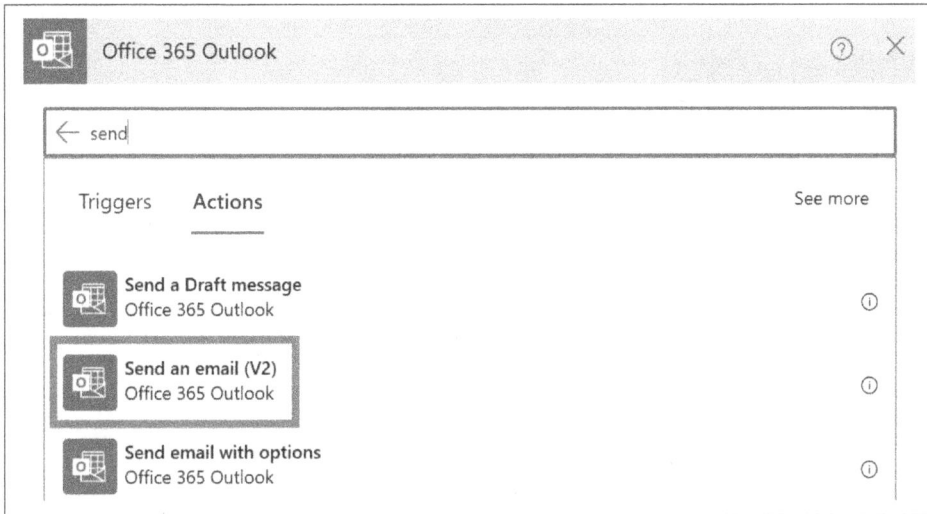

In the To field, type a team member's name and choose the corresponding user account. Note that this field can work as a "people picker" from your organization's accounts. You can type email addresses by switching to Advanced Mode instead of picking accounts:

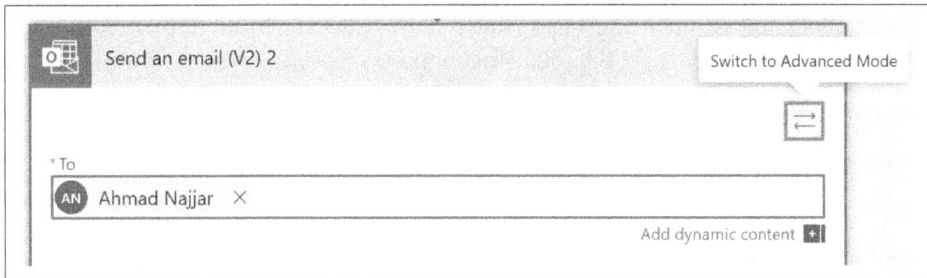

Then, provide a subject for the email, e.g., "Timesheet Reminder." In the Body rich-text field, type the email text reminding your team members to submit their time-sheets by the end of the day:

Finally, check for no error messages (under Flow Checker in the top ribbon), then click Save. Make sure you get the following message once you save the flow:

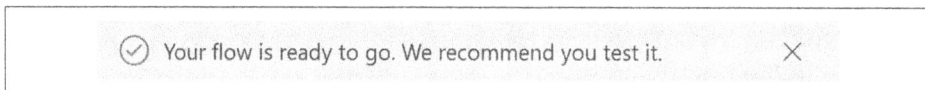

You've now set up a prompt that sends weekly reminders to a group of people (team members). You can make this scenario dynamic by making the team members dynamic, for example, getting the email addresses from an Excel sheet or a Share-Point list, which I will go through later in this book. We can also make the email subject and body more intuitive, for example, by adding an expression in the subject input field to show the week number, or a link to the timesheet site.

You can always check templates related to notifications on the Power Automate website (*https://oreil.ly/mhX0a*).

See Also

- Recipe 3.2, "Sending Daily Weather Forecasts"
- Recipe 4.4, "Sending a Reminder Email for Tasks Due by Tomorrow"
- Recipe 4.5, "Sending Employees Birthday Emails"
- Recipe 7.4, "Sending a Report of Existing Teams and Channels"

3.2 Sending Daily Weather Forecasts

Problem

You want to schedule a recurring daily email notification containing the weather forecast information for the day.

Solution

Create a scheduled cloud flow, setting the required frequency, that gets weather forecast information and then emails the targeted recipients the forecast in the desired email format.

Discussion

For many people, checking the weather is one of the first things they do in the morning, right after waking up. You may want to change this habit and get the weather forecast for the day in your email instead of checking it through your mobile-integrated apps. Remember that this recipe doesn't solely apply to getting the weather forecast; it can apply to any service that Power Automate integrates with, such as news, RSS, etc.

Like the previous recipe, I will start with a recurring trigger by setting up a scheduled flow. I want this flow to run daily on working days (every day except Saturdays and Sundays).

Navigate to the Power Automate home page (*https://oreil.ly/O-MRf*). Then click on Create from the left navigation menu:

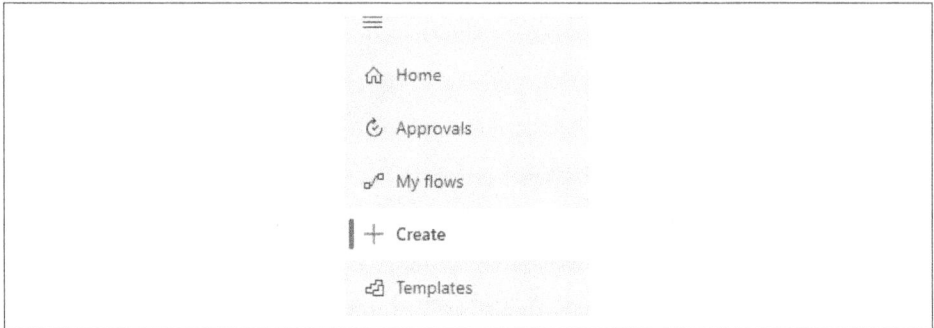

Select "Scheduled cloud flow":

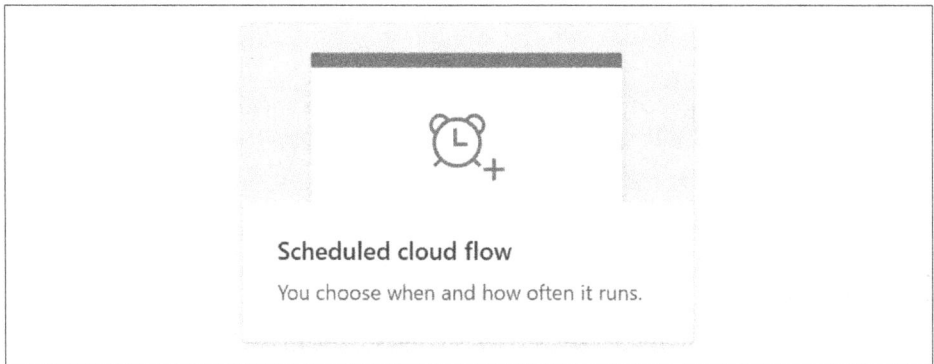

Scheduled cloud flow
You choose when and how often it runs.

In the pop-up window, under "Flow name," provide a name for the flow, such as "Daily Weather Forecasts," and click Create. I'll set up the schedule in the flow designer this time. Note that the flow will not run until you save it from the flow designer. Click on the trigger Recurrence to expand it. Once expanded, change frequency to Week:

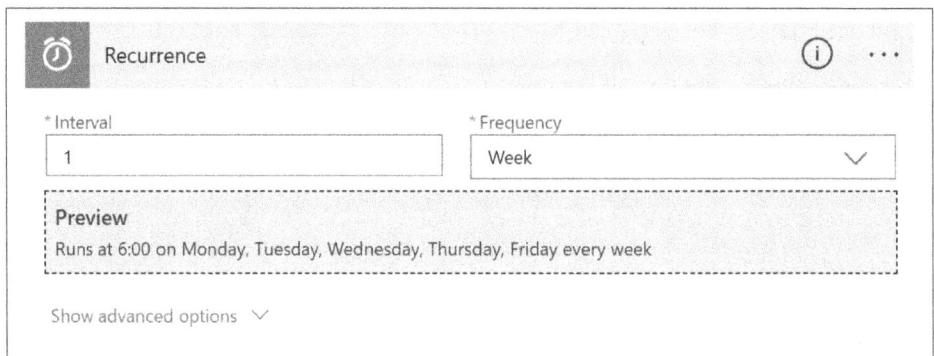

Click on "Show advanced options." Change the "Time zone" to match your own. This will ensure that the flow will run according to your time zone. Then provide a start date and time; there's a maximum of 49 years in the future, and your entry must follow the ISO 8601 date time specification in UTC date time format:

- YYYY-MM-DDThh:mm:ss if you select a time zone
- YYYY-MM-DDThh:mm:ssZ if you don't select a time zone

> For more about ISO 8601 date time specification, see the corresponding Wikipedia entry (*https://oreil.ly/IXHCk*).

I'll set the start date to February 6, 2023, at 6:00 A.M.: 2023-02-06T06:00:00.000Z. Open the drop-down beside "On these days" and unselect Saturday and Sunday:

Monday,Tuesday,Wednesday,Thursday,Friday	∨
☐ Select all	
☑ Monday	
☑ Tuesday	
☑ Wednesday	
☑ Thursday	
☑ Friday	
☐ Saturday	
☐ Sunday	

Open the drop-down next to "At these hours" and select 6. Leave the field beside "At these minutes" blank. This will schedule the flow to run at 6:00 A.M. If you want the flow to run at 6:30 (for example), then enter 30 in the field beside "At these minutes":

At this point, our scheduled trigger is ready. Remember that we can always change the schedule even after saving the flow. Next, click "New step." Then, in the search field, type weather. Choose the MSN Weather connector:

Click "Get forecast for today":

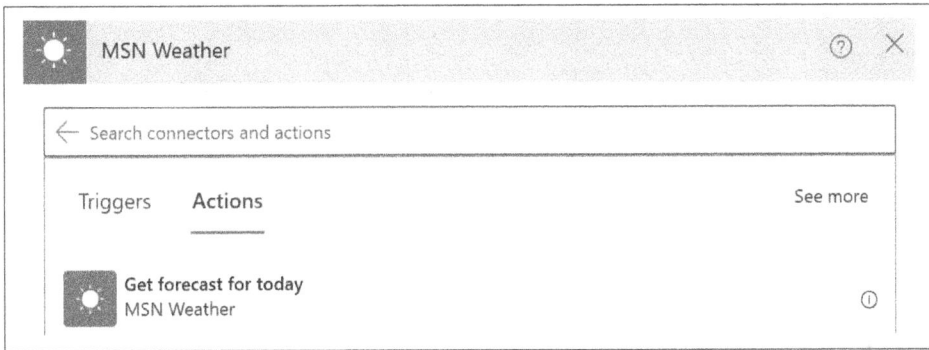

Fill in the Location field. Valid inputs are city, region, state, country, landmark, postal code, or longitude and latitude. Then choose the measurement units (Imperial or Metric):

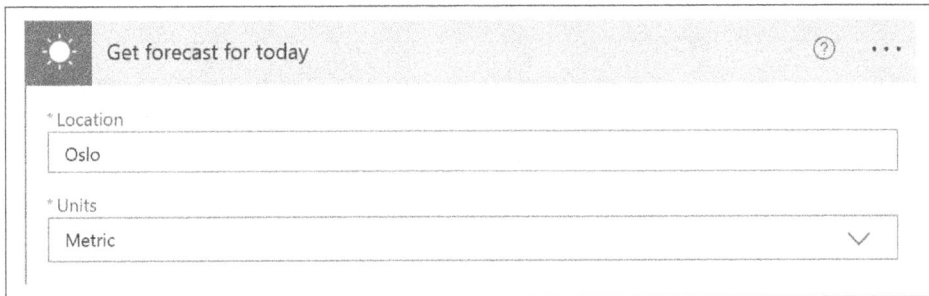

Next, click "New step." Then, in the search field, type office. Choose the Office 365 Outlook connector:

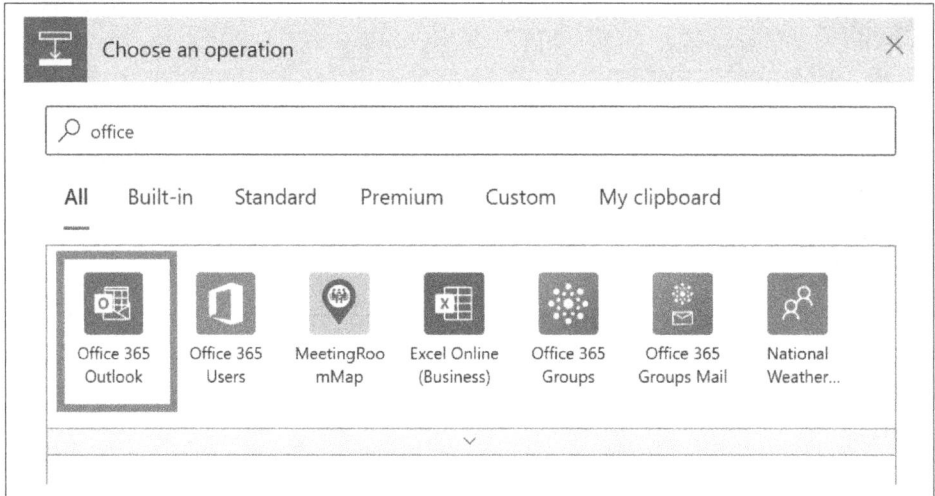

Again, in the connectors search field, type send, then choose "Send an email (V2)":

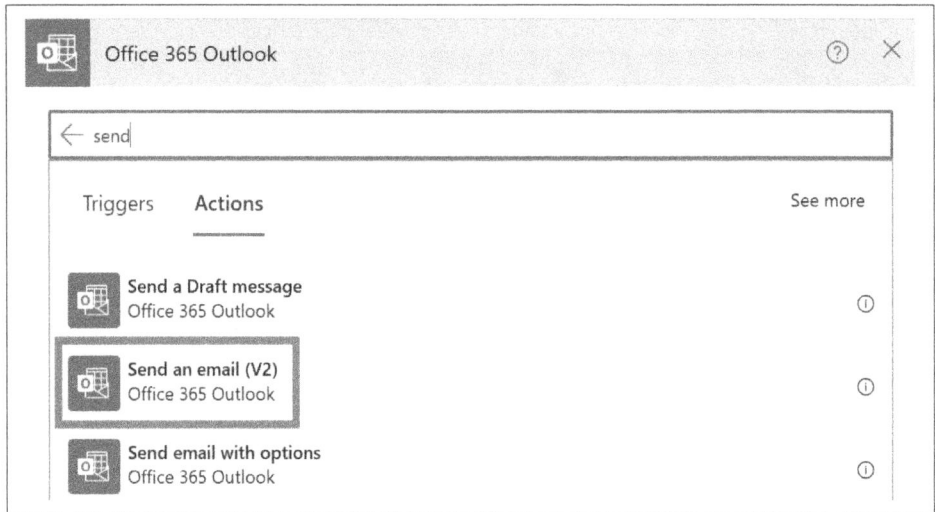

In the To field, type in your name or the email address you want to send the weather forecast to. Enter a subject for the email, e.g., "Today's Weather Forecast." In the Body rich-text field, you can fill in the weather forecast data you are interested in, such as humidity, temperature high, temperature low, conditions, rain chance, UV index, etc.:

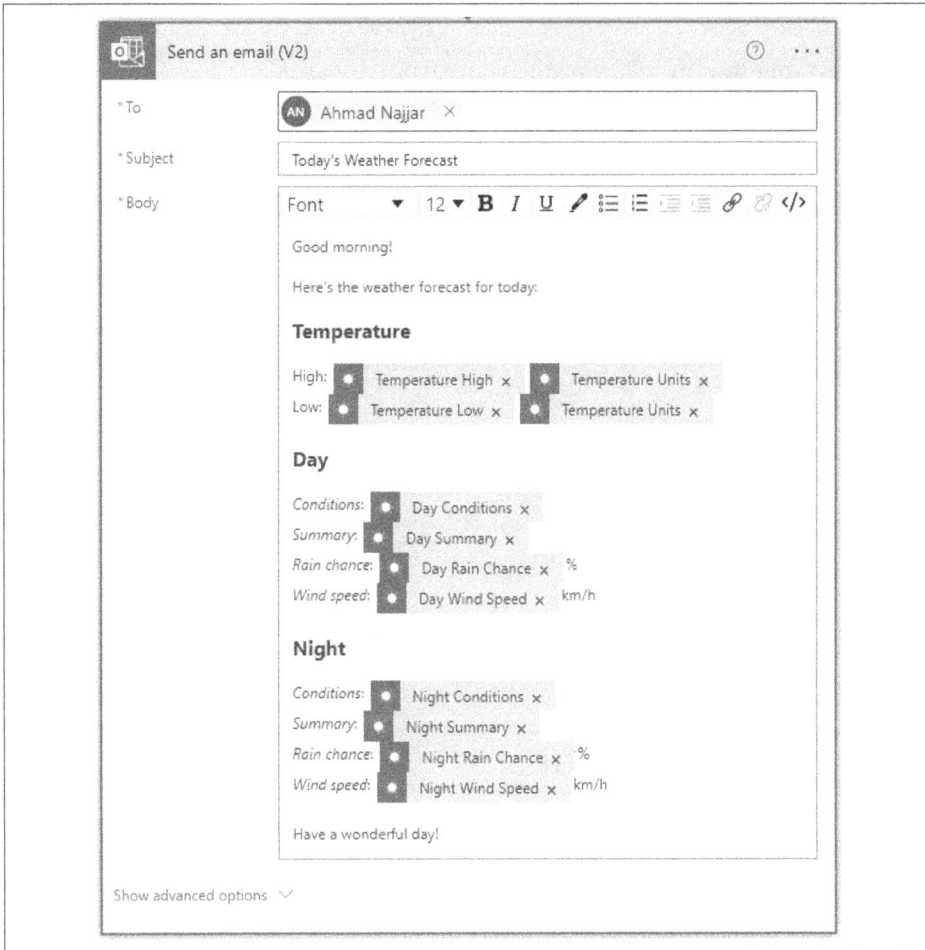

Check that there are no error messages, then click Save. Make sure you get the following message once you save the flow:

> ⊘ Your flow is ready to go. We recommend you test it.　　　　　　✕

Finally, test your flow by following the same steps I discussed in Chapter 2. Your notification email should look something like this:

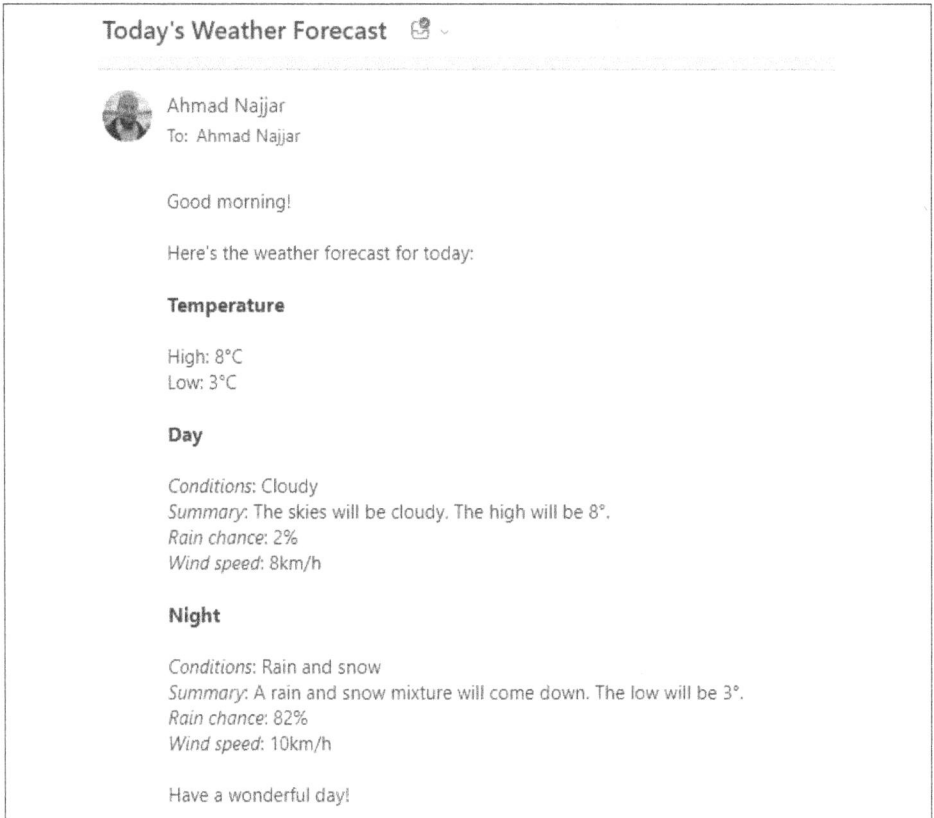

Today's Weather Forecast

Ahmad Najjar
To: Ahmad Najjar

Good morning!

Here's the weather forecast for today:

Temperature

High: 8°C
Low: 3°C

Day

Conditions: Cloudy
Summary: The skies will be cloudy. The high will be 8°.
Rain chance: 2%
Wind speed: 8km/h

Night

Conditions: Rain and snow
Summary: A rain and snow mixture will come down. The low will be 3°.
Rain chance: 82%
Wind speed: 10km/h

Have a wonderful day!

See Also

- Recipe 3.1, "Sending Recurring Reminders"
- Recipe 4.4, "Sending a Reminder Email for Tasks Due by Tomorrow"
- Recipe 4.5, "Sending Employees Birthday Emails"
- Recipe 7.4, "Sending a Report of Existing Teams and Channels"

Push Notifications

A push notification is an alert (typically a pop-up) on a smartphone generated by an application when the application is not open, allowing the user to get app-related events and updates in real time.

Push notifications were introduced in 2009 on Apple's iOS 3 operating system. Over the years, push notifications have become more prevalent as a standard feature of mobile apps, allowing app makers to engage with their users even when they aren't actively using the app. It is a feature that has proved powerful for businesses to drive app activity and engagement and retain users.

In recent years, push notifications have become more sophisticated, with features like personalized messages, geolocation-based alerts, and third-party services like Power Automate app integration. They are now an essential part of the mobile app ecosystem and are used by almost every mobile app to keep users engaged and informed.

In Power Automate, push notifications can be triggered (sent) by countless scenarios, like the completion of a flow, an update on a file or a record, or the occurrence of a specific event or condition. Push notifications can be sent to various devices, including mobile phones and tablets. The recipient(s) will typically need the Power Automate mobile app installed on their device to receive push notifications.

3.3 Getting Push Notifications When You Get an Email from Your Manager

Problem

You want to get a push notification on your mobile when you receive an email from your manager.

Solution

Create a cloud flow from the "Get a push notification when you receive an email from your boss" template.

Discussion

Your mobile might buzz with every update you get through your native apps. Your email native app might be doing the same. However, you might want that to happen only when it matters, such as when you get an email from your boss or an important client.

I'll use an existing template as a starting point for this recipe. To begin, ensure you have installed the Power Automate mobile app on your phone and signed in with your credentials (see "Mobile App" on page 45). Navigate to the Power Automate home page (*https://oreil.ly/O-MRf*) and click Templates from the left navigation menu:

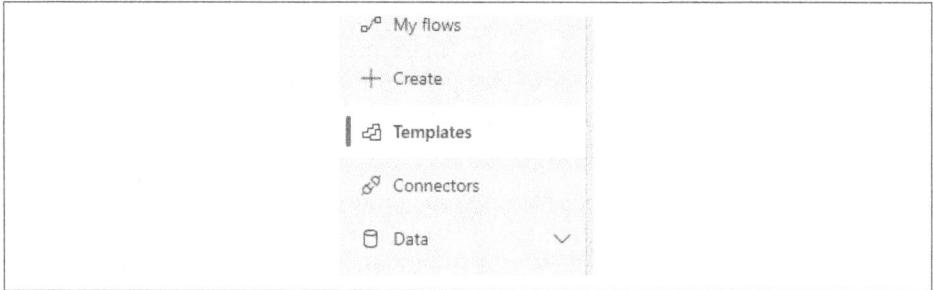

On the templates page, type boss in the search templates text field and hit the Enter key. From the search results, choose "Get a push notification when you receive an email from your boss." On the next page, ensure you are connected/signed in to the required connectors, then click Create Flow:

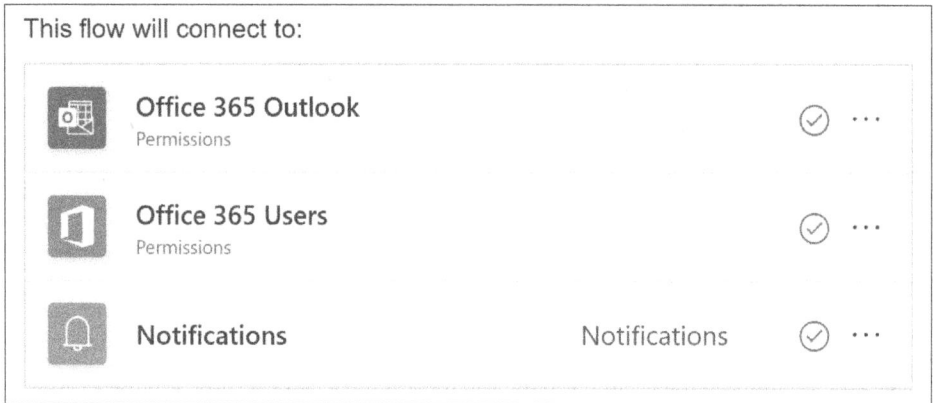

Clicking Create Flow will take you to the flow details page, not to the flow designer experience, since no further configurations or input are needed, meaning this flow is saved and running:

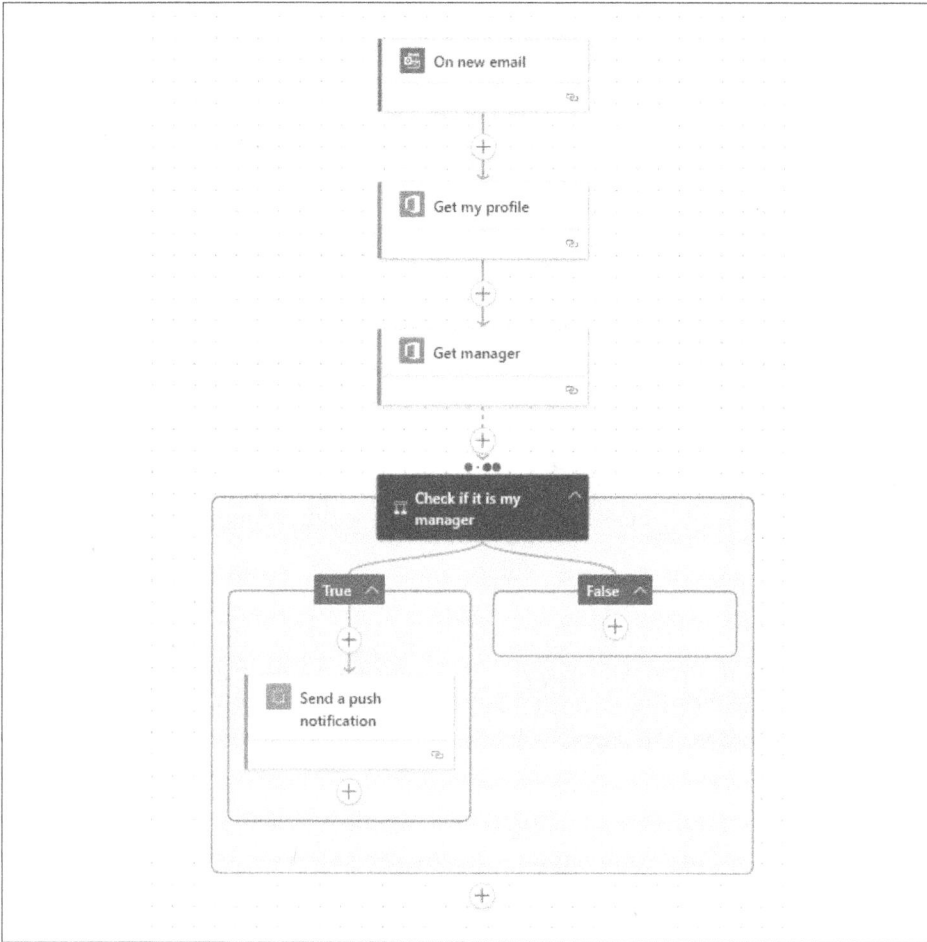

After receiving an email from your manager, a push notification will be sent to your mobile phone via the Power Automate app:

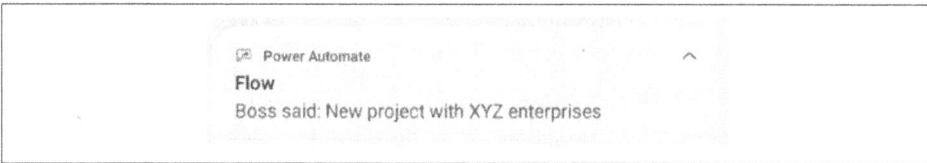

See Also

- Recipe 3.4, "Getting Push Notifications When There Is an Update on the Weather Forecast"
- Recipe 3.5, "Getting Push Notifications When a File Has Been Uploaded to OneDrive for Business"

3.4 Getting Push Notifications When There Is an Update on the Weather Forecast

Problem

You want to get a push notification on your mobile when there is a change in the weather forecast.

Solution

Create an automated cloud flow that monitors weather forecast changes for a specific location and then sends a push notification with the weather condition change.

Discussion

You often want to receive push notifications only when there are updates on a particular service, such as the weather service or when changes happen on a list in Share-Point. This means that you don't have to check updates on the service itself (recurrence). However, the trigger will initiate when there are updates on the service end.

To build a flow to receive push notifications when there is an update on the weather forecast using the MSN Weather connector, you can follow the steps described in this section.

First, ensure that you have installed the Power Automate mobile app on your phone and signed in with your credentials (see "Mobile App" on page 45). Next, go to the Power Automate portal (*https://oreil.ly/O-MRf*) and sign in using your Microsoft account or your organization's account. Before proceeding, verify that you are in the correct Power Automate environment.

Once signed in, navigate to the lefthand navigation bar and click on "My flows," then select "New flow" to create a new automation. Since you want to receive weather condition updates, choose the "Automated cloud flow" option. When prompted with a pop-up, click Skip to proceed to the flow designer experience.

In the flow designer, search for the MSN Weather connector and select the appropriate trigger, which in this case is "When the current conditions change." At this step, you may need to sign in and authenticate your MSN Weather account. Finally, configure the location and units (Metric or Imperial) trigger parameters to determine the weather data you want to receive:

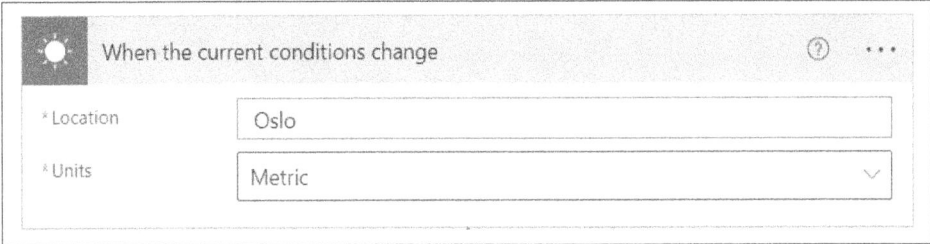

After getting the weather data, you can add an action(s) to send push notifications. Click on "Next step," search for the Notifications connector, and choose the action for your mobile device (e.g., Send a Mobile Notification). Customize the content of your notification with the weather forecast information. You can use dynamic content from the MSN Weather trigger in the notification body. Choose Conditions for the Text parameter. In the Link parameter field, choose Expressions and use the following expression:

```
triggerBody()?['responses']?['source']?['clickThrough']
```

The previous expression uses dynamic content from the MSN Weather trigger (responses), and then it drills down through that content to reach the clickThrough property, the source link for the weather updates. Finally, label the link in the Link parameter field (e.g., "Weather Update"):

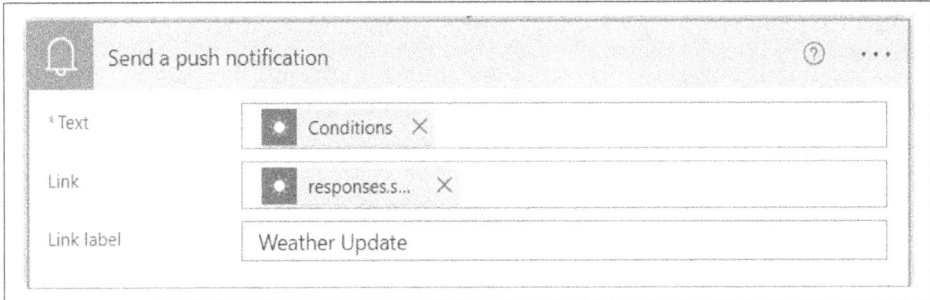

Give your flow a name and then save and test your flow to ensure it works as expected. This flow can't be tested manually; you need a change on the service end. However, the trigger will start eventually:

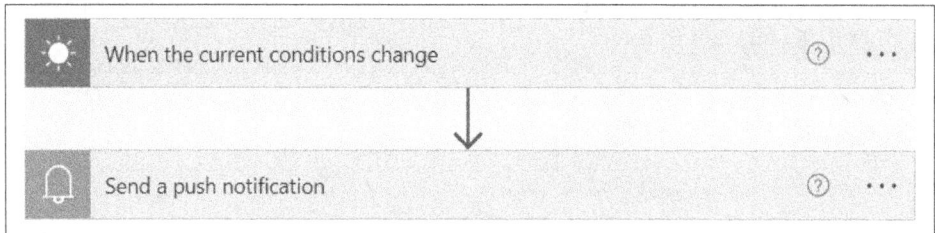

See Also

- Recipe 3.3, "Getting Push Notifications When You Get an Email from Your Manager"
- Recipe 3.5, "Getting Push Notifications When a File Has Been Uploaded to OneDrive for Business"

3.5 Getting Push Notifications When a File Has Been Uploaded to OneDrive for Business

Problem

You want to receive a push notification on your mobile device whenever a file is uploaded to OneDrive for Business.

Solution

Create an automated cloud flow that monitors file creation in a specific folder in OneDrive for Business and then sends a push notification with information about the file creation.

Discussion

There are many scenarios where you may want to get notified when a file is uploaded to a particular repository, such as OneDrive for Business. You might be a project manager who wants to keep track of all files for a particular project. You might be working with an important client on a shared folder and want to be notified whenever the client uploads a file into that folder. Finally, you might be an editor who wants to audit any file uploaded to a shared folder in OneDrive for Business. To be notified, follow the steps described in this section.

Ensure you have installed the Power Automate mobile app on your phone and signed in with your credentials (see "Mobile App" on page 45). Go to the Power Automate portal (*https://oreil.ly/E8BsT*) and sign in with your Microsoft account or your organization's account. Make sure that you're in the correct Power Automate environment. Click on "My flows" in the left navigation bar. Click on "New flow" to create a new flow. Choose a flow type. In this case, you want to be notified when a file is uploaded, so you must choose "Automated cloud flow." Click Skip on the pop-up to navigate to the flow designer experience. Search for the OneDrive for Business connector in the flow designer. You want the trigger to be related to when a file is created (uploaded), so you should choose the "When a file is created (properties only)" trigger. You may need to sign in and authenticate your OneDrive for Business account. Configure the trigger parameters, including folder (the relevant folder or directory in which you want to monitor for file uploads), number of files to return, and whether subfolders should be monitored to trigger the flow when files get created (uploaded) in them:

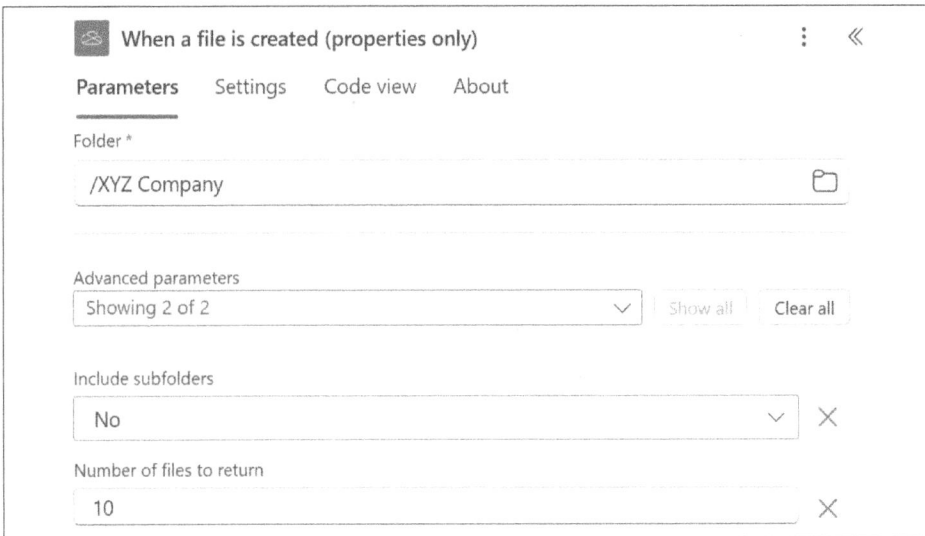

The selected trigger fires on both files and folders. You can skip creating the following condition if you want to be notified when either is created. However, if you'd like to be notified only when files are created (uploaded), then click on "New step," search for "Control," and then select the Control actions. From the list of actions, choose Condition. Configure the condition action by selecting the "Is folder?" property from the trigger dynamic content for the left-side comparison value. Make sure the comparison operator is set to "is equal to," and then for the right-side comparison, in the expression flyout pane, type false and then click Save:

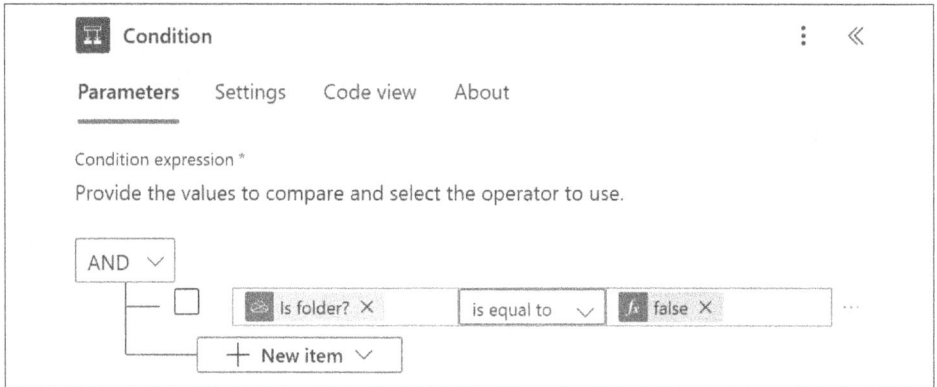

The trigger doesn't provide a property (URL) to access the created/uploaded file directly from the notification alert. This means that you are required to create this within the flow:

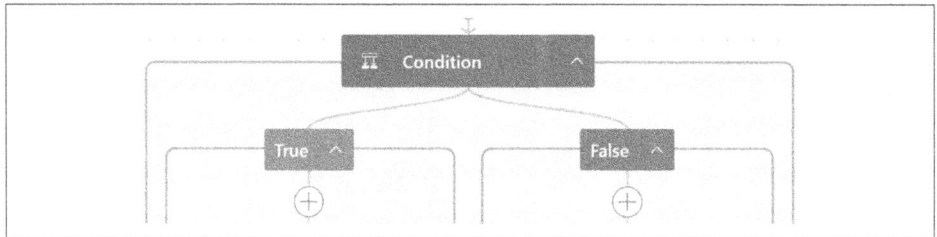

If the condition is true (under the green box), add a new action, search for the One-Drive for Business connector, and then choose the "Create share link" action. Configure the File (the ID of the file from the trigger), Link Type (Edit or View), and Link Scope (where the link can be accessed from, anonymously or only within the organization) action parameters:

| Create share link | ⋮ ≪ |

Parameters   Settings   Code view   Testing   About

File *

🔲 Id ✕   📁

Link type *

View   ⌄

Advanced parameters

Showing 1 of 1   ⌄ | Show all | Clear all

Link scope

Organization   ⌄ ✕

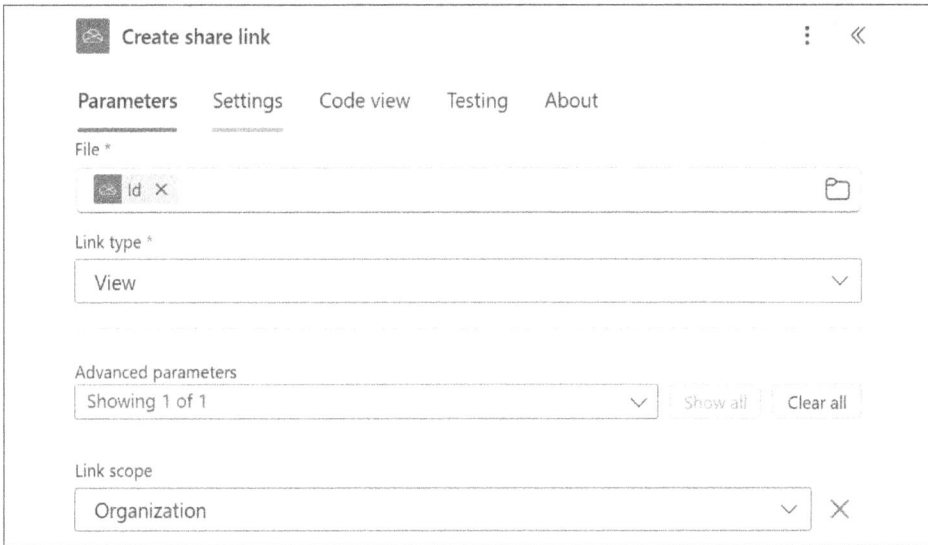

Then, add another action within the condition True box. Search for the Notifications connector and select the "Send me a mobile notification" action. Customize the content of your notification with the file information. You can use the dynamic content from the trigger in the notification body. In the Text field, type A file has been uploaded to OneDrive, or use dynamic content as shown. Finally, use the Web URL property in the Link parameter from the "Create share link" action, then use the Name property from the trigger dynamic content:

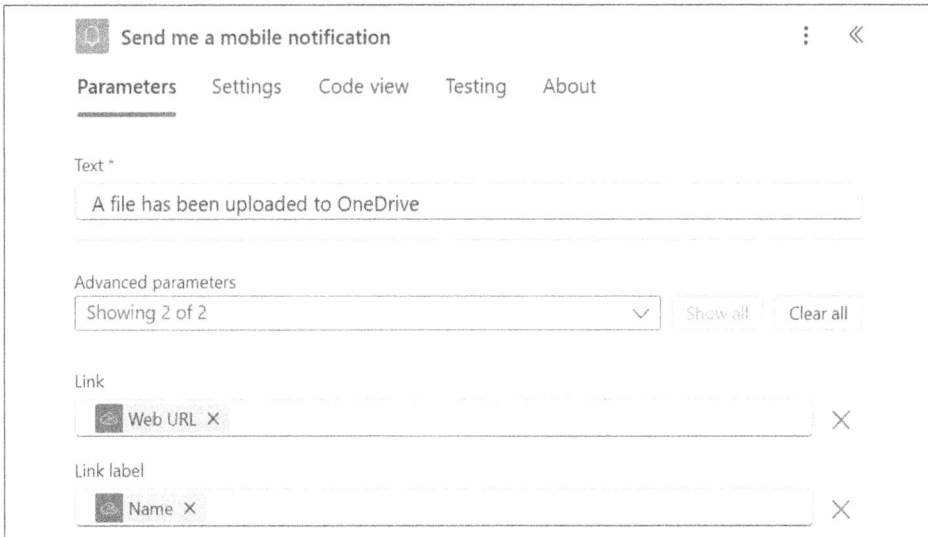

| Send me a mobile notification | ⋮ ≪ |

Parameters   Settings   Code view   Testing   About

Text *

A file has been uploaded to OneDrive

Advanced parameters

Showing 2 of 2   ⌄ | Show all | Clear all

Link

🔲 Web URL ✕   ✕

Link label

🔲 Name ✕   ✕

Give your flow a name and then save and test your flow to ensure it works as expected:

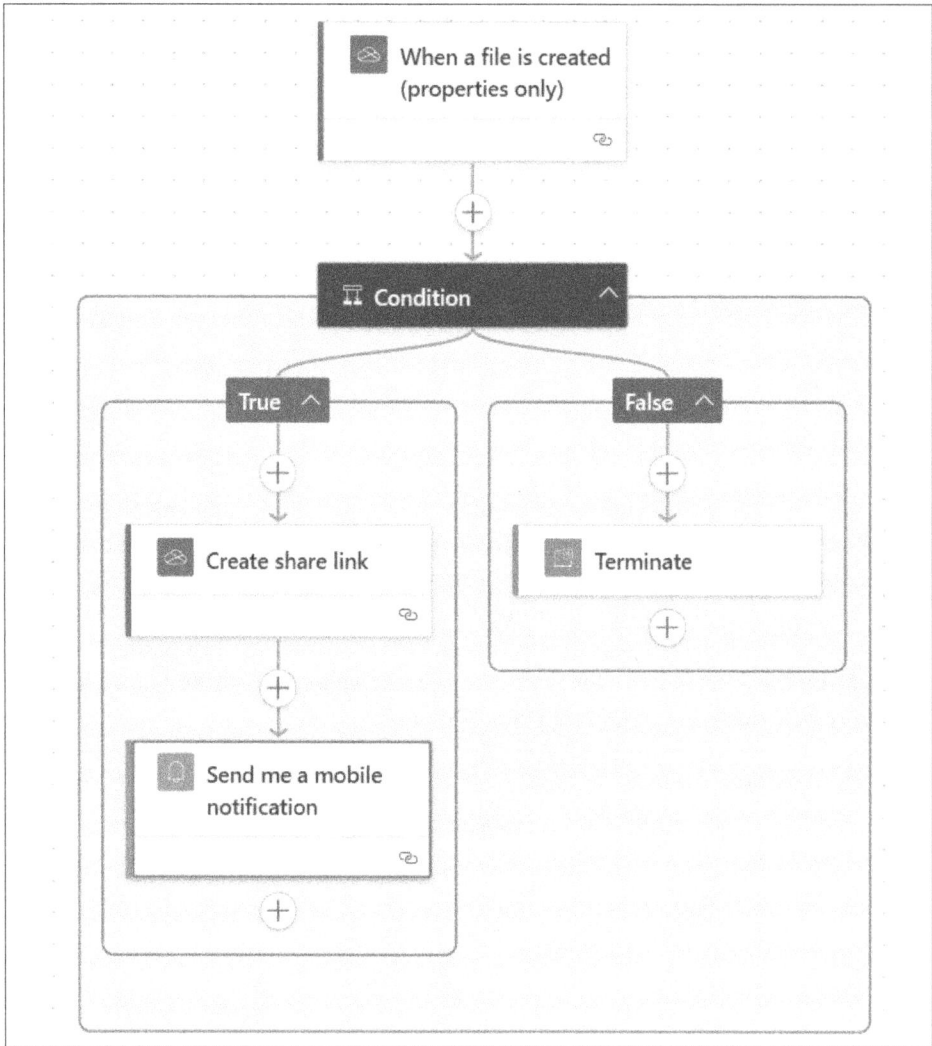

See Also

- Recipe 3.3, "Getting Push Notifications When You Get an Email from Your Manager"
- Recipe 3.4, "Getting Push Notifications When There Is an Update on the Weather Forecast"

Other Notification Types

There are other notification types that could be standard for specific scenarios (projects).

The type of notification used sometimes sets a level of urgency to the receiver. This also might differ from one receiver to another, though the common belief is that Short Message Service (SMS) and automated calls set the highest level of urgency.

Some other services and apps are considered as notification (and communication) platforms, such as Slack, Teams, WhatsApp, and others.

3.6 Getting an SMS When You Receive a Specific Email

Problem

You want to get an SMS when you receive a salary release email in your inbox.

Solution

Create an automated cloud flow that monitors your email inbox for a salary release email and then sends an SMS.

Discussion

SMS notifications serve various purposes. However, receiving an SMS notification indicates a high level of urgency and importance, such as notifications from your bank about transactions, salary releases, or confirmations for clinic appointments. In this capacity, you can also create flows to send SMS notifications when certain events occur, such as when you receive your salary release email from accounting (for example).

> There are no native out-of-the-box SMS services from Microsoft in Power Automate. All SMS services in Power Automate are from third-party service providers such as Twilio, BulkSMS, and others. This means you must create an account and subscribe (additional service fees) to the third-party service to use its connector in Power Automate.

To create a Power Automate cloud flow that sends an SMS when your salary email is received, go to the Power Automate portal (*https://oreil.ly/E8BsT*) and sign in using your Microsoft account or your organization's account. Before proceeding, ensure that you're in the correct Power Automate environment.

Once signed in, navigate to the lefthand navigation bar and click on "My flows," then select "New flow" to create a new automation. Since you want to be notified when you receive your monthly salary email, choose the "Automated cloud flow" option. When prompted with a pop-up, click Skip to proceed to the flow designer experience.

In the flow designer, search for the Office 365 Outlook connector and select the "When a new email arrives (V3)" trigger. At this step, you may need to sign in and authenticate your Office 365 Outlook account. Finally, configure the trigger parameters, specifying the Folder (the inbox folder where you want to monitor new emails) and the From field (the sender's email address, e.g., *salary@xyzcompany.com*). Setting the From parameter ensures that the trigger fires only when you receive an email from that specific address:

For SMS notifications, I suggest using Twilio as the service provider. Therefore, subscribe to the Twilio SMS service to continue with this example.

> Twilio has a free trial subscription. Create a Twilio account (*https://oreil.ly/K2XGu*) to subscribe to the free trial, and follow the instructions to set up your SMS notification service with Twilio. You'll need your Twilio account ID and the associated access token for that account ID.

For the following action, search for the Twilio connector and then choose the Send Text Message (SMS) action. You must create a connection to your Twilio account to use the Twilio service. Configure your connection by giving it a name, and then provide your Twilio Account Id and Twilio Access Token, which you'll find under Keys & Credentials > "API keys & tokens" in your account. Finally, configure the From Phone Number (a configured phone number in the Twilio service to send SMS notifications from), To Phone Number (the mobile number you want to receive notifications on), and Text (which is the message text) action parameters:

Give your flow a name and then save and test your flow to ensure it works as expected:

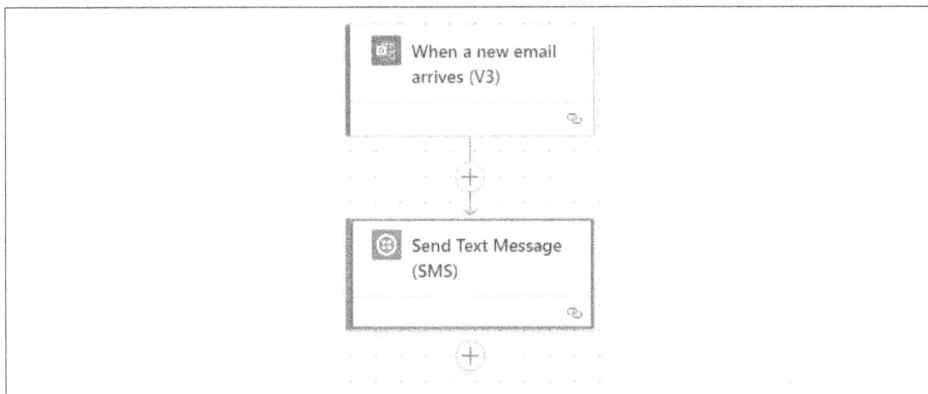

After building the previous flow, you learned how to set up SMS notifications even for more complex flows that fit your needs, such as sending reminders and notifications to your customers on important matters.

See Also

- Recipe 3.7, "Getting a Slack Message When a File Has Been Updated on OneDrive for Business"

3.7 Getting a Slack Message When a File Has Been Updated on OneDrive for Business

Problem

You want to post a message to Slack when a file gets updated on OneDrive for Business.

Solution

Create an automated cloud flow that monitors file modifications in a specific folder in OneDrive for Business and then posts a message to Slack containing information about the updated file.

Discussion

For several reasons, using Slack for notifications with Power Automate flows can be advantageous. Like Microsoft Teams, Slack provides real-time messaging and collaboration capabilities. Integrating with Power Automate enables instant notifications, allowing you and your team to be informed promptly.

You can create channels dedicated to specific projects or topics and notify the relevant teams or individuals when particular events occur. Integrating this feature with Power Automate enhances your notification experience by standardizing the notification platform.

Let's assume that you are working with a team that uses Slack for communication on all matters. There is a set of documents all the team members must collaborate on to finalize. Every update on these documents is essential for the whole team, so they must know what has been updated for further elaboration.

To learn how you can create a Power Automate cloud flow that utilizes Slack for notification when files have been updated on OneDrive for Business, go to the Power Automate portal (*https://oreil.ly/O-MRf*). Sign in with your Microsoft account or your organization's account. Make sure you are in the correct Power Automate environment. Click on "My flows" in the left navigation bar. Click on "New flow" to create a new flow. Choose a flow type. In this case, you want to be notified when a file is updated, so you must choose "Automated cloud flow." Click Skip on the pop-up to navigate to the flow designer experience. Search for the OneDrive for Business connector in the flow designer. You want the trigger to be related to when a file is updated, so choose the "When a file is modified (properties only)" trigger. You may need to sign in and authenticate your OneDrive for Business account. Configure the trigger parameters, including folder (the relevant folder or directory in which you want to monitor for file updates), number of files to return, and whether subfolders should be monitored to trigger the flow when files get modified:

The trigger doesn't provide a property (URL) to access the modified file directly from the notification alert. This means that you're required to create this within the flow. Add a new action, search for the OneDrive for Business connector, and then choose the "Create share link" action. Configure the File (the ID of the file from the trigger), Link Type (Edit or View), and Link Scope (where the link can be accessed from, anonymously or only within the organization) action parameters:

Add an action to post a message into a Slack channel. Search for the Slack connector and select the "Post message (V2)" action. You may need to sign in and authenticate your Slack account. You may also need to consent if a Power Automate connector requests permission to access a Slack workplace. Ensure you allow that request to grant permission for Power Automate to post messages on Slack:

Microsoft Power Platform Connectors is requesting permission to access the Power Automate Cookbook Slack workspace

What will Microsoft Power Platform Connectors be able to view?

👤	Content and info about you	▸
💬	Content and info about channels & conversations	▸
⊞	Content and info about your workspace	▸

What will Microsoft Power Platform Connectors be able to do?

👤	Perform actions as you	▸
💬	Perform actions in channels & conversations	▸

Cancel   **Allow**

Configure the action by providing the Channel Name (the Slack channel you want the message to be posted to). Finally, customize the Message Text parameter (the Slack message to be posted on the chosen channel). You can use the dynamic content from the trigger and the "Create share link" action:

```
File {File DisplayName} has been modified! To check modifications, click on the
 attached link.
{File WebUrl}
```

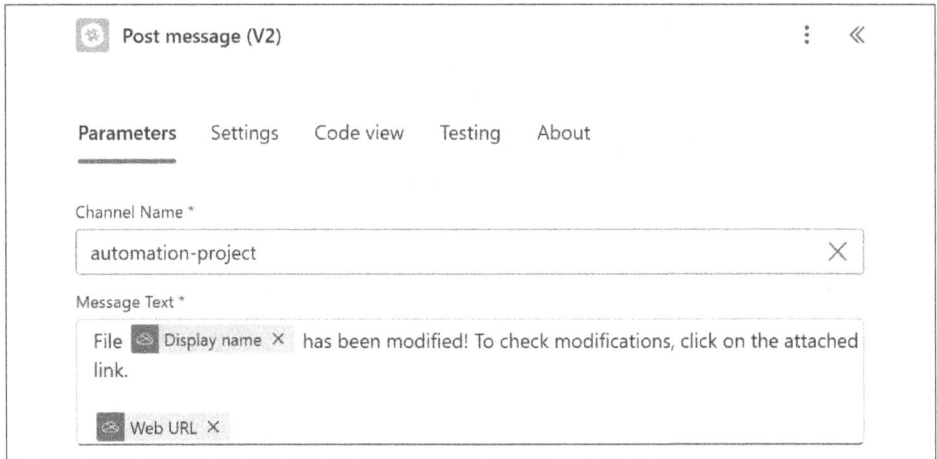

Give your flow a name, then save and test your flow to ensure it works as expected:

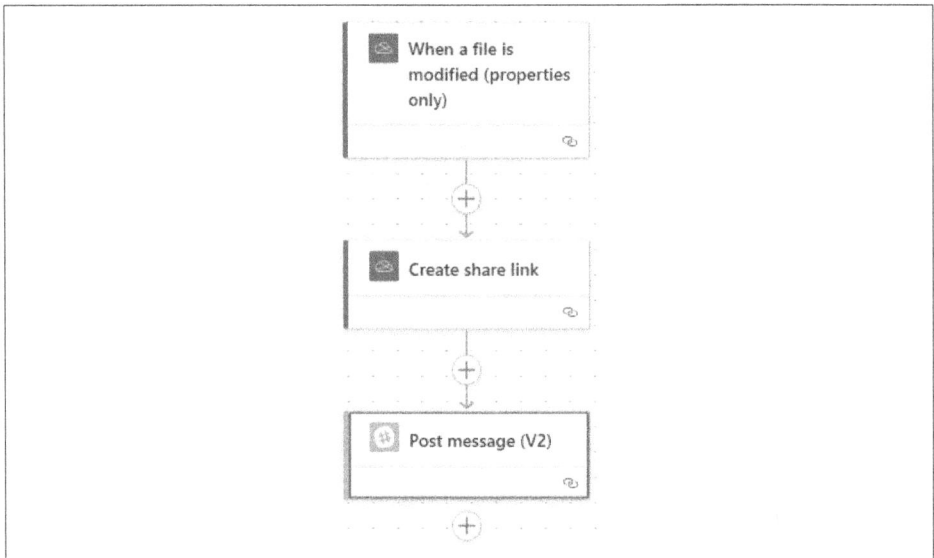

See Also

- Recipe 3.6, "Getting an SMS When You Receive a Specific Email"
- Recipe 4.1, "Posting a Message on Slack and Sending an Email to the Assignee When an Issue Is Created"
- Recipe 4.2, "Posting a Message on Slack When an Issue Status Has Been Modified"
- Recipe 7.2, "Posting a Message on Slack When a Message Is Posted on Teams"

Conclusion

Working with notifications in Power Automate empowers you to streamline communication, enhance productivity, and stay informed in real time. Whether receiving alerts about critical events, automating email notifications, or integrating with collaboration platforms such as Slack and Microsoft Teams, Power Automate offers a versatile and user-friendly solution. By leveraging its capabilities, you can ensure key team members are always in the loop, enabling timely responses to important updates and events. Notifications in Power Automate reduce manual efforts and foster efficient decision making and collaboration across teams, ultimately contributing to improved operational efficiency and agility in the modern workplace!

CHAPTER 4

Power Automate and SharePoint

In this chapter, I'll go through a little bit of Microsoft SharePoint's history, what SharePoint is, and how it became a central collaboration workspace for organizations. Then, I'll go through SharePoint's correlation with automation and how Power Automate and SharePoint became best buddies. Finally, I'll go through common automation scenarios that are based on using SharePoint.

The History of SharePoint

SharePoint has evolved significantly since its inception in the early 2000s. Its journey began with the Microsoft SharePoint Portal Server 2001 release, which marked Microsoft's entry into the enterprise collaboration and content management space. This initial version laid the foundation for document sharing and management within organizations. It allowed users to create web-based portals to store, organize, and share documents and other information.

Microsoft Office SharePoint Portal Server 2003 followed, offering improved collaboration features, enhanced search capabilities, and tighter integration with Microsoft Office applications. The platform underwent a significant transformation with the release of Microsoft Office SharePoint Server 2007 (MOSS 2007), marking a key milestone in SharePoint's evolution. This version introduced features such as document versioning, workflows, and custom web applications, making it a more versatile tool for businesses to manage content and streamline processes.

A major enhancement in MOSS 2007 was its workflow engine, which enabled organizations to automate and optimize business processes. It supported two main types of workflows: built-in workflows for common tasks and custom workflows for more tailored automation needs.

The built-in workflows included essential templates for approval workflows, collecting feedback, and managing document review processes. These out-of-the-box workflows made it easier for users to automate common tasks and approvals without extensive customization. They provided a foundation for businesses to enhance their efficiency and compliance.

Custom workflows, on the other hand, offered greater flexibility. With the introduction of SharePoint Designer 2007, organizations could create custom workflows tailored to their specific needs. This visual design tool allowed users to define workflows without writing code. Organizations could design complex, multistage workflows integrating with SharePoint lists, libraries, and document management processes. This capability enabled businesses to optimize internal processes, automate document routing, and improve collaboration within the SharePoint environment.

Overall, MOSS 2007 was pivotal in bringing workflow automation to SharePoint, offering various options to suit basic and intricate business processes. It laid the groundwork for further workflow advancements in subsequent SharePoint versions, making it a key platform for enhancing organizational productivity and collaboration.

In 2010, Microsoft introduced SharePoint 2010, which built upon the success of its predecessor. This version emphasized enhanced social collaboration, business intelligence, and scalability. It introduced features like the ribbon interface, improved search, and the ability to build custom solutions using SharePoint Designer and Visual Studio.

SharePoint 2013 continued this evolution by focusing on responsive design, making it more accessible across different devices and screen sizes. It also integrated with Microsoft's cloud platform, Azure, providing hybrid deployment options for organizations.

In 2010, the world started shifting from traditional (server) computing to cloud computing. SharePoint Online was initially launched in 2011 as part of Office 365; this cloud-based evolution of Microsoft's SharePoint platform has significantly developed and improved over the years. SharePoint Online became "the cloud" alternative for document management and team collaboration. However, its transformation was marked by a shift toward enhanced collaboration and mobility between 2016 and 2019. This era saw the introduction of modern team sites, tighter integration with Microsoft Teams, and responsive design, providing users with a more versatile and mobile-friendly experience.

In 2020 and 2021, SharePoint Online embraced intelligent content services, with Microsoft incorporating AI-driven features such as SharePoint Syntex for content automation and Project Cortex for knowledge extraction. These advancements aimed to automate content categorization and empower organizations with valuable insights from their data. Search, content management, and security updates were also introduced to align with evolving business needs.

Since 2022, SharePoint Online has continued its growth and integration with Microsoft 365 services and Azure. It emphasizes robust data governance, compliance, and security, catering to the stringent requirements of various industries. Furthermore, Microsoft's commitment to hybrid deployments ensures seamless integration between on-premises SharePoint environments and SharePoint Online, allowing organizations to tailor their collaboration and content management strategies to their unique needs. As SharePoint Online evolves, it remains a powerful platform for modern businesses seeking efficient collaboration, robust content management, and intelligent automation in the cloud.

SharePoint and Automation

Workflows have been integral to SharePoint Online's evolution. SharePoint Online started its journey with basic workflow capabilities but has evolved significantly. In its early years, SharePoint Online offered simple workflows through SharePoint Designer, allowing users to create sequential workflows to automate tasks like document approval or notification routing. However, these workflows needed to be more functional and flexible.

As SharePoint Online matured and became tightly integrated with the broader Microsoft 365 ecosystem, it introduced the SharePoint 2013 workflow platform. This platform brought more advanced workflow capabilities, including the ability to create reusable workflows with SharePoint Designer or custom workflows with Visual Studio. Users could design more complex, multistage workflows that spanned different Microsoft 365 services.

Later in 2015, with the advent of Microsoft Flow (now Power Automate), SharePoint Online workflow capabilities reached new heights. Microsoft Flow allowed users to create automated workflows with a user-friendly, low-code approach. It offered integration with various Microsoft 365 apps and external services, providing multiple automation possibilities. Organizations could now build workflows that spanned SharePoint Online, Outlook, and other Microsoft 365 apps, enabling them to optimize their processes and enhance productivity. In 2017, Microsoft Flow was announced as the successor of SharePoint Designer workflows, and SharePoint Designer was deprecated within a year, while SharePoint Designer support will stop as of 2026. This announcement rushed organizations into using Microsoft Flow for streamlining workflows and process automation, while others got busy converting their SharePoint Designer workflows to Microsoft Flow workflows.

On November 4, 2019, Microsoft Flow was rebranded as Power Automate. This change was part of Microsoft's broader strategy to unify its Power Platform services, including Power Apps and Power BI, under a single branding. The rebranding aimed to better reflect the comprehensive automation capabilities of the service and its integration with the broader suite of Microsoft productivity tools and services, such as Microsoft 365 and Azure.

In recent years, Microsoft has continued to enhance Power Automate and its integration with SharePoint Online, making it the preferred choice for workflow automation. Organizations can leverage this powerful tool to automate document approval, data integration, and business process automation, all within the SharePoint Online environment. As SharePoint Online and Power Automate evolve, businesses can expect even more advanced workflow capabilities and seamless integration with their digital workplace ecosystems.

4.1 Posting a Message on Slack and Sending an Email to the Assignee When an Issue Is Created

Problem

You want to post a message to Slack and email a particular recipient when an issue is created in a SharePoint list.

Solution

Create an automated cloud flow that monitors item creation in the SharePoint list, posts a message to Slack, and sends an email to a particular recipient in the desired email format.

Discussion

Issue tracking in SharePoint is a powerful feature that allows you to manage and monitor various tasks, problems, or projects. With SharePoint's out-of-the-box issue tracking list, you can create, assign, prioritize, and track issues throughout their lifecycle. The issues list lets you capture relevant information, such as issue descriptions, due dates, categories, and assigned personnel.

Furthermore, SharePoint's seamless integration with Power Automate enables you to create workflows, empowering you to automate issue-resolution processes, streamline communication, and ensure timely problem resolution.

Before starting to build this flow, make sure that you have created an issue tracking list in SharePoint or that you have read permissions on the list you want to monitor for newly created issues. First, create an issue tracking list, following the instructions in the SharePoint documentation (*https://oreil.ly/M4RMf*). Go to the Power Automate portal (*https://oreil.ly/O-MRf*). Sign in with your Microsoft account or your organization's account. Make sure you are in the correct Power Automate environment. Click on "My flows" in the left navigation bar. Click on "New flow" to create a new flow. Choose a flow type. In this case, you want to be notified when a new item is created in SharePoint, so you must choose "Automated cloud flow." Click Skip on the pop-up to navigate to the flow designer experience. Search for the SharePoint connector in the flow designer. You want the trigger to be related to when a new item is created in SharePoint, so choose the "When an item is created" trigger. You may need to sign in and authenticate your SharePoint account. Configure the Site Address (the relevant site URL where the issue tracking list resides) and List Name (the SharePoint list to be monitored for newly created items) trigger parameters:

Add an action to post a message into a Slack channel. Search for the Slack connector and select the "Post message (V2)" action. You may need to sign in and authenticate your Slack account. You may also need to consent if a Power Automate connector requests permission to access a Slack workplace. Ensure you allow that request to grant permission for Power Automate to post messages on Slack:

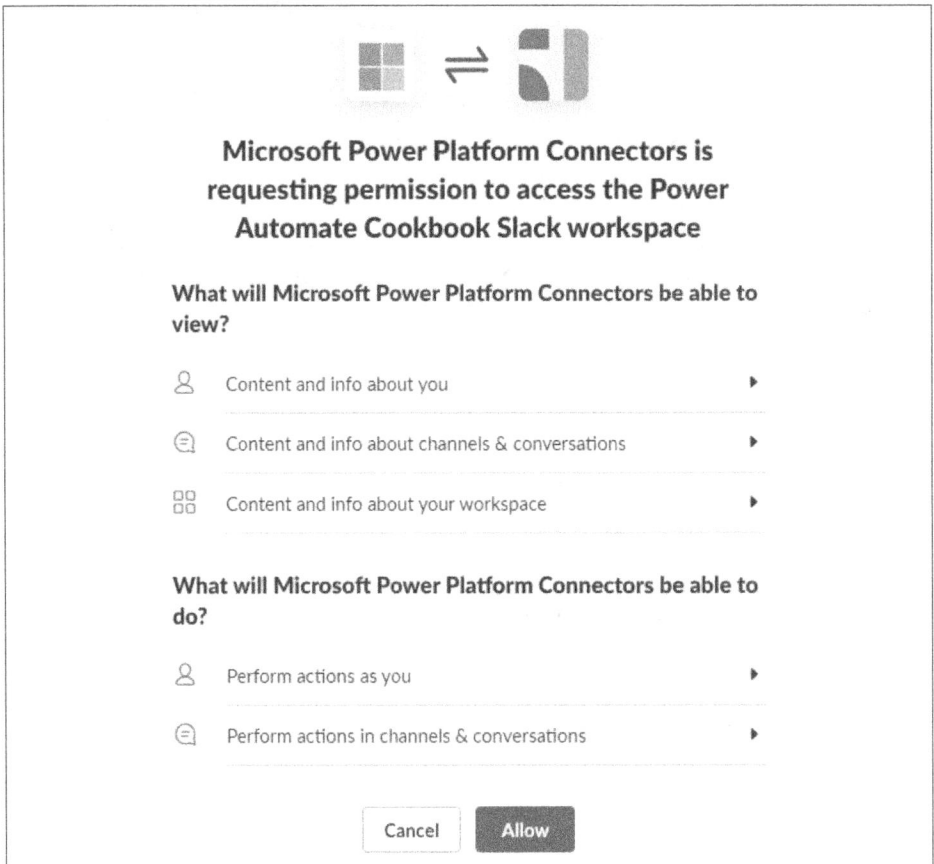

Microsoft Power Platform Connectors is requesting permission to access the Power Automate Cookbook Slack workspace

What will Microsoft Power Platform Connectors be able to view?

    Content and info about you   ▸

    Content and info about channels & conversations   ▸

    Content and info about your workspace   ▸

What will Microsoft Power Platform Connectors be able to do?

    Perform actions as you   ▸

    Perform actions in channels & conversations   ▸

Cancel   **Allow**

Triggers' and actions' version numbers evolve; it's best to select the latest version.

Configure the action by providing the Channel Name (the Slack channel you want the message to be posted to). Then customize the Message Text parameter (the Slack message to be posted on the chosen channel). You can use the dynamic content from the trigger—as shown here—such as Title, Issue, Description, Assigned to Display-Name, Priority, and "Link to item" (the URL to the newly created issue in SharePoint):

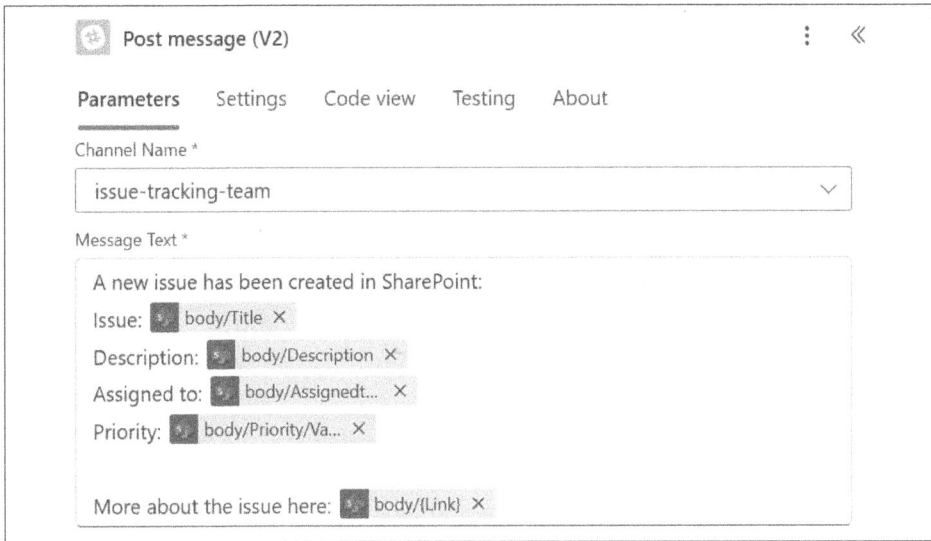

Add an action to send an email to the issue assignee. Search for the Office 365 Outlook connector and select the "Send an email (V2)" action. You may need to sign in and authenticate your Office 365 Outlook account. Then configure the action by providing the To parameter by choosing "Assigned to Email" from the dynamic content. Then provide a subject for the "Send an email" action, such as "An issue has been created and assigned to you." Finally, customize the Body parameter (email text). You can use the dynamic content from the trigger, as follows:

```
Hi {Assigned to DisplayName},

A new issue has been created and assigned to you:
Issue: {Title}
Description: {Description}
Priority: {Priority Value}

More about the issue here: {Link to Item}
```

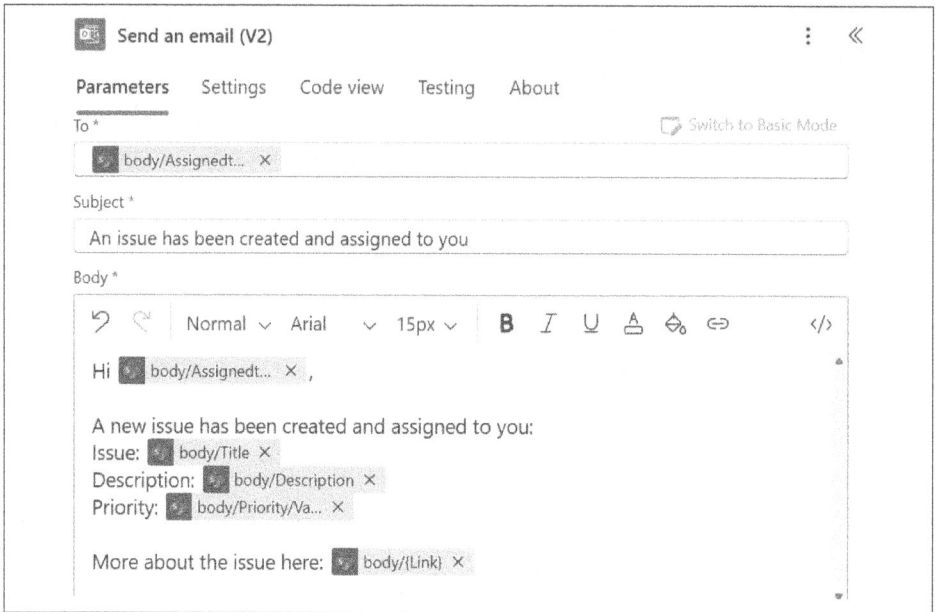

A quick way to configure the Body parameter is by copying the Message Text from the previous action and pasting it into the Body parameter. Then remove the "Assigned to" line. Give your flow a name, and then save and test it to ensure it works as expected:

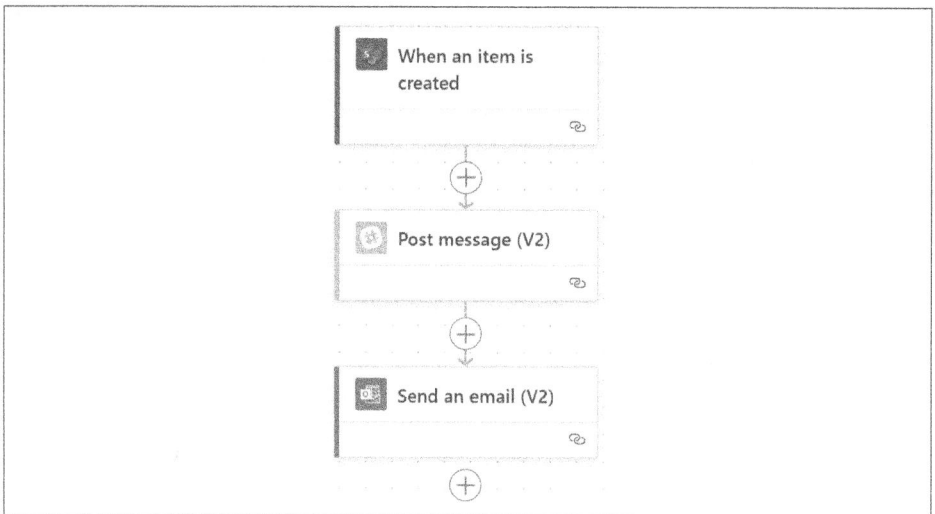

See Also

- Recipe 3.7, "Getting a Slack Message When a File Has Been Updated on OneDrive for Business"
- Recipe 4.2, "Posting a Message on Slack When an Issue Status Has Been Modified"
- Recipe 6.2, "Sending an Email to the Responder When a Response Is Submitted"
- Recipe 7.2, "Posting a Message on Slack When a Message Is Posted on Teams"

4.2 Posting a Message on Slack When an Issue Status Has Been Modified

Problem

You want to post a message to Slack when an item in a SharePoint list has been updated.

Solution

Create an automated cloud flow that monitors item updates in the SharePoint list and then posts a message to Slack containing information about the updated item.

Discussion

Sending a notification when an issue status changes in SharePoint is a seamless way to keep you and your team informed and responsive. By configuring the flow, you can ensure that all of you receive immediate updates when a critical event occurs, such as a change in issue status.

When the flow detects the change, it can automatically send notifications via various channels like email, Slack, or messaging platforms, ensuring that the right individuals are promptly alerted. This streamlined approach accelerates issue resolution and enhances collaboration and transparency within the team, ultimately contributing to improved productivity.

Ensure that you have created an issue tracking list in SharePoint or that you have read permissions on the list you want to monitor for newly created issues. Create an issue tracking list, following the SharePoint instructions (*https://oreil.ly/M4RMf*). Go to the Power Automate portal (*https://oreil.ly/O-MRf*). Sign in with your Microsoft account or your organization's account. Make sure you are in the correct Power Automate environment. Click on "My flows" in the left navigation bar. Click on "New flow" to create a new flow. Choose a flow type. In this case, you want to be notified when an item has been modified in SharePoint, so you must choose "Automated cloud flow."

Click Skip on the pop-up to navigate to the flow designer experience. Search for the SharePoint connector in the flow designer. You want the trigger to be related to when an item has been modified in SharePoint, so choose the "When an item or a file is modified" trigger. You may need to sign in and authenticate your SharePoint account. Configure the Site Address (the relevant site URL where the issue tracking list resides) and List or Library Name (the SharePoint list to be monitored for modified items) trigger parameters:

The configured trigger will monitor the list for any changes regardless of which column has been modified. In contrast, the trigger will return the modified item. However, we want to check if the status column of the modified item has changed. To do so, add an action to get the SharePoint list item changes. Search for the SharePoint connector and select the "Get changes for an item or a file (properties only)" action. Now configure the action parameters, including Site Address (the relevant site URL where the issue tracking list resides), the List or Library Name parameter (the SharePoint list or library to get the changes from), the Id (the ID of the item to get the changes for), Since (the trigger window start token), and Until (the trigger window end token):

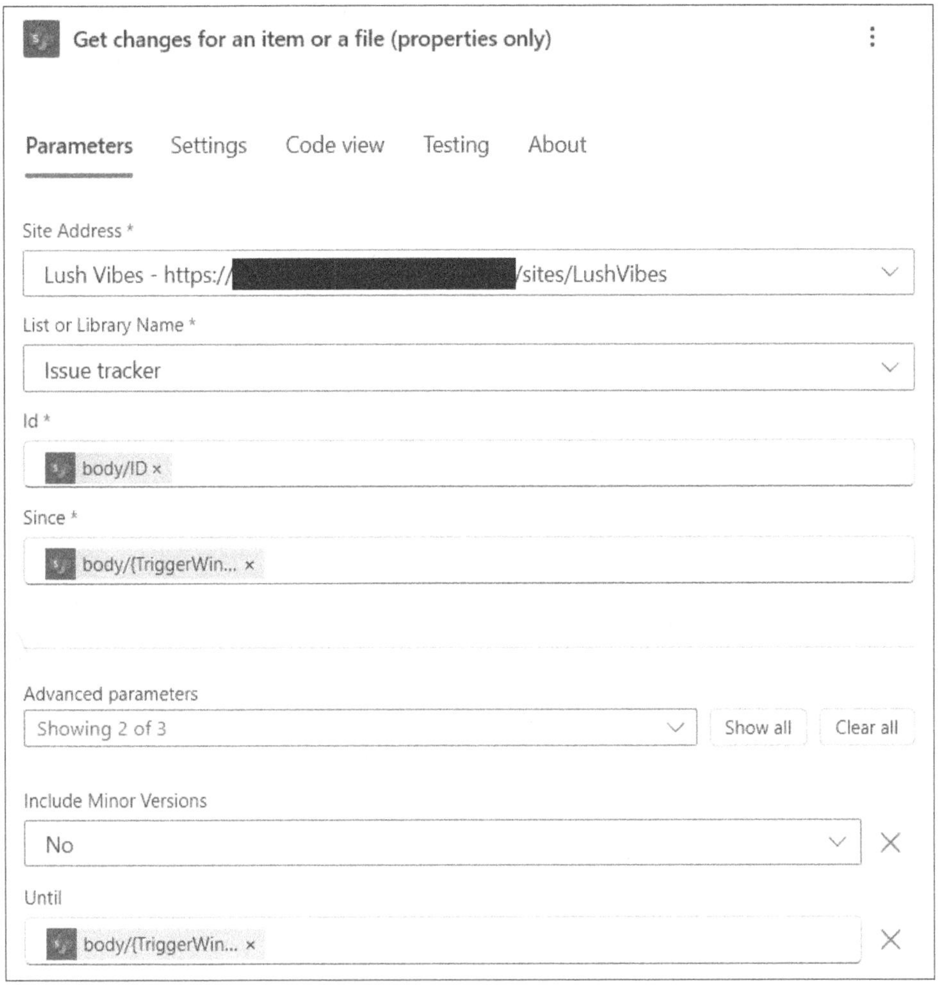

Get changes for an item or a file (properties only)   ⋮

Parameters   Settings   Code view   Testing   About
───────────

Site Address *

Lush Vibes - https://██████████████/sites/LushVibes   ⌄

List or Library Name *

Issue tracker   ⌄

Id *

⬛ body/ID ×

Since *

⬛ body/{TriggerWin... ×

Advanced parameters

Showing 2 of 3   ⌄   Show all   Clear all

Include Minor Versions

No   ⌄   ✕

Until

⬛ body/{TriggerWin... ×   ✕

The Since and Until window period specified in the "Get changes for an item or a file" is the period in which we want to get the changes for a specific SharePoint list item. Luckily, we can get the start and end period from the trigger. Therefore, use the Trigger Window Start Token in the Since parameter field and the Trigger Window End Token in the Until parameter field:

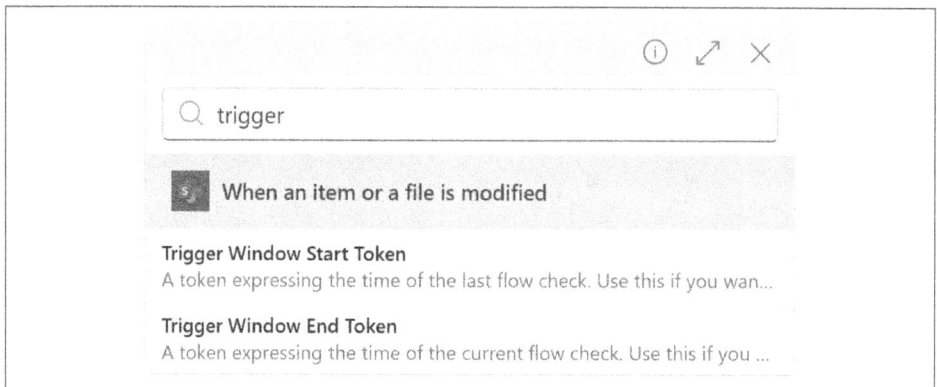

Now that we have the changes for the modified item, we can check if the status column has been modified. Add a new action, search for "Control," and then from the list of actions, choose Condition. Configure the condition action by selecting the Has Column Changed: Status property from the "Get changes for an item or a file (properties only)" dynamic content for the left-side comparison value. Make sure the comparison operator is set to "is equal to," and then for the right-side comparison, in the expression flyout pane, type true and then click Save:

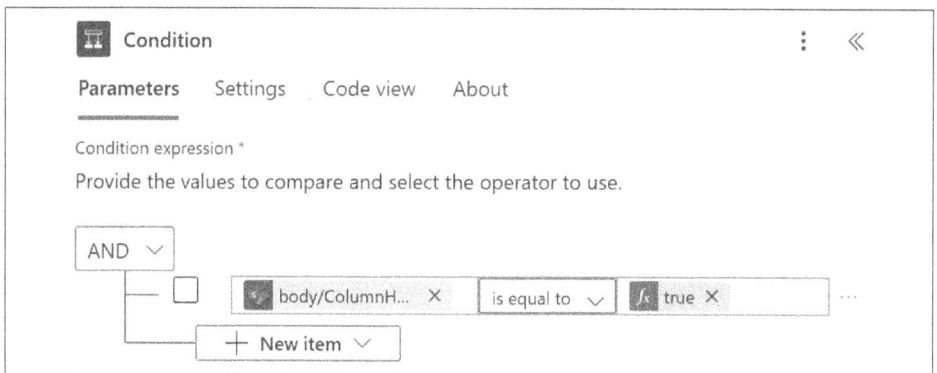

If the condition is true (under True), add an action to post a message into a Slack channel. Search for the Slack connector and select the "Post message (V2)" action. You may need to sign in and authenticate your Slack account. You may also need to consent if a Power Automate connector requests permission to access a Slack workplace. Ensure you allow that request to grant permission for Power Automate to post messages on Slack:

Microsoft Power Platform Connectors is requesting permission to access the Power Automate Cookbook Slack workspace

What will Microsoft Power Platform Connectors be able to view?

⌂	Content and info about you	▶
⌂	Content and info about channels & conversations	▶
⌂	Content and info about your workspace	▶

What will Microsoft Power Platform Connectors be able to do?

⌂	Perform actions as you	▶
⌂	Perform actions in channels & conversations	▶

Cancel   **Allow**

Configure the action by providing the Channel Name (the Slack channel you want the message to be posted to). Then customize the Message Text parameter (the Slack message to be posted on the chosen channel). You can use the dynamic content from the trigger—as shown in the following image—such as Title, Status Value (new status text value), and Link to Item (the URL to the modified issue in SharePoint):

```
Issue "{Title}" status has been updated
New status: {Status Value}
Link to issue: {Link to Item}
```

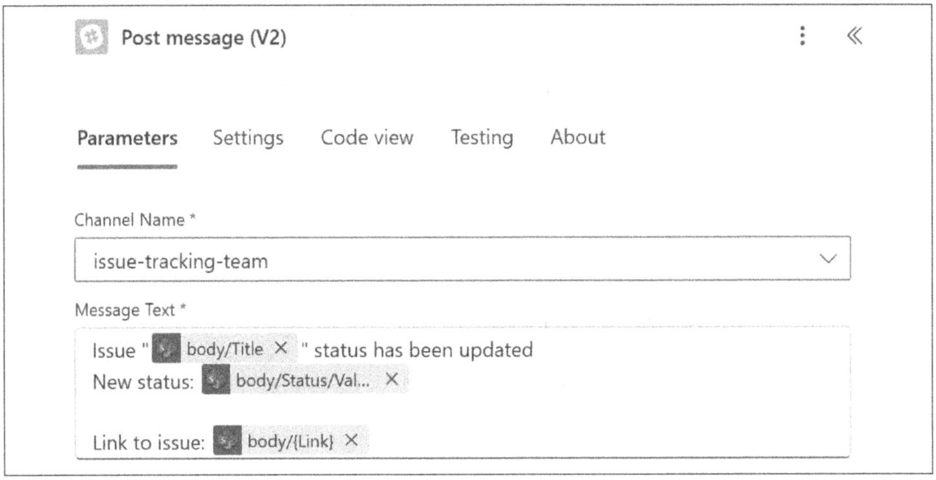

Give your flow a name, and then save and test it to ensure it works as expected:

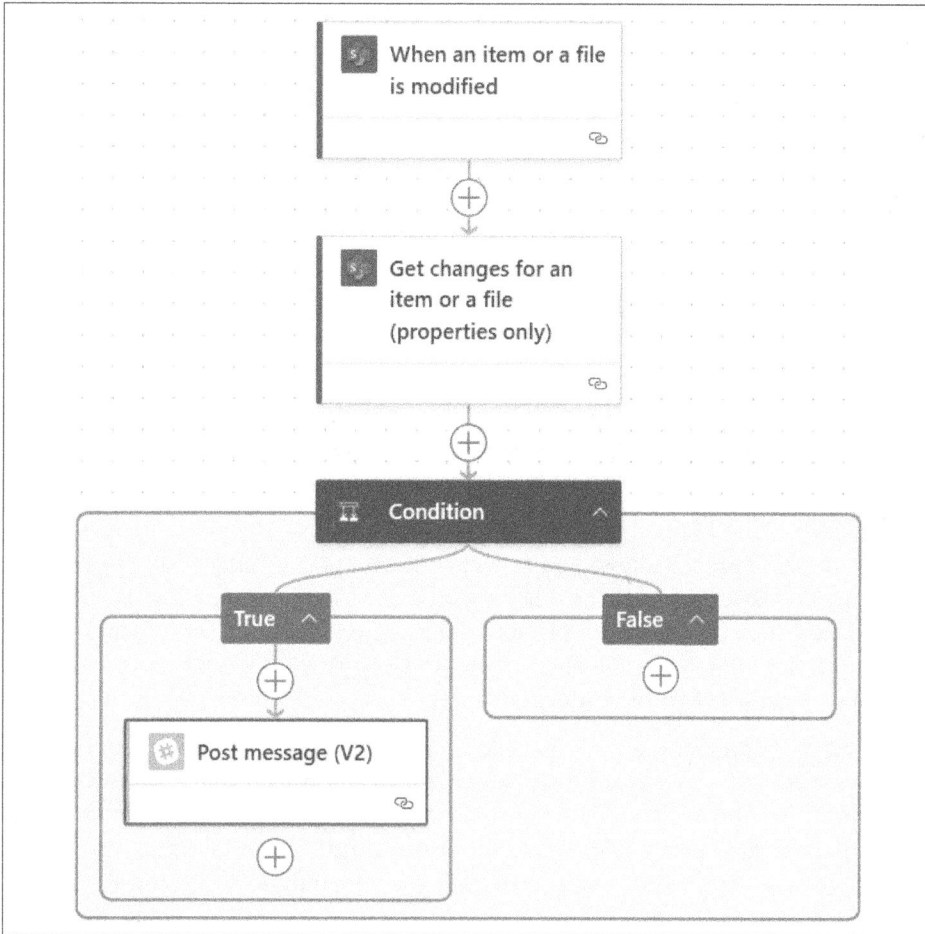

See Also

- Recipe 3.7, "Getting a Slack Message When a File Has Been Updated on OneDrive for Business"
- Recipe 4.1, "Posting a Message on Slack and Sending an Email to the Assignee When an Issue Is Created"
- Recipe 7.2, "Posting a Message on Slack When a Message Is Posted on Teams"

4.3 Sending an Email When an Item Has Been Deleted

Problem

You want to be notified along with stakeholders by email that an item has been deleted from a SharePoint list.

Solution

Create an automated cloud flow that monitors the SharePoint list for item deletion and then sends an email with the desired format to specific users.

Discussion

When an item is deleted in SharePoint, sending an email is an effective way to maintain data governance and keep you informed. With this automated workflow in place, you can swiftly detect when an item is removed, ensuring that necessary personnel are alerted in real time.

This proactive approach allows you to respond promptly, investigate the reasons for deletion, and take appropriate action, such as data recovery or auditing. Whether it's a crucial document, record, or piece of information, this notification mechanism helps maintain data integrity, compliance, and security while providing an added layer of accountability within the organization.

Before building this flow, ensure that the list you want to monitor for item deletion already exists in SharePoint and that you have read permissions on the list you want to monitor. For this recipe, I'm using the out-of-the-box issue tracker list in SharePoint (that I created previously). Go to the Power Automate portal (*https://oreil.ly/O-MRf*). Sign in with your Microsoft account or your organization's account. Make sure you are in the correct Power Automate environment. Click on "My flows" in the left navigation bar. Click on "New flow" to create a new flow. Choose a flow type. In this case, you want to be notified when an item has been deleted in SharePoint, so you must choose "Automated cloud flow." Click Skip on the pop-up to navigate to the flow designer experience. Search for the "SharePoint" connector in the flow designer. You want the trigger to be related to when an item has been deleted in SharePoint, so choose the "When an item is deleted" trigger. You may need to sign in and authenticate your SharePoint account. Configure the Site Address (the relevant site URL where the list you want to monitor resides) and List Name (the SharePoint list to be monitored for item deletion) trigger parameters:

Then add an action to email you and anyone you want to be informed about the item deletion. Search for the Office 365 Outlook connector and select the "Send an email (V2)" action. You may need to sign in and authenticate your Office 365 Outlook account. Configure the action by providing the To parameter by adding your user account and stakeholders' user accounts. Then provide a subject for the "Send an email" action, such as "An issue has been deleted." Finally, customize the Body parameter (email text). You can use the dynamic content from the trigger:

```
Hi,

This is to inform you that issue "{Name}" with Id "String({ID})" has been
 deleted by {DeletedBy}

To recycle the issue item back to the list use this {link}.

Thank you,
Issue tracking monitoring
```

In the Body parameter, I have used the following dynamic content from the trigger:

- Name
- ID
- Deleted by

I have used an expression to stringify the ID:

```
string(triggerOutputs()?['body/ID'])
```

I also have added a link to the site's recycle bin in case you want to recover the deleted item. To add a link to the Body parameter, click on the link icon and then provide a Link Title and Link Target. If you want to open the link in a new window, check the corresponding checkbox, then click Add:

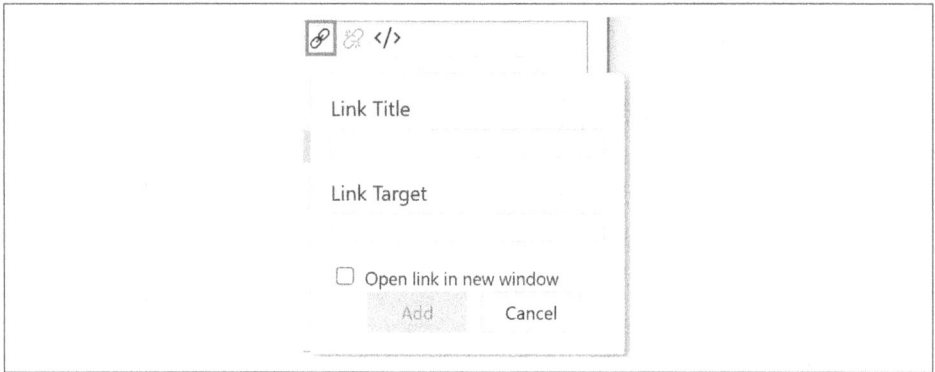

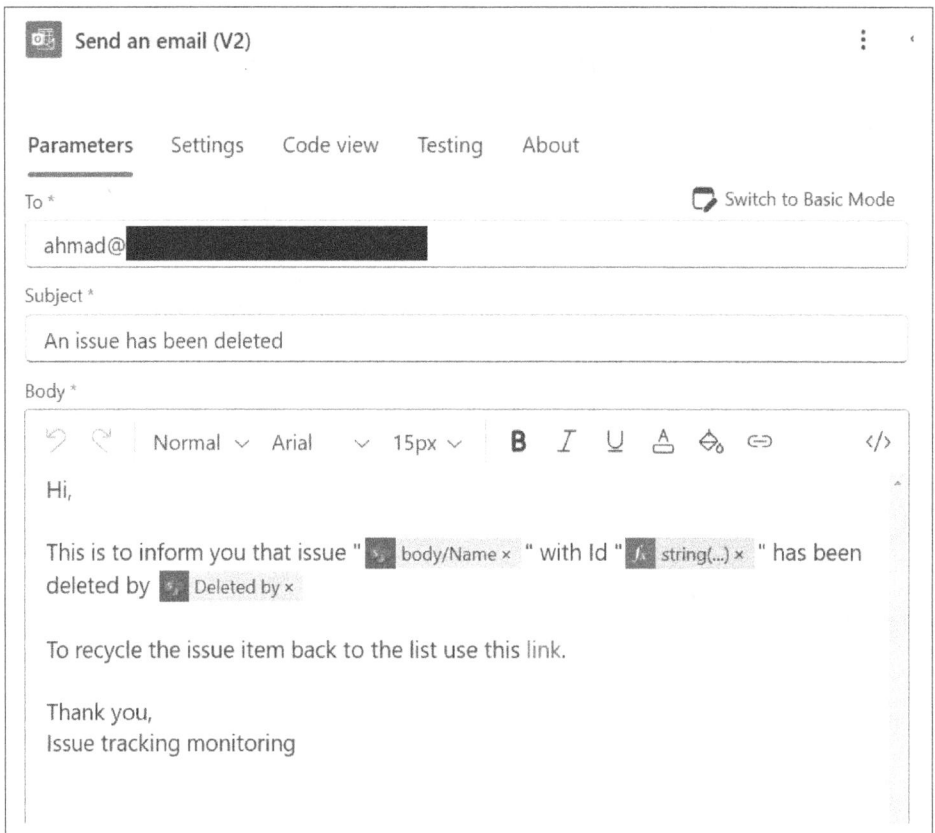

Give your flow a name and then save and test your flow to ensure it works as expected:

See Also

- Recipe 4.1, "Posting a Message on Slack and Sending an Email to the Assignee When an Issue Is Created"

- Recipe 4.2, "Posting a Message on Slack When an Issue Status Has Been Modified"

- Recipe 6.2, "Sending an Email to the Responder When a Response Is Submitted"

4.4 Sending a Reminder Email for Tasks Due by Tomorrow

Problem

You want to email task assignees for tasks due by tomorrow.

Solution

Create a scheduled cloud flow that runs daily, checks for tasks due by tomorrow in the SharePoint list, and then sends an email to the task assignee using the desired email format.

Discussion

Sending a reminder notification for tasks in a SharePoint list is a smart way to ensure that important deadlines are met efficiently. With this automated flow, you can proactively notify yourself—or task assignees—about impending due dates, keeping you well-prepared and on track.

By leveraging the power of SharePoint's task management and Power Automate's capabilities, you can save time and minimize the risk of missed deadlines. This reminder system improves task management and enhances productivity and effective collaboration, as you can focus on completing tasks rather than worrying about tracking deadlines.

Before building this flow, ensure that you have created a SharePoint list that has at least the following columns:

- Title (a single line of text; you get this column by default when creating any custom list)
- Description (multiple lines of text; optional column)
- Due date (date and time)
- Assigned to (person or group)

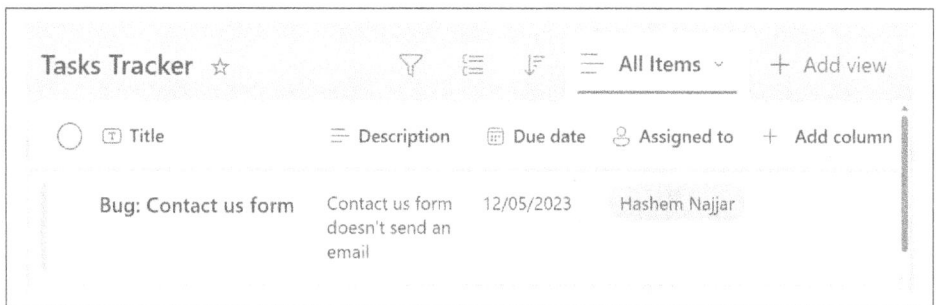

Tasks Tracker ☆			
⊤ Title	Description	Due date	Assigned to
Bug: Contact us form	Contact us form doesn't send an email	12/05/2023	Hashem Najjar

To create a new flow in Power Automate, start by visiting the Power Automate portal (*https://oreil.ly/O-MRf*). Sign in using your Microsoft account or your organization's account, and ensure that you are in the correct Power Automate environment. In the left navigation bar, click on "My flows," and then select "New flow" to initiate the creation process. Since you want to set up a flow that checks for tasks due tomorrow on a daily basis, choose the "Scheduled cloud flow" option. Give your flow a suitable name, and provide the necessary parameters to determine when the flow should run. Set the starting date and time, and configure the flow to repeat once every day:

Flow name

Sending a reminder email for tasks due by tomorrow

Run this flow *

Starting   6/5/23   📅 *   at   08:00 AM   ∨

Repeat every   1   *   Day   ∨ *

This flow will run:

Every day

Skip   **Create**   Cancel

Click Create on the pop-up to navigate to the flow designer experience. Then add a new action (step) and search for "Variable" in the flow designer. Choose "Initialize variable" and set the Name ("Tomorrow's start of day") and Type (choose String) action parameters. Use the following expression for Value:

```
startOfDay(addDays(utcNow(),1))
```

{x}   **Tomorrow - Start of day**   ⋮   ≪

Parameters   Settings   Code view   About

Name *

Tomorrow's start of day

Type *

String   ∨

Value

fx startOfDay(...) ✕

Add another Variable action by adding a new action (step) and searching for "Variable," then choose "Initialize variable" and set the Name ("Tomorrow's end of day") and Type (choose String) action parameters. Use the following expression for Value:

```
startOfDay(addDays(utcNow(),2))
```

I will use these variables in the following action (step). I created them to set a "date and time" range to pass to the SharePoint "Get items" action to fetch only the tasks within the given range. This is how the search works with SharePoint regarding dates, meaning you can't send a filter query to a SharePoint action where "Due date" is equal to so-and-so. Add a new action (step) and search for "SharePoint," then choose the "Get items" action. You may need to sign in and authenticate your SharePoint account. Configure the Site Address (the relevant site URL where the tasks list resides) and List Name (the SharePoint tasks list) action parameters. One additional parameter needs to be set: click on "Show advanced options" in the "Get items" action and set the Filter Query parameter as follows:

```
Duedate gt datetime 'Tomorrow's start of day' and
   Duedate lt datetime 'Tomorrow's end of day'
```

The following table explains the elements of the Filter Query:

Query element	Description
Duedate	SharePoint column internal name.
gt	Greater-than comparison operator.
datetime	Datetime conversion operator.
'Tomorrow's start of day'	Our first variable; "the next day, start of day."
and	The expression on each side of the logical and operator must be true for the full expression to return true.
lt	Less-than comparison operator.
'Tomorrow's end of day'	Our second variable; "the next day, end of day."

Add a new action (step), search for "Control," and then select the Control actions. From the list of actions, choose "Apply to each." Then configure the "Apply to each" action by setting the Select An Output From Previous Steps parameter by selecting the "value" from the "Get items" dynamic content:

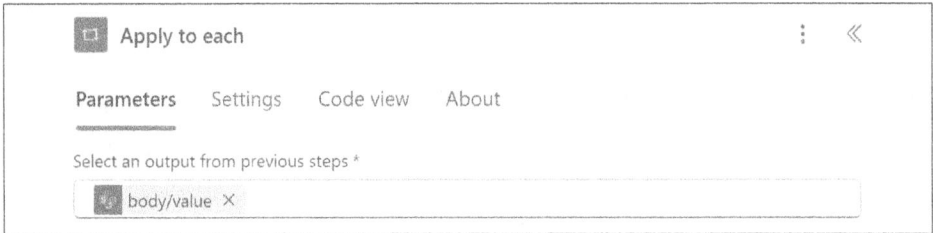

In the "Apply to each" action, add a new action, search for the Office 365 Outlook connector, and select the "Send an email (V2)" action. You may need to sign in and authenticate your Office 365 Outlook account. Configure the action by providing the To parameter by adding the "Assigned to email" from the dynamic content. Then, provide a subject for the "Send an email" action, such as "Task 'Title' is due by tomorrow." Finally, customize the Body parameter (email text). You can use the dynamic content to do so.

In the Body parameter, I have used the following dynamic content:

- Assigned to Displayname
- Title
- Link to item (the URL to the item in SharePoint)

```
Hi {Assigned to DisplayName},

Your task {Title} is due tomorrow formatDateTime({Duedate},'dd-MM-yyyy').
Follow this link to access your task: {Link to item}

Thank you!
```

I have used an expression to format and stringify Duedate:

```
formatDateTime(items('Apply_to_each')?['Duedate'],'dd-MM-yyyy')
```

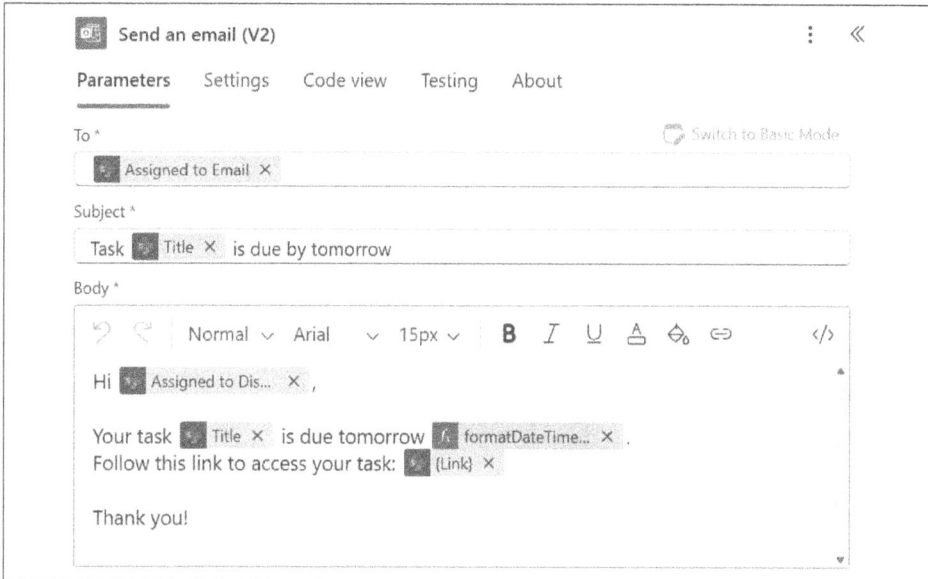

Save and test your flow to ensure it works as expected:

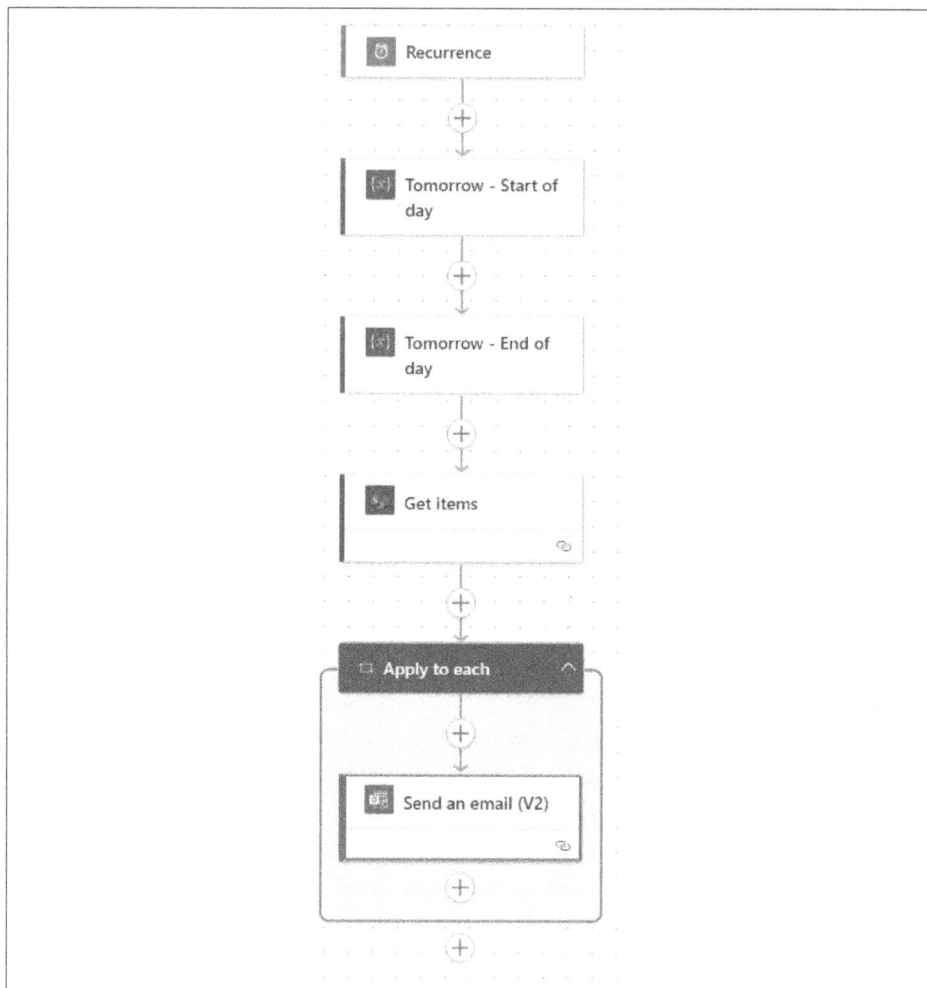

See Also

- Recipe 3.1, "Sending Recurring Reminders"
- Recipe 3.2, "Sending Daily Weather Forecasts"
- Recipe 4.5, "Sending Employees Birthday Emails"
- Recipe 7.4, "Sending a Report of Existing Teams and Channels"

4.5 Sending Employees Birthday Emails

Problem

You want to send a birthday email to the employees celebrating their birthday today.

Solution

Create a scheduled cloud flow that runs daily, checks the SharePoint employee list for birthdays matching today's date, and then sends an email to them using the desired email format.

Discussion

Sending employees a happy birthday email using a Power Automate linked to data stored in a SharePoint list is a thoughtful way to foster a positive work environment and acknowledge your team members' special days.

This automated workflow allows you to create personalized birthday greetings by extracting employee data from the SharePoint list, such as their names and email addresses. The flow then sends out timely birthday emails to celebrate team members' milestones, fostering a sense of camaraderie and appreciation within the workplace. Such gestures boost employee morale and contribute to a more engaged and motivated workforce, reinforcing the importance of recognizing and celebrating the individuals who form the heart of any organization.

Before building this flow, ensure that you have created the employees' SharePoint list that has at least the following columns:

- Title (a single line of text; you get this column by default when creating any custom list)
- Employee (person or group)
- Birthday day of month (number)
- Birthday month (number)

	Employee	Title	Birthday day o...	Birthday month	
	Hashem Najjar	Technical Architect	6	11	
	Randa Najjar	Developer	27	9	

Employees list — All Items — + Add view

To create a new flow in Power Automate, start by visiting the Power Automate portal (*https://oreil.ly/O-MRf*). Sign in with your Microsoft account or your organization's account, and ensure you are in the correct Power Automate environment. From the left navigation bar, click on "My flows," and then select "New flow" to begin creating a new flow. Since your goal is to check for birthdays every day, choose the "Scheduled cloud flow" option. Give your flow a name and input the required parameters to specify when the flow should run. Set the starting date and time, and configure the flow to repeat once every day:

Click Create on the pop-up to navigate to the flow designer experience. Once in the flow designer, expand the Recurrence trigger and set the "Time zone" trigger parameter to your local time zone. Power Automate cloud flows run on the UTC zone by default. Now, search for the Date Time connector and select the "Convert time zone" action. This action is necessary to get the current date/time in your time zone.

In the Base Time parameter field, pass the following expression:

```
utcNow()
```

Fill in the rest of the action parameters:

- *Source time zone*: Select (UTC) Coordinated Universal Time.
- *Destination time zone*: Select your time zone, e.g., (UTC +01:00).
- *Time unit*: Select "Short date pattern."

Convert time zone

Parameters Settings Code view About

Base time *

fx utcNow() ✕

Source time zone *

(UTC) Coordinated Universal Time ⌄

Destination time zone *

(UTC+01:00) Amsterdam, Berlin, Bern, Rome, Stockholm, Vienna ⌄

Time unit

Short date pattern - 6/15/2009 [d] ⌄

Add a new action (step) and search for "Variable." Choose "Initialize variable" and set the Name (Day) and Type (choose Integer) action parameters. Use the following expression for Value:

```
int(formatDateTime(body('Convert_time_zone'),'dd'))
```

{x} Day

Parameters Settings Code view About

Name *

Day

Type *

Integer ⌄

Value

fx int(...) ✕

Add another Variable action by adding a new action (step) and searching for "Variable," then choose "Initialize variable" and set the Name (Month) and Type (choose Integer) action parameters. For Value, use this expression:

```
int(formatDateTime(body('Convert_time_zone'),'MM'))
```

The expressions used in the previous two actions will extract the day of the month in the first variable and the month of the year from the Convert Time Zone output. Add a new action (step) and search for "SharePoint," then choose the "Get items" action. You may need to sign in and authenticate your SharePoint account. Configure the Site Address (the relevant site URL where the employees' birthday list resides) and List Name (the SharePoint employees list) action parameters. One additional parameter needs to be set: click on "Show advanced options" in the "Get items" action and set the Filter Query parameter as follows:

```
Birthdaydayofmonth eq 'Day' and 'Birthdaymonth' eq 'Month'
```

The following table explains the elements of the Filter Query:

Query element	Description
`Birthdaydayof month`	SharePoint column internal name.
`eq`	"Equals" comparison operator.
`'Day'`	Our first variable; "day of the month."
`and`	The expression on each side of the logical and operator must be true for the full expression to return true.
`Birthdaymonth`	SharePoint column internal name.
`'Month'`	Our second variable; "the current month."

Next, add a new action (step), search for "Control," and then select the Control actions. From the list of actions, choose "Apply to each." Configure the "Apply to each" action, setting the "Select an output from previous steps" parameter by selecting the "value" from the "Get items" dynamic content:

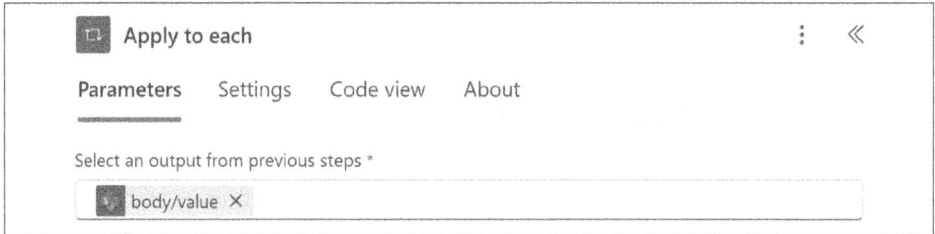

In the "Apply to each" action, add a new action, search for the Office 365 Outlook connector, and select the "Send an email (V2)" action. You may need to sign in and authenticate your Office 365 Outlook account. Configure the action by providing the To parameter by adding the "Employee email" from the dynamic content. Then, provide a subject for the "Send an email" action, such as "Happy Birthday." Finally, customize the Body parameter (email text). You can use the dynamic content from the "Get items" action.

In the Body parameter, I have used Employee Displayname as my dynamic content:

```
Hi {Employee DisplayName},

XYZ company and all its employees wish you a happy birthday.

Thank you,
XYZ HR
```

Customize the rest of the Body parameter (email text). You can use the text as shown in the image:

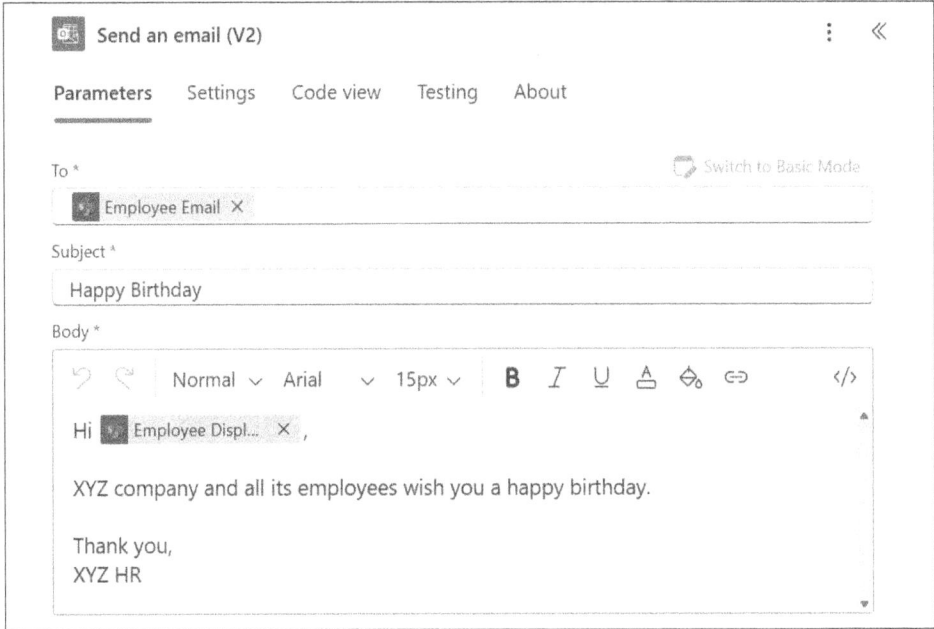

Save and test your flow to ensure it works as expected:

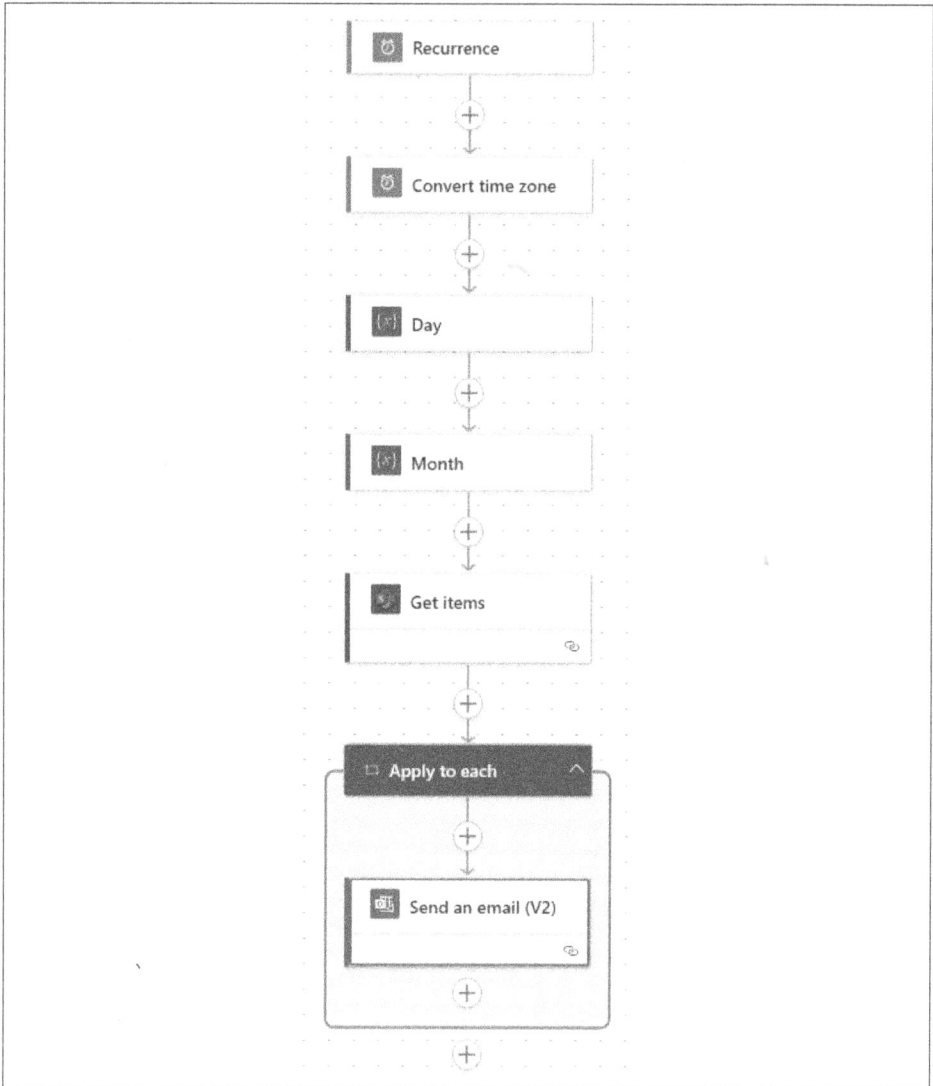

See Also

- Recipe 3.1, "Sending Recurring Reminders"
- Recipe 3.2, "Sending Daily Weather Forecasts"
- Recipe 4.4, "Sending a Reminder Email for Tasks Due by Tomorrow"
- Recipe 7.4, "Sending a Report of Existing Teams and Channels"

Conclusion

The collaboration between Power Automate and SharePoint has revolutionized how organizations manage and automate their workflows. The examples discussed in this chapter illustrate the adaptability and versatility of this integration in addressing various business needs. By posting messages on Slack and sending emails when issues are created, or their statuses change, teams can respond to challenges with agility and accuracy. This immediate communication is a critical component in problem-resolution and decision-making processes.

Moreover, the automated responses to item deletions and the proactive reminder emails for impending tasks contribute to data protection and task management, ensuring that nothing falls through the cracks. These automations save time and reduce the margin for human error, resulting in a more efficient and reliable workflow.

Finally, sending personalized birthday emails to employees showcases the human side of automation. Recognizing and celebrating team members' birthdays fosters a positive workplace culture, boosting morale and team cohesion. These small gestures, combined with the power of automation, have a lasting impact on employee satisfaction and engagement.

As organizations seek ways to improve efficiency, communication, and employee well-being, integrating Power Automate and SharePoint will undoubtedly play a pivotal role in shaping the future of business operations. It is a powerful tool that empowers organizations to adapt, innovate, and thrive in an ever-evolving digital landscape.

CHAPTER 5

Working with Files

In this chapter, I'll briefly go through the history of working with files in OneDrive and SharePoint and how automation came into play as a vital enabler in document management. Finally, I'll go through common automation scenarios in conjunction with files that are based on the use of OneDrive and SharePoint.

Working with Files in OneDrive and SharePoint

Working with files in OneDrive for Business and SharePoint represents a fundamental aspect of modern collaboration and document management within organizations. OneDrive for Business provides users with a personal cloud storage solution, while SharePoint serves as a shared, collaborative workspace. Both platforms offer robust file storage and sharing capabilities.

OneDrive for Business is designed for individual users, allowing them to store, access, and sync files across devices. It offers a familiar file management experience and integrates seamlessly with the Microsoft 365 suite. Users can collaborate in real time on documents, share files with colleagues, and maintain version history. On the other hand, SharePoint is a team-oriented platform that provides a central repository for files and resources. It is structured with document libraries, making it ideal for group collaboration and organization-wide knowledge sharing. Users can access files, set permissions, and create workflows within SharePoint, ensuring a structured approach to document management.

The value of Power Automate in this context is its ability to automate and streamline file-related tasks and processes. Power Automate can create automated workflows that trigger actions in response to file-related events in OneDrive for Business or SharePoint. For example, when a file is uploaded, modified, or deleted, Power Automate can automatically notify team members, move the file to a specific folder, update a database, or perform other tasks. This automation reduces manual work, ensures consistency, and accelerates processes.

Additionally, Power Automate can facilitate cross-platform integrations, bridging the gap between OneDrive for Business, SharePoint, and other tools and services. It can connect with external apps and services, enabling data transfer and synchronization. For instance, Power Automate can automatically back up files from OneDrive for Business to SharePoint or send notifications to other team-collaboration platforms such as Microsoft Teams or Slack. This flexibility extends the capabilities of OneDrive for Business and SharePoint, making them integral parts of a broader ecosystem.

Furthermore, Power Automate supports conditional logic, enabling users to create sophisticated workflows based on specific file conditions or attributes. Organizations can implement custom approval processes, content routing, or compliance checks. For example, Power Automate can trigger approval workflows when specific documents are uploaded to SharePoint, ensuring critical documents go through the necessary review process.

Working with files in OneDrive for Business and SharePoint is foundational to modern document management and collaboration. Power Automate adds significant value by automating processes, facilitating integrations, and enhancing collaboration across the Microsoft 365 ecosystem. Its ability to create custom workflows and integrate with external services makes it a powerful tool for organizations looking to streamline file-related tasks.

5.1 Saving Email Attachments to OneDrive for Business

Problem

You want to save email attachments (when an email arrives) to a particular folder in OneDrive for Business.

Solution

Create an automated cloud flow that monitors email with attachments and then saves the email attachments to a specific folder in OneDrive for Business.

Discussion

Saving email attachments to OneDrive for Business using Power Automate is game-changing. This automation eliminates the manual and time-consuming task of downloading and saving email attachments to a local computer or manually uploading them to OneDrive. Instead, Power Automate does the heavy lifting, automatically detecting email attachments and efficiently transferring them to a designated OneDrive for Business folder. This automation reduces the risk of data loss or misplacement and ensures that files are securely stored in the cloud, making them accessible from anywhere and on any device.

The added advantage of this automation is the seamless integration it offers between email communication and file storage. It simplifies how files are stored and improves collaboration by centralizing data in a shared location within OneDrive for Business. This makes accessing, sharing, and collaborating on files easier without searching through cluttered email inboxes. It is a significant step toward enhanced productivity and data organization.

Before building this flow, ensure you have created a folder in your OneDrive for Business called "Attachments," then go to the Power Automate portal (*https://oreil.ly/O-MRf*). Sign in with your Microsoft account or your organization's account. Make sure you are in the correct Power Automate environment. Click on "My flows" in the left navigation bar. Click on "New flow" to create a new flow. Choose a flow type. In this case, you want to start the flow when an email with attachments is received, so you must choose "Automated cloud flow." Click Skip on the pop-up to navigate to the flow designer experience. Search for the Office 365 Outlook connector in the flow designer. You want the trigger to be related to when an email has been received, so choose the "When a new email arrives (v3)" trigger. You may need to sign in and authenticate your Office 365 Outlook account. Configure the Folder trigger parameter (the email folder to be monitored for arriving emails) and ensure that "Only with Attachments" and Include Attachments are set to Yes:

Add a new action (step), search for "Control," and then select the Control actions. From the list of actions, choose "Apply to each." You'll want to configure the "Apply to each" action, setting the "Select an output from previous steps" parameter by selecting the Attachments from the trigger dynamic content. In the "Apply to each" action, add a new action and search for the OneDrive for Business connector, and select the "Create file" action. You may need to sign in and authenticate your OneDrive for Business account. Then configure the action by providing the Folder Path parameter by selecting the Attachments folder created in the prerequisites. Then, provide a File Name (from the dynamic content Attachments Name) and File Content (from the dynamic content Attachments Content):

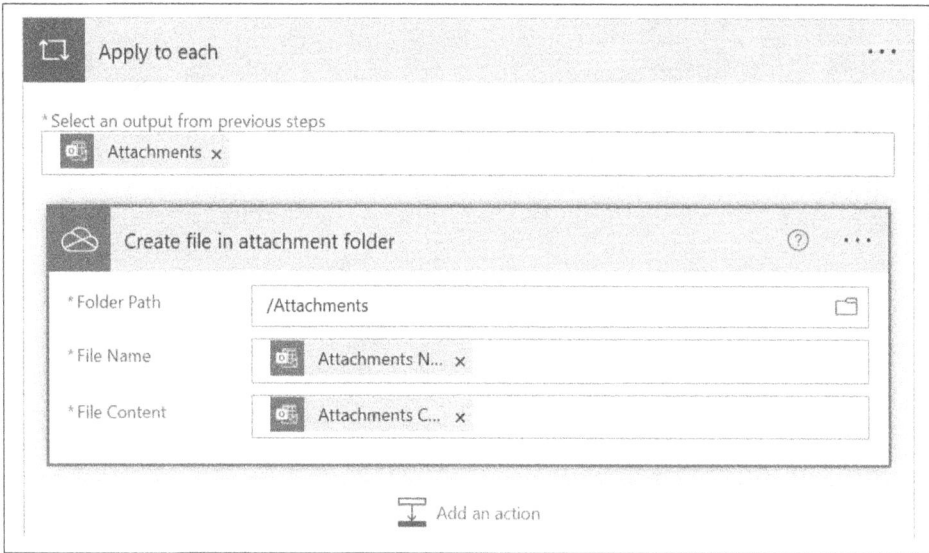

Give your flow a name and then save and test your flow to ensure it works as expected:

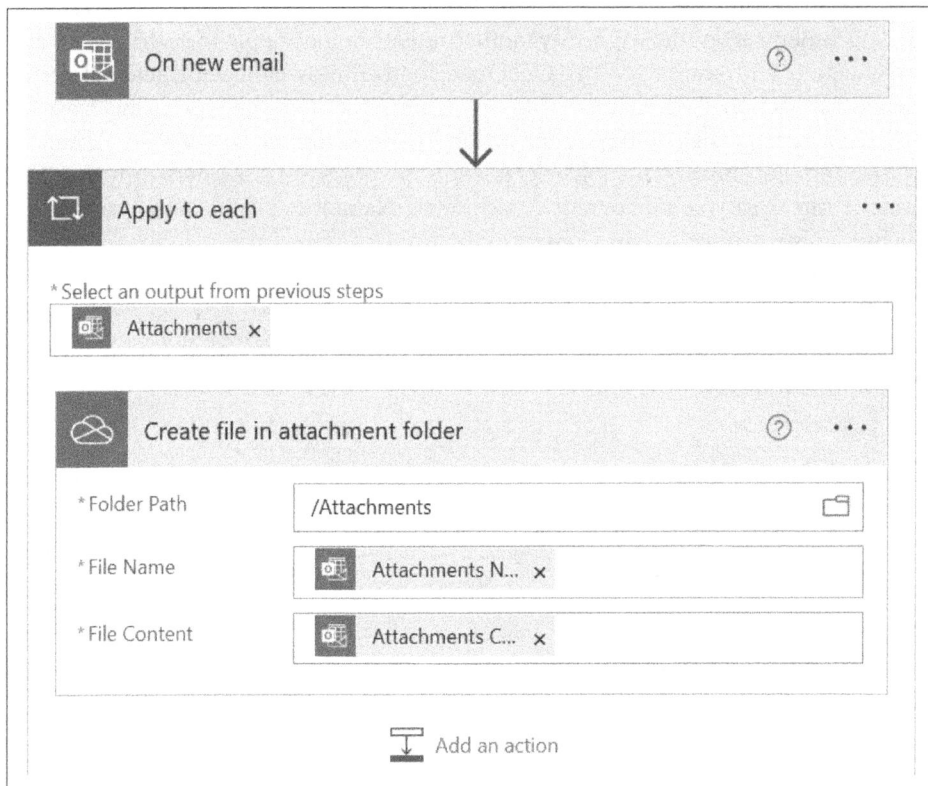

See Also

- Recipe 5.2, "Moving Documents Between SharePoint Libraries"
- Recipe 5.3, "Archiving SharePoint Documents"
- Recipe 5.4, "Converting a Word Document to PDF"

5.2 Moving Documents Between SharePoint Libraries

Problem

You want to move documents between SharePoint libraries based on a value in a particular column.

Solution

Create a scheduled cloud flow that runs once a week, checking the source SharePoint documents library (documents pool) and then rerouting (moving) the documents to their corresponding destination SharePoint library based on a particular column.

Discussion

Using Power Automate represents a significant enhancement in document management and organization. Such automation streamlines the process of reorganizing and categorizing documents, ensuring that files are placed in the right location within SharePoint. Power Automate can be configured to move documents automatically based on predefined criteria, such as document type, metadata, or specific keywords, reducing the manual effort required for file reorganization. This not only saves time but also minimizes the risk of human errors associated with manual document transfers.

Additionally, the ability to move documents between SharePoint libraries using Power Automate contributes to improved data security and access control. With precise workflows in place, you can ensure that confidential or sensitive documents are placed in secure, restricted-access libraries, while public or general-use files are located in more open areas. This allows for a highly tailored approach to document management within SharePoint and ensures that files are consistently organized and secure. Ultimately, this automation empowers you to maintain a structured and efficient SharePoint environment, making it easier for users to locate and collaborate on documents while enhancing data governance and security.

Before building this flow, ensure that you have created three SharePoint libraries:

- Documents pool (a library to receive all unsorted documents)
- HR (HR-related documents)
- IT (IT-related documents)

🗐 Documents pool	Document library	
🗐 Form Templates	Document library	
🗐 HR	Document library	
🗐 IT	Document library	

Add a "Rerouted to" column to the "Documents pool" library, selecting Choice and adding HR and IT:

Name and Type

Type a name for this column.

Column name:

Rerouted to

The type of information in this column is:
- ○ Single line of text
- ○ Multiple lines of text
- ● Choice (menu to choose from)
- ○ Number (1, 1.0, 100)
- ○ Currency ($, ¥, €)
- ○ Date and Time

Additional Column Settings

Specify detailed options for the type of information you selected.

Description:

Require that this column contains information:
- ○ Yes ● No

Enforce unique values:
- ○ Yes ● No

Type each choice on a separate line:

HR
IT

To create a new flow in Power Automate, start by visiting the Power Automate portal (*https://oreil.ly/O-MRf*). Sign in with your Microsoft or organization's account. Ensure you are in the correct Power Automate environment, then navigate to "My flows" in the lefthand menu and click on "New flow" to create a new flow. Since you want to check for sorted documents ready for routing on a weekly basis, choose the "Scheduled cloud flow" option. While it's possible to check for documents daily, this example focuses on a weekly schedule. Give your flow a name and enter the necessary parameters to set when it should run. Set the starting date to today's date and the time to 9:00 P.M. (21:00). Under the "Repeat every" setting, choose once every week, and for the "On these days" parameter, uncheck all days except Friday. Finally, click Create on the pop-up to enter the flow designer experience:

Add an action to get SharePoint documents in "Documents pool." Search for the SharePoint connector and select the "Get files (properties only)" action. You may need to sign in and authenticate your SharePoint account. Next, configure the Site Address (the relevant site URL where the Documents pool library resides) and Library Name (the SharePoint library to get the files from: "Documents pool") action parameters:

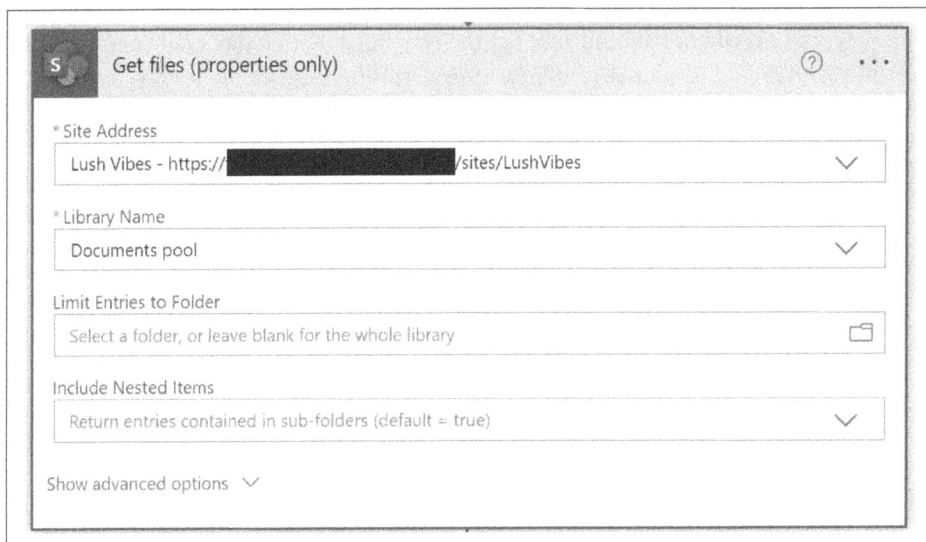

Add a new action (step), search for "Control," and then select the Control actions. From the list of actions, choose "Apply to each." Then configure the "Apply to each" action by setting the Select An Output From Previous Steps parameter by selecting the "value" from the previous action's dynamic content. In the "Apply to each" action, add a new action (step), search for "Control," and then select the Switch action. Next, configure the Switch action by setting the On parameter to "Route to" from the dynamic content (the SharePoint column in the "Documents pool" library).

Then, add the HR and IT cases in the Switch action:

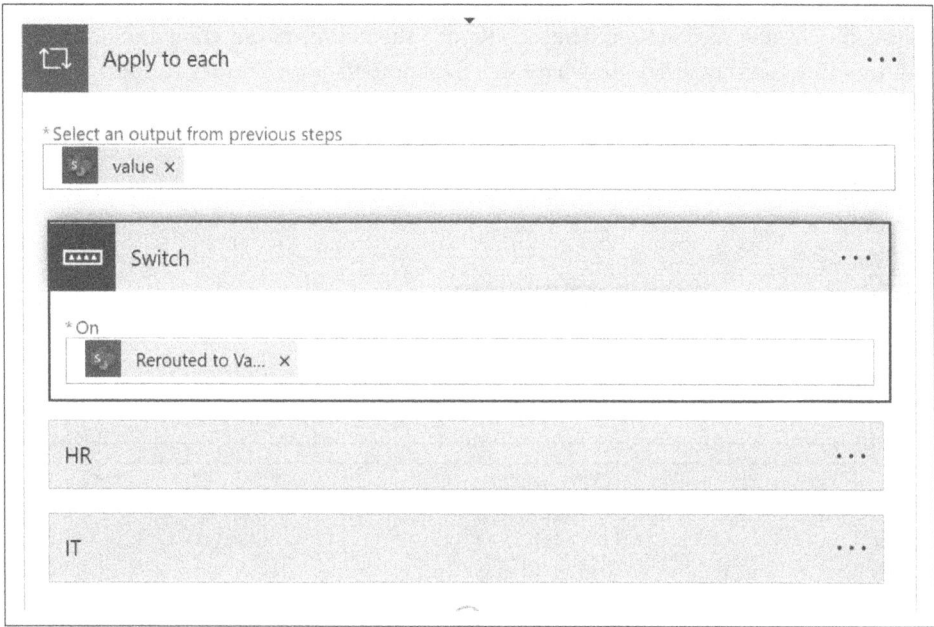

Under the HR case, add an action to copy the document from the "Documents pool" document library to the HR document library. Search for the SharePoint connector and select the "Copy file" action. Next, configure the action parameters, including Current Site Address (the relevant site URL where the "Documents pool" library resides), File to Copy (the Identifier dynamic content), Destination Site Address (the relevant site URL where the HR library resides), Destination Folder (the relevant folder where the document will be copied to, /HR in this case), and the "If another file is already there" parameter ("Copy with a new name"):

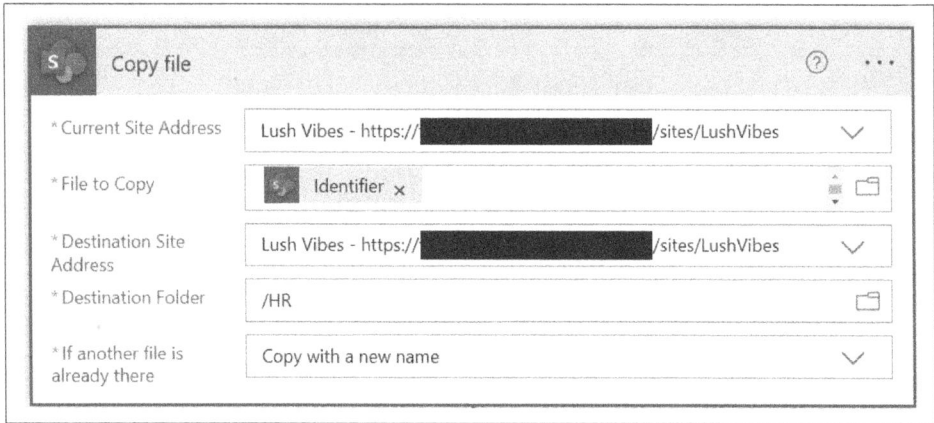

The copied file should then be deleted. Add an action to delete the document from the "Documents pool" document library. Search for the SharePoint connector and select the "Delete file" action. Then configure the action parameters, including Site Address (the relevant site URL where the "Documents pool" library resides) and File Identifier (the Identifier dynamic content from the "Get files" action):

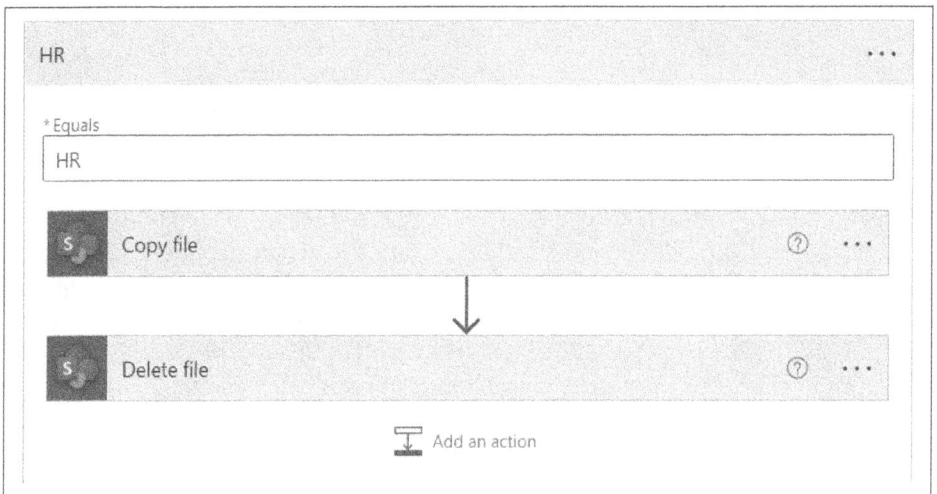

Under the IT case, repeat the previous four steps. However, in the Destination Folder, choose */IT* instead of */HR*:

Finally, save and test your flow to ensure it works as expected:

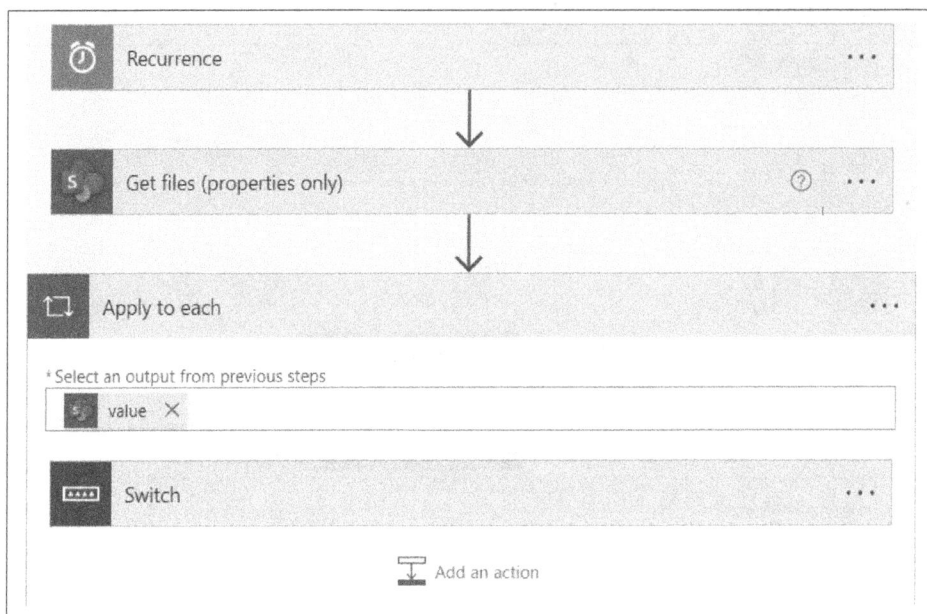

See Also

- Recipe 5.1, "Saving Email Attachments to OneDrive for Business"
- Recipe 5.3, "Archiving SharePoint Documents"
- Recipe 5.4, "Converting a Word Document to PDF"

5.3 Archiving SharePoint Documents

Problem

You want to archive documents in a SharePoint library that haven't been modified for some time.

Solution

Create a scheduled cloud flow that checks for documents in a SharePoint library that haven't been modified for a certain amount of time and then archives (moves) the documents to the archive SharePoint library.

Discussion

Using Power Automate is a strategic approach to document management, archiving, and compliance. This automation ensures that outdated or less frequently accessed documents are systematically moved to an archival location, keeping the primary document library clutter-free and easy to navigate. By automating the archival process, you improve data organization and enhance user productivity by reducing the time spent on manual clean-up tasks.

Furthermore, archiving SharePoint documents with Power Automate is crucial in ensuring regulatory compliance and adhering to data retention policies. Many industries have stringent data retention requirements, mandating that documents be retained for a specific period before archiving or disposal. Power Automate allows you to set up precise workflows that automatically enforce these policies. This guarantees that documents are archived per regulatory mandates, reducing the risk of compliance violations and legal complications. As a result, this automation fosters operational efficiency and robust data governance within SharePoint environments.

Before building this flow, ensure that you have created the following two SharePoint libraries:

- Documents (documents to be archived, the source)
- Documents Archive (archive document library, the destination)

🗂	Documents	Document library
🗂	Documents Archive	Document library

Go to the Power Automate portal (*https://oreil.ly/O-MRf*). Sign in with your Microsoft account or your organization's account. Make sure you are in the correct Power Automate environment. Click on "My flows" in the left navigation bar. Click on "New flow" to create a new flow. Choose a flow type. In this case, you want to check for documents ready for archiving (every week), so you must choose "Scheduled cloud flow." You can check for documents ready for archiving every day; this recipe is just an example. Give your flow a name and then enter the required parameter to set when to run this flow. Set the starting date to today's date. Set the starting time to 9:00 P.M. (21:00). Set the "Repeat every" to once weekly. Then, unselect all days and keep Saturday (S) selected for the "On these days" parameter:

Click Create on the pop-up to navigate to the flow designer experience. Then add a new action (step) and search for "Variable." Choose "Initialize variable" and set the Name ("Two weeks ago") and Type (choose String) action parameters. Use the following expression for Value:

```
addDays(utcNow(),-14)
```

The value in the previous action will return the date of two weeks ago. The value in the variable will be used to fetch all documents that haven't been modified in the past two weeks. You can change the date (longer or shorter) based on your needs:

Add an action to get SharePoint documents in the Documents library. Search for the SharePoint connector and select the "Get files (properties only)" action. You may need to sign in and authenticate your SharePoint account. Then configure the Site Address (the relevant site URL where the Documents library resides) and Library Name (the SharePoint library to get the documents to be archived from Documents) action parameters. One additional parameter needs to be set: click on "Show advanced options" in the "Get files" action and set the Filter Query parameter as follows:

```
Modified lt datetime 'Two weeks ago'
```

The following table explains the elements of the Filter Query:

Query element	Description
`Modified`	SharePoint built-in column internal name
`lt`	Less-than comparison operator
`datetime`	Datetime conversion operator
`'Two weeks ago'`	Our defined variable

Next, add a new action (step), search for "Control," and then select the Control actions. From the list of actions, choose Condition. The condition will ensure that the following steps will execute only if there are documents to be archived. Otherwise, it terminates the flow. Then configure the condition action using the following expression for the left-side comparison value:

```
length(outputs('Get_files_(properties_only)')?['body/value'])
```

This expression uses the `length()` function to check if the "value" dynamic content from the "Get files" action contains items. Make sure the comparison operator is set to "is greater than," and then for the right-side comparison, type 0:

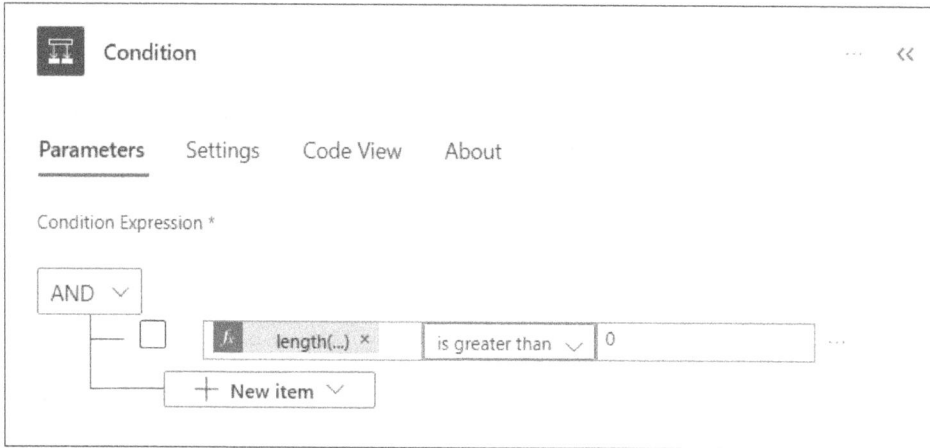

If the condition is not met, under False, add an action to terminate the flow. Search for "Control" actions and then select Terminate from the list of actions. Next, configure the Status action parameter by selecting Succeeded from the list of possible values:

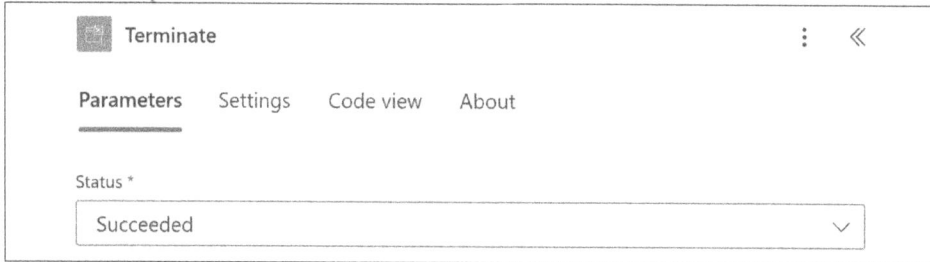

Now, if the condition is met, under True, add an action to create a folder in the archive document library. Search for the SharePoint connector and select the "Create new folder" action. Configure the action parameters, including Site Address (the relevant site URL where the archive document library resides), List or Library (the name of the SharePoint library where documents will be archived), and Folder Path (the relevant folder path in the destination document library). For the Folder Path parameter, type a forward slash (/) in the field and add the following expression:

```
string(formatDateTime(utcNow(),'dd-MM-yyyy'))
```

This expression formats the current time "dd-MM-yyyy" and then stringifies that value:

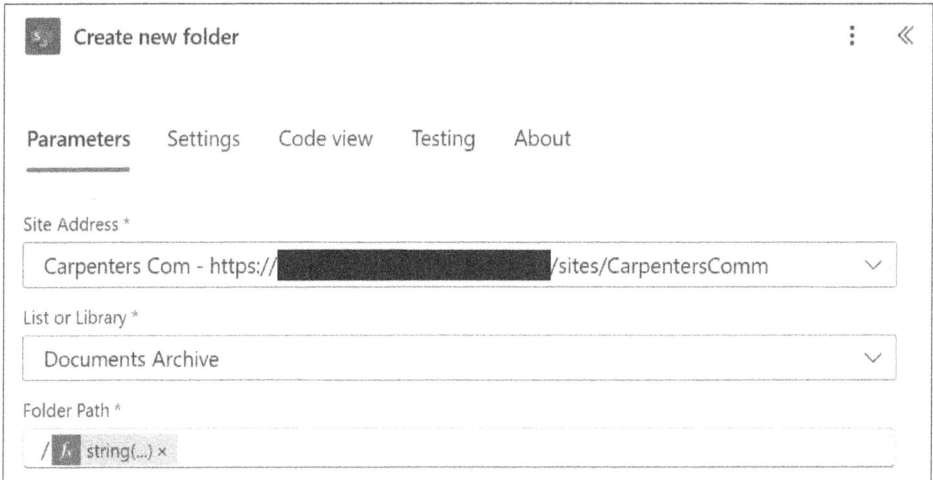

⑤ Create new folder	⋮ ≪

Parameters   Settings   Code view   Testing   About
───────────

Site Address *

Carpenters Com - https://████████████████/sites/CarpentersComm	⌄

List or Library *

Documents Archive	⌄

Folder Path *

/ ƒx string(...) ×

Add a new action (step), search for "Control," and then select the Control actions. From the list of actions, choose "Apply to each." Then configure the "Apply to each" action by setting the "Select an output from previous steps" parameter by selecting the "value" from the "Get files" action dynamic content:

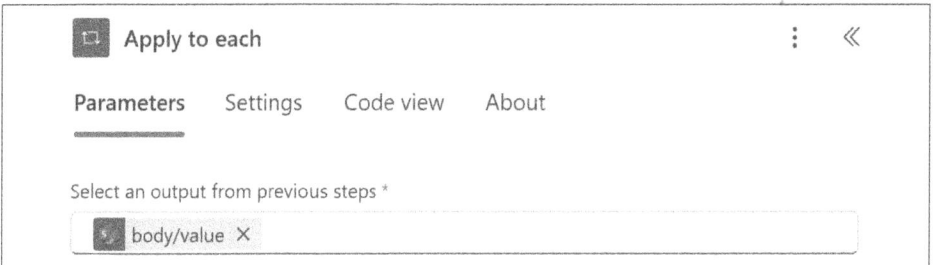

⊡ Apply to each	⋮ ≪

Parameters   Settings   Code view   About
───────────

Select an output from previous steps *

⑤ body/value ×

In the "Apply to each" action, add a new action (step), search for "SharePoint," and then select the "Move file" action. Next, configure the action parameters, including Current Site Address (the relevant site URL where the document library resides, the source), File To Move (the document Identifier from the "Get files" action dynamic content), Destination Site Address (the relevant site URL where the archive document library resides, the destination), and Destination Folder (the full relative folder where the document will be moved/archived. Provide the Full Path (from the "Create new folder" action dynamic content) and "If another file is already there" (select "Move with a new name"):

Move file	⋮ ≪

Parameters Settings Code view Testing About

Current Site Address *

> Carpenters Com - https://████████████/sites/CarpentersComm ⌄

File to Move *

> {Identifier} ×   📁

Destination Site Address *

> Carpenters Com - https://████████████/sites/CarpentersComm ⌄

Destination Folder *

> Full Path ×   📁

If another file is already there *

> Move with a new name ⌄

Finally, save and test your flow to ensure it works as expected:

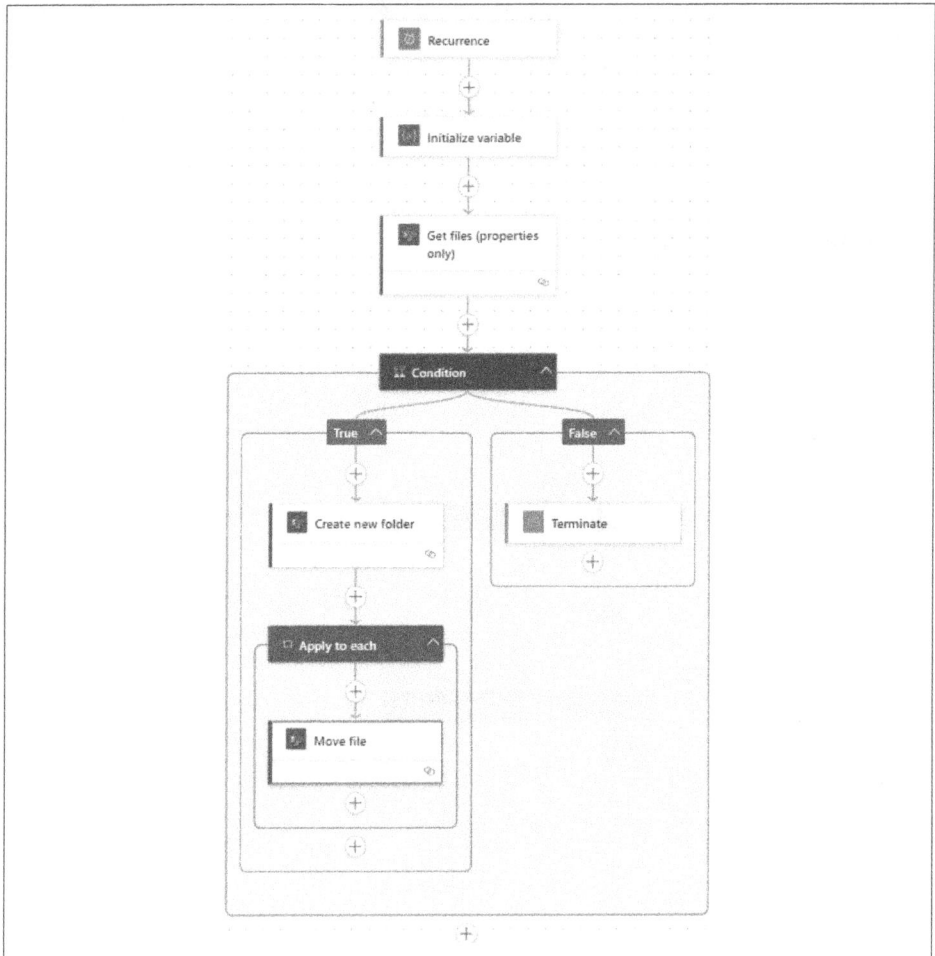

Documents Archive 📚 ⌄

📄	Name ⌄	Modified ⌄	Modified By ⌄
📁	13-05-2023	May 13	Ahmad Najjar
📁	Monday 05-11-2018 07--29	November 5, 2018	Ahmad Najjar
📁	Monday 17-09-2018 02--41	September 17, 2018	Ahmad Najjar

See Also

- Recipe 5.1, "Saving Email Attachments to OneDrive for Business"
- Recipe 5.2, "Moving Documents Between SharePoint Libraries"
- Recipe 5.4, "Converting a Word Document to PDF"

5.4 Converting a Word Document to PDF

Problem

You want to convert all Word documents created/uploaded to a particular SharePoint library to PDF.

Solution

Create an automated cloud flow that monitors Word file creation (upload) in a particular SharePoint library and then converts the created/uploaded file to PDF using OneDrive for Business.

Discussion

Using Power Automate to convert a Word document to PDF is a straightforward and crucial process for businesses and individuals alike. This automation simplifies converting important documents into a universally accessible format, ensuring consistency and compatibility. Whether you're dealing with reports, proposals, or any other Word document, this automation provides a seamless solution that reduces the need for manual conversions and eliminates the risk of formatting discrepancies.

Moreover, converting Word documents to PDFs boosts efficiency and consistency in document management. With automated workflows in place, you can easily ensure that all Word documents are automatically transformed into PDFs as they're uploaded. This saves time and establishes a standardized approach to document distribution, making it easier to share, view, and collaborate on documents across various platforms and devices. This automation simplifies the process of preparing documents for sharing, whether for internal team collaboration, client communication, or public distribution, ultimately streamlining document management and enhancing productivity.

Before building this flow, create a folder in your OneDrive for Business named "Temp." Additionally, ensure that you have created the following two SharePoint libraries:

- Converted to PDF (converted Word files Document library, the destination)
- Documents (documents to be converted to PDF, the source)

	Name	Type
	Converted to PDF	Document library
	Documents	Document library

To create a new flow in Power Automate, go to the Power Automate portal (*https://oreil.ly/O-MRf*). Sign in using your Microsoft or organization's account. Ensure that you are in the correct Power Automate environment, then click on "My flows" in the left navigation bar and select "New flow" to begin. Since you want to trigger the flow when a Word document is uploaded or created, choose the "Automated cloud flow" option. On the pop-up, click Skip to proceed to the flow designer. In the flow designer, search for the SharePoint connector, and select the "When a file is created (properties only)" trigger. You may need to sign in and authenticate your SharePoint account. Finally, configure the trigger's parameters, including the Site Address (the URL of the site where the Word Documents library is located) and Library Name (the library from which the Word files, to be converted, will be retrieved, typically Documents):

Add a new action (step) and search for "Variable" in the flow designer. Then choose "Initialize variable" and set the Name (File Extension) and Type (choose String) action parameters. Use the following expression for Value:

```
toLower(last(split(triggerOutputs()?['body/{FilenameWithExtension}'],'.')))
```

The previous expression will extract file extension and convert it to lowercase letters. Then, we want to check whether the uploaded file is a Word document based on the extracted value in the variable/expression. Add a new action, search for "Control," and then from the list of actions, choose Condition. Configure the condition action by selecting the File Extension property from the variable dynamic content for the left-side comparison value. Make sure the comparison operator is set to "is equal to," and then for the right-side comparison, type docx:

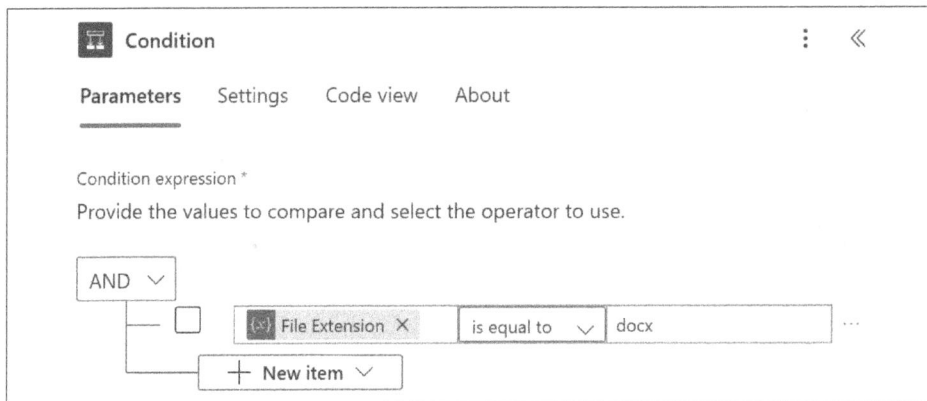

If the condition is not met, under False, add an action to terminate the flow. Search for "Control" actions, and then select Terminate from the list of actions. Next, configure the Status action parameter by selecting Succeeded from the list of possible values:

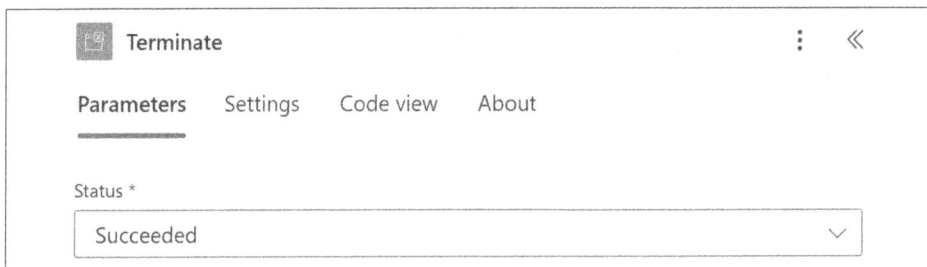

Now, if the condition is met, under True, add an action to get the file content (binaries) from the document library. Search for the SharePoint connector and select the "Get file content" action. Configure the action parameters, including Site Address (the relevant site URL where the Word documents library resides), File Identifier (the Identifier dynamic content from the trigger), and Infer Content Type (set to Yes):

Now I'll utilize OneDrive for Business to convert the Word file to PDF, but the file must be created (or uploaded) to a OneDrive repository to carry out the conversion. Add a new action, search for the OneDrive for Business connector, and select the "Create file" action. You may need to sign in and authenticate your OneDrive for Business account. Next, configure the action by providing the Folder Path parameter by selecting the Temp folder created in the prerequisites. Then, provide a File Name (from the dynamic content of the trigger "File name with extension") and File Content (from the dynamic content of the "Get file content" action):

Add a new action and search for the OneDrive for Business connector, then select the "Convert file" action. Then configure the action by providing the File (the file identifier dynamic content from the "Create file" action) and Target Type (show "Advanced parameters," then select PDF from the list):

Now that the file is created and converted in OneDrive for Business, it must be created in SharePoint. Add an action to create the PDF file in the destination document library. Search for the SharePoint connector and select the "Create file" action. Configure the action parameters, including "Site Address (the relevant site URL where the PDF document library resides), Folder Path (the folder path for the PDF document library created in the prerequisites, *Converted to PDF*), File Name (the filename from the "Convert file" action), and File Content (the file content from the "Convert file" action):

Finally, the created file in the Temp folder in OneDrive must be deleted. Add a new action, search for the OneDrive for Business connector, and select the "Delete file" action. Configure the action by providing the File (the file identifier dynamic content from the "Create file" action):

Give your flow a name and then save and test your flow to ensure it works as expected:

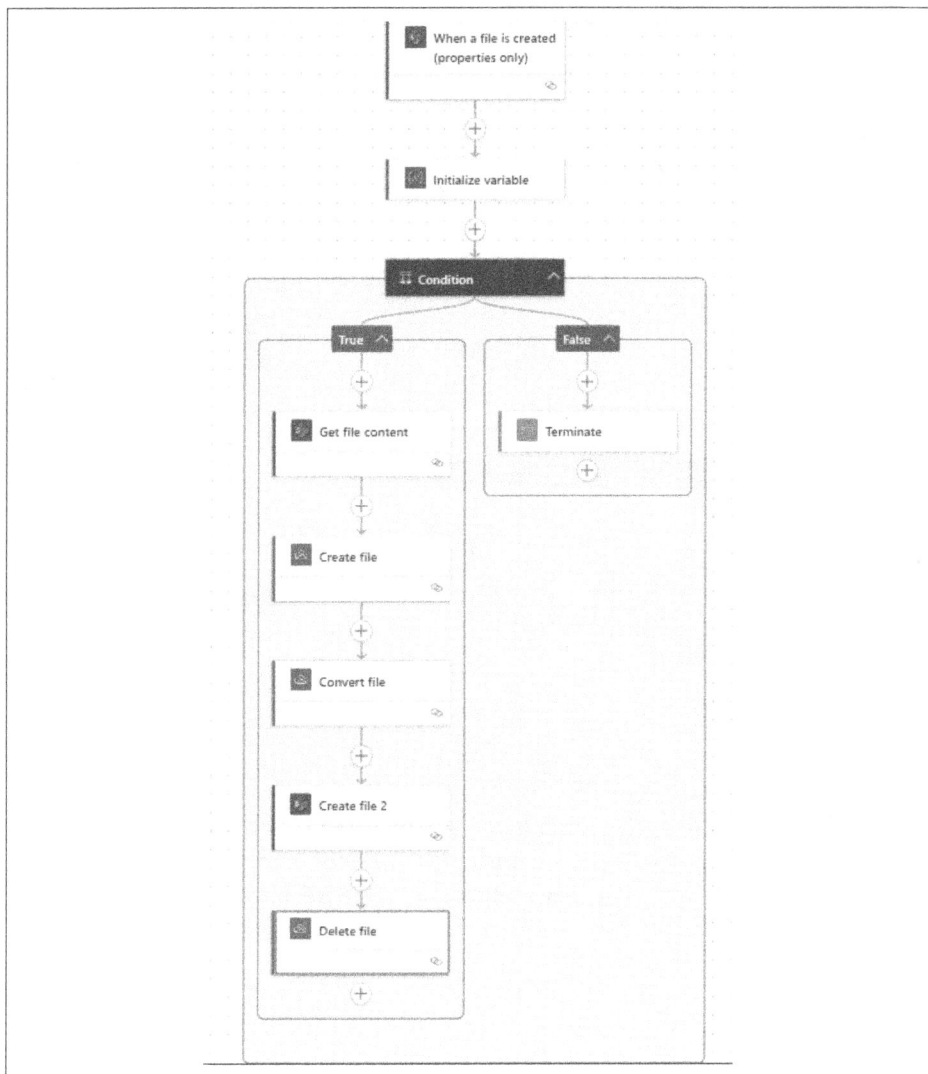

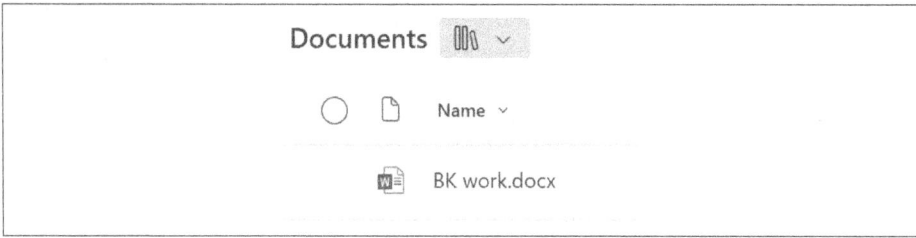

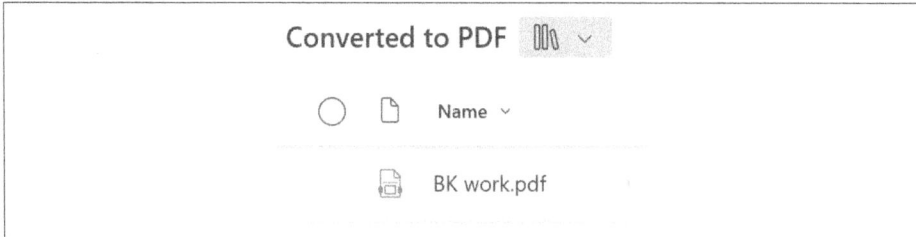

Documents ▯▯ ⌄

○　▯　Name ⌄

　　　📄 BK work.docx

Converted to PDF ▯▯ ⌄

○　▯　Name ⌄

　　　📄 BK work.pdf

See Also

- Recipe 5.1, "Saving Email Attachments to OneDrive for Business"
- Recipe 5.2, "Moving Documents Between SharePoint Libraries"
- Recipe 5.3, "Archiving SharePoint Documents"

Conclusion

Exploring the interplay of Power Automate with OneDrive for Business and Share-Point, this chapter revealed a game-changing fusion of tools that fundamentally transform how organizations handle files and document management. The examples showcased in this chapter underline the remarkable efficiency and versatility that this harmony brings to the realm of document management.

Integrating Power Automate with OneDrive for Business and SharePoint epitomizes file management and automation within the modern workplace. It simplifies file handling and contributes to increased productivity. This partnership offers a strategic advantage as organizations navigate their evolving digital landscape. By harnessing the combined capabilities of Power Automate with OneDrive for Business and Share-Point, businesses can significantly boost operational efficiency, reduce manual workload, and position themselves for success in a rapidly evolving data-centric business environment. In this digital transformation era, this integration is not merely a convenience; it's a linchpin for a future of enhanced file management and seamless workflow automation.

The collaboration between Power Automate, OneDrive for Business, and SharePoint extends beyond just convenience. It forms the cornerstone of modern information management, enabling organizations to adapt to the dynamic needs of today's digital workplace. As remote work and distributed teams become increasingly prevalent, this integration offers a pivotal solution for unifying and simplifying file handling, regardless of team members' locations. It empowers businesses to optimize their document management, streamline routine tasks, and reduce the risk of data errors or loss. As organizations continue to embrace the digital revolution, this strategic alignment of Power Automate with OneDrive for Business and SharePoint is a forward-thinking approach to achieving unparalleled efficiency, enhancing collaboration, and securing a future of agile and robust information management.

CHAPTER 6

Power Automate and Microsoft Forms

In this chapter, I'll start by defining what Microsoft Forms is, give a brief history of Microsoft Forms, and describe how Microsoft Forms and Power Automate became integral components of the Microsoft 365 ecosystem, offering organizations powerful tools for data collection, automation, and workflow management. Finally, I'll present two common scenarios for automating Microsoft Forms with Power Automate.

What Is Microsoft Forms?

Microsoft Forms is a user-friendly platform for creating surveys, quizzes, and feedback forms. Its intuitive interface makes it accessible to users across various skill levels, from educators gathering student feedback to businesses conducting market research. With a range of question types and the ability to collect responses in real time, Forms enables organizations to make informed decisions and engage with their audience effectively.

The History of Microsoft Forms

Introduced in 2016, Forms has undergone a noteworthy journey of development and expansion. Initially designed for the educational sector, Forms soon extended its reach to commercial customers of Office 365 (Microsoft 365 today) in 2018. This broad availability marked the transition from an education-focused tool to a versatile solution for businesses and organizations worldwide. One of the significant turning points came in 2019 when Forms was integrated into the Power Platform. This integration allowed users to create more complex, automated workflows by connecting Forms with various Microsoft 365 services and external applications.

Throughout the 2020s, Microsoft Forms added features, making it more versatile and user-friendly. Introducing branching logic, advanced collaboration and sharing options, and integration with Microsoft Teams enhanced its utility. Furthermore, integrating Forms Pro, a premium version of Microsoft Forms, and Dynamics 365 Customer Voice solidified its position as a robust tool for gathering feedback and managing surveys in a business context. Microsoft's commitment to ongoing development ensures that Forms remains relevant and adaptable, making it an indispensable component of the Microsoft ecosystem. With its evolution, Microsoft Forms has become a powerful asset for education, data collection, and engagement with audiences in the business world.

Microsoft Forms and Power Automate are integral components of the Microsoft 365 ecosystem, offering organizations powerful tools for data collection, automation, and workflow management.

Power Automate integration with Microsoft Forms is particularly valuable, allowing users to trigger actions based on form responses. For example, when a survey is submitted, Power Automate can automatically send follow-up emails, update SharePoint lists, or initiate approval processes. This dynamic combination saves time and enhances productivity by reducing manual intervention and ensuring data and information flow seamlessly across various applications and services. Microsoft Forms and Power Automate together offer a comprehensive solution for data collection and automation, catering to the diverse needs of both educational and business users.

6.1 Saving Microsoft Forms Responses to SharePoint

Problem

You want to save Microsoft Forms responses to a particular SharePoint list.

Solution

Create an automated cloud flow that monitors certain Microsoft Forms responses and then saves the response details to a particular SharePoint list.

Discussion

Leveraging Power Automate to save Microsoft Forms responses to SharePoint is a powerful automation that streamlines the collection, organization, and accessibility of survey data. This automation bridges Microsoft Forms, a versatile survey and data collection tool, and SharePoint, a robust records management platform. By setting up this workflow, every response submitted through Microsoft Forms is automatically transferred to a designated location within SharePoint. This eliminates the need for manual data entry and ensures that all responses are uniformly organized, making it easier for you to access, review, and collaborate on the collected data.

Integrating Power Automate with Microsoft Forms and SharePoint mainly benefits those who rely on data-driven decision making. By centralizing survey responses in SharePoint, you can effortlessly search, filter, and analyze data to gain valuable insights. Additionally, the automation ensures that data remains secure and accessible, enhancing governance and compliance. This flow of data between Microsoft Forms and SharePoint significantly reduces the manual effort required for data management, allowing you to focus on extracting insights and making informed decisions based on the collected responses.

Before building this flow, create a Microsoft Forms survey (Workshop Feedback). To learn how to create a Microsoft Form, go to the Microsoft Forms documentation (*https://oreil.ly/ox5Ix*). Then add the following fields:

- What is your name? (required text field)
- What is your occupation? (required text field)
- What do you think of the workshop? (required numbers rating field to level 10)
- Any other comments or suggestions? (optional long text field)

Additionally, ensure that you have created a SharePoint list that has the following corresponding columns to save the form's responses:

- Title (default, single line of text)
- Occupation (single line of text)
- Rating (number)
- Suggestions (multiple lines of text)

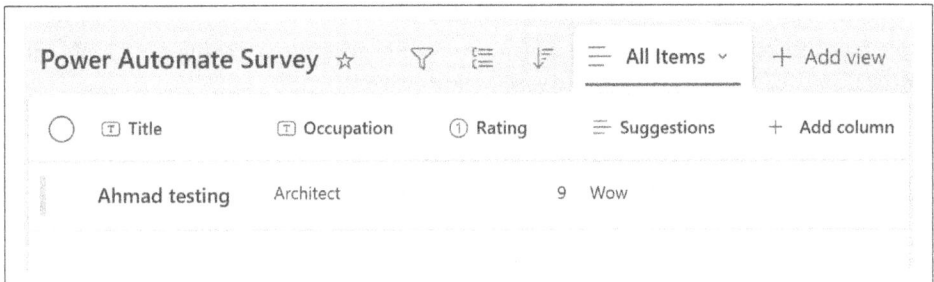

To create a new flow in Power Automate, visit the Power Automate portal (*https://oreil.ly/O-MRf*). Sign in with your Microsoft or organization's account. Ensure that you're in the correct Power Automate environment, then click on "My flows" in the left navigation bar and select "New flow" to begin. Since you want the flow to start when a response is submitted, choose the "Automated cloud flow" option. On the pop-up, click Skip to access the flow designer. In the designer, search for the Microsoft Forms connector and select the "When a new response is submitted" trigger. You may need to sign in and authenticate your Microsoft Forms account. Finally, configure the trigger's parameter, selecting the Form Id of the Microsoft form from which you want to collect responses:

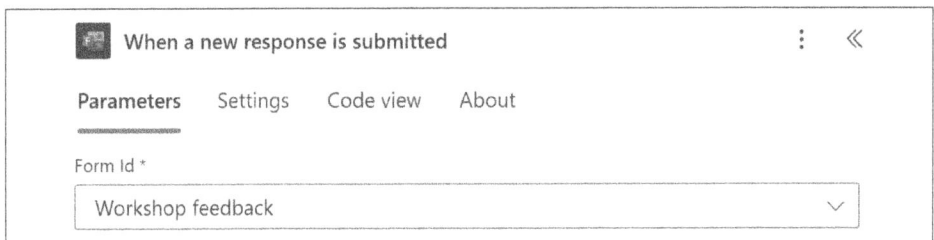

Add a new action (step) and search for Microsoft Forms in the flow designer. Choose "Get response details" to collect the data from the submitted response. Then configure the action's parameters, including Form Id (the relevant Microsoft form from which you want to collect the responses) and Response Id (the corresponding response ID from the trigger's dynamic content):

Add a new action (step) and search for SharePoint in the flow designer. Choose "Create item" to save the data from the submitted response to SharePoint. Finally, configure the action's parameters, including the Site Address (the relevant site URL where the form responses will be saved) and List Name (the list where the response's details will be saved), and then set the SharePoint item values to their respective values from the "Get response details" action:

- *Title*: What is your name?
- *Occupation*: What is your occupation?
- *Rating*: What do you think of the workshop?
- *Suggestions*: Any other comments or suggestions?

Create item   ⋮

Parameters   Settings   Code view   Testing   About
‾‾‾‾‾‾‾‾‾‾

Site Address *

| Lush Vibes - https://████████████/sites/LushVibes   ⌄ |

List Name *

| Power Automate Survey   ⌄ |

Title *

| ⬚ body/r126563061... × |

Advanced parameters

| Showing 3 of 5   ⌄ | Show all | Clear all |

Occupation

| ⬚ body/r856a3b1d9... × | ✕

Rating

| ⬚ body/r5da136338... × | ✕

Suggestions

| ⬚ body/r2003180fe... × | ✕

Give your flow a name and then save and test your flow to ensure it works as expected:

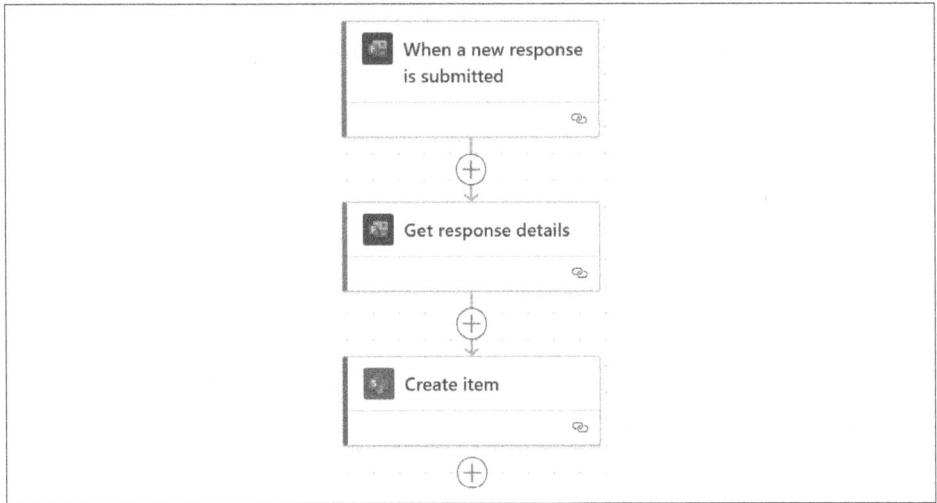

See Also

- Recipe 6.2, "Sending an Email to the Responder When a Response Is Submitted"

6.2 Sending an Email to the Responder When a Response Is Submitted

Problem

You want to email the Microsoft Forms form responder when a response is submitted.

Solution

Create an automated cloud flow that monitors certain Microsoft Forms form responses and then emails the responder using the desired email format.

Discussion

This automation adds a personalized and efficient touch to data collection and engagement. It creates a real-time connection between the survey process and communication, ensuring that responders receive acknowledgment and confirmation upon submitting their responses. This provides instant feedback and fosters a sense of engagement and responsiveness, showing that their input is valued. It's a simple yet impactful way to improve the user experience and demonstrate effective communication.

Additionally, this integration enhances the efficiency of data processing. By using Power Automate, you can automate sending personalized confirmation emails to responders, which would be a cumbersome and time-consuming task if done manually. This not only saves time and resources but also ensures that responders receive prompt and consistent communication, contributing to a positive interaction between you and your audience. Overall, this automation streamlines the response collection process and enhances the user experience, making data collection more efficient, engaging, and user-friendly.

Before building this flow, create a Microsoft Forms survey (Workshop Feedback). Then add the following fields:

- What is your name? (required text field)
- What is your occupation? (required text field)
- What do you think of the workshop? (required numbers rating field to level 10)
- Any other comments or suggestions? (optional long text field)

Ensure you set the "Who can fill out this form" setting to one of the following:

- Only people in Organization Name can respond
- Specific people in Organization Name can respond

To create a new flow in Power Automate, go to the Power Automate portal (*https://oreil.ly/O-MRf*). Sign in with your Microsoft or organization's account. Ensure that you're in the correct Power Automate environment, then click on "My flows" in the left navigation bar and select "New flow" to start. Since you want the flow to trigger when a response is submitted, choose the "Automated cloud flow" option. Afterward, click Skip on the pop-up to enter the flow designer. In the flow designer, search for the Microsoft Forms connector and select the "When a new response is submitted" trigger. You may need to authenticate your Microsoft Forms account. Finally, configure the trigger's parameter by selecting the relevant Form Id of the Microsoft form from which you want to collect responses:

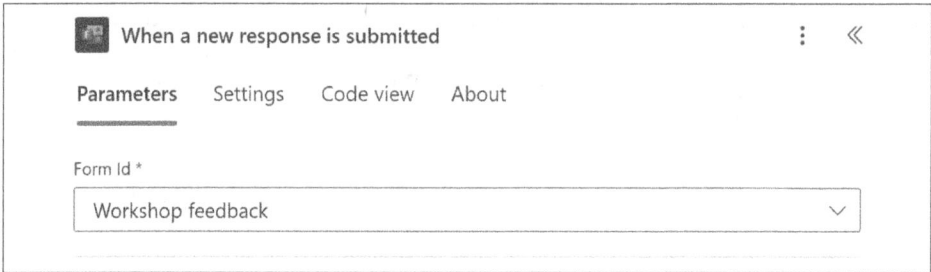

When a new response is submitted

Parameters   Settings   Code view   About

Form Id *

Workshop feedback

Add a new action (step) and search for Microsoft Forms in the flow designer. Choose "Get response details" to collect the data from the submitted response. Configure the action's parameters, including Form Id (the relevant Microsoft form from which you want to collect the responses) and Response Id (the corresponding response ID from the trigger's dynamic content):

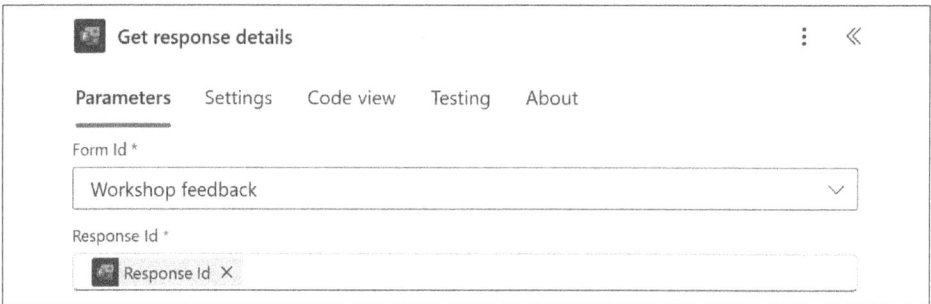

Get response details

Parameters   Settings   Code view   Testing   About

Form Id *

Workshop feedback

Response Id *

Response Id X

Add a new action (step), search for "Control," and then select the Control actions. From the list of actions, choose Condition. The condition will ensure that the following steps will execute only if the user is identified. That way, the email can be fetched from the response details. Otherwise, the flow should be terminated. Configure the condition action comparison value to the left to Responder from the dynamic content of the "Get response details." Ensure that the operator is set to "is not equal to," and then type anonymous in the comparison value to the right:

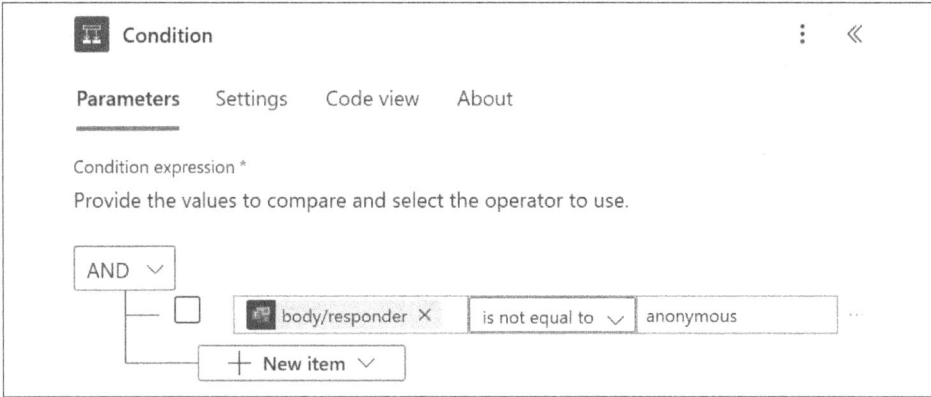

If the condition is not met, under False, add an action to terminate the flow. Search for "Control" actions and then select Terminate from the list of actions:

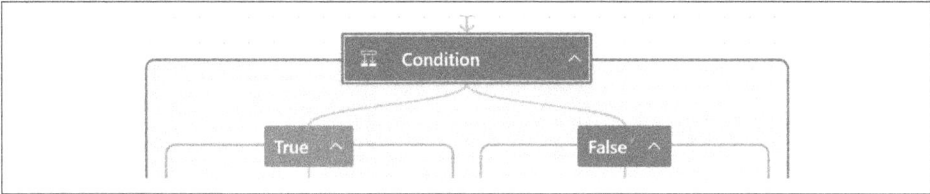

Configure the Status action parameter by selecting Succeeded from the list of possible values:

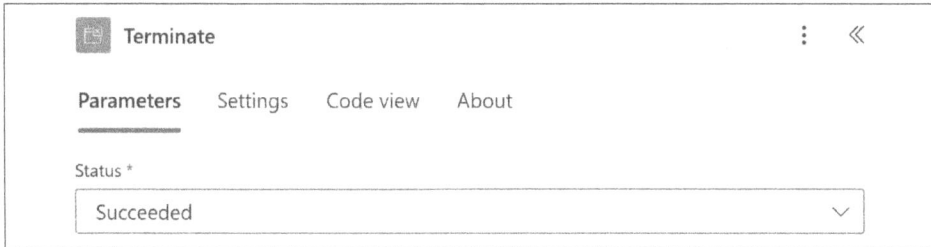

Now, if the condition is met, under True, add an action to email the responder. Search for the Office 365 Outlook connector and select the "Send an email (V2)" action. You may need to sign in and authenticate your Office 365 Outlook account. Configure the action by providing the To parameter by adding the Responder Email from the dynamic content. Then, provide a subject for the "Send an email" action, such as "Microsoft Form Response," in addition to "Submission time" from the dynamic content. Finally, customize the Body parameter (email text). In the following example, all text in {} are dynamic content from the "Get response details" action:

```
Microsoft Forms response has been submitted by {Responder Email}
    at {Submission time}
```

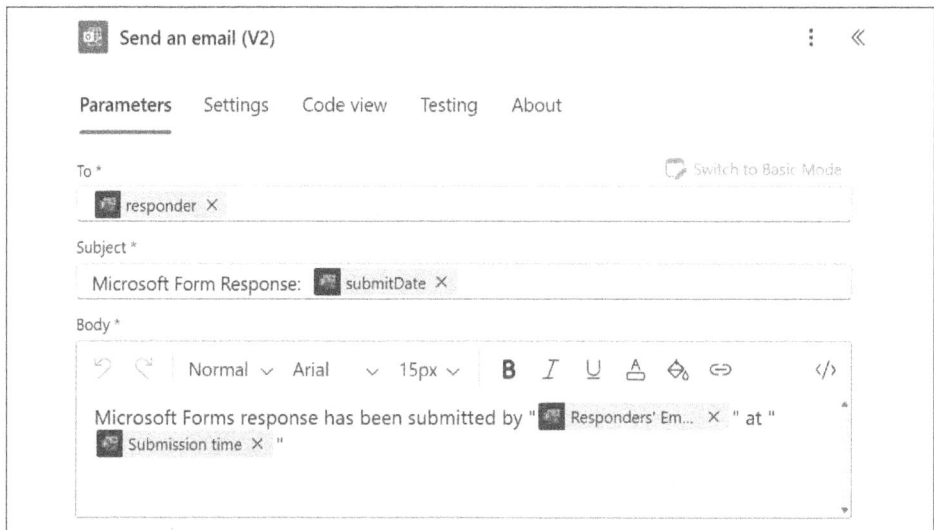

Give your flow a name and then save and test your flow to ensure it works as expected:

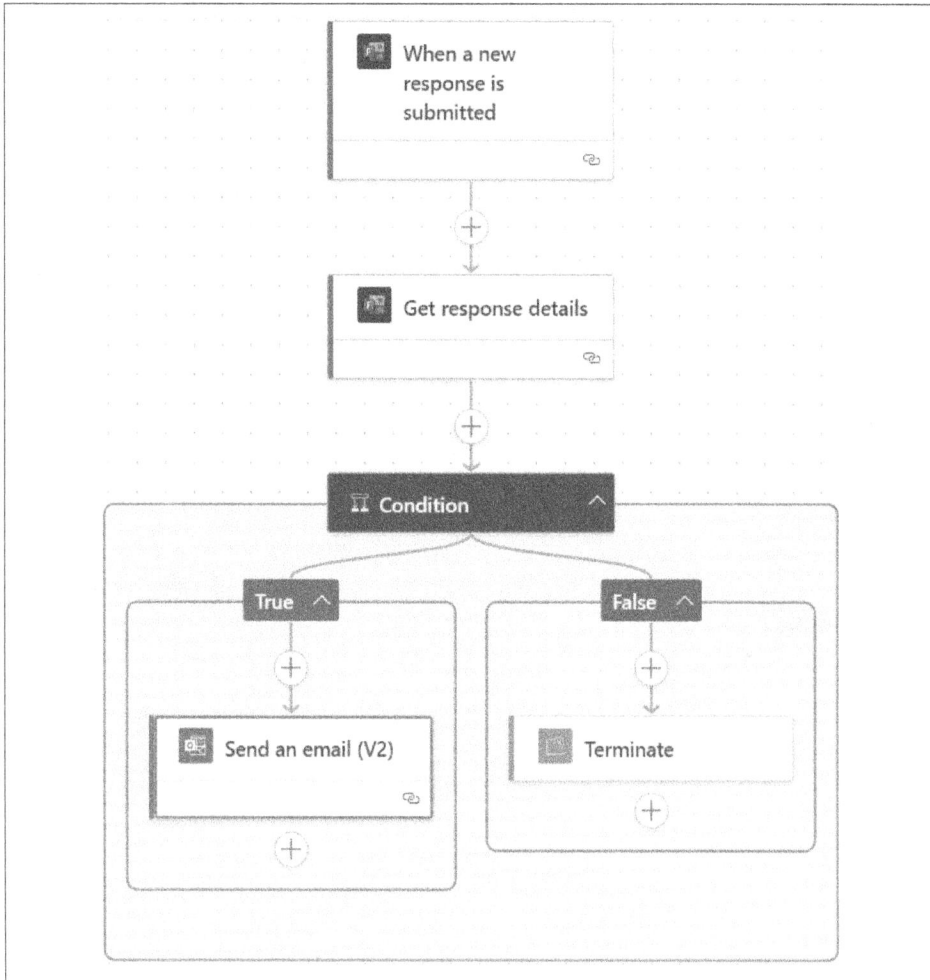

See Also

- Recipe 6.1, "Saving Microsoft Forms Responses to SharePoint"

Conclusion

The synergy between Power Automate and Microsoft Forms has redefined how organizations collect and manage data, streamlining processes and improving communication. Through the examples discussed in this chapter, we've witnessed the power of automation in action. By saving Microsoft Forms responses to SharePoint, organizations can effortlessly centralize data, ensuring easy access and efficient management. Furthermore, the ability to store these responses and post corresponding messages to Microsoft Teams channels exemplifies the versatility of this integration. It fosters real-time collaboration and ensures that relevant stakeholders are promptly informed.

The potential of Power Automate and Microsoft Forms extends far beyond these examples, offering organizations an arsenal of tools to enhance productivity and data-driven decision making. Harnessing the full potential of Power Automate and Microsoft Forms is not just an option; it's a strategic advantage that can drive operational excellence and success in today's data-driven and collaborative business environment.

CHAPTER 7

Power Automate and Microsoft Teams

In this chapter, I'll go through the history of Microsoft Teams and how it has evolved from a basic messaging tool into a comprehensive platform facilitating collaboration across organizations through features like chat, video conferencing, and file sharing. I'll briefly highlight the expansion of Microsoft Teams, the various user-centric features, and its integration with Power Automate, which significantly boosts workflow efficiency and productivity by automating tasks and facilitating the creation of custom apps and bots. Finally, I'll go through common and useful automation scenarios using Power Automate and Microsoft Teams.

The History of Microsoft Teams

Microsoft Teams, launched in March 2017, is a comprehensive collaboration platform that has revolutionized how organizations communicate, collaborate, and share information. As part of the Microsoft 365 suite, Teams provides a unified hub for chat, video conferencing, file sharing, and project management. Its primary goal is to streamline teamwork and enhance productivity within the modern workplace.

The development of Microsoft Teams has been a dynamic journey of growth and innovation. Microsoft Teams was introduced to compete with popular collaboration tools such as Slack and to address the increasing demand for seamless digital teamwork. Initially designed for chat and messaging, Teams has since evolved into a full-fledged collaboration ecosystem. In 2018, Microsoft introduced the free Teams version, further expanding its user base. Subsequent years witnessed continuous updates and features, including integrations with other Microsoft 365 apps, third-party applications, and AI-driven features for tasks like meeting transcription and automated responses.

The onset of the COVID-19 pandemic in 2020 propelled Teams to the forefront, with its usage skyrocketing as remote work and virtual meetings became the norm. The platform became increasingly versatile, accommodating educational institutions, healthcare providers, and businesses of all sizes. In 2021, Microsoft announced a significant development by introducing the Teams Essentials subscription for small businesses, underlining the platform's adaptability to various user needs.

The synergy between Microsoft Teams and Power Automate creates a dynamic environment for seamless collaboration and workflow automation within organizations. Microsoft Teams, as a hub for communication and collaboration, is enhanced by Power Automate's automation capabilities. With this integration, users can automate routine tasks, receive notifications, and trigger actions directly within their Teams channels. This ensures that relevant information is readily accessible and that work processes flow smoothly.

One key aspect of this correlation is the ability to automate processes triggered by Microsoft Teams activities. For instance, when a new message or file is posted in a Teams channel, Power Automate can instantly initiate workflows, such as sending notifications to specific team members, updating a shared document in SharePoint, or creating tasks in Microsoft Planner. This integration saves time and ensures that critical information is promptly acted upon, increasing overall efficiency.

Moreover, incorporating Power Automate within Teams empowers users to build custom apps and bots to further enhance collaboration. Teams users can create custom flows within Power Automate, seamlessly integrating with their channel conversations. This facilitates data retrieval, task management, and other automation processes, making Teams a central hub for communication and action. Therefore, the correlation between Microsoft Teams and Power Automate is a powerful means of optimizing team productivity and enabling a more agile and responsive approach to business operations.

7.1 Posting the Weather Forecast to a Teams Channel

Problem

You want to post the daily weather forecast to a Microsoft Teams channel.

Solution

Create a scheduled cloud flow that runs daily, gets the weather forecast information, and then posts the information to a particular Teams channel.

Discussion

This automation is a practical application in enhancing team collaboration and staying informed in real time. This flow lets you proactively provide channel members with essential weather updates directly within Microsoft Teams. You can configure workflows to fetch weather forecasts and share them in designated Teams channels by integrating with MSN Weather and Power Automate. This not only streamlines the process of accessing weather information but also ensures that teams are well-prepared and informed, especially in situations where weather conditions can impact their work activities or travel plans.

Furthermore, this flow underscores the adaptability and versatility of Power Automate in extending the functionality of Microsoft Teams. It empowers you to access many external data sources and bring that information into your Team's workspace, enabling more efficient communication. Automating weather updates can enhance situational awareness, improve planning, and foster a more agile and responsive work environment. Ultimately, the ability to post weather forecasts in Teams is just one example of how Power Automate can customize and enrich the Teams experience, turning it into a central hub for internal collaboration and external data access.

Before building this flow, create a dedicated team in Teams, such as "Weather." Then, create a channel for posting weather updates, such as "Daily Weather Forecast":

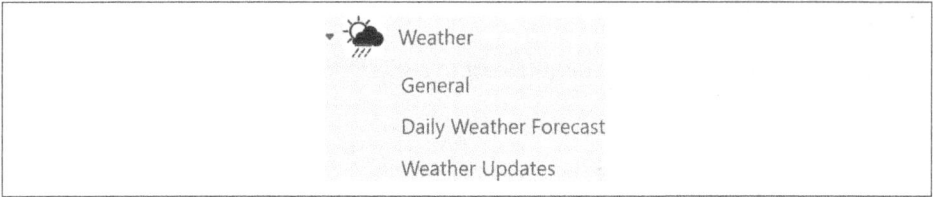

To create a new flow in Power Automate, begin by visiting the Power Automate portal (*https://oreil.ly/O-MRf*) and signing in with your Microsoft or organization's account. Ensure that you are in the correct Power Automate environment, then click on "My flows" in the left navigation bar and select "New flow" to initiate the creation process. Since you want the flow to retrieve the weather forecast daily, choose the "Scheduled cloud flow" option. Assign a name to your flow, and enter the necessary parameters to determine when it should run, setting the starting date to today's date and the time to 6:00 A.M. Finally, configure the flow to repeat once every day:

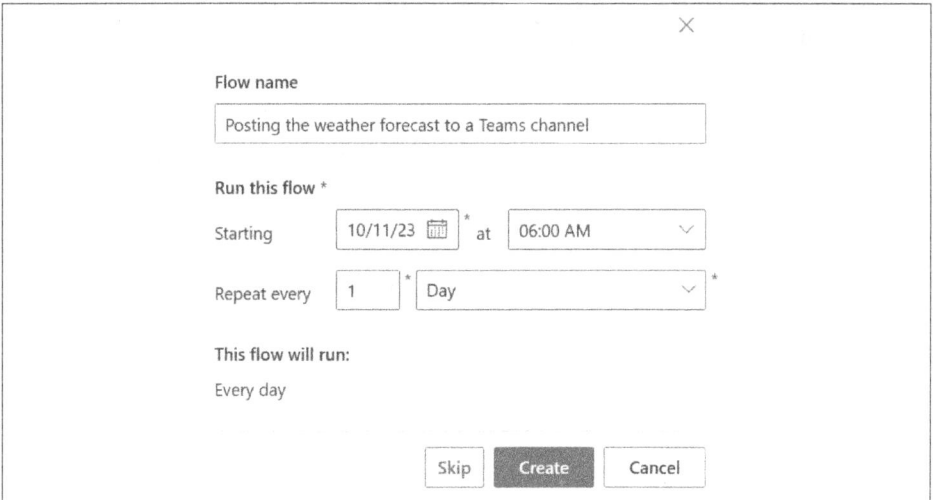

Click Create on the pop-up to navigate to the flow designer experience. Once in the flow designer, expand the Recurrence trigger and set the "Time zone" trigger parameter to your local time zone. Power Automate cloud flows run on the UTC zone by default:

⏱ Recurrence	⋮ ≪

Parameters   Settings   Code view   About

Recurrence *

Interval *

1

Frequency *

Day	⌄

Time zone

(UTC+01:00) Amsterdam, Berlin, Bern, Rome, Stockholm, Vienna	⌄

Start time

Example: 2017-03-24T15:00:00Z

At these hours

6	⌄

At these minutes

Enter the valid minute values (from 0 to 59) separated by comma, e.g., 15,30

Preview
Runs at 6:00 every day

Add an action to get today's weather forecast. Search for the MSN Weather connector and select the "Get forecast for today" action. You may need to sign in and authenticate your MSN Weather account. Configure the Location (city, region, country, postal code, longitude, and latitude) and Units (Imperial or Metric) action parameters:

⬤ Get forecast for today	⋮ ≪

Parameters   Settings   Code view   Testing   About

Location *

Oslo

Units *

Imperial	⌄

🔗 Connected to MSN Weather.   Change connection

Add an action to post to the created Teams channel. Search for the Microsoft Teams connector and select the "Post message in a chat or channel" action. You may need to sign in and authenticate your Microsoft Teams account. Then configure the action parameters, including "Post as" (choose "Flow bot"), "Post in" (choose Channel), Team (choose the created team in the prerequisites, Weather), and Channel (the designated channel to post weather forecasts in Daily Weather Forecast). Finally, compose a message to post to the Teams channel in the Message parameter. In the following example, all text in {} is dynamic content from the "Get forecast for today" action:

```
Good Morning! Today's forecast for Oslo will be {Conditions} with a High of
{Temperature High} and a Low of {Temperature Low} and a {Rain Chance}% chance
of rain.
```

Save and test your flow to ensure it works as expected:

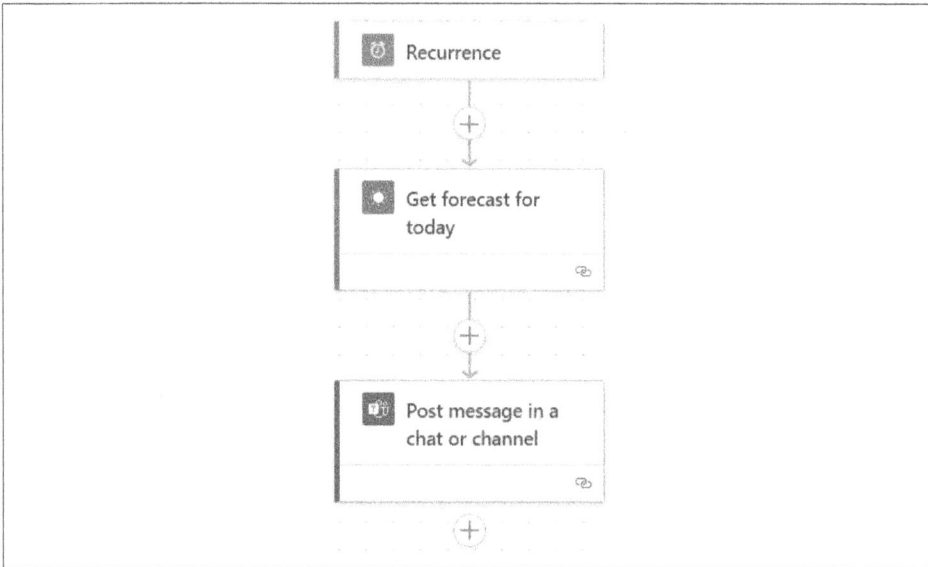

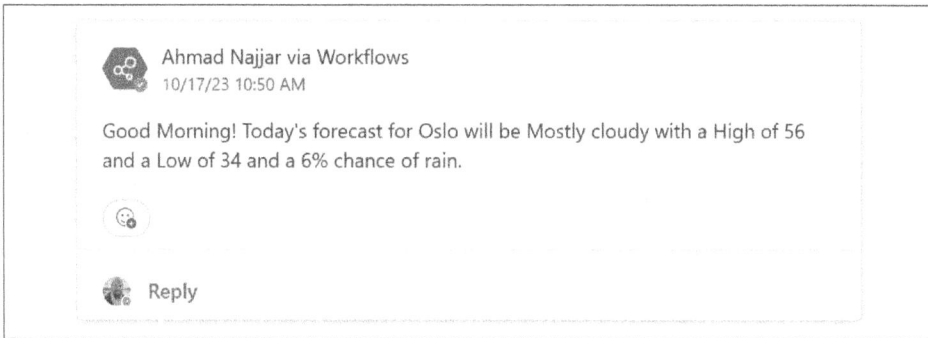

Ahmad Najjar via Workflows
10/17/23 10:50 AM

Good Morning! Today's forecast for Oslo will be Mostly cloudy with a High of 56 and a Low of 34 and a 6% chance of rain.

Reply

See Also

- Recipe 7.2, "Posting a Message on Slack When a Message Is Posted on Teams"
- Recipe 7.3, "Posting a Message to Microsoft Teams When an Email Arrives"

7.2 Posting a Message on Slack When a Message Is Posted on Teams

Problem

You want to post a message to a particular Slack channel when a message is posted on a Microsoft Teams channel.

Solution

Create an automated cloud flow that monitors a particular Microsoft Teams channel for posted messages and then posts the message to a Slack channel.

Discussion

This flow is a prime illustration of how automation can break down communication barriers and foster a more interconnected digital workspace. This automation bridges the gap between the two popular collaboration platforms, allowing for seamless communication and information sharing. With this integration, messages and updates from Teams can be instantly mirrored on Slack, ensuring that team members are well-informed, regardless of which platform they prefer or use most frequently. This synchronization improves internal communication and minimizes the risk of information silos by ensuring everyone stays on the same page.

The beauty of this automation lies in its ability to streamline communication while reducing redundancy. Rather than manually duplicating messages across platforms, Power Automate takes care of this task, freeing up time for you to focus on more critical activities. This integration underscores the adaptability and efficiency of modern workplace technology, enabling you to leverage the strengths of multiple platforms while maintaining a cohesive and collaborative communication environment. In the era of remote work and distributed teams, automation like this is pivotal in ensuring that information flows seamlessly and team members can effectively collaborate, regardless of their location or preferred communication tools.

Before building this flow, first identify or create a dedicated Teams team, such as "Development," that you want to monitor for new messages. Additionally, identify or create a dedicated Slack channel, such as "Bugs Broadcast," where you want to post the new messages. Choose the flow type; in this case, since you want to start the flow when a message is posted to a specified Teams channel, select the "Automated cloud flow" option. Click Skip on the pop-up to access the flow designer experience. In the designer, search for the Microsoft Teams connector and choose the trigger related to new messages in Microsoft Teams by selecting the "When a new channel message is added" trigger. You may need to sign in and authenticate your Microsoft Teams account. Finally, configure the trigger's parameters by selecting the relevant Microsoft

Teams team and the specific channel from which you want to collect posted messages:

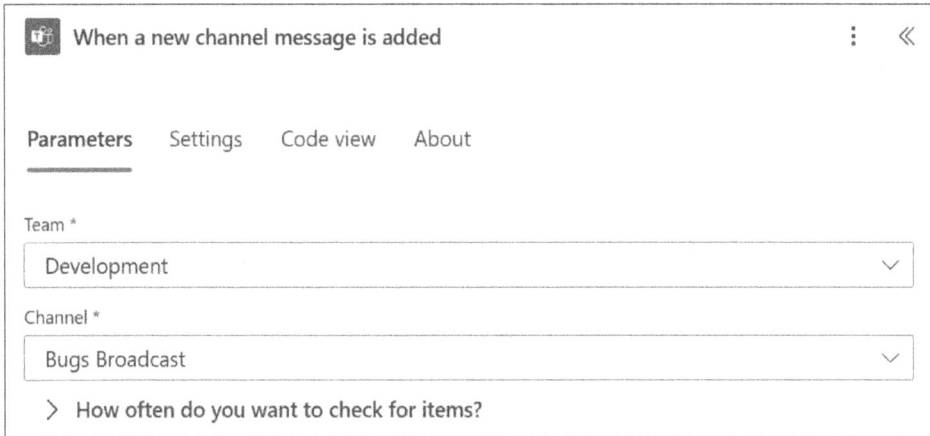

Microsoft Teams messages are posted in HTML format. Therefore, you need to extract the plain text before posting to Slack. Search for the Content Conversion connector and select the "Html to text" action. Configure the Content action parameter (the content you want to clean the HTML tags from). In this case, you want to pass in the "Message body content" from the dynamic content of the trigger:

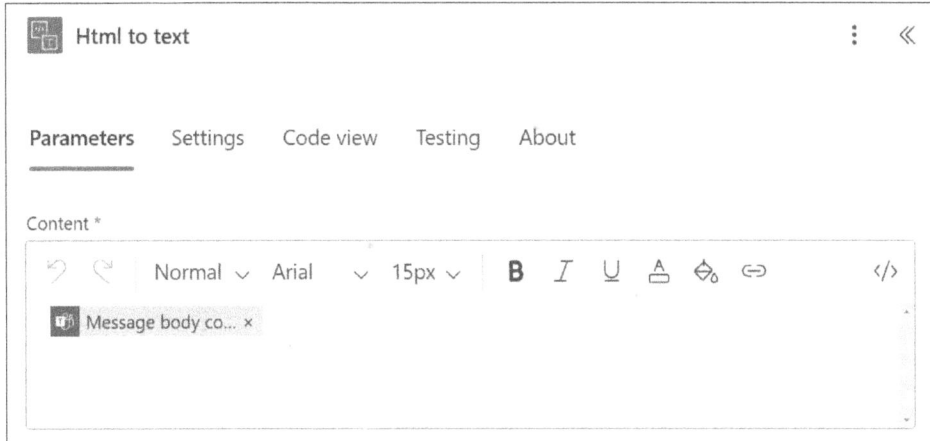

Add an action to post a message to a Slack channel. Search for the Slack connector and select the "Post message (V2)" action. You may need to sign in and authenticate your Slack account. You may also need to consent if a Power Automate connector requests permission to access a Slack workplace. Ensure that you allow that request to grant permission for Power Automate to post messages on Slack:

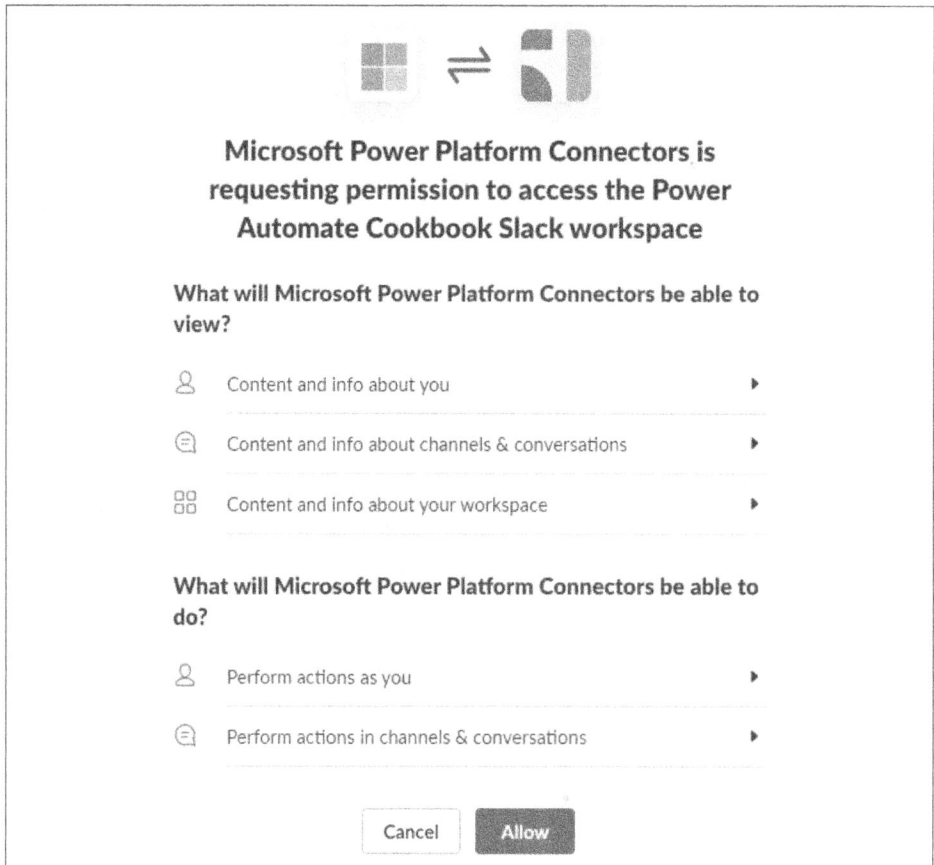

Microsoft Power Platform Connectors is requesting permission to access the Power Automate Cookbook Slack workspace

What will Microsoft Power Platform Connectors be able to view?

   Content and info about you   ▸

   Content and info about channels & conversations   ▸

   Content and info about your workspace   ▸

What will Microsoft Power Platform Connectors be able to do?

   Perform actions as you   ▸

   Perform actions in channels & conversations   ▸

Cancel   **Allow**

Configure the action by providing the Channel Name (the Slack channel you want the message to be posted to) and the Message Text parameter (the Slack message to be posted on the chosen channel). You can use the dynamic content from the trigger. Therefore, you need to pass {`Message body content`}:

Give your flow a name, and then save and test your flow to ensure it works as expected:

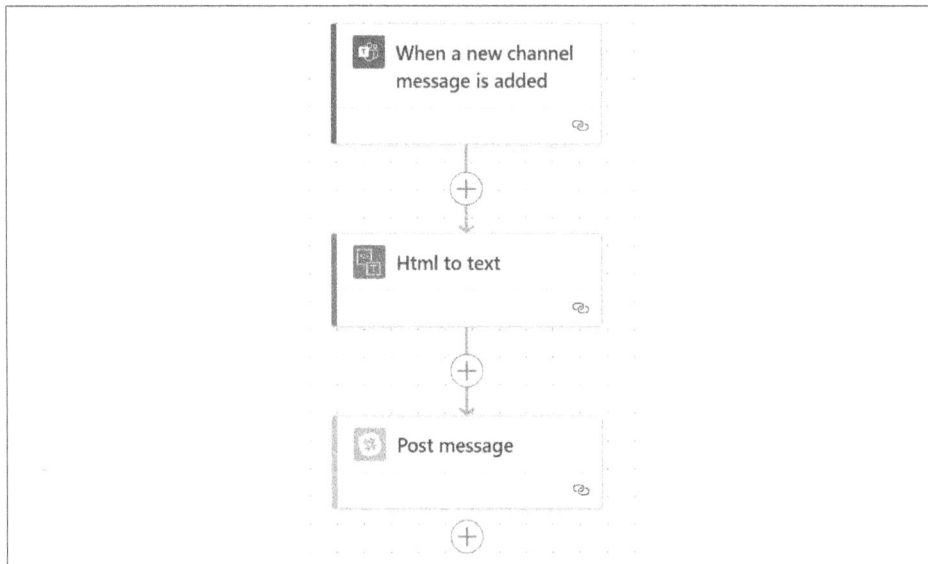

> **Microsoft Power Platform Connectors** `APP` 4:50 PM
> Markdown formatting (e.g., bold, italic, and bullet points) does not render
> correctly and instead displays raw syntax. This issue occurs only in this
> channel, while formatting works fine elsewhere. Users can manually edit messages
> after sending to apply formatting as a temporary workaround. Tested on Teams
> version 1.6.00.12345 across Windows 11, macOS Monterey, Edge 119, and Chrome
> 118. Issue confirmed by multiple users. Needs investigation for a fix in the
> next update.

See Also

- Recipe 7.1, "Posting the Weather Forecast to a Teams Channel"
- Recipe 7.3, "Posting a Message to Microsoft Teams When an Email Arrives"

7.3 Posting a Message to Microsoft Teams When an Email Arrives

Problem

You want to be notified on Microsoft Teams (channel) when an email arrives in a particular folder.

Solution

Create an automated cloud flow that monitors a particular folder in your email for new emails and then posts a message to a particular Microsoft Teams channel.

Discussion

This automation is a strategic move to enhance communication and streamline information sharing. This flow facilitates the real-time dissemination of critical information. As soon as an email lands in an Outlook inbox, Power Automate can trigger a notification or message in a designated Teams channel when an email contains a specific keyword, ensuring that you are promptly informed and can take immediate action if necessary. This instant notification system eliminates the need to constantly monitor email inboxes and promotes a more agile and responsive work environment.

Moreover, this integration of Power Automate with Teams and Outlook brings together the strengths of both platforms to create a well-rounded communication ecosystem. It capitalizes on the quick and structured communication of Teams while ensuring that critical information from Outlook is effortlessly integrated. This helps reduce the risk of overlooked emails and ensures that you see crucial updates or messages without delay. In a world where timely and efficient communication is paramount, this automation optimizes the flow of information and empowers you to make quicker decisions and stay well-informed.

Before building this flow, create a dedicated Teams channel, such as "Email Notification." Next, visit the Power Automate portal (*https://oreil.ly/O-MRf*) and sign in with your Microsoft or organization's account. Ensure that you are in the correct Power Automate environment, then click on "My flows" in the left navigation bar and select "New flow" to start creating a new flow. Since you want the flow to initiate when an email is received, choose the "Automated cloud flow" option. On the pop-up, click Skip to enter the flow designer experience. In the designer, search for the Office 365 Outlook connector and select the trigger that corresponds to when an email is received, specifically the "When a new email arrives (V3)" trigger. You may need to sign in and authenticate your Office 365 Outlook account. Finally, configure the trigger parameters, selecting the Folder that will be monitored for incoming emails:

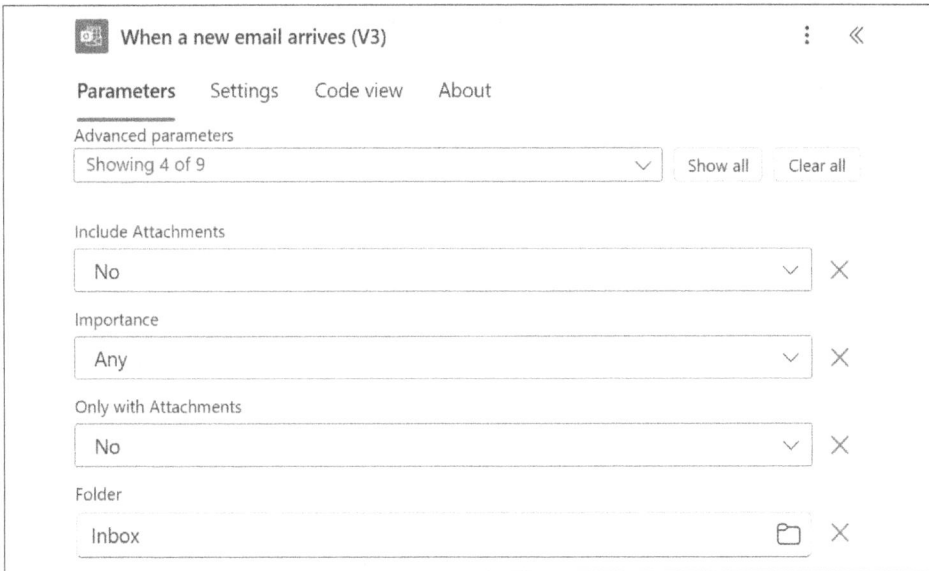

Then, add a new action (step), search for "Control," and then select the Control actions. From the list of actions, choose Condition. The condition will ensure that the following steps will execute only if the email body contains a specific keyword. Otherwise, it terminates the flow. Next, configure the condition action by setting the left-side comparison value to {Body} from the dynamic content of the trigger. Ensure the comparison operator is set to "contains." Then, type `Project XYZ` (the keyword) in the right-side comparison value:

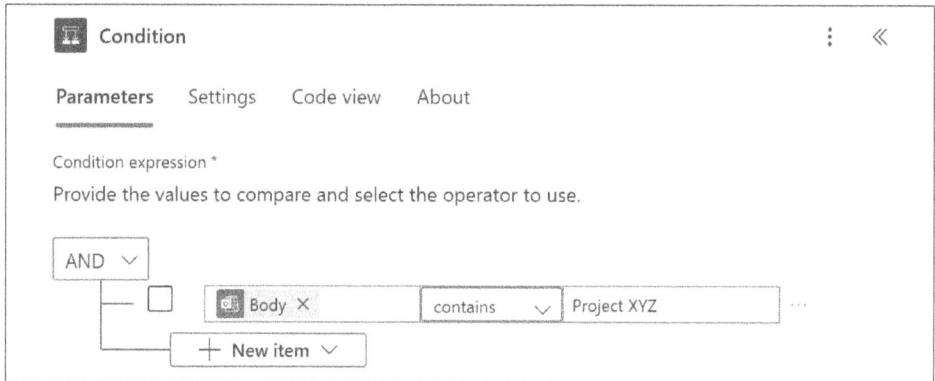

If the condition is not met, under False, add an action to terminate the flow. Search for "Control" actions, and then select Terminate from the list of actions. Configure the Status action parameter by selecting Succeeded from the list of possible values:

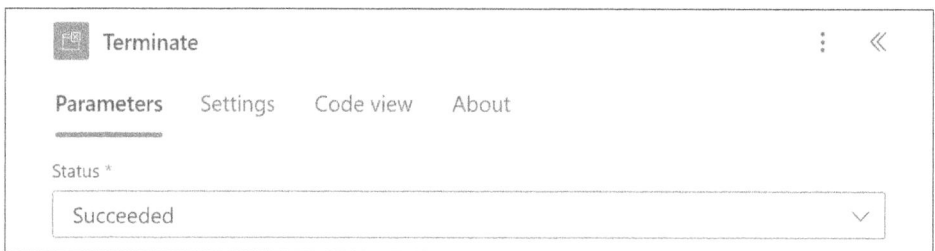

Now, if the condition is met, under True, add an action to post the message to Microsoft Teams. Search for the Microsoft Teams connector and select the "Post message in a chat or channel" action. You may need to sign in and authenticate your Microsoft Teams account. Configure the action parameters, including Post As (choose "Flow bot"), Post In (choose Channel), Team (choose the Teams team you want to post to), and Channel (the designated channel to post the email preview to). Finally, compose a message to post to the Teams channel in the Message parameter. In the following example, all text in braces ({}) is dynamic content from the trigger:

```
Hi!
The following email contains "Project XYZ"; you may want to follow up on it.
{Subject}
{Body Preview}

- - - -
Email preview taken from Office 365 Outlook email.
```

◻ Post message in a chat or channel   ⋮   ≪

Parameters   Settings   Code view   Testing   About

Post as *

| Flow bot | ⌄ |

Post in *

| Channel | ⌄ |

Team *

| NASA | ⌄ |

Channel *

| Apollo 8 | ⌄ |

Message *

↺ ↻   Normal ⌄ Arial ⌄ 15px ⌄   **B** *I* U̲ A̲ ✎ ⌸   ⟨/⟩

Hi!
The following email contains "Project XYZ"; you may want to follow up on it.
▣ Subject ✕
▣ Body Preview ✕

- - - -
Email preview taken from Office 365 Outlook email.

Give your flow a name, and then save and test your flow to ensure it works as expected:

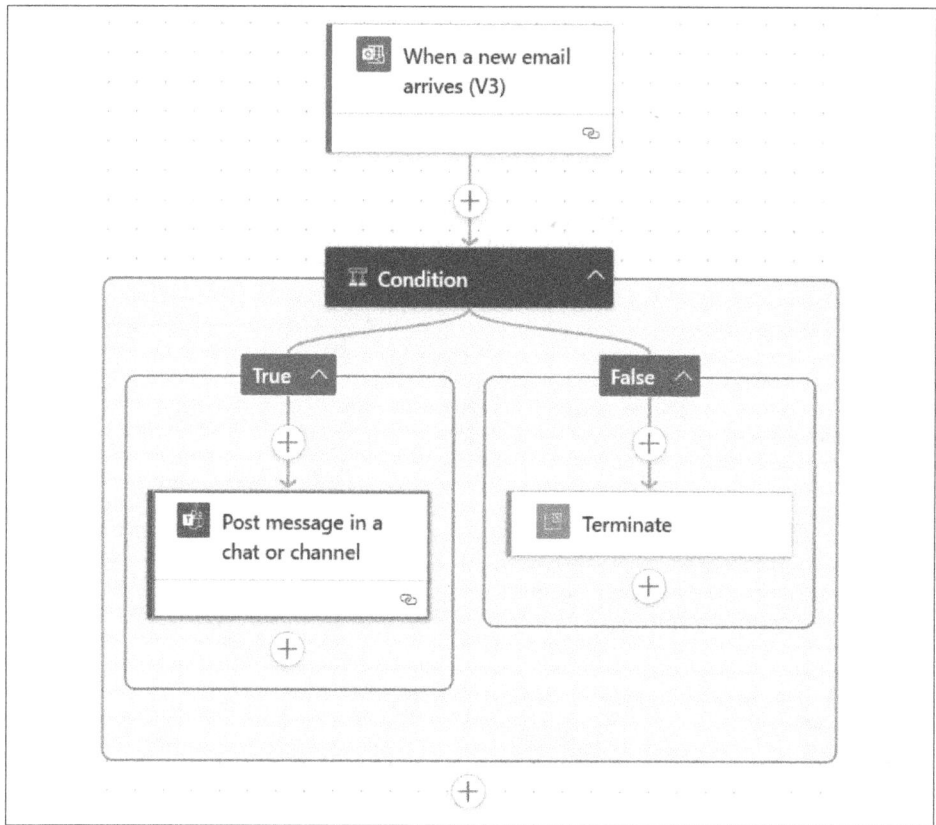

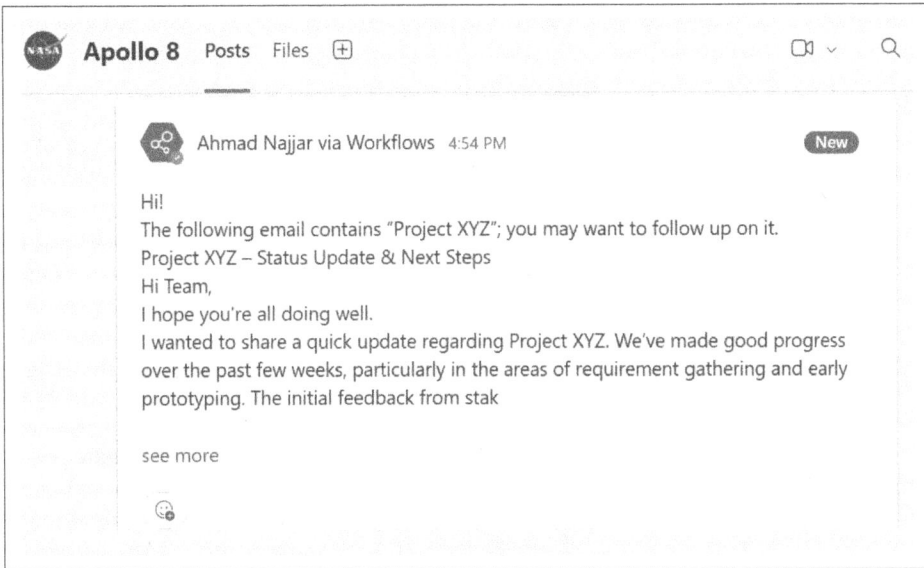

See Also

- Recipe 7.1, "Posting the Weather Forecast to a Teams Channel"
- Recipe 7.2, "Posting a Message on Slack When a Message Is Posted on Teams"

7.4 Sending a Report of Existing Teams and Channels

Problem

You want to receive a monthly report by email showing the existing Microsoft Teams teams and channels.

Solution

Create a monthly scheduled cloud flow that retrieves the required information from Microsoft Teams and then emails the information to you (and stakeholders).

Discussion

This automation is a strategic approach to enhancing team collaboration and ensuring you have a clear overview of the organization's digital workspace. This flow simplifies generating regular updates by automatically compiling a comprehensive report of all teams and channels within Microsoft Teams. It then delivers this report via email to you (or any intended recipients), providing a snapshot of the current state of collaboration. This streamlined and consistent reporting mechanism ensures you can easily monitor and manage teams and channels, fostering a more organized and productive digital workspace.

Furthermore, this integration of Power Automate enhances the efficiency of team and channel management. Rather than relying on manual processes or ad hoc reporting, you can schedule and automate the delivery of these reports, reducing the burden on administrators and team owners. This not only saves time but also promotes a more proactive approach to workspace governance and oversight. With regular email reports, you can keep a close eye on the evolving digital landscape of their Teams environment, ensuring that teams and channels are structured, used efficiently, and aligned with organizational goals. Ultimately, this automation optimizes team collaboration and channel management, making it easier to maintain an organized and productive workspace within Microsoft Teams.

To create a new flow in Power Automate, begin by visiting the Power Automate portal (*https://oreil.ly/O-MRf*) and signing in with your Microsoft or organization's account. Ensure that you're in the correct Power Automate environment, then click on "My flows" in the left navigation bar and select "New flow" to initiate the creation process. Since your goal is to collect all Microsoft Teams teams and their respective channels monthly, choose the "Scheduled cloud flow" option. Assign a name to your flow and enter the necessary parameters to determine when it should run, setting the starting date to today's date and configuring the flow to repeat once every month. Finally, click Create on the pop-up to access the flow designer experience:

Add a new action (step) and search for "Variable" in the flow designer. Then choose "Initialize variable" and set the Name ("Report") and Type (choose String) action parameters. Leave the Value empty:

{x} Initialize variable	⋮ ≪

Parameters   Settings   Code view   About

Name *

Report

Type *

String   ∨

Value

Next, add an action to list all Microsoft Teams teams. Search for the Microsoft Teams connector and select the "List teams" action. You may need to sign in and authenticate your Microsoft Teams account. Include a new action (step), search for "Control," and then select the Control actions. From the list of actions, choose "Apply to each." Configure the "Apply to each" action by setting the "Select an output from previous steps" parameter by selecting the Teams List from the "List teams" action dynamic content:

▢ Apply to each	⋮ ≪

Parameters   Settings   Code view   About

Select an output from previous steps *

▣ Teams List ✕

In the "Apply to each" action, add an action to list all Microsoft Teams channels. Search for the Microsoft Teams connector and select the "List channels" action. Configure the "List channels" action by providing the "Team" parameter by selecting "Custom value." Then, provide the Team Id from the "List teams" dynamic content:

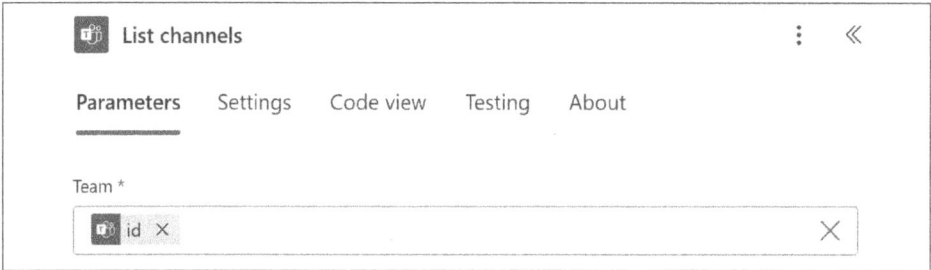

Add a new action (step) in the "Apply to each" scope, search for "Control," and then select the Control actions. From the list of actions, choose "Apply to each." Configure the "Apply to each" action, setting the "Select an output from previous steps" parameter by selecting the Channel List from the "List channels" action dynamic content:

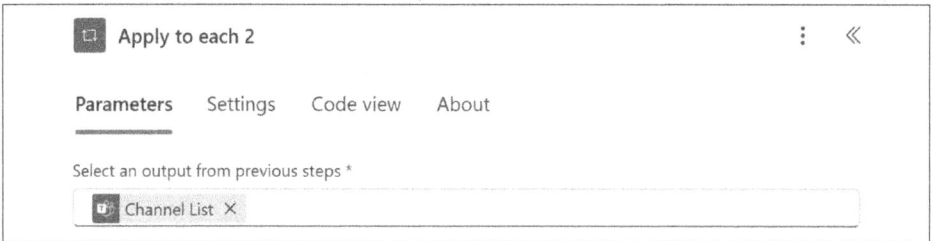

In the "Apply to each 2" action, add an action. Search for "Variable," and choose "Append to string variable." Configure the "Append to string variable" action by selecting Report (the previously initialized variable). Then, customize the value (all text shown in braces is dynamic content from the previous actions): {Team Name} - {Channel Name}
:

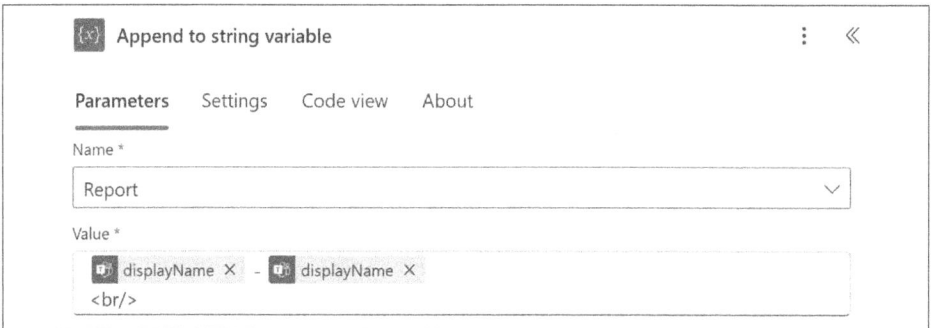

Now, outside the scope of both "Apply for each" actions, add an action to send an email to yourself (and all stakeholders). Search for the Office 365 Outlook connector and select the "Send an email (V2)" action. You may need to sign in and authenticate your Office 365 Outlook account. Configure the action by providing the To parameter by choosing your user account (and stakeholders' accounts). Then provide a subject for the "Send an email" action, such as "Monthly Microsoft Teams Report." Finally, customize the Body parameter (email text) as follows:

```
Hi!

This is the list of Teams and their correspondent channels:

{Report}

Thank you!
```

Save and test your flow to ensure it works as expected:

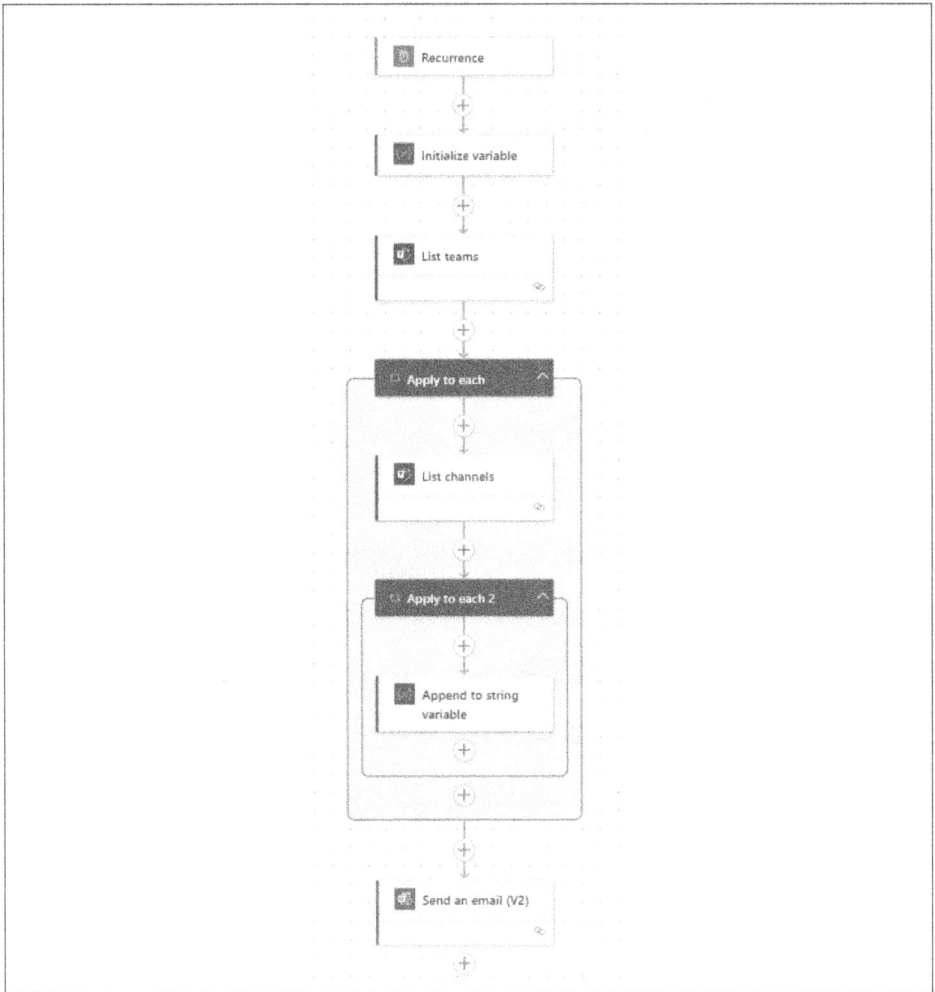

An example of the expected result of this flow should look something like the following:

Monthly Microsoft Teams Report

Ahmad Najjar

To: ⊗ Ahmad Najjar

Hi!

This is the list of Teams and their correspondent channels:

Music Corner - Scratching Beats
Music Corner - House and Techno
Music Corner - General
Music Corner - DJ Flow
Carpenters Com - Lush Vibes
Carpenters Com - Groovy Old Times
Carpenters Com - General
Carpenters Com - Now or Never
NASA - Apollo 8
NASA - Space X
NASA - General
NASA - To The Moon and Back
NASA - Mars Expedition
Weather - Weather Updates
Weather - Daily Weather Forecast
Weather - General
Events Collaboration - General
Events Collaboration - Collaboration Summit (ECS)

Thank you!

See Also

- Recipe 3.1, "Sending Recurring Reminders"
- Recipe 3.2, "Sending Daily Weather Forecasts"
- Recipe 4.4, "Sending a Reminder Email for Tasks Due by Tomorrow"
- Recipe 4.5, "Sending Employees Birthday Emails"

Conclusion

Power Automate and Microsoft Teams have unrivaled correlations that can revolutionize how teams collaborate, communicate, and automate various tasks. The examples explored in this chapter demonstrate the myriad possibilities and added efficiencies this integration brings. Providing real-time weather forecasts and uplifting quotes of the day within Teams channels can boost engagement and productivity and foster a positive work environment. Additionally, the capability to present forms for data collection and effortlessly send reports of existing Teams and channels deepens the integration's utility in real-world business operations.

The powerful combination of Power Automate and Microsoft Teams represents more than just a convenient collaboration tool; it's a strategic enabler for the digital workplace. As remote work, virtual meetings, and the need for streamlined communication continue to define the modern workspace, this alliance stands as a pivotal solution. It empowers organizations to adapt, thrive, and lead in a rapidly changing business landscape.

The seamless integration of these tools facilitates the streamlining of communication and collaboration and the automation of routine tasks, reducing manual effort and ensuring that essential information is promptly accessible. It positions organizations to tackle the challenges of today's dynamic business environment and create a more agile, data-driven, and collaborative future. By embracing the full potential of Power Automate and Microsoft Teams, organizations are modernizing their workflows and shaping how work gets done in the digital age.

CHAPTER 8

Power Automate and Approvals

In this chapter, I'll explain how approval processes have evolved from manual, paper-based methods to more automated systems. Manual processes were slower, error-prone, and required substantial physical storage space. I'll go through the key characteristics of approvals, which are documentation, signing and authorization, communication tracking, accountability and reliability, and auditing and compliance. I'll emphasize the critical role of automating approval processes within organizations, highlighting how doing so enhances efficiency, compliance, and control. Automated approvals streamline decision making by reducing time, minimizing human errors, and ensuring consistency. They also facilitate compliance with internal and external regulations by enforcing rules and providing an audit trail. As organizations grow, automated systems can scale effectively, handling increased approval requests without additional administrative burden. I'll trace the evolution of Microsoft's automation tools from early SharePoint workflows to the more advanced Power Automate, which integrates with various applications and services, offering robust, scalable, and user-friendly solutions for approval automation. Finally, I'll go through common and useful approval recipes where Power Automate and SharePoint go hand-in-hand, enhancing effectiveness.

Manual Approvals and Characteristics

Before the advent of automation (modern tech), approval processes were markedly different, relying heavily on manual and paper-based processes. These processes were more time-consuming, prone to errors, and often required significant physical space for document storage. Whether approvals are automated or not, certain characteristics must be present to achieve the goal behind them, such as the following:

Documentation

Virtually all approval processes historically relied on paper documents, but many have since transitioned to digital documents. Proposals, purchase orders, leave requests, and other forms had to be physically prepared, printed, and then hand-carried or mailed to the next person in the approval chain.

Signing and authorization

Physical signatures were necessary to authorize documents, requiring the approver's physical presence. In situations where multiple approvals were needed, documents were circulated among all relevant parties, sometimes leading to considerable delays if individuals were out of the office or if the documents were misplaced.

Tracking and communication

Keeping track of which documents had been approved, which were pending, and where they physically were at any given time was a substantial administrative task. Large filing systems were necessary to store these documents, and significant effort was required to retrieve and review them when needed. The status of approvals relied on phone calls, memos, or face-to-face conversations. This could further slow down the process, especially in larger organizations where approvers might be in different locations.

Accountability and reliability

Tracking down who had a document (the approval) at any given time could be difficult, and there was no easy way to verify if an approver had reviewed the material before signing off. Therefore, it took more work to maintain visibility over the approval process and ensure accountability. Furthermore, due to the slow circulation of paperwork, the manual process was susceptible to various errors, including lost or damaged documents, missing signatures, or approvals based on outdated information.

Auditing and compliance

Auditing and ensuring compliance with internal or external regulations was a labor-intensive process. Auditors would need to manually review large volumes of paperwork to verify that proper approvals were obtained and that processes were followed correctly.

Despite these challenges, organizations introduced meticulous platforms and developed procedures to manage approvals effectively. The introduction of automation into these processes has addressed many of these inefficiencies, transforming how decisions are made and actions are authorized within organizations. Therefore, any automation of approval processes must address the highlighted characteristics previously discussed, which, in turn, means that such automation platforms require robust documentation, collaboration, and communication capabilities.

Today, the emphasis is on streamlining workflows, enhancing transparency, and ensuring compliance through automation, which has significantly improved the speed and reliability of approvals.

The Importance of Approvals Automation

The importance of approvals and automating its processes in any organization cannot be overstated. They are central to maintaining efficiency, compliance, and control over various operational aspects, contributing significantly to the organization's overall success and adaptability. When implementing automated approvals, it's essential to choose a platform that integrates well with other tools the organization uses, is flexible enough to handle the specific types of approvals needed, and is accessible to all relevant members. Training and support are also vital in ensuring everyone understands how to use the system effectively.

Automating approvals streamlines the decision-making process. It reduces the time taken to get approvals for various processes, from expenditure to project timelines, by eliminating the need for physical paperwork and the necessity of chasing individuals for signatures. This, in turn, speeds up operations and allows projects to move forward more quickly.

Automation reduces the likelihood of human error. Manual processes can lead to mistakes, such as lost documents or overlooked approvals, which can delay processes and have implications. Automated approvals ensure that requests are processed consistently and error-free.

Compliance with internal policies and external regulations is non-negotiable in many industries. Automated approval processes help ensure compliance by enforcing predefined rules and requirements for each type of approval. Additionally, they provide an audit trail of all actions taken, including who approved what and when, making it easier to demonstrate compliance during audits.

Automated approval processes offer real-time visibility into the status of each request. Managers can quickly see which requests are pending, approved, or denied and take action as necessary. This level of visibility improves control over the processes and helps identify bottlenecks or inefficiencies.

Manual approval processes that work for a small team can quickly become unmanageable as organizations grow, and the required approvals can increase exponentially. Automated approval processes, however, can quickly scale to handle an increasing volume of requests without a corresponding increase in administrative workload.

Power Automate, aided by Microsoft 365, provides a suite of possibilities contributing to meeting the latter criteria and benefits.

Approvals from SharePoint to Microsoft 365

For many years, automation tools have been coupled with collaboration platforms either as a native service in that platform, like SharePoint, or as a third-party product. SharePoint has been considered one of the best platforms for approval automation, given its native collaboration features.

In the early days, SharePoint 2001 and 2003 offered basic document management and collaboration features. Over time, Microsoft introduced workflows, enabling users to automate business processes. SharePoint 2007 marked a significant upgrade with built-in workflows for tasks such as document approvals, which could be customized using SharePoint Designer or Visual Studio. SharePoint 2010 and 2013 introduced more sophisticated workflow capabilities, including reusable workflows and improved user interfaces (UIs) for designing them. SharePoint 2013 enhanced the workflow engine, offering more robust and scalable solutions for approvals and automating business processes. Nevertheless, SharePoint Designer was mostly used in basic approval automation scenarios, while third-party tools were used for complex scenarios.

In 2016, Microsoft introduced Microsoft Flow. Flow integrates with SharePoint and was designed to be more user-friendly and focused on comprehensively automating tasks and approvals. After the rebrand of Microsoft Flow to Power Automate to better align with Microsoft's Power Platform, Power Automate emphasized the tool's capabilities in automating processes, including approvals, not just in SharePoint but expanding beyond Microsoft services.

Power Automate significantly expanded the possibilities for approval automation. It introduced more intuitive and powerful tools for creating approval workflows, including customizable approval emails, integration with Microsoft Teams for notifications, and the ability to create complex multistage approval processes. Microsoft continues to update Power Automate with new features and integrations, enhancing its usability and functionality. This includes AI-based tools and deeper integrations with Microsoft 365 apps, making approvals and overall workflow automation more efficient and integrated into daily work processes.

The journey from SharePoint workflows to Power Automate represents a shift from localized, intra-platform automation toward a broader, more interconnected approach to workflow automation across an entire suite of applications and services not limited to Microsoft 365 but extending beyond the intended collaboration platform.

With the evolution from basic SharePoint workflows to the advanced capabilities of Power Automate, organizations now have more powerful and flexible tools at their disposal to streamline approvals and other business processes. Power Automate's versatility allows for the automation of complex workflows that integrate seamlessly with Microsoft 365 and beyond. To help you unlock the full potential of Power Automate, I'll now explore some practical recipes that can be easily implemented to enhance your organization's approval processes, improving overall efficiency.

8.1 Requesting Expense Approval

Problem

You want to automate the process of requesting expense approval.

Solution

Create an automated cloud flow that monitors item creation in an expense tracker SharePoint list, initiates an approval process, and sends an email to the expense creator when the expense item is approved or rejected.

Discussion

Automating the process of requesting expense approval enhances efficiency by streamlining the approval process, reducing the time employees spend on manual tasks. With automated notifications, managers can approve or reject expenses promptly, minimizing delays. This leads to faster processing times and ensures that employees are reimbursed in a timely manner, which can boost morale and productivity. Additionally, it reduces the risk of human error, such as data entry mistakes, ensuring that expense reports are accurate and compliant with company policies.

Power Automate provides improved tracking throughout its approval process. This visibility helps identify bottlenecks and optimizes the process for better performance. Moreover, the system can be customized to enforce specific approval hierarchies and conditions, ensuring that only authorized expenses are approved. This not only enhances compliance but also helps with better budget management and financial oversight, as all expense data is centralized and can be analyzed to identify spending patterns and areas for cost savings.

Before starting to build this flow, make sure that you have created an expense tracker list in SharePoint or that you have read permissions on the list you want to monitor for newly created expenses. Create an expense tracker list in SharePoint, following the instructions in the documentation (*https://oreil.ly/M4RMf*). After you create the list, add the following fields:

- Approver comments (optional, multiple lines of text field)
- Approval status (optional, choice field), and add the following choices:
  — Awaiting approval
  — Approved
  — Rejected

Go to the Power Automate portal (*https://oreil.ly/O-MRf*). Sign in with your Microsoft account or your organization's account. Make sure you're in the correct Power Automate environment. Click on "My flows" in the left navigation bar. Click on "New flow" to create a new flow. Choose a flow type. In this case, you want to kick-start the approval process when a new expense is created in SharePoint, so you must choose "Automated cloud flow." Click Skip on the pop-up to navigate to the flow designer experience. Search for the SharePoint connector in the flow designer. Select the trigger for when a new item is created in SharePoint by choosing the "When an item is created" trigger. You may need to sign in and authenticate your SharePoint account. Configure the trigger parameters, including Site Address (the relevant site URL where the expense tracker list resides) and List Name (the SharePoint list to be monitored for newly created expenses):

When an item is created   ⋮   ‹

Parameters   Settings   Code view   About

Site Address *

| Lush Vibes - https://███████████████/sites/LushVibes | ⌄ |

List Name *

| Expense tracker | ⌄ |

Next, add an action to update the SharePoint list item with corresponding approval status, which is awaiting approval. Search for the SharePoint connector and select the "Update item" action. Configure the action parameters, including Site Address (the relevant site URL where the expense tracker list resides), List Name (the SharePoint list tracking expenses), Id (the ID of the expense item that triggered the flow), and Approval Status Value (the column indicating the approval status of the expense item). Select "Awaiting approval":

Then, add an action to start the approval process and wait for a response from the approver. Search for the Approvals connector and select the "Start and wait for an approval" action. Fill the approval action parameters as follows (the text in braces is dynamic content from the trigger):

- *Approval Type*: Approve/Reject - Everyone must approve
- *Title*: A new expense awaiting your approval (or the text of your choice)
- *Assigned To*: the email address of the approver (your manager)
- *Details*:

    ## A new expense has been submitted by {Created by DisplayName}

    {Description}

- *Item Link*: {Link to Item}
- *Item Link Description*: {Title}

> **Start and wait for an approval**   ⋮
>
> **Parameters**   Settings   Code View   Testing   About
> ────────────
>
> Approval Type *
> ┌──┐
> │ Approve/Reject - Everyone must approve   ∨ │
> └──┘
> Title *
> ┌──┐
> │ A new expense awaiting your approval   │
> └──┘
> Assigned To *
> ┌──┐
> │ mymanager@company.com   │
> └──┘
> Details
> ┌──┐
> │ ## A new expense has been submitted by ▣ Author.D... ×   │
> │   │
> │ ▣ Descripti... ×   │
> └──┘
> Item Link
> ┌──┐
> │ ▣ {Link} ×   │
> └──┘
> Item Link Description
> ┌──┐
> │ ▣ Title ×   │
> └──┘

Next, add a new action, search for "Control," and then from the list of actions, choose Condition. Configure the condition action by selecting the Outcome property from the "Start and wait for an approval" dynamic content for the left-side comparison value. Make sure the comparison operator is set to "is equal to," and then for the right-side comparison, type Approve:

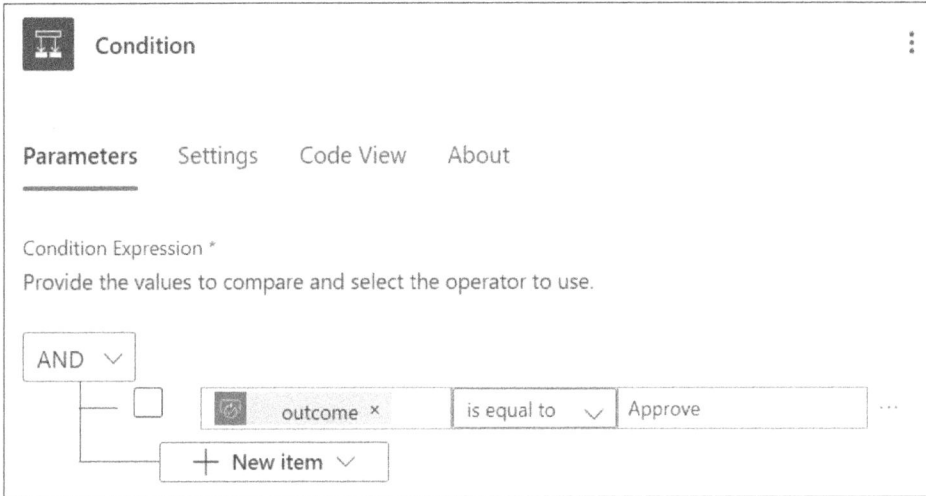

Following that, the outcome property returns a standard text value, returning "Approve" if the request is approved and "Reject" if the request is rejected. If the condition is met, under True, add an action to update the expense approval status with the corresponding approval status, Approved. Search for the SharePoint connector and select the "Update item" action. Configure the action parameters, including Site Address (the relevant site URL where the expense tracker list resides), List Name (the SharePoint list tracking expenses), Id (the ID of the expense item that triggered the flow), and Approval Status Value (the column indicating the approval status of the expense item; select Approved):

Update item - Approved   ⋮

Parameters   Settings   Code view   Testing   About

Site Address *

Lush Vibes - https:// ███████████████ /sites/LushVibes   ∨

List Name *

Expense tracker   ∨

Id *

⚡ ID ×

Advanced parameters

Showing 2 of 9   ∨   Show all   Clear all

Approver Comments

fx first(...) ×   ✕

Approval Status Value

Approved   ∨   ✕

If the condition is not met, under False, add an action to update the expense approval status with the corresponding approval status, Rejected. Search for the SharePoint connector and select the "Update item" action. Configure the action parameters, including Site Address (the relevant site URL where the expense tracker list resides), List Name (the SharePoint list tracking expenses), Id (the ID of the expense item that triggered the flow), and Approval Status Value (the column indicating the approval status of the expense item; select Rejected):

	Update item - Rejected	⋮

Parameters   Settings   Code view   Testing   About

Site Address *

Lush Vibes - https://▬▬▬▬▬/sites/LushVibes	⌄

List Name *

Expense tracker	⌄

Id *

ID ×

Advanced parameters

Showing 2 of 9	⌄	Show all	Clear all

Approver Comments

first(...) ×	×

Approval Status Value

Rejected	⌄	×

Subsequently, for the Approver Comments parameter, for both the "Update item" actions (Approved and Rejected), add the following expression:

```
first(body('Start_and_wait_for_an_approval')?['responses'])?['comments']
```

Note that the Responses dynamic value from the approval action is a collection of data for one or multiple approvers. However, we have only one approver in this scenario, so we get the first item. Then, we'll want to get the comments from that response, so we'll add ?['comments']:

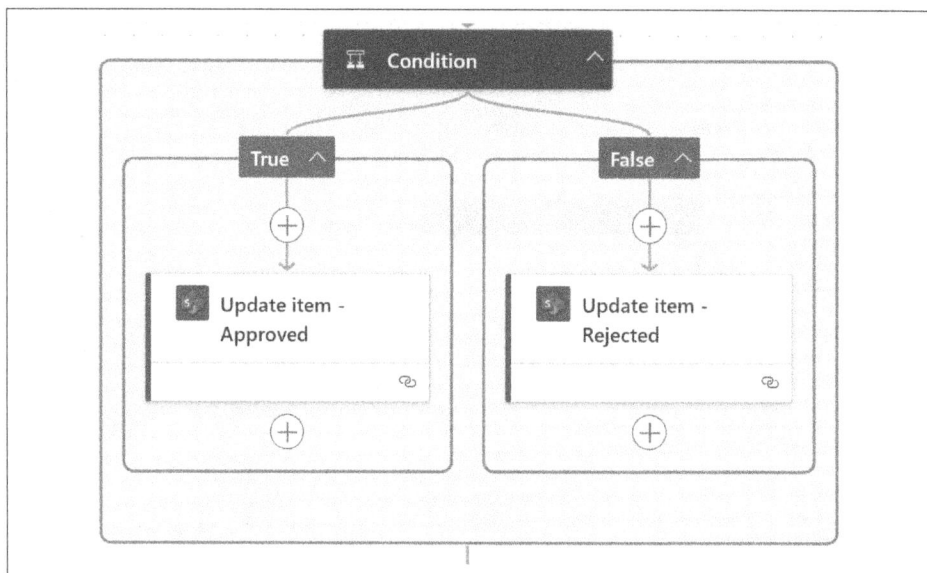

After the condition, add an action to send an email to the expense creator (requester). Search for the Office 365 Outlook connector and select the "Send an email (V2)" action. You may need to sign in and authenticate your Office 365 Outlook account.

Fill the "Send an email (V2)" action parameters as follows (the text in braces is dynamic content from the trigger):

- *To*: {Created by Email}
- *Subject*: Expense Approval :: {Title}
- *Body*:

    Hi {Created By DisplayName},

    Your expense "{Title}" has been {*expression*}

    You'll be reimbursed on the next salary release if your expense has been approved by your manager.

Thank you.

where {*expression*} is:

```
if(equals(body('Start_and_wait_for_an_approval')?['outcome'],'Approve'),
'approved','rejected')
```

| ⊡ | Send an email (V2) | ⋮ |

Parameters   Settings   Code View   Testing   About

To *

| 🔄 Author.E... × | ✕ |

Subject *

Expense Approval :: 🔄 Title ×

Body *

⟲ ⟳ | Normal ⌄ Arial ⌄ 15px ⌄ | **B** *I* U ∞ A⌄ 🖉⌄ ⟨⟩

Hi 🔄 Author.D... × ,

Your expense " 🔄 Title × " has been 𝑓ₓ if(...) ×

You'll be reimbursed on the next salary release if your expense has been approved by your manager.

Thank you.

Next, the expression in the Body parameter will check whether the expense is approved or rejected. Accordingly, it will return "Approved" or "Rejected" text based on the Outcome dynamic value. Finally, name your flow, save it, and test it to ensure it works as expected.

See Also

- Recipe 8.2, "Requesting Document Content Approval (Sequential Approval)"
- Recipe 8.3, "Requesting Vacation Approval (Parallel Approval)"
- Recipe 8.4, "Requesting Proposal Approval (Approval with Escalation)"

8.2 Requesting Document Content Approval (Sequential Approval)

Problem

You want to automate the process of requesting document content approval that requires the sequential consent of two stakeholders.

Solution

Create an automated cloud flow that monitors file creation/upload in a SharePoint document library, starting an approval process for the first stakeholder and terminating it if rejected. If the first approval is granted, it starts the second approval process. Finally, it sends an email to the content creator when the content item is either approved or rejected.

Discussion

In traditional settings, documents often pass through multiple hands for review, which can be time-consuming and prone to errors or delays. Automation addresses these issues by creating a structured path for document progression, ensuring that each stage is completed before the document moves to the next reviewer. This not only speeds up the approval process but also enhances accountability and transparency, as each action taken on the document is tracked and recorded. Automated notifications and reminders ensure that reviewers are alerted promptly, reducing the likelihood of bottlenecks.

Furthermore, automated sequential approval systems can integrate with various tools and platforms (like SharePoint), facilitating smoother collaboration and communication among stakeholders. SharePoint comes with version control, which helps maintain a clear record of changes and the rationale behind them. By incorporating predefined rules and criteria, this automation can also enforce compliance with your organizational policies and regulatory requirements. This not only improves efficiency but also reduces the risk of noncompliance.

Before starting to build this flow, make sure that you have created a document library in SharePoint (such as Company Public News) or that you have read permissions on the library you want to monitor for newly created content.

After you create the library, add the following fields:

- Editor comments (optional, multiple lines of text)
- Managing editor comments (optional, multiple lines of text)
- Approval status (optional, choice), and add the following choices:
  - Awaiting approval
  - Approved
  - Rejected

Go to the Power Automate portal (*https://oreil.ly/O-MRf*). Sign in with your Microsoft account or your organization's account. Make sure you're in the correct Power Automate environment. Click on "My flows" in the left navigation bar. Click on "New flow" to create a new flow. Choose a flow type. In this case, you want to kick start the approval process when a new file is created/uploaded in SharePoint, so you must choose "Automated cloud flow." Click Skip on the pop-up to navigate to the flow designer experience. Search for the SharePoint connector in the flow designer. You want the trigger to be related to when a new file is created in SharePoint, so choose the "When a file is created (properties only)" trigger. You may need to sign in and authenticate your SharePoint account. Configure the trigger parameters, including Site Address (the relevant site URL where the document library resides) and Library Name (the SharePoint library to be monitored for newly created files):

When a file is created (properties only)	⋮ ≪

Parameters   Settings   Code view   About

Site Address *

| Lush Vibes - https://█████████████/sites/LushVibes | ∨ |

Library Name *

| Company Public News | ∨ |

Next, add an action to update the SharePoint library item with corresponding approval status (awaiting approval). Search for the SharePoint connector and select the "Update item" action. Configure the action parameters, including Site Address (the relevant site URL where the document library resides) and List Name (the SharePoint document library name), then choose "Enter custom value" and type the name of the document library. Then, configure the Id (the ID of the file item that triggered the flow). Now, open the "Advanced parameters" drop-down and check the Approval Status Value (the column indicating the approval status of the file item). Select "Awaiting approval":

Then, add an action to start the approval process and wait for a response from the editor. Search for the Approvals connector and select the "Start and wait for an approval" action. Rename your action to "Start and wait for an approval - Editor."

Fill the approval action parameters as follows (the text in braces is dynamic content from the trigger):

- *Approval Type*: Approve/Reject - First to respond
- *Title*: Public news content approval (or the text of your choice)
- *Assigned To*: the email address of the approver (the editor)
- *Details*: ## A new content for public news submitted by {Created by DisplayName} awaiting your approval
- *Item Link*: {Link to Item}
- *Item Link Description*: {Name}

⟳ **Start and wait for an approval - Editor**   ⋮

Parameters   Settings   Code View   Testing   About

Approval Type *

| Approve/Reject - First to respond   ⌄ |

Title *

| Public news content approval |

Assigned To *

| editor@company.com |

Details

| ## A new content for public news submitted by [s] Author.D... × awaiting your approval |

Item Link

| [s] {Link} × |

Item Link Description

| [s] {Name} × |

Add a new action, search for "Control," and then from the list of actions, choose Condition. Rename your condition to "Check editor approval response." Configure the condition action by selecting the Outcome property from the "Start and wait for an approval - Editor" dynamic content for the left-side comparison value. Ensure the comparison operator is set to "is equal to," and then type Approve for the right-side comparison:

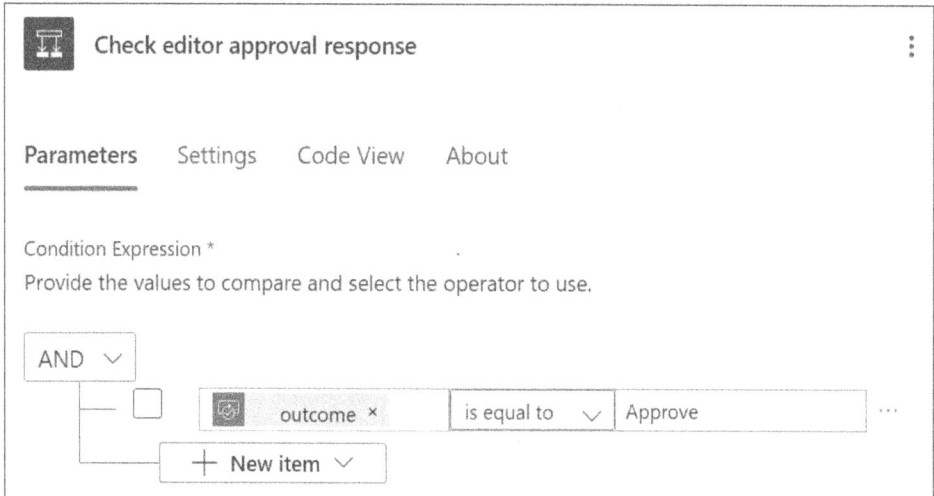

The outcome property returns a standard text value, returning "Approve" if the request is approved and "Reject" if the request is rejected:

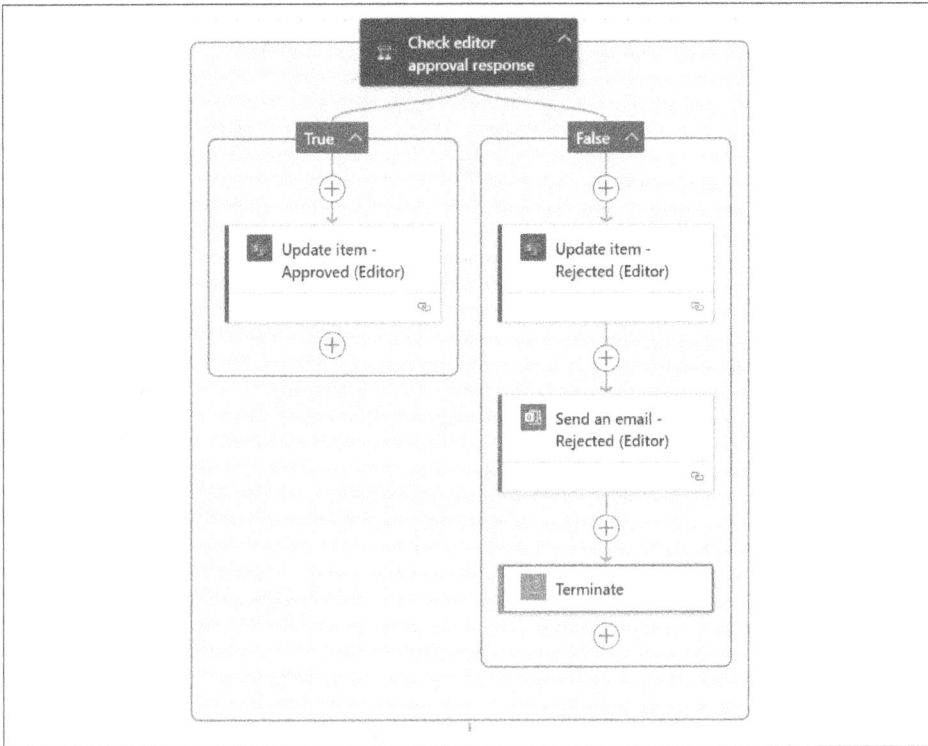

If the condition is met, under True, add an action to update the file item with the editor comments. Search for the SharePoint connector and select the "Update item" action. Rename the action to "Update item - Approved (Editor)." Configure the action parameters, including Site Address (the relevant site URL where the document library resides) and List Name (the SharePoint document library name), then choose "Enter custom value" and type the name of the document library. Then, configure the Id (the ID of the file item that triggered the flow). Now, open the "Advanced parameters" drop-down and check Editor Comments, then add the following expression:

```
first(body('Start_and_wait_for_an_approval_-_Editor')?['responses'])
?['comments']
```

Note that the Responses dynamic value from the approval action contains a collection of data for one or multiple approvers; however, since there is only one approver in this scenario, we will focus on the first item. If the condition is not met, under False, add an action to update the file item's approval status to the corresponding approval status ("Rejected") and also update the Editor Comments. To do this, search for the SharePoint connector and select the "Update item" action. Rename this action to "Update item - Rejected (Editor)."

Next, configure the action parameters, including the Site Address, which is the relevant site URL where the document library resides, and List Name, which should be the name of the SharePoint document library. Choose "Enter custom value" and type in the name of the document library, then configure the Id parameter to match the ID of the file item that triggered the flow. After that, open the "Advanced parameters" drop-down and check the boxes for "Editor comments" and "Approval status Value." For "Editor comments," use the same expression that was used four steps earlier, and for the "Approval status Value," select Rejected, which indicates the approval status of the file item:

After the "Update item - Rejected (Editor)," add an action to send an email to the content creator (requester). Search for the Office 365 Outlook connector and select the "Send an email (V2)" action. You may need to sign in and authenticate your Office 365 Outlook account. Rename the action to "Send an email - Rejected (Editor)."

Fill the "Send an email (V2)" action parameters as follows (the text in braces is dynamic content from the trigger and "Update item - Rejected (Editor)" action):

- *To*: {Created by Email}
- *Subject*: Public News Content Approval :: {Name}

- *Body*:

  Hi {CreatedBy DisplayName},

  Your public news content "{Name}" has been rejected by the editor. The editor left you the following comments:

  {Editor comments}

  Thank you.

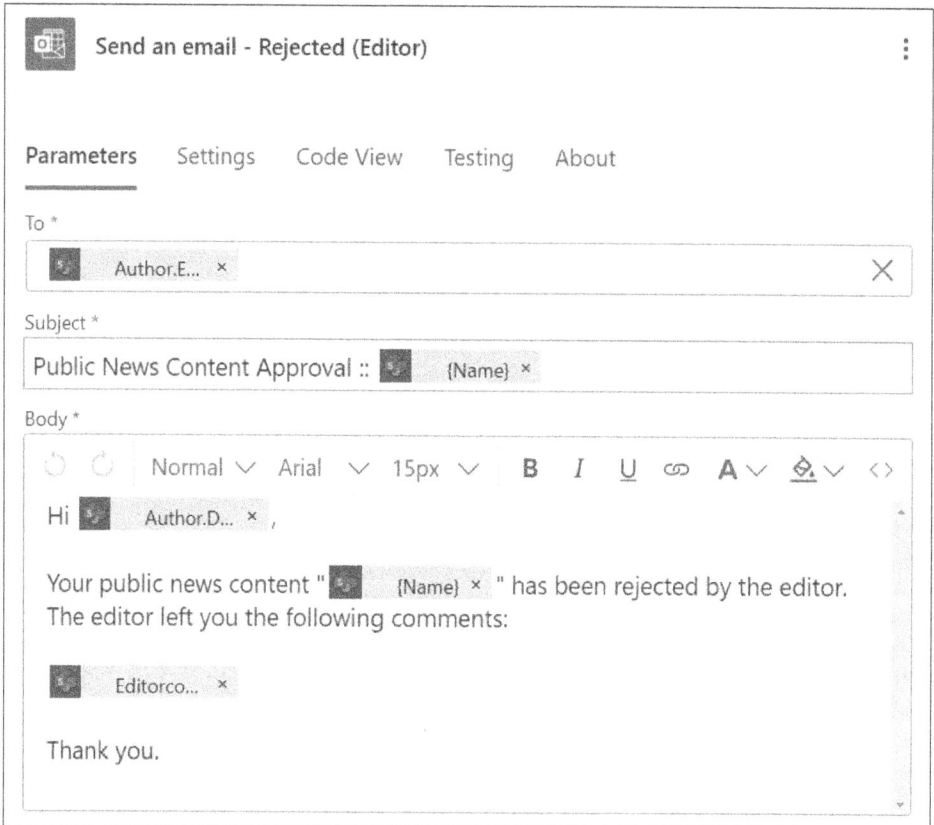

Now, add an action to terminate the flow. Search for "Control" actions, and then select Terminate from the list of actions. Configure the Status action parameter by selecting Succeeded from the list of possible values:

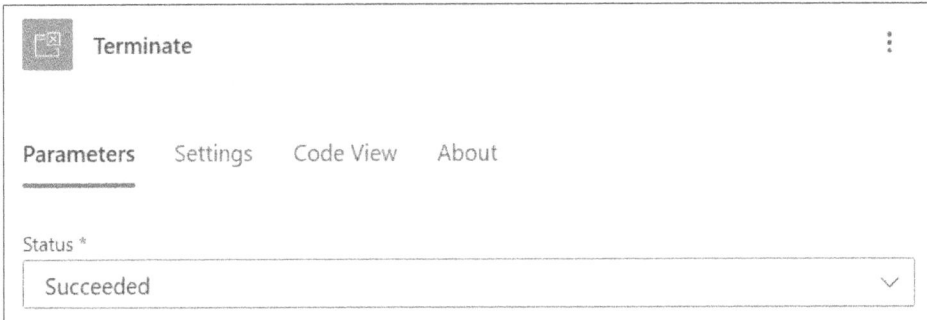

Terminate	⋮
Parameters Settings Code View About	
Status *	
Succeeded	∨

After the condition, add another action to start and wait for an approval. Search for the Approvals connector and select the "Start and wait for an approval" action. Rename the action to "Start and wait for an approval - Managing editor."

Fill the approval action parameters as follows (the text in braces is dynamic content from the trigger):

- *Approval Type*: Approve/Reject - First to respond
- *Title*: Public news content approval (or the text of your choice)
- *Assigned To*: the email address of the approver (the managing editor)
- *Details*: ## A new content for public news submitted by {Created by DisplayName} and approved by public news editor awaiting your approval
- *Item Link*: {Link to Item}
- *Item Link Description*: {Name}

Start and wait for an approval - Managing editor

⋮

Parameters   Settings   Code View   Testing   About

Approval Type *

Approve/Reject - First to respond ⌄

Title *

Public news content approval

Assigned To *

managing.editor@company.com

Details

A new content for public news submitted by 🔲 Author.D... ✕ and approved
by public news editor awaiting your approval

Item Link

🔲 {Link} ✕

Item Link Description

🔲 {Name} ✕

Then add a new action, search for "Control," and then from the list of actions, choose Condition. Rename your condition to "Check managing editor approval response":

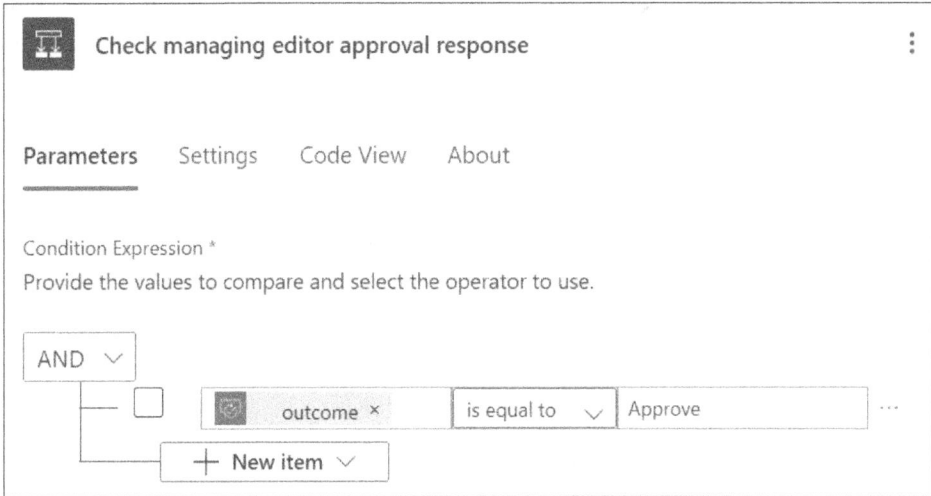

Next, configure the condition action by selecting the Outcome property from the "Start and wait for an approval - Managing editor" dynamic content for the left-side comparison value. Make sure the comparison operator is set to "is equal to," and then for the right-side comparison, type Approve:

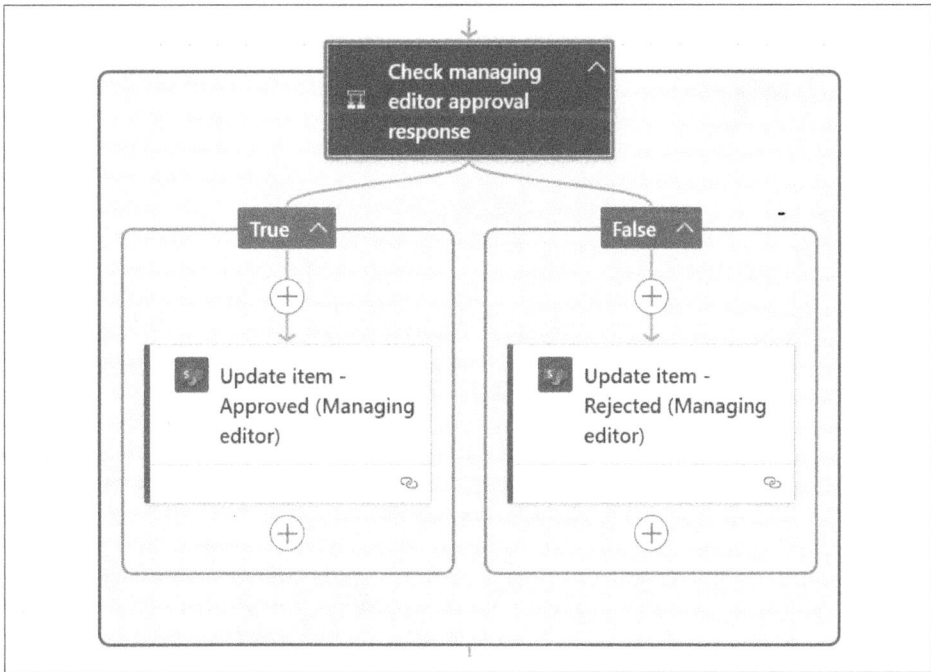

If the condition is met, under True, add an action to update the file item with the managing editor comments and the corresponding approval status. Search for the SharePoint connector and select the "Update item" action. Rename the action to "Update item - Approved (Managing editor)." Configure the action parameters, including Site Address (the relevant site URL where the document library resides) and List Name (the SharePoint document library name), then choose "Enter custom value" and type the name of the document library. Then, configure the Id (the ID of the file item that triggered the flow).

Now, open the "Advanced parameters" drop-down and check "Managing editor comments" and "Approval status Value," then add the following expression for the "Managing editor comments" parameter:

```
first(body('Start_and_wait_for_an_approval_-_Managing_editor')?['responses'])
?['comments']
```

Then, select Approved for the "Approval status Value":

Update item - Approved (Managing editor)

Parameters   Settings   Code view   Testing   About

Site Address *

Lush Vibes - https://████████████████/sites/LushVibes

List Name *

Company Public News

Id *

ID ×

Advanced parameters

Showing 2 of 7   Show all   Clear all

Managing editor comments

fx first(...) ×

Approval status Value

Approved

Note that the Responses dynamic value from the approval action is a collection of data for one or multiple approvers. However, we have only one approver in this scenario, so we get the first item. If the condition is not met, under False, add an action to update the file item approval status with the corresponding approval status (Rejected) and update "Managing editor comments." Search for the SharePoint connector and select the "Update item" action. Rename the action to "Update item - Rejected (Managing editor)." Configure the action parameters, including Site Address (the relevant site URL where the document library resides) and List Name (the SharePoint document library name), then choose "Enter custom value" and type the name of the document library. Then, configure the Id (the ID of the file item that triggered the flow).

For the "Managing editor comments" parameter, use the same expression used four steps before. Then, select Rejected in the "Approval status Value" field:

After the condition, add an action to send an email to the content creator (requester). Search for the Office 365 Outlook connector and select the "Send an email (V2)" action. Rename the action to "Send an email - Managing editor."

Fill the "Send an email - Managing editor" action parameters as follows (the text in braces is dynamic content from the trigger):

- *To*: {Created by Email}
- *Subject*: Public News Content Approval :: {Name}
- *Body*:

    Hi {Created By DisplayName},

    Your public news content "{Name}" has been *{expression1}*.
    The managing editor left you the following comments:

    {expression2}

    The editor left the following comments:

    {expression3}

    Thank you.

  where *{expression1}* is as follows:

    if(equals(body('Start_and_wait_for_an_approval_-_Managing_editor')
    ?['outcome'],'Approve'),'approved','rejected')

  and *{expression2}* is:

    first(body('Start_and_wait_for_an_approval_-_Managing_editor')
    ?['responses'])?['comments']

  and *{expression3}* is:

    first(body('Start_and_wait_for_an_approval_-_Editor')?['responses'])
    ?['comments']

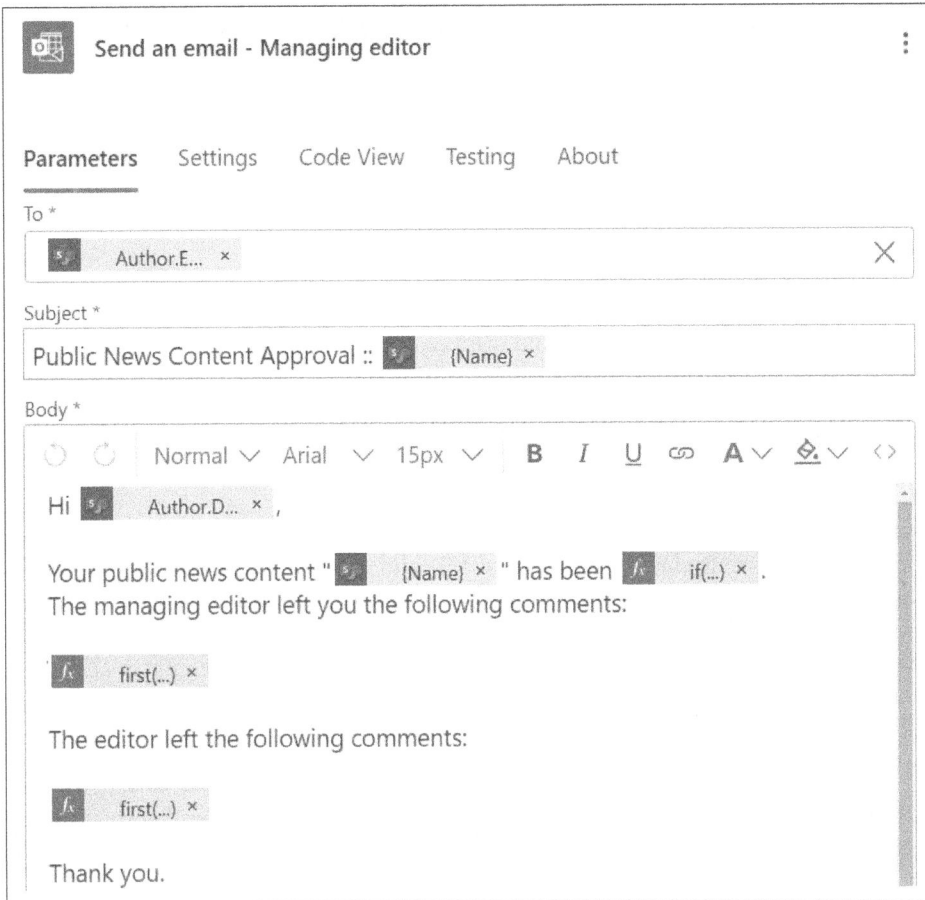

Send an email - Managing editor

Parameters   Settings   Code View   Testing   About

To *

[sᵧ] Author.E... ✕   ✕

Subject *

Public News Content Approval :: [sᵧ]   {Name} ✕

Body *

⟲   ⟳   Normal ∨   Arial ∨   15px ∨   **B**   *I*   U̲   ⌘   **A** ∨   🖋 ∨   ‹›

Hi [sᵧ]   Author.D... ✕ ,

Your public news content " [sᵧ]   {Name} ✕ " has been [*fx*]   if(...) ✕ .
The managing editor left you the following comments:

[*fx*]   first(...) ✕

The editor left the following comments:

[*fx*]   first(...) ✕

Thank you.

In the Body parameter, *expression1* will check whether the content has been approved or rejected by the managing editor. Accordingly, it will return "Approved" or "Rejected" text based on the Outcome dynamic value of the "Start and wait for an approval - Managing editor" action. *expression2* and *expression3* will get the comments from the managing editor and the news editor, respectively. Finally, name your flow, save it, and test it to ensure it works as expected.

See Also

- Recipe 8.1, "Requesting Expense Approval"
- Recipe 8.3, "Requesting Vacation Approval (Parallel Approval)"
- Recipe 8.4, "Requesting Proposal Approval (Approval with Escalation)"

8.3 Requesting Vacation Approval (Parallel Approval)

Problem

You want to automate the approval process of requesting vacations, which requires the simultaneous consent of two stakeholders.

Solution

Create an automated cloud flow that monitors the creation of items in a SharePoint vacation requests list. The flow should start an approval process for the first and second stakeholders simultaneously, check the responses, and then email the vacation requester when the vacation request is approved or rejected.

Discussion

Unlike sequential approval, where requests are handled one after another, parallel approval allows multiple approvers to review and approve requests simultaneously. This approach significantly reduces the time it takes for a vacation request to be processed, as there is no need to wait for one approver to finish before another begins. Automated notifications ensure that all relevant approvers are promptly alerted to new requests, and real-time tracking allows both employees and managers to monitor the status of each request. Combining HR approval with the manager's approval can further ensure that staffing levels are maintained and conflicts are avoided.

Furthermore, parallel approval automation enhances transparency and accountability within the approval process. Each approver's decision is recorded, creating a clear audit trail that can be reviewed if necessary. Overall, automating the parallel approval of vacation requests leads to improved operational efficiency, greater employee satisfaction, and better resource management.

Before starting to build this flow, make sure that you have created a vacation requests list in SharePoint or that you have read permissions on the list you want to monitor for newly created vacation requests. Create a vacation requests list in SharePoint from blank. After you create the list, add the following fields:

- From (required, date and time field, don't include time)
- To (required, date and time field, don't include time)
- Manager comments (optional, multiple lines of text field)
- HR comments (optional, multiple lines of text field)

- Approval status (optional, choice field), and add the following choices:
  — Awaiting approval
  — Approved
  — Rejected

Go to the Power Automate portal (*https://oreil.ly/O-MRf*). Sign in with your Micro-soft account or your organization's account. Make sure you're in the correct Power Automate environment. Click on "My flows" in the left navigation bar. Click on "New flow" to create a new flow, then choose a flow type. In this case, you want to kick-start the approval process when a new vacation request is created in SharePoint, so you must choose "Automated cloud flow." Click Skip on the pop-up to navigate to the flow designer experience. Search for the SharePoint connector in the flow designer. You want the trigger to be related to when a new item is created in SharePoint, so choose the "When an item is created" trigger. You may need to sign in and authenticate your SharePoint account. Configure the Site Address (the relevant site URL where the vacation requests list resides) and List Name (the SharePoint list to be monitored for newly created requests) trigger parameters:

Next, add an action to update the SharePoint list item with the corresponding appro-val status, awaiting approval. Search for the SharePoint connector and select the "Update item" action. Configure the action parameters, including Site Address (the relevant site URL where the vacation requests list resides), List Name (the SharePoint list tracking vacation requests), Id (the ID of the vacation request item that triggered the flow), Title (the Title from the dynamic values of the trigger), and From and To (from the dynamic values of the trigger).

Now, open the "Advanced parameters" drop-down and check the "Approval status Value" (the column indicating the approval status of the request item). Then, select "Awaiting approval." Next, add an action to start the approval process and wait for a response from the manager. Search for the Approvals connector and select the "Start and wait for an approval" action:

Rename your action to "Start and wait for an approval - Manager." Fill the approval action parameters as follows (the text in braces is dynamic content from the trigger):

- *Approval Type*: Approve/Reject - First to respond
- *Title*: `Vacation approval` (or the text of your choice)
- *Assigned To*: the email address of the approver (the manager)
- *Details*: `### A new vacation submitted by {Created by DisplayName} awaiting your approval`
- *Item Link*: `{Link to Item}`
- *Item Link Description*: `{Title}`

Start and wait for an approval - Manager

Parameters   Settings   Code View   Testing   About

Approval Type *

| Basic | ✕ |

Title *

Vacation approval

Assigned To *

mymanager@company.com

Details

A new vacation submitted by ⬛   Author.Disp... awaiting your approval

Item Link

⬛   {Link}

Item Link Description

⬛   Title

Click on the plus sign above the approval action, then click on "Add a parallel branch":

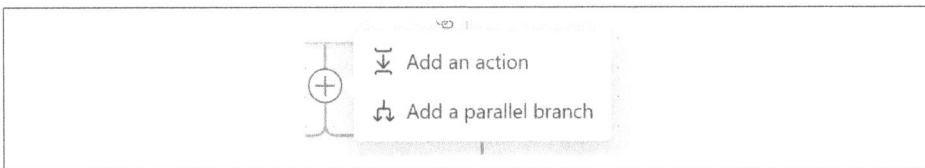

⊥   ⊼ Add an action
    ⊼ Add a parallel branch

In the new branch, add an action to start the approval process and wait for a response from HR. Search for the Approvals connector and select the "Start and wait for an approval" action. Rename your action to "Start and wait for an approval - HR":

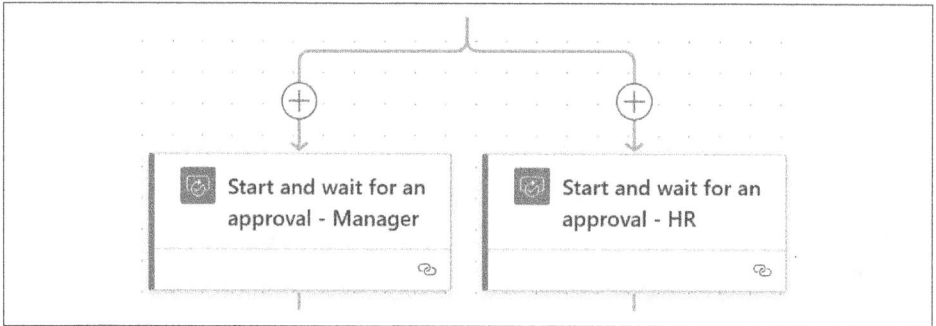

Fill the approval action parameters as follows (the text in braces is dynamic content from the trigger):

- *Approval Type*: Approve/Reject - First to respond
- *Title*: Vacation approval (or the text of your choice)
- *Assigned To*: the email address of the approver (HR)
- *Details*: ### A new vacation submitted by {Created by DisplayName} awaiting your approval
- *Item Link*: {Link to Item}
- *Item Link Description*: {Title}

Start and wait for an approval - HR

⋮

Parameters   Settings   Code View   Testing   About

Approval Type *

Approve/Reject - First to respond ⌄

Title *

Vacation approval

Assigned To *

hr@company.com

Details

A new vacation submitted by 🔲 Author.D... × awaiting your approval

Item Link

🔲 {Link} ×

Item Link Description

🔲 Title ×

After the "Start and wait for an approval - HR" action, add a new action, search for "Control," and then from the list of actions, choose Condition. From the Settings tab, under Run After, click Select Actions and choose "Start and wait for an approval - Manager." This will consolidate the parallel branches into one branch:

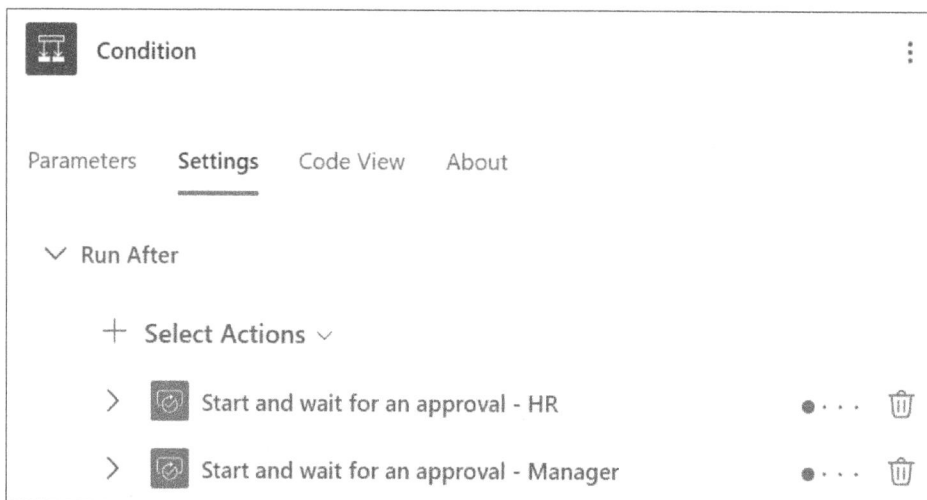

Now, click on the Parameters tab, and configure the condition action by selecting the Outcome property from the "Start and wait for an approval - Manager" dynamic content for the left-side comparison value. Make sure the comparison operator is set to "is equal to," and then for the right-side comparison, type Approve. The condition requires examining the approval response from HR too. Click on "New item" and choose "add row." Configure the second condition row by selecting the Outcome property from the "Start and wait for an approval - HR" dynamic content for the left-side comparison value. Make sure the comparison operator is set to "is equal to," and then for the right-side comparison, type Approve:

If the condition is met, under True, add an action to update the vacation request item with the approver's comments and response. Search for the SharePoint connector and select the "Update item" action. Rename the action to "Update item - Approved":

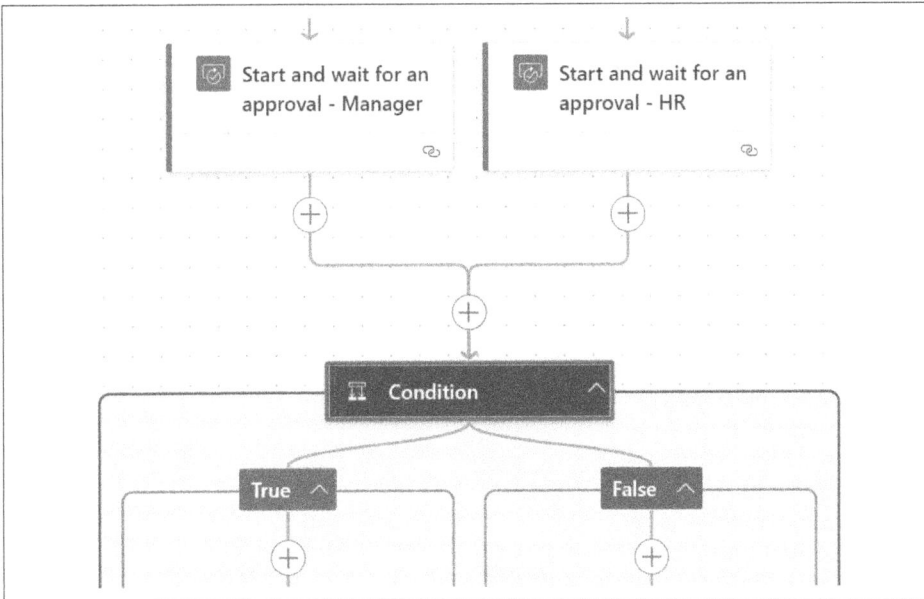

Configure the action parameters, including Site Address (the relevant site URL where the vacation requests list resides), List Name (the SharePoint list tracking vacation requests), Id (the ID of the vacation request item that triggered the flow), Title (the title from the dynamic values of the trigger), and From and To (from the dynamic values of the trigger):

Now, open the "Advanced parameters" drop-down and check Manager Comments, HR Comments, and the Approval Status Value (the column indicating the approval status of the request item).

Use the following expression for the Manager Comments parameter:

```
first(outputs('Start_and_wait_for_an_approval_-_Manager')?['body/responses'])
?['comments']
```

Then, use the following expression for the HR Comments parameter:

```
first(outputs('Start_and_wait_for_an_approval_-_HR')?['body/responses'])
?['comments']
```

Select Approved for the Approval Status Value:

| Parameters | Settings | Code View | Testing | About |

Advanced parameters

| Showing 3 of 4 | ∨ | Show all | Clear all |

Manager Comments

| *fx*   first(...) ✕ | ✕ |

HR Comments

| *fx*   first(...) ✕ | ✕ |

Approval Status Value

| Approved | ∨ | ✕ |

If the condition is not met, under False, add an action to update the request item approval status with the corresponding approval status ("Rejected") alongside the comments from both HR and the manager. Search for the SharePoint connector and select the "Update item" action. Rename the action to "Update item - Rejected."

Configure the action parameters, including Site Address (the relevant site URL where the vacation requests list resides), List Name (the SharePoint list tracking vacation requests), Id (the ID of the vacation request item that triggered the flow), Title (the title from the dynamic values of the trigger), and From and To (from the dynamic values of the trigger):

Now, open the "Advanced parameters" drop-down and check Manager Comments, HR Comments, and the Approval Status Value (the column indicating the approval status of the request item). Use the same expressions as in the "Update item - Approved" action for both the Manager Comments and the HR Comments parameters. Select Rejected for the Approval Status Value:

After the condition, add an action to send an email to the vacation requester. Search for the Office 365 Outlook connector and select the "Send an email (V2)" action.

Fill the "Send an email (V2)" action parameters as follows (the text in braces is dynamic content from the trigger):

- *To*: {Created by Email}
- *Subject*: Vacation approval :: {Title}
- *Body*:

    Hi {Created By DisplayName},

    Your vacation request "{Title}" has been {*expression1*}.
    Your manager left the following comments:

    {*expression2*}

    HR left the following comments:

    {*expression3*}

    Thank you.

where {*expression1*} is as follows:

```
if(and(equals(body('Start_and_wait_for_an_approval_-_Manager')?
['outcome'],'Approve'),equals(body('Start_and_wait_for_an_approval_-_HR')
?['outcome'],'Approve')),'approved','rejected')
```

and {*expression2*} is:

```
first(body('Start_and_wait_for_an_approval_-_Manager')?['responses'])
?['comments']
```

and {*expression3*} is:

```
first(body('Start_and_wait_for_an_approval_-_HR')?['responses'])
?['comments']
```

In the Body parameter, *expression1* will check whether the content has been approved or rejected by the manager and HR. Accordingly, it will return "Approved" or "Rejected" text based on the Outcome dynamic values of the "Start and wait for an approval - Manager" and "Start and wait for an approval - HR" actions. *expression2* and *expression3* will get the comments from the manager and HR, respectively. Finally, name your flow, save it, and test it to ensure it works as expected.

See Also

- Recipe 8.1, "Requesting Expense Approval"
- Recipe 8.2, "Requesting Document Content Approval (Sequential Approval)"
- Recipe 8.4, "Requesting Proposal Approval (Approval with Escalation)"

8.4 Requesting Proposal Approval (Approval with Escalation)

Problem

You want to automate the proposal approval process, which requires the consent of a senior approver and escalates if the request has not been processed within three days.

Solution

Create an automated cloud flow that monitors file creation or upload to a SharePoint document library, starts an approval process for the senior approver, and waits for a response. If no response is received within three days, it escalates and starts a new approval process. Finally, it sends an email to the content creator when the proposal is approved or rejected.

Discussion

Escalations in automated approval processes are critical mechanisms designed to handle situations where initial approvals are not completed within a specified time frame or when certain conditions are met that necessitate higher-level intervention. In an automated workflow, an escalation typically triggers when a request remains pending beyond a certain due date, automatically routing the request to a higher authority or an alternative approver to ensure timely resolution. This is essential for maintaining operational efficiency and preventing bottlenecks that can disrupt the workflow. For example, if a manager is unavailable to approve a vacation request, the workflow can escalate the approval to the next level in the hierarchy, ensuring that requests are processed without undue delay.

Furthermore, escalations in automated approvals help enforce accountability and transparency. By establishing clear escalation paths and criteria, you can ensure that all requests are handled appropriately and according to predefined policies. This reduces the risk of requests being overlooked or ignored. This flexibility allows you to tailor the escalation process to your unique needs, ultimately enhancing overall efficiency and ensuring that critical decisions are made in a timely manner.

Before starting to build this flow, make sure that you have created a document library in SharePoint (such as Proposal approval requests) or that you have read permissions on the library you want to monitor for newly created proposals.

After you create the library, add the following fields:

- Senior approver comments (optional, multiple lines of text field)
- Managing approver comments (optional, multiple lines of text field)
- Approval status (optional, choice field), and add the following choices:
  — Awaiting approval
  — Approved
  — Rejected

Go to the Power Automate portal (*https://oreil.ly/O-MRf*). Sign in with your Microsoft account or your organization's account. Make sure you're in the correct Power Automate environment. Click on "My flows" in the left navigation bar. Click on "New flow" to create a new flow. Choose a flow type. In this case, you want to kick-start the approval process when a new file is created/uploaded in SharePoint, so you must choose "Automated cloud flow." Click Skip on the pop-up to navigate to the flow designer experience. Search for the SharePoint connector in the flow designer.

You want the trigger to be related to when a new file is created in SharePoint, so choose the "When a file is created (properties only)" trigger. You may need to sign in and authenticate your SharePoint account. Configure the Site Address (the relevant site URL where the document library resides) and Library Name (the SharePoint library to be monitored for newly created files) trigger parameters:

Next, add an action to update the SharePoint library item with the corresponding approval status (awaiting approval). Search for the SharePoint connector and select the "Update item" action. Configure the Site Address (the relevant site URL where the document library resides) and List Name (the SharePoint document library name) action parameters, then choose "Enter custom value" and type the name of the document library. Then, configure Id (the ID of the file item that triggered the flow). Now, open the "Advanced parameters" drop-down and check the "Approval status Value" (the column indicating the approval status of the file item). Then, select "Awaiting approval":

Add an action to start the approval process and wait for a response from the approver. Search for the Approvals connector and select the "Start and wait for an approval" action.

Fill the approval action parameters as follows (the text in braces is dynamic content from the trigger):

- *Approval Type*: Approve/Reject - First to respond
- *Title*: Proposal approval request (or the text of your choice)
- *Assigned To*: the email address of the approver (senior proposal approver)
- *Details*: ## A new proposal approval request submitted by {Created by DisplayName} awaiting your approval
- *Item Link*: {Link to Item}
- *Item Link Description*: {Name}

Click on the Settings tab, then under General, type P3D for the Action Timeout. This will set the timeout for this action to three days. Note that timeout duration must be specified in ISO 8601 format.

> ISO 8601 duration format represents time intervals in a standardized way. It uses a P (period, indicating duration) followed by time values (years, months, days, hours, minutes, and seconds; a T is used to separate date and time components). For example:
>
> - P1Y2M3D → 1 year, 2 months, 3 days
> - P2DT12H → 2 days, 12 hours
>
> To learn more about ISO 8601, visit the corresponding Wikipedia entry (*https://oreil.ly/B10wb*).

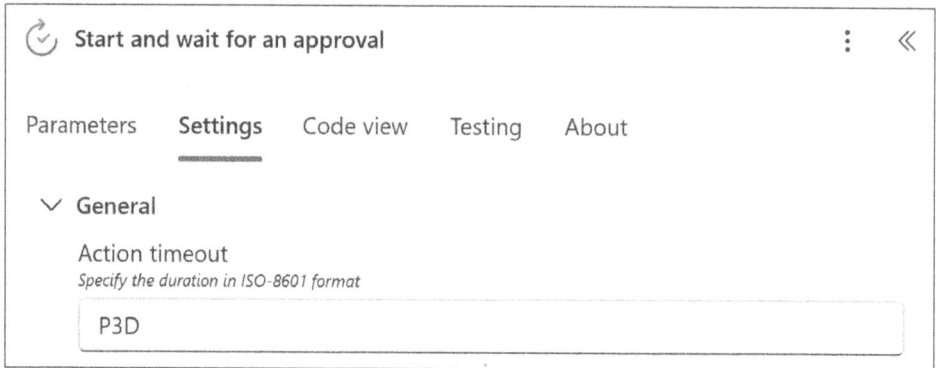

Start and wait for an approval   ⋮ ≪

Parameters   **Settings**   Code view   Testing   About

∨ General

Action timeout
Specify the duration in ISO-8601 format

P3D

Add a new action, search for "Control," and then from the list of actions, choose Condition. Next, configure the Condition action by selecting the Outcome property from the "Start and wait for an approval" dynamic content for the left-side comparison value. Make sure the comparison operator is set to "is equal to," and then for the right-side comparison, type `Approve`:

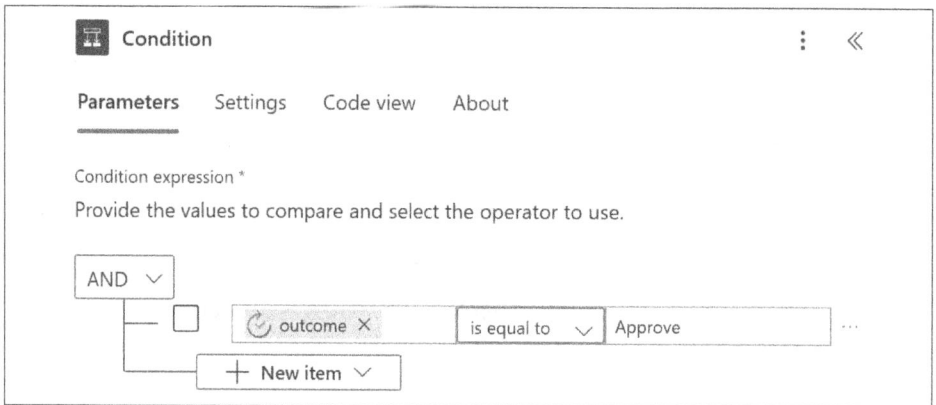

Condition   ⋮ ≪

Parameters   Settings   Code view   About

Condition expression *
Provide the values to compare and select the operator to use.

AND ∨

☐   outcome ✕ | is equal to ∨ | Approve   ···

+ New item ∨

The outcome property returns a standard text value, returning "Approve" if the request is approved and "Reject" if the request is rejected. If the condition is met, under True, add an action to update the file item with the senior approver comments. Search for the SharePoint connector and select the "Update item" action. Rename the action to "Update item - Approved":

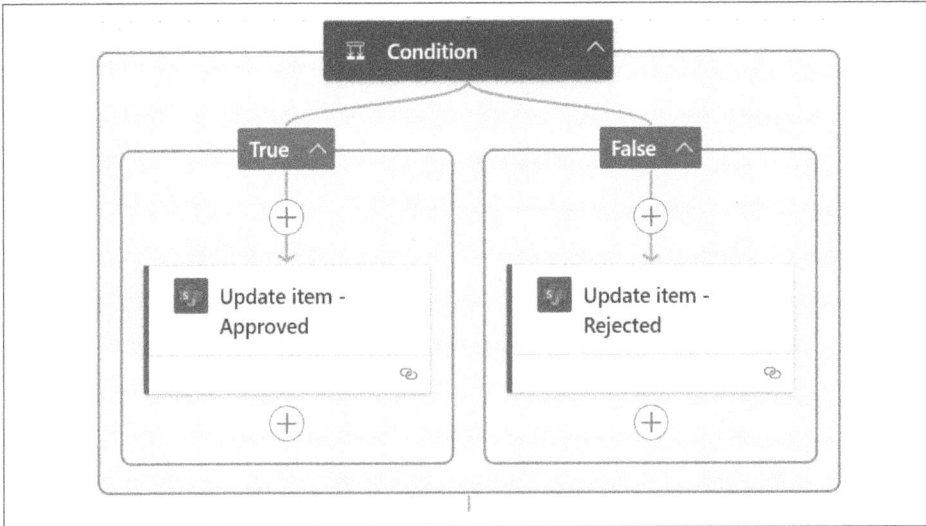

Configure the Site Address (the relevant site URL where the document library resides) and List Name (the SharePoint document library name) action parameters, then choose "Enter custom value" and type the name of the document library. Then, configure Id (the ID of the file item that triggered the flow). Now, open the "Advanced parameters" drop-down and check "Senior approver comments" and "Approval status value." Next, select Approved for the "Approval status value" (the column indicating the approval status of the file item). Then, add the following expression in the "Senior approver comments":

```
first(body('Start_and_wait_for_an_approval')?['responses'])?['comments']
```

Update item - Approved

Parameters   Settings   Code view   Testing   About

Site Address *

Lush Vibes - https:// ███████████████████ /sites/LushVibes   ⌄

List Name *

Proposal approval requests   ✕

Id *

ID ✕

Advanced parameters

Showing 2 of 7   ⌄   Show all   Clear all

Senior approver comments

fx first(...) ✕   ✕

Approval status Value

Approved   ⌄   ✕

Note that the Responses dynamic value from the approval action is a collection of data for one or multiple approvers. However, we have only one approver in this scenario, so we get the first item. If the condition is not met, under False, add an action to update the file item approval status with the corresponding approval status ("Rejected") and update "Senior approver comments." Search for the SharePoint connector and select the "Update item" action. Rename the action to "Update item - Rejected." Configure the Site Address (the relevant site URL where the document library resides) and List Name (the SharePoint document library name) action parameters, then choose "Enter custom value" and type the name of the document library. Then, configure Id (the ID of the file item that triggered the flow). Now, open the "Advanced parameters" drop-down and check the "Senior approver comments" and "Approval status Value."

For "Senior approver comments," use the same expression used in configuring the "Update item - Approved" action. As for "Approval status Value" (the column indicating the approval status of the file item), select Rejected:

Update item - Rejected	⋮ ‹

Parameters   Settings   Code view   Testing   About

Site Address *

Lush Vibes - https:// ████████████████ /sites/LushVibes	⌄

List Name *

Proposal approval requests	✕

Id *

5 ID ×	

Advanced parameters

Showing 2 of 7	⌄	Show all	Clear all

Senior approver comments

ƒₓ first(...) ×	✕

Approval status Value

Rejected	⌄	✕

After the condition, add an action to send an email to the content creator (requester). Search for the Office 365 Outlook connector and select the "Send an email (V2)" action.

Fill the "Send an email (V2)" action parameters as follows (the text in braces is dynamic content from the trigger):

- *To*: {Created by Email}
- *Subject*: Proposal approval request :: {Name}
- *Body*:

      Hi {Created By DisplayName},

      Your proposal approval request "{Name}" has been {*expression1*}.

The senior approver left you the following comments:

{expression2}

Thank you.

where *{expression1}* is as follows:

```
if(equals(body('Start_and_wait_for_an_approval')?['outcome'],'Approve'),
'approved','rejected')
```

and *{expression2}* is:

```
first(body('Start_and_wait_for_an_approval')?['responses'])?['comments']
```

Send an email (V2)   ⋮

Parameters   Settings   Code View   Testing   About

To *

> Author.E... ×   ✕

Subject *

> Proposal approval request :: {Name} ×

Body *

> ↺ ↻   Normal ∨   Arial ∨   15px ∨   **B**   *I*   U̲   ⊖   A ∨   ◇ ∨   <>
>
> Hi Author.D... × ,
>
> Your proposal approval request " {Name} × " has been *fx* if(...) × .
> The senior approver left you the following comments:
>
> *fx* first(...) ×
>
> Thank you.

In the Body parameter, *expression1* will check whether the content has been approved or rejected by the senior approver. Accordingly, it will return "Approved" or "Rejected" text based on the Outcome dynamic value of the "Start and wait for an approval" action; *expression2* will get the comments from the senior approver.

Just before the Condition action, click on the plus sign above, then click on "Add a parallel branch":

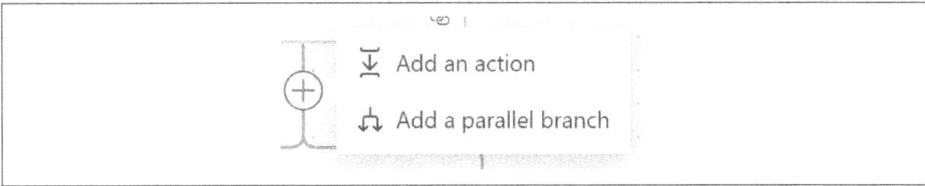

In the new branch, add an action to start the approval process with the managing approver. Search for the Approvals connector and select the "Start and wait for an approval" action:

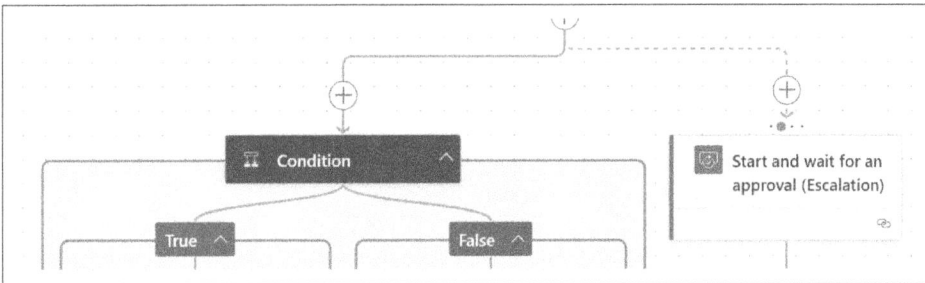

Rename your action to "Start and wait for an approval (Escalation)."

Fill the approval action parameters as follows (the text in braces is dynamic content from the trigger):

- *Approval Type*: Approve/Reject - First to respond
- *Title*: Proposal approval request :: Escalated (or the text of your choice)
- *Assigned To*: the email address of the approver (managing proposal approver)
- *Details*: ## A new proposal approval request submitted by {Created by DisplayName} has been escalated and is awaiting your approval
- *Item Link*: {Link to Item}
- *Item Link Description*: {Name}

Start and wait for an approval (Escalation)

Parameters   Settings   Code View   Testing   About

Approval Type *

| Approve/Reject - First to respond | ⌄ |

Title *

Proposal approval request :: Escalated

Assigned To *

managingapprover@company.com

Details

A new proposal approval request submitted by   Author.D... ×   has been escalated and is awaiting your approval

Item Link

{Link} ×

Item Link Description

{Name} ×

Click on the Settings tab, then under Run After, under Select Actions, open "Start and wait for an approval" by clicking on it. Then, uncheck "Is successful" and check "Has timed out." Make sure that "Has timed out" is the only checked option. This will allow the current action to run if and only if the previous action has timed out:

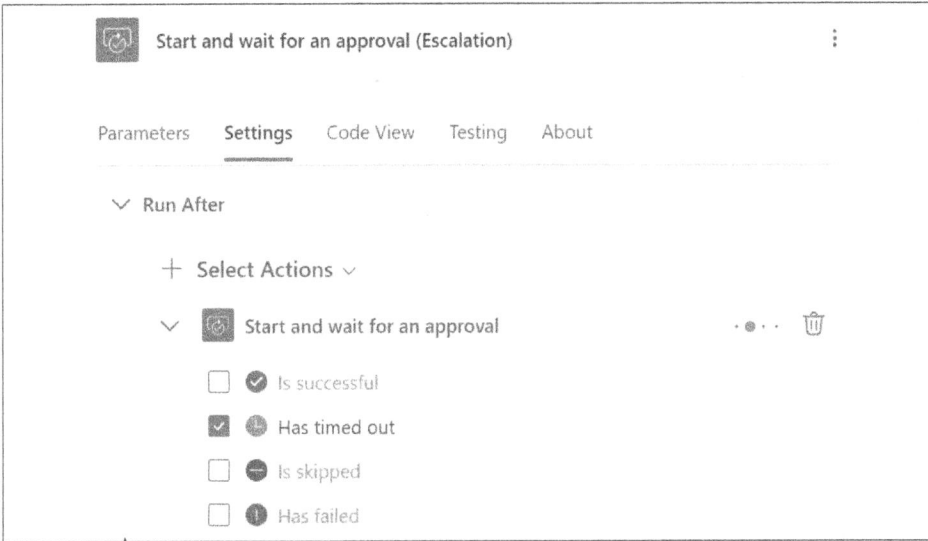

Now add a new action, search for "Control," and then from the list of actions, choose Condition. Rename your condition to "Check Escalated Approval." Then configure the condition action by selecting the Outcome property from the "Start and wait for an approval (Escalation)" dynamic content for the left-side comparison value. Make sure the comparison operator is set to "is equal to," and then for the right-side comparison, type Approve:

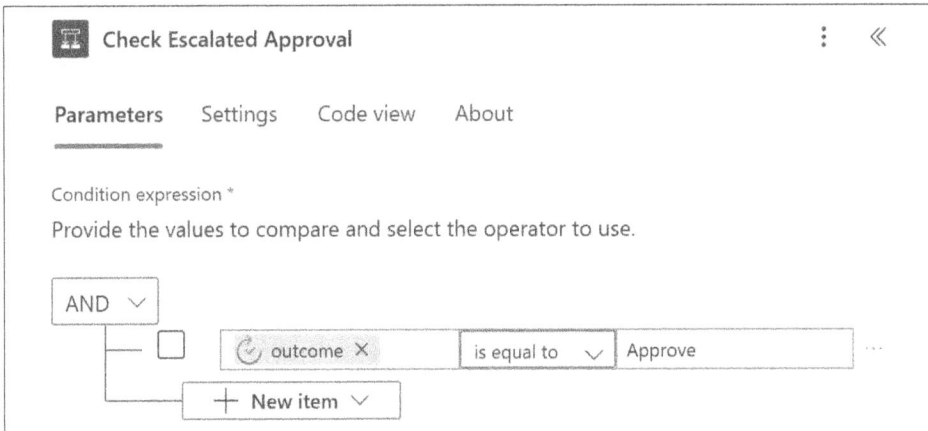

If the condition is met, under True, add an action to update the file item with the managing approver comments. Search for the SharePoint connector and select the "Update item" action. Rename the action to "Update item - Escalated (Approved)":

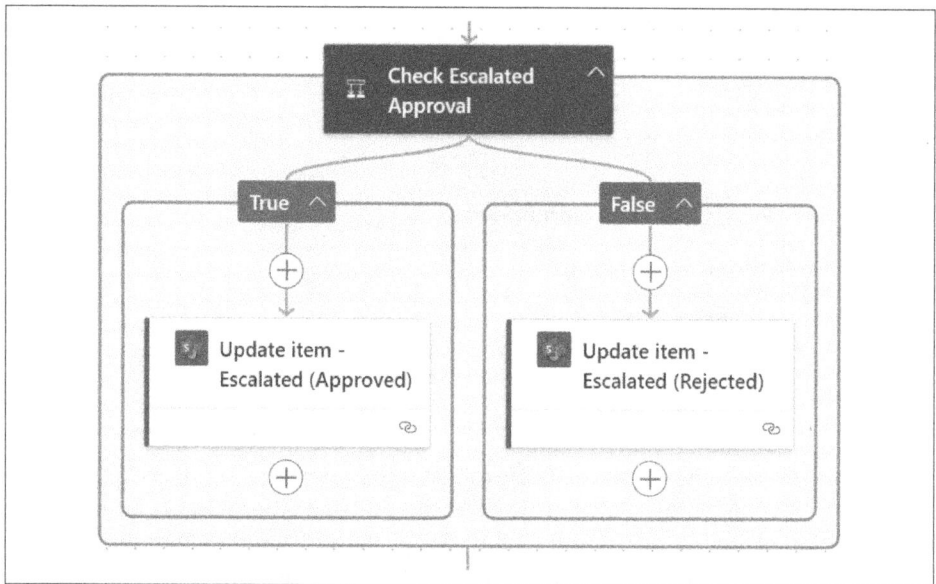

Configure the Site Address (the relevant site URL where the document library resides) and List Name (the SharePoint document library name) action parameters, then choose "Enter custom value" and type the name of the document library. Then, configure Id (the ID of the file item that triggered the flow). Now, open the "Advanced parameters" drop-down and check "Managing approver comments" and "Approval status Value." Select Approved for the "Approval status Value" (the column indicating the approval status of the file item).

Then, add the following expression in the "Managing approver comments":

```
first(body('Start_and_wait_for_an_approval_(Escalation)')?['responses'])
?['comments']
```

Update item - Escalated (Approved)

Parameters   Settings   Code view   Testing   About

Site Address *

Lush Vibes - https://[redacted]/sites/LushVibes

List Name *

Proposal approval requests   ✕

Id *

⬛ ID ✕

Advanced parameters

Showing 2 of 7   ⌄   Show all   Clear all

Managing approver comments

ƒx first(...) ✕   ✕

Approval status Value

Approved   ⌄   ✕

If the condition is not met, under False, add an action to update the file item approval status with the corresponding approval status ("Rejected") and update "Managing approver comments." Search for the SharePoint connector and select the "Update item" action. Rename the action to "Update item - Escalated (Rejected)." Next, configure the Site Address (the relevant site URL where the document library resides) and List Name (the SharePoint document library name) action parameters, then choose "Enter custom value" and type the name of the document library. Then, configure Id (the ID of the file item that triggered the flow).

Now, open the "Advanced parameters" drop-down and check "Managing approver comments" and "Approval status Value." For "Managing approver comments," use the same expression used in configuring the "Update item - Escalated (Approved)" action. As for "Approval status Value" (the column indicating the approval status of the file item), select Rejected:

Update item - Escalated (Rejected)

Parameters   Settings   Code view   Testing   About

Site Address *

| Lush Vibes - https://█████████████/sites/LushVibes | ∨ |

List Name *

| Proposal approval requests | ✕ |

Id *

| ▪ ID ✕ |

Advanced parameters

| Showing 2 of 7 | ∨ | Show all | Clear all |

Managing approver comments

| ƒₓ first(...) ✕ | ✕ |

Approval status Value

| Rejected | ∨ | ✕ |

After the condition, add an action to send an email to the content creator (requester).
Search for the Office 365 Outlook connector and select the "Send an email (V2)"
action. Rename the action to "Send an email - Escalated."

Fill the "Send an email - Escalated" action parameters as follows (the text in braces is
dynamic content from the trigger):

- *To*: {Created by Email}
- *Subject*: Proposal approval request :: {Name}
- *Body*:

      Hi {Created By DisplayName},

      Your proposal approval request "{Name}" has been escalated
       and {expression1}.
      The managing approver left you the following comments:

      {expression2}

Thank you.

where {*expression1*} is as follows:

```
if(equals(body('Start_and_wait_for_an_approval_(Escalation)')
?['outcome'],'Approve'),'approved','rejected')
```

And {*expression2*} is:

```
first(body('Start_and_wait_for_an_approval_(Escalation)')
?['responses'])?['comments']
```

Send an email - Escalated   ⋮

Parameters   Settings   Code View   Testing   About

To *

| Author.E... × | × |

Subject *

Proposal approval request :: [Name] ×

Body *

↺ ↻   Normal ∨   Arial ∨   15px ∨   **B** *I* U̲ ∞ A∨ ⬧∨ <>

Hi   Author.D... × ,

Your proposal approval request " {Name} × " has been escalated and
if(...) × .
The managing approver left you the following comments:

first(...) ×

Thank you.

In the Body parameter, *expression1* will check whether the content has been approved or rejected by the managing approver. Accordingly, it will return "Approved" or "Rejected" text based on the Outcome dynamic value of the "Start and wait for an approval" action; *expression2* will get the comments from the managing approver. Finally, name your flow, save it, and test it to ensure it works as expected.

See Also

- Recipe 8.1, "Requesting Expense Approval"
- Recipe 8.2, "Requesting Document Content Approval (Sequential Approval)"
- Recipe 8.3, "Requesting Vacation Approval (Parallel Approval)"

Conclusion

The shift from manual, paper-based approval processes to automated systems has revolutionized organizational efficiency. Manual approvals, though functional in the past, were slow, error-prone, and required substantial effort to track, store, and manage documents. Power Automate, in particular, represents a significant leap forward by enabling the creation of more complex, scalable, and flexible approval workflows that integrate seamlessly with both Microsoft 365 and third-party applications. This flexibility and ease of use have made automation accessible to a broader range of users, reducing administrative burdens and enhancing compliance, accountability, and auditability.

As organizations continue to grow and the need for rapid decision making becomes critical, automated approval processes will remain essential for maintaining operational efficiency. The powerful tools now available allow organizations to customize and optimize workflows, ensuring faster approvals and better control, all while minimizing the risks associated with manual processes.

CHAPTER 9

Power Automate Instant Flows

In this chapter, I'll introduce instant flows, a feature of Power Automate that enables users to manually trigger workflows when needed. These flows can be started on demand by various methods, providing flexibility with how and when processes are initiated. Then, I'll introduce the different methods where workflows are triggered manually, such as button flows, HTTP requests, etc. Finally, I'll go through very interesting and useful recipes where Power Automate instant flows provide simplicity and productivity.

Instant Flows: On-Demand Automation Made Simple

The ability to trigger workflows on demand allows individuals and organizations alike to respond quickly to changing events, simplify redundant tasks, and unlock new levels of productivity. This is where instant flows shine, delivering a versatile solution that puts the power of automation directly in the hands of users! Whether it's initiating a process with the press of a button or triggering workflows from specific data points, instant flows offer a dynamic approach to automation that aligns with the diverse needs of modern digitalization.

At its core, instant flows empower users to initiate actions at the right moment, tailoring workflows to fit real-time requirements. These flows offer a unique blend of control and flexibility by enabling manual triggers, making them ideal for scenarios that demand precision and timing. Unlike scheduled or automated flows that operate on predefined rules, instant flows place decision making directly with the user, ensuring that processes run only when they are most relevant. This capability is particularly valuable in environments where human judgment and situational awareness are key.

With instant flows, Power Automate bridges the gap between user-driven decisions and seamless automation. By providing various trigger options, users can design workflows that align with their specific needs. This not only simplifies complex processes but also empowers individuals across all levels of an organization to harness the power of automation without requiring extensive technical expertise.

Instant flows are part of the suite of tools offered by Power Automate, designed to be initiated by a manual trigger. This allows users to start workflows on demand, such as clicking a button, offering flexibility with when and how processes are initiated.

Instant flows can be categorized based on their initiation method:

Button flows
> Triggered by pressing a virtual button in the Power Automate app or an actual button (Flic or Bttn). These are ideal for on-the-go scenarios.

For a selected item
> Triggered when a user selects an item, a file, or a message in a supported service, such as SharePoint, OneDrive, or Teams, and chooses the flow from the integrated menu.

For a selected row
> Similar to the selected item trigger, but specifically for rows in a database or a table in services such as SQL Server or Excel.

HTTP request
> Triggered when receiving an HTTP request (a URL is called). This is very useful for integrating Power Automate with external services, systems, applications, or even Power Automate flow, which can send HTTP requests.

Power Apps or Copilot Studio
> Specifically designed to trigger from a Power Apps app, such as a click of a button, or through a dedicated action in Copilot Studio to call a Power Automate flow on demand.

Instant flows in Power Automate offer a user-friendly way to trigger automations manually, providing flexibility and efficiency in managing workflows. From simple task automation to complex business processes, instant flows empower users to create customized solutions that meet their specific operational needs.

9.1 Taking a Sick Leave

Problem

You want to take a sick leave with a click of a button on your mobile.

Solution

Create a manually triggered flow by pressing a virtual button in the Power Automate app that emails your manager to inform them that you're taking a sick day.

Discussion

By simply pressing a virtual button within the Power Automate app (on your cell phone), you can instantly send a prewritten email template to your manager. This ensures that you communicate your absence promptly without the need to open your Outlook app or spend time composing an email from scratch. The convenience of this automation allows you to rest without any added stress or effort, making it an ideal solution for those unexpected sick days.

First, go to the Power Automate portal (*https://oreil.ly/O-MRf*). Sign in with your Microsoft account or your organization's account. Make sure you're in the correct Power Automate environment. Click on "My flows" in the left navigation bar. Click on "New flow" to create a new flow. Choose a flow type. In this case, you want to kick-start the flow when you click the virtual button on your Power Automate app, so you must choose "Instant cloud flow." You want the trigger related to when a flow button for cell phone is clicked, so choose the "Manually trigger a flow" trigger. Then click Create. No need to do any further configurations for the trigger. Next, you want to get your manager's email and name to use in your prewritten email template. Therefore, you need to get the required information as follows. Add an action to get your own Microsoft 365 profile information. Search for the Office 365 Users connector and select the "Get my profile (V2)" action. You may need to sign in and authenticate your Office 365 Users account. Then, add another action after to get your manager's Microsoft 365 profile information. Search for the Office 365 Users connector and select the "Get manager (V2)" action. Configure the action by selecting the Id property from the "Get my profile (V2)" dynamic content:

Get manager (V2)

Parameters   Settings   Code View   Testing   About

User (UPN) *

```
Id ×
```

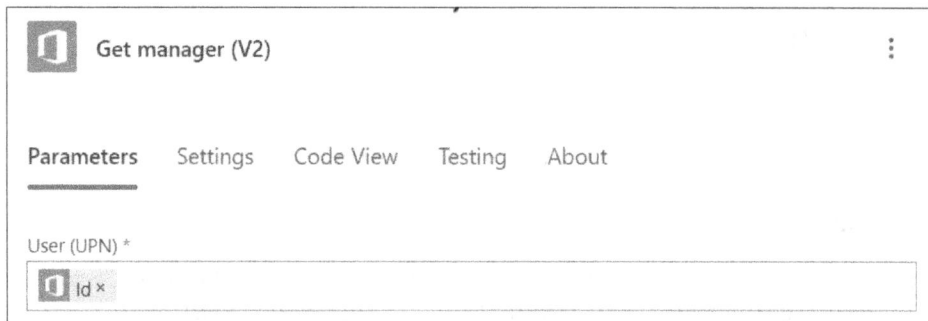

Now, add an action to send an email to your manager. Search for the Office 365 Outlook connector and select the "Send an email (V2)" action. You may need to sign in and authenticate your Office 365 Outlook account.

Fill the "Send an email (V2)" action parameters as follows (the text in braces is dynamic content):

- *To*: {Email} (from the "Get manager (V2)" action)
- *Subject*: Sick Leave
- *Body*:

  Good morning {DisplayName},

  I'm feeling sick. I want to inform you that I'm taking a sick leave for today {Date}.

  Thank you,
  {DisplayName}

where the first {DisplayName} instance is dynamic content from the "Get manager (V2)" action, the {Date} is from the "Manually trigger a flow" trigger, and the second {DisplayName} instance is from the "Get my profile (V2)" action.

For further configuration, in case you want to send this to your project manager (or coworker), open the "Advanced parameters" drop-down and check CC and Importance. Then select High for the Importance parameter and fill in the email addresses of your project manager and coworkers (separated by a semicolon). Finally, name your flow, save it, and test it to ensure it works as expected.

See Also

- Recipe 9.2, "Requesting a Daily Leave"
- Recipe 9.3, "Simulating a Warehouse Doorbell"
- Recipe 9.4, "Sending a Document for (Ad Hoc) Approval in SharePoint"
- Recipe 9.5, "Registering a Guest Visit"

9.2 Requesting a Daily Leave

Problem

You want to request a daily leave with a click of a button on your mobile without the need to log in to internal systems.

Solution

Create a manually triggered flow by pressing a virtual button in the Power Automate app that takes the daily leave information details, sends an approval request to your manager, and emails you upon approval or rejection.

Discussion

Once again, this manually triggered flow provides an effortless way to send a daily leave request to your manager and initiate an approval process on the fly. This automation is especially beneficial when you want to send that request before or after working hours, eliminating the need to log in to the organization's internal system to request your absence.

By simply pressing a virtual button within the Power Automate app (on your cell phone), you can instantly initiate the approval request with your manager. This ensures that you communicate your leave promptly when you remember it without the need to spend time composing an email to request a leave.

Go to the Power Automate portal (*https://oreil.ly/O-MRf*). Sign in with your Microsoft account or your organization's account. Make sure you're in the correct Power Automate environment. Click on "My flows" in the left navigation bar. Click on "New flow" to create a new flow. Choose a flow type. In this case, you want to kick-start the flow when you click the virtual button on your Power Automate app, so you must choose "Instant cloud flow." You want the trigger to be related to when a flow button for cell phone is clicked, so pick the "Manually trigger a flow" trigger. Then click Create. Configure the trigger to take the following inputs (parameters) by clicking on "Add an input" under the Parameters tab:

- Add a Date input and rename it to "When."
- Add a Number input and rename it to "Duration (h)."
- Add a Text input and rename it to "Reason."

Manually trigger a flow

Parameters Settings Code View About

When	Please enter or select a date (YYYY-MM-DD)	
Duration (h)	Please enter a number	
Reason	Please enter your input	

+ Add an input

Next, you want to get your manager's email address and name to use in the approval action. Therefore, you need to get the required information in two steps, as follows.

First, add an action to get your own Microsoft 365 profile information. Search for the Office 365 Users connector and select the "Get my profile (V2)" action. You may need to sign in and authenticate your Office 365 Users account.

Then, add another action to get your manager Microsoft 365 profile information. Search for the Office 365 Users connector and select the "Get manager (V2)" action. Configure the action by selecting the Id property from the "Get my profile (V2)" dynamic content:

Get manager (V2)

Parameters Settings Code View Testing About

User (UPN) *

Id ×

Add an action to start and wait for the approval process from your manager. Search for the Approvals connector and select the "Start and wait for an approval" action.

Fill the approval action parameters as follows (the text in braces is dynamic content):

- *Approval Type*: Approve/Reject - First to respond
- *Title*: `Daily leave request` (or the text of your choice)
- *Assigned To*: {`Mail`} (the email address of your manager, from "Get manager (V2)")
- *Details*:

      ## A new daily leave request awaiting your approval
      {Display Name} has requested a daily leave on {Date}
      for {Duration (h)} hours.
      Reason: {Reason}

  where {`Display Name`} is dynamic content from the "Get my profile (V2)" action and {`Date`}, {`Duration (h)`}, and {`Reason`} are from the "Manually trigger a flow" trigger.

Next, add a new action. Search for "Control," and then, from the list of actions, choose Condition. Configure the condition action by selecting the Outcome property from the "Start and wait for an approval" dynamic content for the left-side comparison value. Make sure the comparison operator is set to "is equal to," and then for the right-side comparison, type `Approve`:

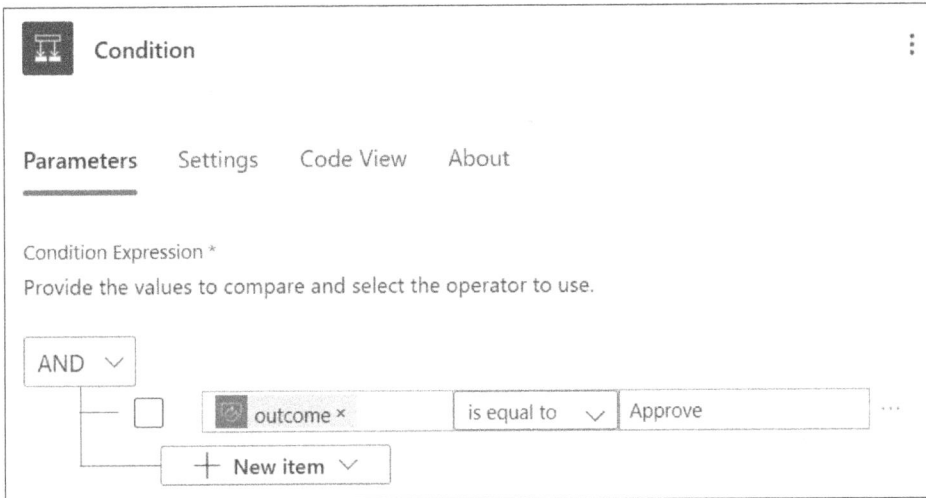

🎚 Condition	⋮

Parameters   Settings   Code View   About

Condition Expression *
Provide the values to compare and select the operator to use.

AND ∨			
☐	🖼 outcome ×	is equal to ∨	Approve	⋯
	➕ New item ∨		

If the condition is met, under True, add an action to send an email informing you that the request has been approved. Search for the Office 365 Outlook connector and select the "Send an email (V2)" action. You may need to sign in and authenticate your Office 365 Outlook account.

Rename the action to "Send an email (V2) - Approved," then fill the action parameters as follows (the text in braces is dynamic content):

- *To*: {`Email`} (from the "Get my profile (V2)" action)
- *Subject*: `Daily leave request`
- *Body*:

    `Hi {DisplayName},`

    `Your leave request on {When} for {Duration (h)} hours has been approved.`

    `Your manager left the following comments:`
    `{expression1}`

    `Thank you.`

where {DisplayName} is dynamic content from the "Get my profile (V2)" action, {When} and {Duration (h)} are from the "Manually trigger a flow" trigger, and {*expression1*} is as follows:

```
first(body('Start_and_wait_for_an_approval')?['responses'])?['comments']
```

📧 **Send an email (V2) - Approved**   ⋮

Parameters   Settings   Code View   Testing   About
─────────────

To *

┌───┐
│ 📧 Mail ×   ✕ │
└───┘

Subject *

┌───┐
│ Daily leave request   │
└───┘

Body *

┌───┐
│ ↺ ↻   │ Normal ∨ Arial   ∨ 15px ∨ **B** *I* U̲ **A** 🖌 ∞ <>│
│   │
│ Hi 📧 Display Name × ,   ▲│
│   │
│ Your leave request on 🔔 When × for 🔔 Duration (h) × hours has been │
│ approved.   │
│   │
│ Your manager left the following comments: │
│ ƒx first(...) ×   │
│   │
│ Thank you.   │
└───┘

If the condition is not met, under False, add an action to send an email informing you that the request has been rejected. Search for the Office 365 Outlook connector and select the "Send an email (V2)" action. Rename the action to "Send an email (V2) - Rejected," then fill the action with exactly the same parameters for the "Send an email (V2) - Approved" action (changing "approved" to "rejected" in the Body parameter):

Finally, name, save, and test your flow to ensure it works as expected.

See Also

- Recipe 9.1, "Taking a Sick Leave"
- Recipe 9.3, "Simulating a Warehouse Doorbell"
- Recipe 9.4, "Sending a Document for (Ad Hoc) Approval in SharePoint"
- Recipe 9.5, "Registering a Guest Visit"

9.3 Simulating a Warehouse Doorbell

Problem

You want to simulate a warehouse doorbell to notify doorkeepers that a delivery has arrived at the warehouse door/gate.

Solution

Create a manually triggered flow by pressing an actual physical button. This triggers a Power Automate flow, which in turn notifies the doorkeepers through SMS that a delivery has arrived at the warehouse.

Discussion

This automation can significantly enhance the efficiency of warehouse operations, particularly in managing deliveries. By integrating an actual physical button with a Power Automate flow, the process of notifying doorkeepers about a delivery becomes seamless and immediate. When the button is pressed, the flow is triggered to send an SMS notification to all doorkeepers on shift, informing them that a delivery has arrived. This instant communication reduces the waiting time for delivery personnel and ensures that the delivery process is handled promptly, minimizing disruptions and delays in the warehouse operations.

Moreover, this offers several benefits beyond immediate communication. It improves accountability by providing a clear, time-stamped record of when the delivery notification was sent, ensuring that all parties are informed simultaneously. This reduces the chances of miscommunication and ensures that deliveries are not overlooked. By implementing this automation, warehouses can enhance their operational efficiency, improve response times, and maintain better control over their delivery management processes.

Before starting to build this flow, make sure that you have bought the actual physical button that integrates with Power Automate.

For this example, I'm using a Flic (*https://oreil.ly/2JBC9*) for the physical button.

To configure the Flic button with your mobile device, follow the configuration instructions from Microsoft (*https://oreil.ly/S7fHp*).

Configure your Flic button with a cell phone or tablet (it requires Bluetooth). This means that the button and the device need to be within Bluetooth range of each other.

For SMS notifications, I'm using Twilio as the service provider for this example. Therefore, subscribe to Twilio SMS service for this scenario.

> To subscribe (*https://oreil.ly/K2XGu*) to a free trial of Twilio, follow the instructions to set up your SMS notification service. You'll need your Twilio account ID and the associated access token for that account ID.

Create a SharePoint list (e.g., "Warehouse doorkeepers") that has the following columns:

- Title (single line of text; you get this column by default when creating any custom list)
- Doorkeepers (person or group; allow multiple selections)

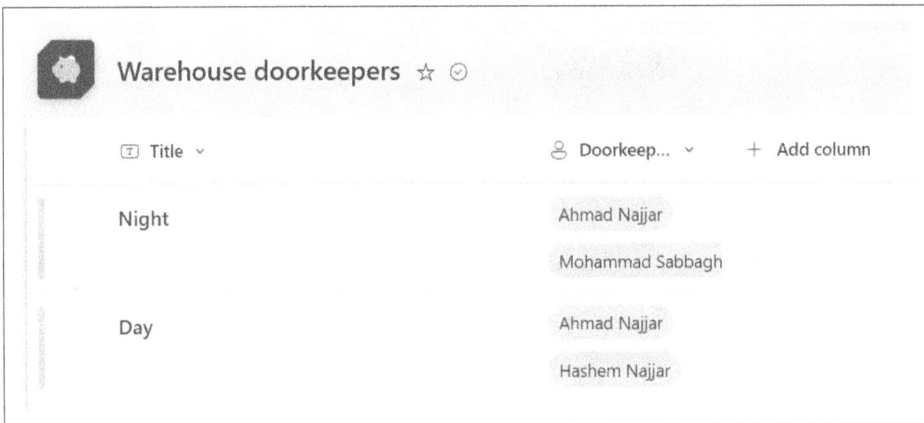

In this scenario, I'm assuming that there are only two shifts: "Day" (from 6:00 A.M. to 6:00 P.M.) and "Night" (from 6:00 P.M. to 6:00 A.M.). Accordingly, I added two items titled "Night" and "Day" to the SharePoint list, each with the corresponding doorkeepers assigned to their respective shifts.

To create a flow, go to the Power Automate portal (*https://oreil.ly/O-MRf*) and sign in with your Microsoft or organization's account. Ensure that you're in the correct Power Automate environment, click on "My flows" in the left navigation bar, and select "New flow." Since you want to initiate the flow when a physical button is clicked, choose "Instant cloud flow," and then click Skip. In the flow designer, select your flow's trigger by searching for Flic and choosing "When a Flic is pressed":

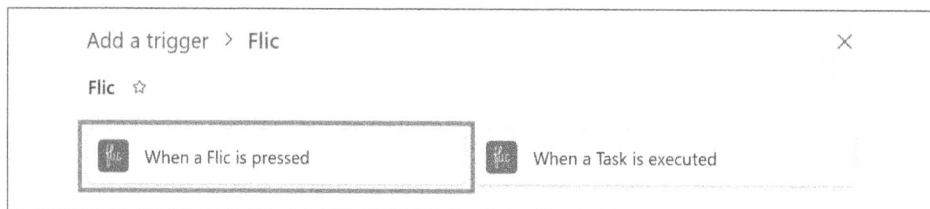

In the Flic button trigger, select the drop-down arrow and then select the Flic button you previously added (in the second step). For Events, select "click":

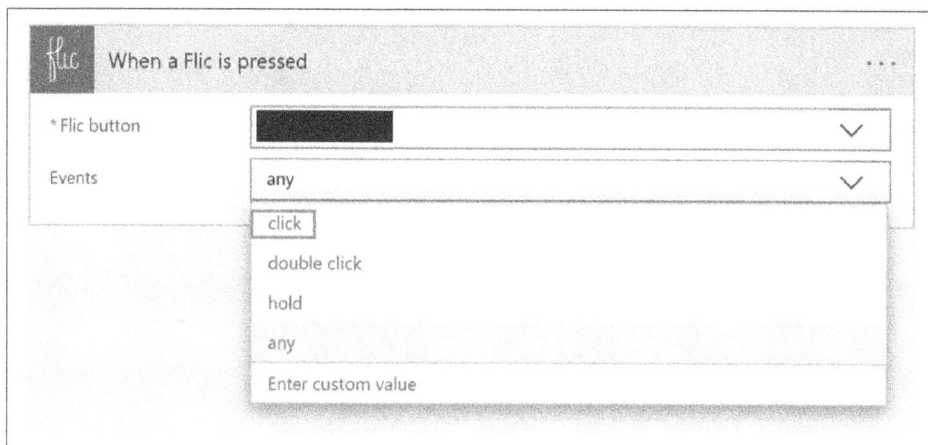

Next, get the current local time (when the button is pressed) to obtain the working shift. You'll need to acquire the information needed in multiple steps, as follows. Add an action to get the current time. Search for the Date Time connector and select the "Convert time zone" action.

Fill in the action parameters as follows:

- *Base Time*: utcNow() (expression)
- *Source Time Zone*: (UTC) Coordinated Universal Time
- *Destination Time Zone*: Your local time zone
- *Time Unit*: Select "Enter custom value," then type HH:mm.

Add an action to initialize a variable. This variable will hold the ID of the working shift when fetched from the SharePoint List. Search for the Variable connector and select the "Initialize variable" action.

Configure the action parameters as follows:

- *Name*: Shift Id
- *Type*: Integer

Now rename the action to "Initialize variable - Shift Id":

{x} **Initialize variable - Shift Id**   ⋮

Parameters   Settings   Code View   About
_____

Name *

Shift Id

Type *

Integer   ⌄

Value

Enter initial value

Next, add a new action, search for "Control," and then from the list of actions, choose Condition. Configure the condition action by adding the following expression for the left-side comparison value:

```
int(formatDateTime(body('Convert_time_zone'),'HH'))
```

Set the comparison operator to "is greater or equal to," and for the right-side comparison, type 18. The condition requires you to examine if the current time is the night shift. So, it's not enough to check that with one logical statement. Click on "New item" and choose "add row." Configure the second condition row by adding the same expression from the first row for the left-side comparison value. Set the comparison operator to "is less or equal to," and then for the right-side comparison, type 6. Then change the logical operators for the rows from AND to OR:

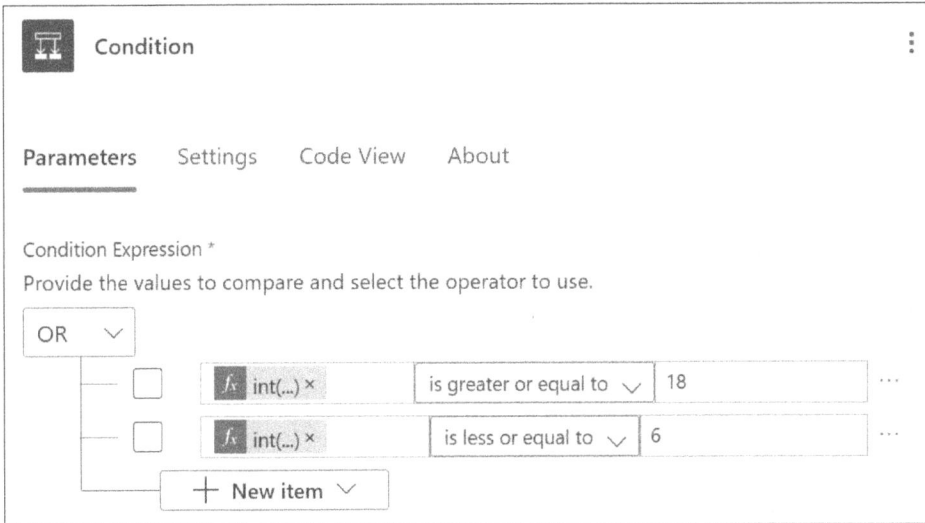

If the condition is met, under True, add an action to get the night shift item from the SharePoint list. Search for the SharePoint connector and select the "Get items" action. You may need to sign in and authenticate your SharePoint account. Configure the Site Address (the relevant site URL where the warehouse doorkeepers list resides) and List Name (the SharePoint list name) action parameters. Now, open the "Advanced parameters" drop-down and check the Filter Query parameter. Then, type `Title eq 'Night'`. The filter query will get all the items where the Title column is equal to "Night." However, only one item in the SharePoint list meets this query. Finally, rename the action to "Get items - Night shift":

Then, right after the "Get items - Night shift" action, add an action to set the Shift Id variable with the shift item ID in SharePoint. Search for the Variable connector and select the "Set variable" action. Rename the action to "Set variable - Night."

Configure the action parameters as follows:

- *Name*: Select Shift Id.
- *Value*: Use the following expression:

```
first(outputs('Get_items_-_Night_shift')?['body/value'])?['Id']
```

The expression in the Value field will get the first item's ID. If the condition is not met, under False, add an action to get the day shift item from the SharePoint list. Search for the SharePoint connector and select the "Get items" action. Configure the Site Address (the relevant site URL where the warehouse doorkeepers list resides) and List Name (the SharePoint list name) action parameters. Do the same for the action under True. Now, open the "Advanced parameters" drop-down and check the Filter Query parameter. Then, type `Title eq 'Day'`. The filter query will get all the items where the Title column is equal to "Day." However, only one item in the SharePoint list meets this query. Rename the action to "Get items - Day shift":

Right after the "Get items - Day shift" action, add an action to set the Shift Id variable with the shift item ID in SharePoint. Search for the Variable connector and select the "Set variable" action. Rename the action to "Set variable - Day."

Configure the action parameters as follows:

- *Name*: Select Shift Id.
- *Value*: Use the following expression:

```
first(outputs('Get_items_-_Day_shift')?['body/value'])?['Id']
```

After the condition action, add an action to get the shift item by ID. Search for the SharePoint connector and select the "Get items" action:

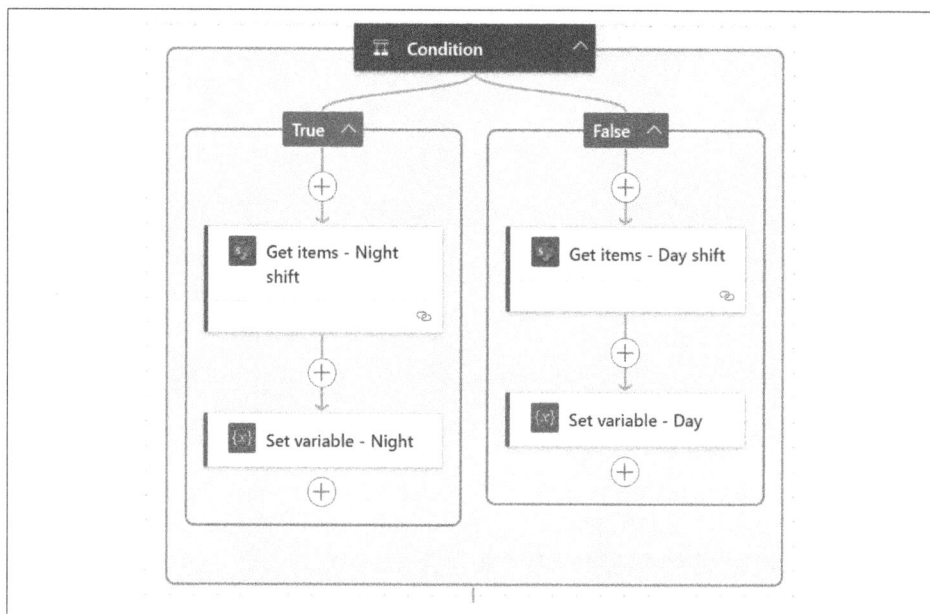

Configure the Site Address (the relevant site URL where the warehouse doorkeepers list resides) and List Name (the SharePoint list name) action parameters. Then, set the Id parameter to Shift Id variable from the dynamic content. Rename the action to "Get item - Working Shift":

Now, add an action to loop through the doorkeepers of that shift. Search for the Control connector and select the "Apply to each" action. Configure the action by choosing Doorkeepers from the "Get item - Working Shift" action dynamic content:

In the "Apply to each" action scope, add an action to get the doorkeeper user profile. Search for the Office 365 Users connector and select the "Get user profile (V2)" action. You may need to sign in and authenticate your Office 365 Users account. Configure the action by setting the User (UPN) parameter to Email (the doorkeeper's email address) from the "Get item - Working Shift" action dynamic content:

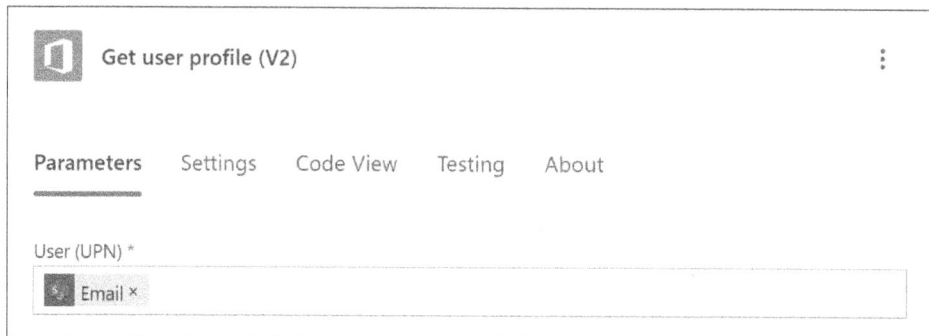

Finally, add an action to send an SMS to the corresponding doorkeeper user profile. Search for the Twilio connector and then choose the Send Text Message (SMS) action. You must create a connection to your Twilio account to use the Twilio service. Configure your connection by giving it a name, and then provide your Twilio Account Id and Twilio Access Token, which you'll find under Keys & Credentials > "API keys & tokens" in your account.

Configure the action parameters as follows:

- *From Phone Number*: a pre-configured phone number in the Twilio service to send SMS notifications from
- *To Phone Number*: {Mobile Phone} (from "Get user profile (V2)")
- *Text*:

      Hi {Display Name},

      Warehouse delivery has arrived and is waiting by the door.
      Please head over to open for them.

      Thank you,
      Warehouse delivery services

where {Display Name} is dynamic content from the "Get user profile (V2)" action.

Send Text Message (SMS)

Parameters | Settings | Code view | Testing | About

From Phone Number *

+12████████

To Phone Number *

1 Mobile Phone ×

Text *

Hi 1 Display Name × ,

Warehouse delivery has arrived and is waiting by the door. Please head over to open for them.

Thank you,
Warehouse delivery services

Name your flow, save it, and test it to ensure it works as expected.

See Also

- Recipe 9.1, "Taking a Sick Leave"
- Recipe 9.2, "Requesting a Daily Leave"
- Recipe 9.4, "Sending a Document for (Ad Hoc) Approval in SharePoint"
- Recipe 9.5, "Registering a Guest Visit"

9.4 Sending a Document for (Ad Hoc) Approval in SharePoint

Problem

You want to start an (ad hoc) approval process for a specific document in a SharePoint library.

Solution

Create a Power Automate flow that triggers manually on a selected file in a Share-Point library, takes approval details parameters, starts an approval process, and then sends an email to the approval initiator upon approval/rejection.

Discussion

The flow handles the approval request, sending it to the designated approvers and capturing their decisions. Upon approval or rejection, the initiator receives an auto-mated email notification with the outcome, ensuring timely communication.

Unlike the previous recipes in this chapter, this flow can only be triggered manually from a SharePoint library. However, it can be applied for lists and libraries (items and documents) in SharePoint as well.

Before building this flow, ensure you have created a SharePoint document library. After you create the library, add an Approval Status field (optional, choice field) with the following choices:

- Awaiting approval
- Approved
- Rejected

To create a new flow in Power Automate, begin by going to the Power Automate por-tal (*https://oreil.ly/O-MRf*) and signing in with your Microsoft or organization's account. Ensure that you're in the default Power Automate environment, as manually triggered flows from SharePoint can be activated only if they are created in this envi-ronment. Next, click on "My flows" in the left navigation bar and select "New flow." Since you want to initiate the flow for a selected file in SharePoint, choose the "Instant cloud flow" option. Then, select the trigger related to a selected file in Share-Point by picking the "For a selected file" trigger and clicking Create. Finally, configure the trigger parameters, including the Site Address, which is the relevant site URL where the document library resides, and Library Name, which refers to the name of the SharePoint library.

Configure the trigger to take the following inputs (parameters) by clicking on "Add an input" under the Parameters tab for the trigger:

- Add an Email input and rename it to "Approver."
- Add a Text input and rename it to "Comments."

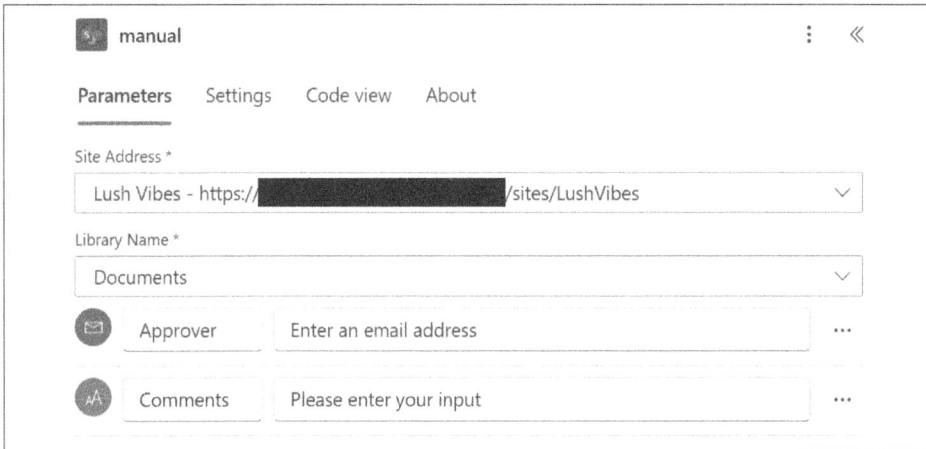

Now, add an action to get the initiator user profile. Search for the Office 365 Users connector and select the "Get user profile (V2)" action. You may need to sign in and authenticate your Office 365 Users account.

Configure the action by setting the User (UPN) parameter to the following expression:

```
triggerOutputs()?['headers']?['x-ms-user-id']
```

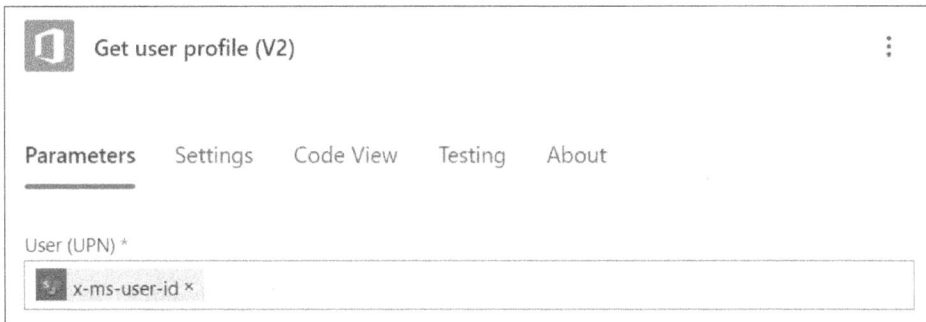

This expression will get the initiator's email address from the trigger. Next, add an action to update the SharePoint library item with the corresponding approval status, which is awaiting approval. Search for the SharePoint connector and select the "Update item" action. Configure the action parameters, including Site Address (the relevant site URL where the SharePoint document library resides), List Name (the SharePoint document library name), and Id (the ID of the document item that triggered the flow). Now, open the "Advanced parameters" drop-down and check the

"Approval status Value" parameter (the column indicating the approval status of the document item). Select "Awaiting approval":

Add an action to start and wait for the approval process from your approver (the input parameter in the trigger). Search for the Approvals connector and select the "Start and wait for an approval" action.

Fill the approval action parameters as follows (the text in braces is dynamic content):

- *Approval Type*: Approve/Reject - First to respond
- *Title*: Document approval (or the text of your choice)
- *Assigned To*: {Approver} (the input parameter from the trigger)
- *Details*:

    ## A new document approval request submitted by {Display Name}
    awaiting your approval

    Comments:
    {Comments}

where {Display Name} is dynamic content from the "Get user profile (V2)" action and {Comments} is from the trigger.

- *Item Link*: {itemUrl} (from the trigger)
- *Item Link Description*: {fileName} (from the trigger)

Start and wait for an approval   ⋮

Parameters   Settings   Code View   Testing   About
━━━━━━━━━

Approval Type *

Approve/Reject - First to respond   ⌄

Title *

Document approval

Assigned To *

Approver ×

Details

A new document approval request submitted by Display Name × awaiting
your approval

Comments:
Comments ×

Item Link

itemUrl ×

Item Link Description

fileName ×

Next, add a new action, search for "Control," and then from the list of actions, choose Condition. Configure the condition action by selecting the Outcome property from the "Start and wait for an approval" dynamic content for the left-side comparison value. Make sure the comparison operator is set to "is equal to," and then for the right-side comparison, type Approve:

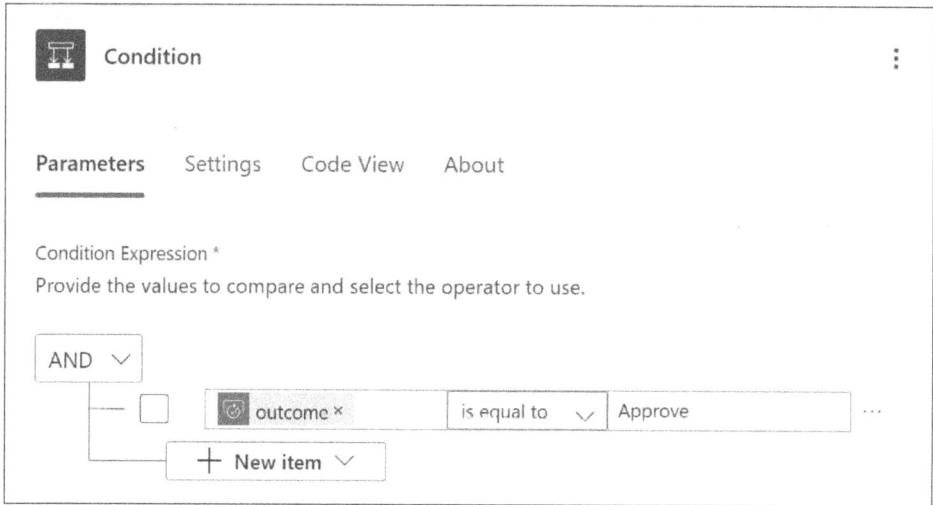

Condition

Parameters · Settings · Code View · About

Condition Expression *
Provide the values to compare and select the operator to use.

AND ⌄

☐ ⊙ outcome × | is equal to ⌄ | Approve | …

＋ New item ⌄

If the condition is met, under True, add an action to update the document approval status with the corresponding approval status, Approved. Search for the SharePoint connector and select the "Update item" action. Configure the action parameters, including Site Address (the relevant site URL where the document library resides), List Name (the SharePoint document library name), and Id (the ID of the document item that triggered the flow). Now, open the "Advanced parameters" drop-down and check the "Approval status Value" parameter (the column indicating the approval status of the document item). Select "Approved":

Update item - Approved

Parameters   Settings   Code view   Testing   About

Site Address *

Lush Vibes - https:// ███████████ /sites/LushVibes   ⌄

List Name *

Documents   ✕

Id *

⬚ ID ✕

Advanced parameters

Showing 2 of 6   ⌄   Show all   Clear all

Approver comments

_fx_ first(...) ✕   ✕

Approval status Value

Approved   ⌄   ✕

If the condition is not met, under False, add an action to update the document approval status with the corresponding approval status, Rejected. Search for the SharePoint connector and select the "Update item" action. Configure the action parameters, including Site Address (the relevant site URL where the document library resides), List Name (the SharePoint document library), and Id (the ID of the document that triggered the flow). Then, open the "Advanced parameters" drop-down and check the "Approval status Value" parameter (the column indicating the approval status of the document item). Select "Rejected":

Update item - Rejected

Parameters   Settings   Code view   Testing   About

Site Address *

| Lush Vibes - https://████████████████/sites/LushVibes | ⌄ |

List Name *

| Documents | ✕ |

Id *

| 🔷 ID ✕ |

Advanced parameters

| Showing 2 of 6 | ⌄ | Show all | Clear all |

Approver comments

| _fx_ first(...) ✕ | ✕ |

Approval status Value

| Rejected | ⌄ | ✕ |

After the condition, add an action to send an email to the flow initiator. Search for the Office 365 Outlook connector and select the "Send an email (V2)" action. You may need to sign in and authenticate your Office 365 Outlook account.

Fill the "Send an email (V2)" action parameters as follows (the text in braces is dynamic content):

- *To*: {Mail} (from "Get user profile (V2)")
- *Subject*: Document approval :: {fileName} (from the trigger)
- *Body*:

    Hi {Display Name},

    Your document approval request "{fileName}" has been {*expression1*}.

    The approver left you the following comments:

```
{expression2}

Thank you.
```

where {Display Name} and {fileName} are dynamic content from the trigger. {expression1} is as follows:

```
if(equals(body('Start_and_wait_for_an_approval')?['outcome'],'Approve'),
'approved','rejected')
```

And {expression2} is:

```
first(body('Start_and_wait_for_an_approval')?['responses'])?['comments']
```

Finally, name your flow, save it, and test it to ensure it works as expected.

See Also

- Recipe 9.1, "Taking a Sick Leave"
- Recipe 9.2, "Requesting a Daily Leave"

- Recipe 9.3, "Simulating a Warehouse Doorbell"
- Recipe 9.5, "Registering a Guest Visit"

9.5 Registering a Guest Visit

Problem

You want to register guests' visits at the reception area through a Power Apps app and trigger a Power Automate flow on registration to notify visitees.

Solution

Create a manually triggered flow from a Power Apps app that receives registration information details and sends an SMS to the visitee upon registration.

Discussion

This automation improves the efficiency of the reception area by digitizing the visitor registration process, reducing the need for manual recordkeeping and minimizing wait times for guests. The automated SMS notification ensures that visitees are immediately aware of their guests' arrival, leading to more timely and organized meetings. This can enhance overall visitor satisfaction and improve your organization's professionalism.

This recipe is simple and straightforward. However, additional aspects can be added to this automation to ensure better data management and security. For example, storing all visitor records digitally makes it easy to retrieve and analyze visitor data when needed. You can use this data to maintain security protocols, track visitor patterns, and generate reports. Overall, this solution not only streamlines visitor management but also enhances communication and operational efficiency within your organization.

Before creating this flow, make sure that you have created the registration app described in section "Creating a Registration App (Power Apps)" on page 357.

For reference purposes, the app takes three pieces of information from the visitor:

- Name (text)
- Cell phone number (number)
- Visitee (text; user ID)

For SMS notifications, I'm using Twilio as the service provider for this example. Therefore, you need to subscribe to the Twilio SMS service for this scenario.

Refer to Chapter 3 to learn how to create a free trial subscription to Twilio.

To create a new flow in Power Automate, start by visiting the Power Automate portal (*https://oreil.ly/O-MRf*) and signing in with your Microsoft or organization's account. Ensure that you're in the same Power Automate environment where you created the registration app. Next, click on "My flows" in the left navigation bar and select "New flow" to begin creating a new flow. Since you want to initiate the flow from Power Apps, choose the "Instant cloud flow" option. Then, select the trigger related to Power Apps by picking the "When Power Apps calls a flow (V2)" trigger and click Create to proceed.

Configure the trigger to take the following inputs (parameters) by clicking on "Add an input" under the Parameters tab for the trigger:

- Add a Text input and rename it to "Guest."
- Add a Number input and rename it to "Mobile."
- Add a Text input and rename it to "Visitee Id."

These parameters will pass from the Power Apps registration app. Now, add an action to get the visitee user profile. Search for the Office 365 Users connector and select the "Get user profile (V2)" action. You may need to sign in and authenticate your Office 365 account. Configure the action by setting the User (UPN) parameter to Visitee Id input from the trigger:

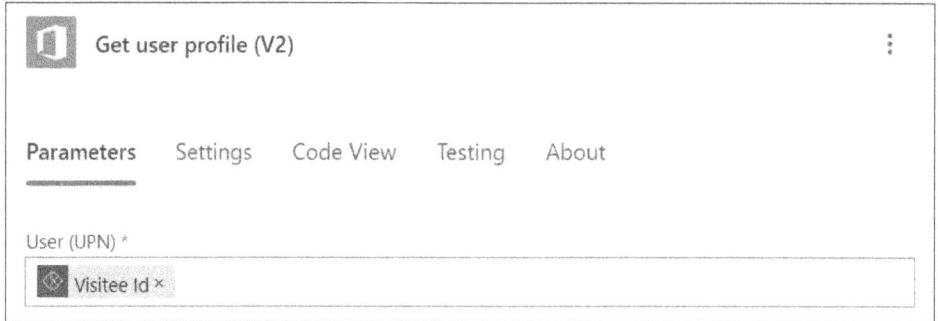

Finally, add an action to send an SMS to the corresponding visitee. Search for the Twilio connector, and then choose the Send Text Message (SMS) action. You must create a connection to your Twilio account to use the Twilio service. Configure your connection by giving it a name, and then provide your Twilio Account Id and Twilio Access Token, which you'll find under Keys & Credentials > "API keys & tokens" in your account.

Configure the action parameters as follows:

- *From Phone Number*: a pre-configured phone number in the Twilio service to send SMS notifications from
- *To Phone Number*: {Mobile Phone} (from "Get user profile (V2)")
- *Text*:

    ```
    Hi {Display Name},

    Your visitor {Guest} has arrived and is waiting at the reception desk.
    You can contact your visitor through this number {Mobile}.

    Thank you,
    Reception desk services
    ```

    where {Display Name} is dynamic content from the "Get user profile (V2)" action and {Guest} and {Mobile} are from the "When Power Apps calls a flow (V2)" trigger.

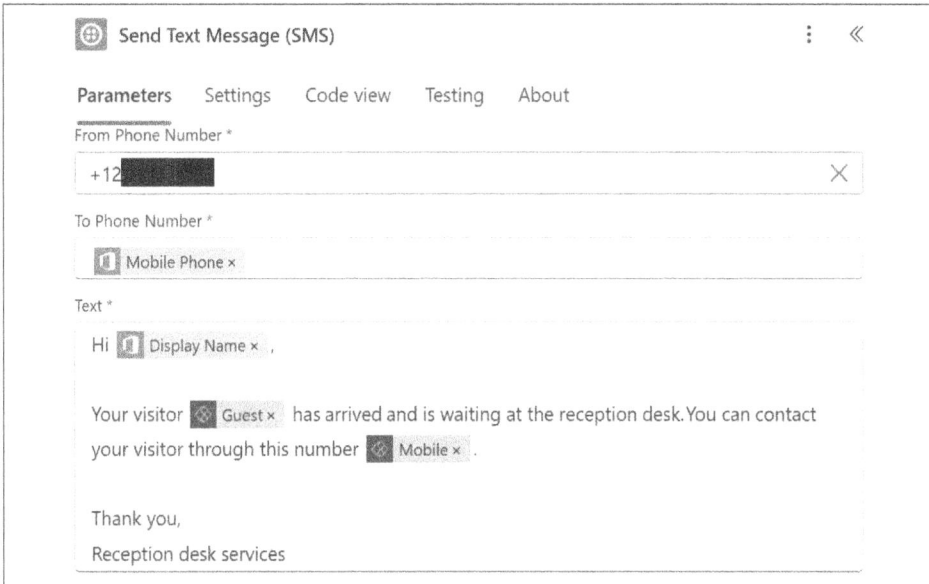

Give your flow a name, save it, and test it to ensure it works as expected.

See Also

- Recipe 9.1, "Taking a Sick Leave"
- Recipe 9.2, "Requesting a Daily Leave"
- Recipe 9.3, "Simulating a Warehouse Doorbell"
- Recipe 9.4, "Sending a Document for (Ad Hoc) Approval in SharePoint"

Conclusion

Instant flows in Power Automate provide a powerful and adaptable solution for on-demand automation. By offering control, flexibility, and ease of use, they enable users to respond to real-time needs efficiently, simplify tasks, and enhance productivity. This capability empowers individuals and organizations to bridge the gap between human decision making and automated processes, driving smarter, more agile workflows.

CHAPTER 10

Power Automate and Dataverse

In this chapter, I'll give an overview of Microsoft Dataverse. Then, I'll explain how Dataverse is used for storing and managing data in structured tables and highlight its key features, such as security, scalability, and compliance. I'll also describe how Dataverse integrates with Power Automate to automate workflows and business processes, making it easier to manage data-driven tasks without extensive coding. Finally, I'll go through common and simple useful recipes where Power Automate and Dataverse go hand-in-hand, enhancing productivity.

Dataverse at a Glance

Microsoft Dataverse is a cloud-based data source designed to store and manage data used by business applications. It serves as the underlying data platform for Microsoft's Power Platform, including Power Automate. Dataverse provides a secure, scalable, and structured environment where you can manage your data, create relationships between entities, enforce business rules, and interact with other data services, such as Dynamics 365 and Azure services.

At its core, Microsoft Dataverse is a relational data source. It allows you to store data in a structured format using tables. Each table contains rows (records) and columns (fields), similar to how data is organized in traditional databases like SQL Server or Oracle Database Server. The platform provides built-in support for creating relationships between tables, allowing for more complex data models and queries. It also integrates seamlessly with other Microsoft cloud services and offers APIs for integration with third-party systems.

Microsoft Dataverse was initially introduced as the Common Data Service (CDS) in 2016. CDS was part of the Power Platform, which was created to help organizations build custom business solutions without requiring deep development expertise. Over time, CDS evolved to include a richer set of features, supporting more complex data models and integrating with a broader range of services. In late 2020, Microsoft rebranded CDS as Dataverse, reflecting its broader capabilities and future potential as a key component of the Microsoft ecosystem. This shift was not just in name but also in functionality. Dataverse began to align more closely with other Microsoft data services, such as Azure Data Lake and Microsoft Fabric, making it more flexible for modern data needs.

Dataverse offers several technical advantages that make it a robust platform for managing business data. It allows users to create structured data models, supporting relationships between different tables. This enables the development of complex business logic and workflows. Tables can be customized with calculated fields, rollups, and different data types, making them highly flexible.

One of Dataverse's strengths is its strong security model. It allows administrators to define role-based access control (RBAC) at various levels, including row-level and field-level security. This ensures that sensitive data is protected while allowing users to interact with the data they're authorized to access.

Dataverse's deep integration with Power Automate (and other Power Platform underlying services) provides a seamless experience for users looking to build custom applications, automate workflows, and generate business insights. For example, Power Automate can use Dataverse as a backend to store automation data.

Dataverse supports custom plug-ins and workflows, allowing developers to extend its capabilities. It also offers a rich set of APIs, which enable programmatic access to data and operations. This makes it a suitable platform for both citizen developers (using Power Platform tools) and professional developers (using custom code).

Built on top of Azure, Dataverse inherits the scalability and performance features of the cloud. It can handle small data sets for lightweight applications or scale up to manage large volumes of data for enterprise solutions.

Finally, Dataverse offers compliance with various industry standards, such as General Data Protection Regulation (GDPR) and others. It provides auditing and logging features to ensure data integrity and traceability.

In summary, Microsoft Dataverse is more than just a data source. It's a platform designed to handle complex business data, enforce rules, integrate with multiple services, and provide a secure and scalable foundation for business applications. Over the years, it has evolved from a simple common data model to a powerful, enterprise-grade data platform that can be used by both developers and business users alike.

Power Automate and Dataverse Integration

Microsoft Dataverse and Power Automate are tightly integrated, enabling automation of workflows and processes that interact with data stored in Dataverse. This integration allows users to trigger workflows based on specific data events, such as creating, updating, or deleting records in Dataverse. For example, when a new record is added to a table in Dataverse, Power Automate can trigger a flow to perform tasks such as sending notifications, updating related records, or enforcing business rules. This event-driven integration provides a powerful way to automate routine tasks and ensure that business processes run smoothly without manual intervention.

Beyond event triggers, Power Automate can manipulate data in Dataverse by creating, updating, retrieving, or deleting records. This functionality simplifies data management, as workflows can automatically handle data modifications, eliminating the need for custom code. The ability to work with Dataverse data in a structured, automated manner enhances consistency in business operations.

The conditional logic and looping capabilities in Power Automate can be applied to Dataverse data. This allows workflows to process multiple records at once, enforce conditional logic, or branch based on data values in the Dataverse tables. This flexibility is particularly useful for complex business logic or when interacting with large data sets. For example, a flow might loop through a set of records in Dataverse, identify those that meet certain conditions, such as overdue tasks, and then send reminder emails or escalate actions based on predefined business rules.

One of the most significant advantages of integrating Dataverse with Power Automate is the ability to connect Dataverse with other services, both within the Microsoft ecosystem and with third-party applications. Power Automate provides a vast library of connectors, allowing workflows to synchronize data between systems, trigger actions across multiple platforms, or move data between different cloud services. This seamless integration reduces manual data entry and improves efficiency across platforms.

The integration between Microsoft Dataverse and Power Automate provides a highly flexible and powerful platform for automating data-driven business processes. With event triggers, data manipulation capabilities, conditional logic, and broad integration with other services, Power Automate enables users to streamline their workflows and ensure that their Dataverse data is managed efficiently, making this integration a strong solution for both simple and complex business scenarios.

10.1 Following Up with Newly Added Customers

Problem

You need to follow up on records added to your Dataverse customers table and create a task with a due date to track the follow-up process.

Solution

Create a flow that is automatically triggered when a new record (customer) is added to your Dataverse table, and then create a Microsoft To Do task with the corresponding data.

Discussion

Creating a cloud flow that automatically generates a task in Microsoft To Do when a new record is added to a Dataverse table ensures that follow-up actions are never missed.

These new records can come from various sources, such as a Power App submission, an integration with another system, or manual data entry in Dataverse. Whether it's for sales or customer service, every new record—like a lead, inquiry, or support ticket—requires timely attention. Automating task creation removes the need for manual tracking and ensures that you stay organized and on top of critical tasks without any additional effort.

This workflow also helps you reduce human error and increases efficiency by standardizing how tasks are generated and tracked. By linking the task directly to the record's data, you can easily access relevant information to take immediate action. This way, you can improve response times, manage higher volumes of records, and ultimately provide better service to your customers.

Before starting to build this flow, make sure that you have created a custom table in Dataverse in the environment of your choice. To create a Dataverse table, you can follow the steps in the section "Creating a Custom Table in Dataverse" on page 363. Begin by defining the following columns:

- Primary Name Column (e.g., "Customer Name")
- Email (single line of text; email format)
- Phone Number (single line of text; phone number format)
- Company (single line of text; text format)
- Follow-up notes (single line of text; text area format)

Alternatively, you can use the table named "Contact" that comes with the default Dataverse data store. Go to the Power Automate portal (*https://oreil.ly/O-MRf*). Sign in with your Microsoft account or your organization's account. On the lefthand navigation pane, select Create. Choose Automated cloud flow. In the "Choose your flow's trigger" field, search for and select the Dataverse trigger "When a row is added, modified or deleted." Then, click Create. Set up the trigger by choosing the Change Type drop-down, then select Added (since you want the flow to trigger only when a new record is added). Choose the table name you created earlier ("Customers"). Finally, select Organization in the Scope, unless you need a different scope. Optionally, you can add a filter if you want the flow to trigger only under certain conditions (e.g., only when a customer is from a specific country):

Add a new step to create a task in Microsoft To Do. In the search bar, type `Microsoft To Do`. Then, choose "Add a to-do (V3)."

Fill the "Add a to-do (V3)" action parameters as follows (the text in braces is dynamic content from the trigger):

- *To-Do List*: Choose Tasks. Alternatively, you can create your own to-do list under Microsoft To Do.
- *Title*: `Follow up with {Customer Name}`

- *Due Date*: addDays(utcNow(),14) (an expression returning the date two weeks from now). Alternatively, you can create a column to make the due date dynamic based on a column in the "Customer" table.

- *Body Content*:

  ```
  Here is some extra information to help with this task:
  Customer: {Customer Name}
  Company: {Company}
  Phone: {Phone number}
  Email: {Email}
  Notes: {Follow up notes}
  ```

Add a to-do (V3)   ⋮

Parameters   Settings   Code view   Testing   About

To-Do List *

| Tasks | ⌄ |

Title *

| Follow up with 🔘 Customer Name × |

Due Date

| YYYY-MM-DDThh:mm:ss |

Reminder Date-Time

| YYYY-MM-DDThh:mm:ss |

Importance

| *Low, normal or high.* | ⌄ |

Status

| *Indicates state or progress of the to-do - not started, in progress, completed, waiting o...* | ⌄ |

Body Content

| ↺ ↻   Normal ⌄   Arial   ⌄   15px ⌄   **B**   *I*   U̲   A   ◬   ∞   ⟨⟩ |

Here is some extra infomation to help with this task:
Customer: 🔘 Customer Name × .
Company: 🔘 Company ×
Phone: 🔘 Phone Number ×
Email: 🔘 Email ×
Notes: 🔘 Follow up notes ×

Name your flow, save it, and test it to ensure it works as expected.

See Also

- Recipe 10.2, "Generating a Weekly Report on Newly Added Leads"
- Recipe 10.3, "Syncing Service Request Tickets from Dataverse to SharePoint"

10.2 Generating a Weekly Report on Newly Added Leads

Problem

You want to create a weekly report containing newly added leads in your Dataverse table and then send it to your manager (or sales management).

Solution

Create a weekly scheduled cloud flow that lists rows in Dataverse, filtering by the creation date to get lead records added within the last week, and then emails the information to your manager (or the stakeholder of your choice).

Discussion

This flow is useful for keeping your manager informed about new data entries without manual effort. If your organization collects new customer registrations, leads, or other important information daily, weekly, or monthly, this automation ensures that everyone stays updated with a simple email. It saves time by eliminating the need to check data sources or systems manually, especially when tracking multiple records each week.

Additionally, it helps you maintain accountability and quick action. By having a weekly report sent directly to the inbox of relevant stakeholders, you make sure no new records are overlooked. It's an efficient way to keep everyone aligned and make sure that follow-ups or next steps are handled promptly.

Before starting to build this flow, make sure that you have created a custom table in Dataverse in the environment of your choice. To create a Dataverse table, you can follow the steps in the section "Creating a Custom Table in Dataverse" on page 363. Start by defining the following columns:

- Primary Name Column (e.g., "Lead Name")
- Email (single line of text; email format)
- Phone Number (single line of text; phone number format)
- Company (single line of text; text format)

Alternatively, you can use any table of your choice to track newly added data entries. Go to the Power Automate portal (*https://oreil.ly/O-MRf*). Sign in with your Microsoft account or your organization's account. On the lefthand navigation pane, select Create. Choose "Scheduled cloud flow." In the Recurrence section, set the start date and time to the desired time. Set the frequency to Week and the interval to 1. Unselect all days except Friday under "On these days." Then, click Create:

Add a new action to list all rows. Then search for Dataverse and choose the List Rows action. In the Table Name parameter, select the Dataverse table you created earlier (e.g., "Leads").

In the Filter Rows parameter, enter the following OData filter to retrieve only records created in the last week (seven days):

```
createdon gt '{expression1}'
```

where {*expression1*} is as follows:

```
addDays(utcNow(), -7)
```

This filter ensures that only records created in the last seven days are retrieved. Remember that to make this flow meaningful and the data consistent, the recurring interval must match the filter elapsed time since the last run. For example, if you want to generate this report daily, then change the recurrence to daily and then change the OData filter expression to -1 instead of -7.

Next, add a new action and search for "Initialize variable." Name the variable HTML Table. Set the Type to String. Then, enter the following in Value:

```
<table>
  <tr>
    <th>Lead Name</th>
    <th>Email</th>
    <th>Phone</th>
    <th>Company</th>
    <th>Created On</th>
  </tr>
```

```
{x}   Initialize variable                                              ⋮   ≪

Parameters    Settings    Code view    About

Name *
HTML Table

Type *
String                                                                    ∨

Value
<table>
 <tr>
  <th>Lead Name</th>
  <th>Email</th>
  <th>Phone</th>
  <th>Company</th>
  <th>Created On</th>
 </tr>
```

Now you need to iterate over the records. Add a new action, search for "Apply to each," and select it. In the Select An Output From Previous Steps parameter, choose value from the dynamic content from the List Rows action (this refers to the list of new records):

```
⊡   Apply to each                                                       ⋮   ≪

Parameters    Settings    Code view    About

Select An Output From Previous Steps *
 ⊙ body/value ×
```

Next, inside the "Apply to each" loop, add a new action, search for "Append to string variable," and choose it. Set Name to the variable you initialized earlier (e.g., "HTML Table").

In the Value parameter field, add dynamic content to format each record into an HTML table row as follows (the text in braces is dynamic content from the List Rows action):

```
<tr>
  <td>{Lead Name}</td>
  <td>{Email}</td>
  <td>{Phone Number}</td>
  <td>{Company}</td>
  <td>{Created On}</td>
</tr>
```

After the loop, add another "Append to string variable" action to close the HTML table. Set Name to the variable you initialized earlier (e.g., "HTML Table"). Then, type `</table>` in Value:

Finally, add an action to send an email to whom this might concern. Search for "Send an email (V2)" under Office 365 Outlook and choose it. Next, fill the "Send an email

"(V2)" action parameters as follows (the text in braces is dynamic content from the variable you initialized earlier):

- *To*: Your manager
- *Subject*: `Leads :: Weekly Report`
- *Body*:

  `Hi,`

  `Below is a report of the leads added in the past seven days.`

  `{HTML Table}`

  `Thank you.`

Finally, name your flow, save it, and test it to ensure it works as expected.

See Also

- Recipe 7.4, "Sending a Report of Existing Teams and Channels"
- Recipe 10.1, "Following Up with Newly Added Customers"
- Recipe 10.3, "Syncing Service Request Tickets from Dataverse to SharePoint"

10.3 Syncing Service Request Tickets from Dataverse to SharePoint

Problem

You want to automatically sync service request tickets (created or updated) in Dataverse to a SharePoint list.

Solution

Create an automated flow that triggers when a record is added or updated in your Dataverse Tickets table and then creates or updates the corresponding ticket with the relevant data.

Discussion

This flow is useful when you need to keep data synchronized between Dataverse and SharePoint, especially if different teams work on different platforms. For example, if one team manages service request tickets in Dataverse and another tracks them in SharePoint, this flow ensures that everyone has the latest information without needing to manually update both systems.

Additionally, this automation eliminates the risk of missing or inconsistent data across platforms. It saves time by reducing manual data entry and minimizes errors, making sure both systems stay in sync. This is especially helpful in larger organizations where collaboration across multiple platforms is necessary.

Before starting to build this flow, make sure that you have created a custom table in Dataverse in the environment of your choice. To create a Dataverse table, you can follow the steps in the section "Creating a Custom Table in Dataverse" on page 363.

Begin by defining the following columns:

- Primary Name Column (e.g., "Id")
- Description (single line of text; text area format)
- Status (choice), with three choices:
  - Open (set as default)

— In progress

— Closed

- Due date (date and time; date-only format)

Create a ticket-tracking list (custom list) in SharePoint to sync data into from the table in Dataverse. Add the following columns:

- Title (single line of text; you get this column by default when creating any custom list; use for the ID)
- Description (multiple lines of text)
- Status (string)
- Due date (date and time)

Go to the Power Automate portal (*https://oreil.ly/O-MRf*). Sign in with your Microsoft account or your organization's account. On the lefthand navigation pane, select Create. Choose "Automated cloud flow." In the "Choose your flow's trigger" field, search for and select the Dataverse trigger "When a row is added, modified or deleted." Then, click Create. Set up the trigger by choosing the Change Type dropdown and selecting "Added or Modified." Choose the table name you created earlier (Tickets). Finally, select Organization in the Scope, unless you need a different scope:

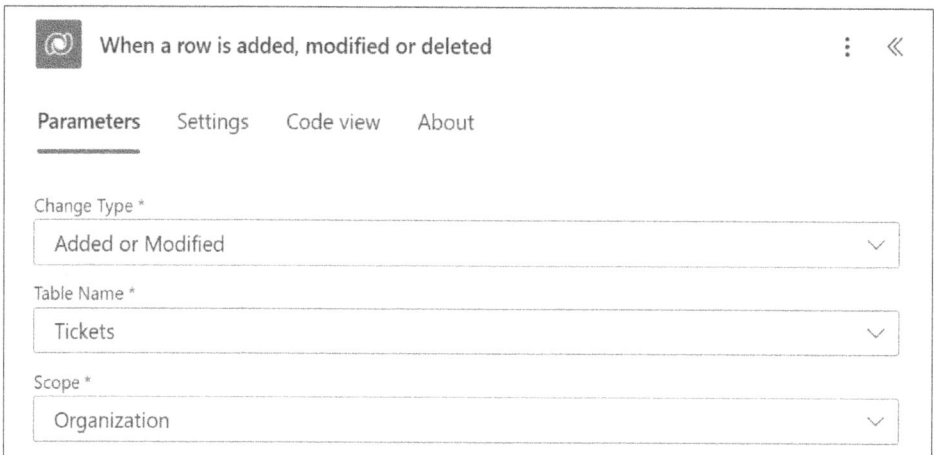

First, you want to check if the ticket exists in the SharePoint list. Add a new action (step) and search for SharePoint, then choose the "Get items" action. You may need to sign in and authenticate your SharePoint account. Then configure the Site Address (the relevant site URL where the tickets list resides) and List Name (the SharePoint tickets list) action parameters.

One additional parameter needs to be set. Click on "Advanced parameters" in the "Get items" action, then select and set the Filter Query parameter as follows:

```
Title eq '{Id}'
```

The following table explains the elements of the Filter Query:

Query element	Description
Title	SharePoint column internal name
eq	"Equals" comparison operator
'{Id}'	The value of the Id column from the Tickets Dataverse table

Then, add a new action (step), search for "Control," and then select the Control actions. From the list of actions, choose Condition. The condition will ensure that the following steps will execute only if there are documents to be archived. Otherwise, it terminates the flow.

Configure the condition action using the following expression for the left-side comparison value:

```
length(outputs('Get_items')?['body/value'])
```

This expression uses the `length()` function to check whether the value from the "Get items" action contains items. Make sure the comparison operator is set to "is greater than," and then for the right-side comparison, type 0:

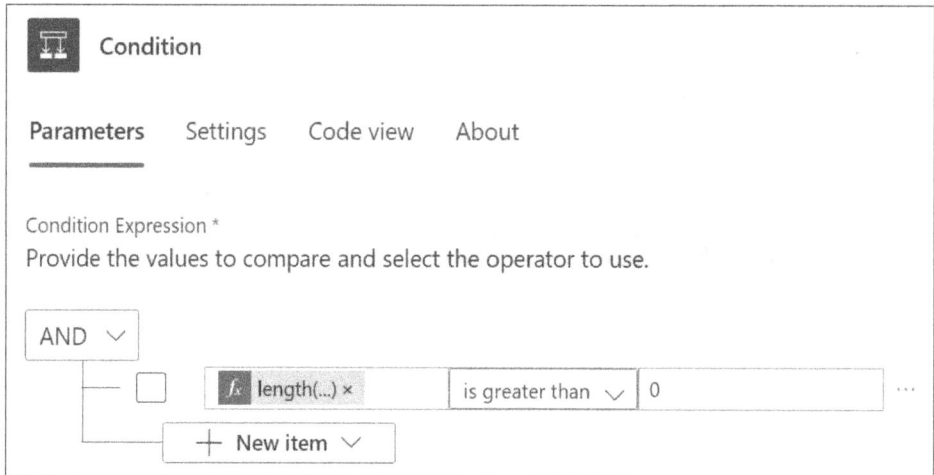

If the condition is not met, under False, add an action to add a new item in Share-Point. Add a new action (step) and search for "SharePoint." Choose "Create item."

Configure the action's parameters, including the Site Address (the relevant site URL where the tickets list resides) and List Name (the list where the ticket item will be created), and then set the SharePoint item values to their respective values from the trigger ("Dataverse record"):

- *Title*: {Id}
- *Description*: {Description}
- *Due date*: {Due Date}

The Status column in Dataverse is of type Choice. If you use the column as is from the trigger, it will use the corresponding value, not the label value. To get the label value, use the following expression:

```
triggerBody()?['_cr304_status_label']
```

The internal name of the status column in Dataverse is `cr304_status`. However, the label value is formatted as `_internalColumnName_label`, where you don't get this out-of-the-box, and you need to use an expression to get a hold of it. Now, if the condition is met under True, add an action to get the specific ticket item in SharePoint. Search for the SharePoint connector and select the "Get item" action.

Configure the Site Address (the relevant site URL where the tickets list resides) and List Name (the SharePoint list name) action parameters. Then, set the Id parameter to the following expression:

```
first(outputs('Get_items')?['body/value'])?['ID']
```

Get item   ⋮   «

Parameters   Settings   Code view   Testing   About
──────────

Site Address *

Lush Vibes - https://████████████████████/sites/LushVibes   ⌄

List Name *

Tickets   ⌄

Id *

fx first(...) ×

This expression will get the first item in the collection dynamic content from the "Get items" action and then return/select the ID value only. Finally, add an action to update the corresponding SharePoint ticket item with the corresponding data from Dataverse. Search for the SharePoint connector and select the "Update item" action. Then configure the action parameters, including Site Address (the relevant site URL where the tickets list resides), List Name (the SharePoint list name), Id (the ID of the SharePoint item from the "Get item" action), Description, Status, and "Due date" (use the same expression you used for the "Create item"):

Give your flow a name, save it, and test it to ensure it works as expected.

See Also

- Recipe 10.1, "Following Up with Newly Added Customers"
- Recipe 10.2, "Generating a Weekly Report on Newly Added Leads"

Conclusion

Power Automate and Dataverse offer a powerful combination for simplifying business processes, automating tasks, and keeping data synchronized across platforms. Through the integration of these tools, users can ease daily tasks, such as creating records, reporting on data, and syncing data, all while ensuring data consistency.

Beyond basic automations, Dataverse can be used in more advanced scenarios, especially within Dynamics 365. For instance, businesses can leverage Dataverse to handle complex workflows involving multiple tables, automate data validation, and create dynamic connections between various tables, helping you to focus more on strategic thinking rather than manual data management.

You can tailor workflows to align with specific business requirements, automate interactions between different departments, and maintain consistent data between multiple systems. Whether it's managing customer relationships, tracking tickets, or handling inventory, Power Automate and Dataverse provide the infrastructure for efficient business processes.

As organizations grow and their processes become more complex, the ability to scale and customize these automations becomes even more valuable. Dataverse's role in handling larger data sets and supporting more intricate workflows within Dynamics 365 opens up opportunities in advanced scenarios.

CHAPTER 11

Power Automate and Planner

In this chapter, I will explore the evolution and capabilities of Microsoft Planner, a task management tool within the Microsoft 365 suite that has become essential for team collaboration and project organization. As part of the broader Microsoft 365 suite, it benefits from robust integration and security. It enables organizations to manage tasks within their existing workflows while ensuring compliance and reliability. From sending notifications on task completion to generating summaries of Planner boards, this collaboration facilitates processes, reduces manual effort, and improves task visibility. I will also highlight practical examples, such as creating Microsoft To Do tasks from Planner and automating reminders, to demonstrate how these tools enhance efficiency and support effective team management.

What Is Microsoft Planner?

Microsoft Planner is a task management tool in the Microsoft 365 suite designed to help individuals organize, assign, and track tasks visually. Launched in 2016, Planner was introduced as a lightweight remedy for project and task management, intended for use by both small teams and large organizations. Its integration within the Microsoft ecosystem allows it to work seamlessly alongside tools like Microsoft Teams, SharePoint, and Outlook, enabling users to manage tasks within broader organizational workflows.

Microsoft Planner offers a Kanban-style board interface, where tasks are represented as cards that can be moved across various stages or categories, referred to as "buckets." Each task can contain descriptions, due dates, attachments, checklists, and comments, making it easier for users to manage and keep track of individual responsibilities and group projects.

Historically, Microsoft Planner filled a gap in Microsoft 365 for teams that needed a more lightweight task management tool than Microsoft Project, which is more suited to complex, large-scale projects requiring advanced resource planning and timeline management. Before Planner, smaller teams or those needing only essential task management often had to rely on third-party tools. Planner's introduction as a part of the Microsoft 365 suite meant that organizations could stay within the Microsoft ecosystem for task management, benefitting from the platform's built-in integration and security features. Since its launch, Planner has undergone steady updates, improving its collaboration capabilities, task-tracking features, and integration with other Microsoft tools, particularly Microsoft Teams, which has become a central hub for collaboration in many organizations.

Tasks in Planner can be linked directly to other productivity tools, such as Outlook and Microsoft To Do, allowing users to manage their workload across multiple interfaces. For instance, tasks assigned in Planner can appear in a user's Outlook calendar or in Microsoft To Do for personal task tracking. The seamless flow between these tools helps users stay organized without manually synchronizing their tasks across different platforms. Furthermore, Planner is tightly integrated with Microsoft Teams, allowing work groups to embed Planner boards directly into their Teams channels. This enables task management to happen in the same space where communication and collaboration occur, reducing the need to switch between applications and improving overall productivity.

Another significant strength of Planner is its simplicity in design and functionality. Unlike more complex project management tools, which often entail a steep learning curve, Planner focuses on ease of use. Teams can quickly set up boards, create tasks, and assign responsibilities without formal training. This makes Planner particularly well-suited for smaller projects or work groups that do not require advanced project management features but still need a way to organize their work effectively.

Microsoft Planner is a straightforward, visually intuitive tool for managing tasks and small projects. Its evolution from a basic task management solution to an integrated part of the Microsoft 365 suite has made it a valuable tool for teams looking to stay organized and collaborate effectively. Its strengths lie in its ease of use and seamless integration with other Microsoft tools. While it may not offer the advanced features of dedicated project management platforms, its simplicity makes it a practical choice for teams looking to manage tasks without unnecessary complexity.

Power Automate and Microsoft Planner

Microsoft Planner and Power Automate integration provides a powerful way to automate task management processes. This integration enables users to create workflows that connect Planner with other applications in the Microsoft 365 ecosystem and beyond!

Power Automate can trigger actions in response to specific events in Planner, such as creating, assigning, or completing tasks; automating repetitive processes; and ensuring tasks are tracked consistently. This integration allows users to automate task management across multiple systems. For instance, tasks created in Planner can be automatically copied to a personal task list in Microsoft To Do, enabling users to manage individual and team tasks from a single interface. Similarly, Power Automate flows can create Planner tasks based on data from external sources. For example, a support request submitted via a Microsoft Form can trigger a workflow that creates a task in Planner, assigns it to the appropriate team member, and includes all relevant details in the task description.

Furthermore, Power Automate's ability to loop through multiple tasks in Planner helps automate bulk operations. For example, a workflow can automatically review all overdue tasks in a specific Planner board and send reminders to the task owners. This eliminates the need to manually check task status and helps ensure deadlines are met. Similarly, tasks that require periodic updates, such as monthly or weekly reviews, can be automatically generated and assigned to the appropriate team members based on predefined schedules, ensuring that recurring tasks are handled consistently.

Integration between Planner and other systems through Power Automate allows for more sophisticated automation scenarios. For example, when a project reaches a particular phase in a project management system, Power Automate can automatically create tasks in Planner for the next set of activities, assign them to the relevant team members, and set deadlines based on predefined project timelines. This allows teams to keep tasks aligned with overall project milestones without manual intervention, ensuring better coordination and reducing the risk of oversight.

In addition to workflow automation, Power Automate's integration with Planner allows error handling and task monitoring. For example, suppose a task fails to complete within a specified time frame. In that case, a workflow can trigger notifications to escalate the issue or reassign the task to another team member. This reduces the potential for bottlenecks and ensures that critical tasks are handled promptly.

Incorporating Microsoft Planner and Power Automate enhances task management by automating repetitive processes, enabling seamless coordination between different systems and ensuring that tasks are tracked and completed efficiently. By automating notifications, task creation, and status updates, teams can focus more on completing their work and less on managing task logistics, leading to improved productivity and project outcomes.

11.1 Sending a Notification on Task Completion

Problem

You want to check whether all subtasks are complete and send a notification when a task is marked as completed.

Solution

Create a flow that is automatically triggered when a task is completed in your Planner plan, checking whether all subtasks are completed and then sending a notification to the task creator.

Discussion

Monitoring subtask completion and notifying the task creator brings a significant improvement to task management, especially when handling complex projects where tasks are frequently delegated. By implementing this flow, the person responsible for the primary task is kept informed without having to manually check each subtask, which reduces the load of constantly tracking progress. This also minimizes the chance of delays, as any necessary follow-up action can be taken promptly upon notification, ensuring that projects stay on schedule.

When a task creator is notified of subtask completion, it becomes easier to monitor the task's progress holistically. This allows team members to manage their workloads more effectively, knowing that they'll receive a notification once each subtask is completed, rather than needing to check in periodically. This automation helps to create a self-sustaining flow of information, leading to a smoother, more efficient process where updates are delivered only when necessary. In projects where multiple team members collaborate on a single task, knowing that all subtasks are completed provides assurance that dependencies are met. This allows the primary task creator to move forward with the next steps or to finalize their work with confidence. It also enhances communication within the team, as there is less need for repetitive status updates, freeing up time and resources for more valuable interactions.

Before starting to build this flow, make sure that you have created a plan in Microsoft Planner or that you have the right permissions on the plan you want to monitor for completed tasks. Create a plan in Microsoft Planner using the support documentation (*https://oreil.ly/Ha51d*).

To create a new flow in Power Automate, begin by going to the Power Automate portal (*https://oreil.ly/O-MRf*) and signing in with your Microsoft or organization's account. Next, click on "My flows" in the left navigation bar and select "New flow." Since you want to initiate the flow for tasks checked as completed in Planner, choose the "Automated cloud flow" option. Then, select the trigger related to completed tasks in Planner by choosing the "When a task is completed" trigger and clicking Create. Finally, configure the trigger parameters, including the Group Id, which is the relevant Planner Group (or Teams team) to retrieve the plan, and the Plan Id parameter, which refers to the plan identifier in Microsoft Planner:

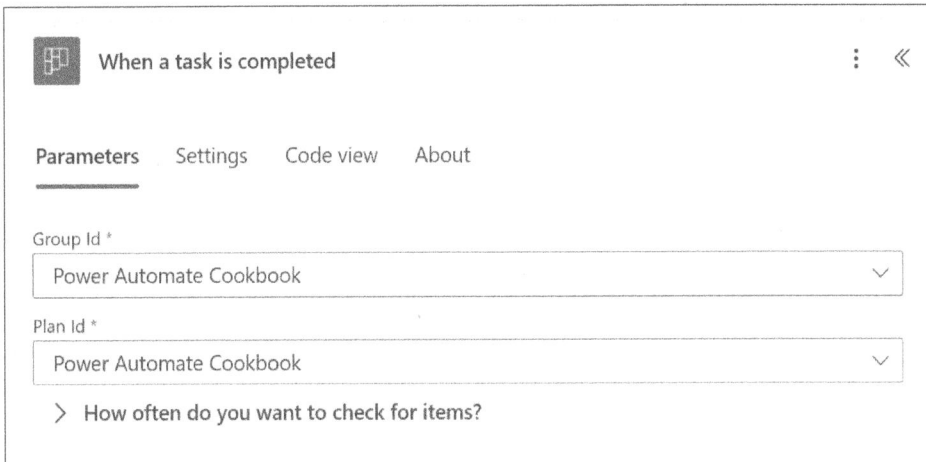

Add the "Get user profile (V2)" action to retrieve details about the user who created the task. Search for the Office 365 Users connector and select the "Get user profile (V2)" action. You may need to sign in and authenticate your Office 365 account. Rename the action to "Get creator profile," and then configure the action by setting the User (UPN) parameter to Created By User Id input from the trigger:

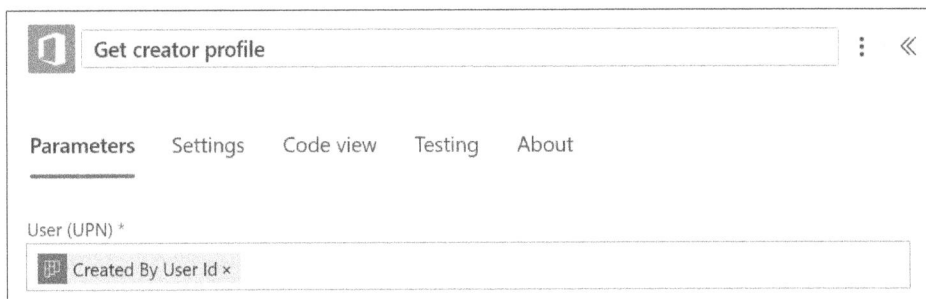

Add another "Get user profile (V2)" action to get the profile details about the user who completed the task. Search for the Office 365 Users connector and select the "Get user profile (V2)" action. Rename the action to "Get completed by profile," and then configure the action by setting the User (UPN) parameter to the following expression:

```
triggerBody()?['completedBy']?['user']?['id']
```

This expression gets the user ID of the person who checked the task as completed. Now, add a variable to store any unchecked subtasks. Search for "Variable." Choose "Initialize variable" and set the name to Unchecked Subtasks, choose Type as String, and keep the Value blank for now. This variable will later collect the names of any subtasks that remain incomplete:

Add a Condition to check if there are unfinished checklist items (subtasks). Search for "Control," and then select the Control actions. From the list of actions, choose Condition. Next, configure the condition action using the following expression for the left-side comparison value:

```
triggerBody()?['activeChecklistItemCount']
```

Make sure the comparison operator is set to "is greater than," and then for the right-side comparison, type 0:

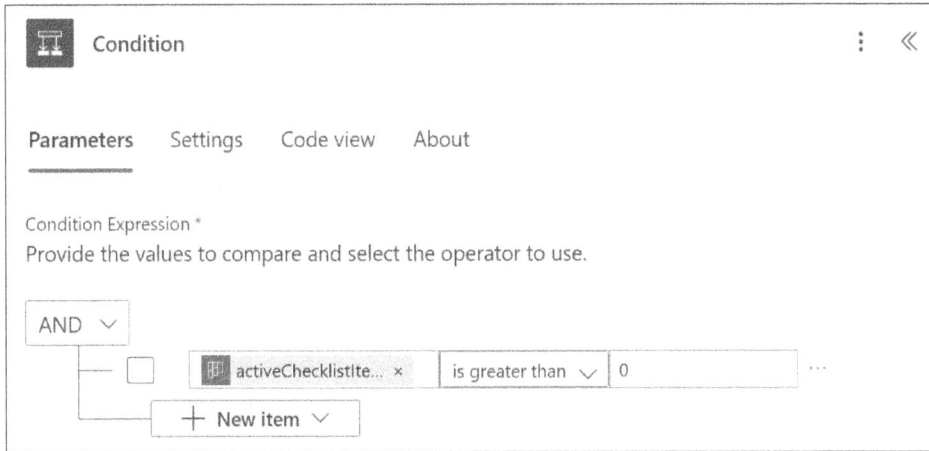

If the condition is not met, under False, it means that all subtasks are checked (or there are no subtasks). Then, add an action to send an email notifying the task creator that a task has been completed. Search for the Office 365 Outlook connector and select the "Send an email (V2)" action. You may need to sign in and authenticate your Office 365 Outlook account. Rename the action to "Send an email (V2) - Completed."

Fill the "Send an email (V2)" action parameters as follows (the text in braces is dynamic content from the trigger, "Get creator profile" action, and "Get completed by profile"):

- *To*: {Mail} (from "Get creator profile")
- *Subject*: Task completed
- *Body*:

      Hi {Display Name},

      Kindly note that task "{Title}" was checked as completed
      by {Display Name}.
      All underlying tasks were checked as complete.

      Thank you!

where the first instance of {Display Name} is dynamic content from the "Get creator profile" action, {Title} is from the "When a task is completed" trigger, and the second instance of {Display Name} is from the "Get completed by profile" action.

If there are active subtasks, under True, then we need to retrieve task details to get all the underlying subtasks. Search for the Microsoft Planner connector and select the "Get task details" action. Finally, configure the action by setting the Task Id to Id from the dynamic content of the trigger:

Next, filter incomplete subtasks returned in the "Get task details" action. Search for the Data Operations actions and select the "Filter array" action. Configure the action by setting the From to Checklist from the dynamic content of the "Get task details" action. Then, in Filter Query, set the lefthand side to "Checklist is Checked," make sure that the operator is set to "is equal to," and set the righthand side to "false":

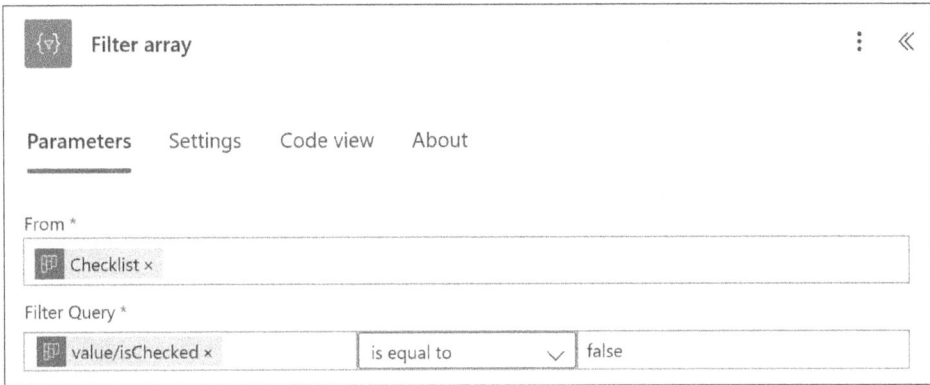

{v}	Filter array	⋮	≪

Parameters   Settings   Code view   About

From *

🔢 Checklist ×

Filter Query *

🔢 value/isChecked ×	is equal to ∨	false

Now, add an "Apply to each" action that loops through the output from the Filter array (i.e., the incomplete subtasks). Search for "Control," and then select the Control actions. From the list of actions, choose "Apply to each." Then configure the "Apply to each" action by setting the Select An Output From Previous Steps parameter by selecting the Checklist from the "Filter array" dynamic content:

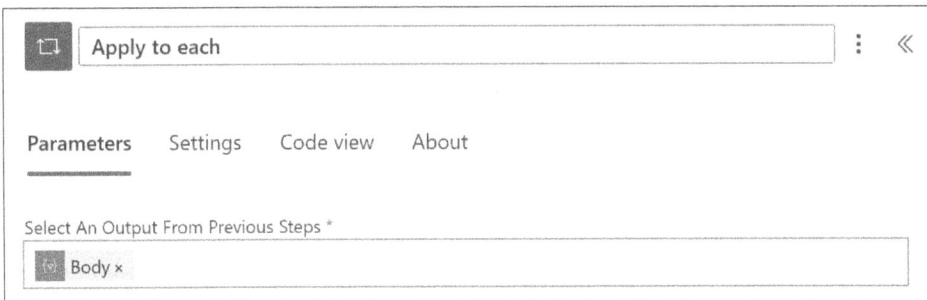

🔲	Apply to each	⋮	≪

Parameters   Settings   Code view   About

Select An Output From Previous Steps *

{v} Body ×

Inside this loop, add the "Append to string variable" action to append each unchecked subtask's title to the "Unchecked subtasks" variable you initialized. This will collect the names of all incomplete subtasks. Search for "Variable" and choose "Append to string variable." Configure the "Append to string variable" action by selecting "Unchecked subtasks" (the previously initialized variable). Then, customize the value as follows:

```
{Checklist Title} <br/>
```

Finally, add a "send an email" action (after the "Apply to each") to send an email to the person who checked the task as completed. Search for the Office 365 Outlook connector and select the "Send an email (V2)" action.

Fill the "Send an email (V2)" action parameters as follows (the text in braces is dynamic content from the trigger, "Unchecked subtasks" variable, "Get creator profile" action, and "Get completed by profile" action):

- *To*: {Mail} (from "Get completed by profile")
- *CC*: {Mail} (from "Get creator profile")
- *Subject*: Task completed with unchecked subtasks
- *Body*:

    ```
    Hi {DisplayName},

    Kindly note that task "{Title}" you checked as completed has
    unchecked subtasks.

    Unchecked subtasks:
    {Unchecked subtasks}

    Make sure that the underlying tasks are checked as complete.

    Thank you!
    ```

where {DisplayName} is dynamic content from the "Get completed by profile" action, {Title} is from the "When a task is completed" trigger, and {Unchecked subtasks} is from our string variable.

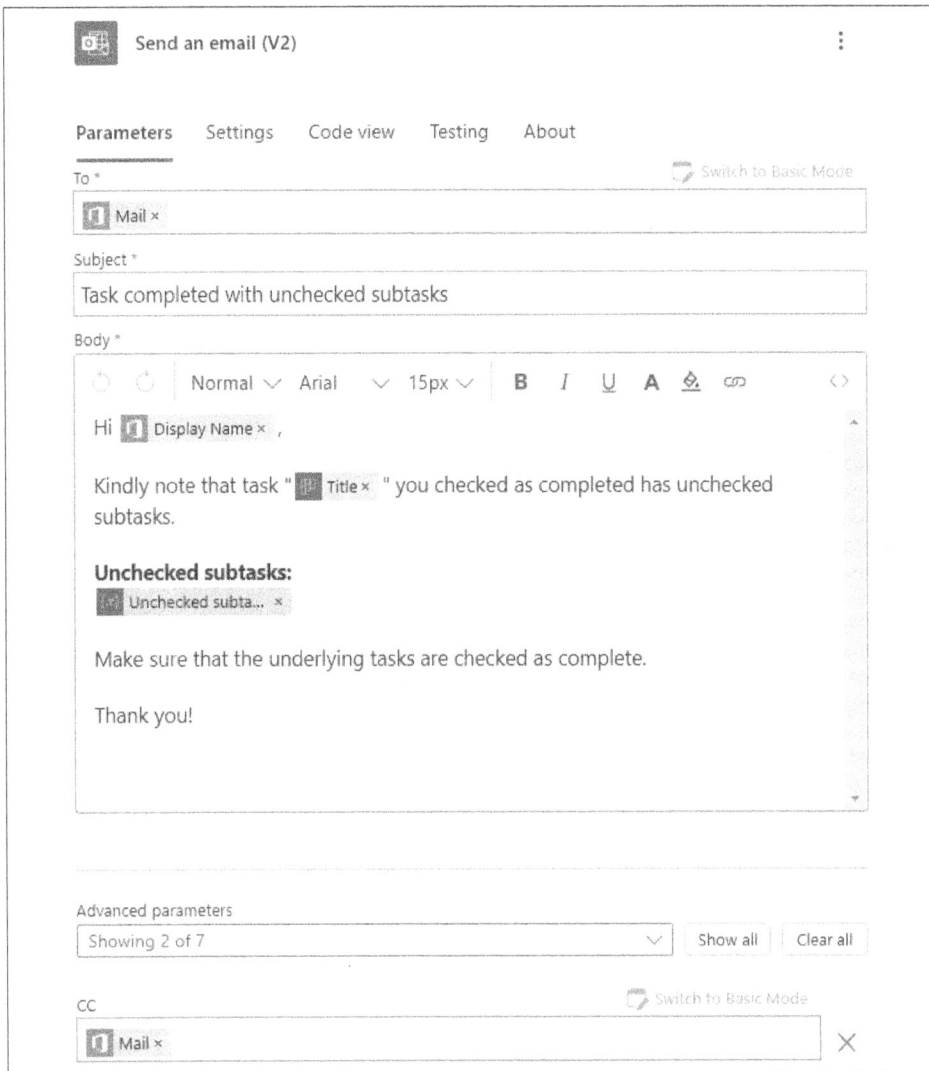

Give your flow a name, save it, and test it to confirm it behaves as expected.

See Also

- Recipe 11.2, "Creating a Microsoft To Do Task from a Microsoft Planner Task"
- Recipe 11.3, "Sending a Summary of Planner Tasks"

11.2 Creating a Microsoft To Do Task from a Microsoft Planner Task

Problem

You want to create a Microsoft To Do task in your personal list when a task is assigned to you in a specific Microsoft Planner plan.

Solution

Create a flow that monitors assignments in a selected Planner plan and, upon detection, generates a corresponding task in Microsoft To Do.

Discussion

Automating the creation of a Microsoft To Do task whenever a Planner task is assigned ensures tasks are centralized, making it easier to manage your responsibilities without constantly switching between applications. By synchronizing tasks across platforms, you reduce the risk of missing assignments, especially when working within multiple projects or teams. This automation brings all tasks assigned to you directly into your Microsoft To Do, aligning personal task management with collaborative project efforts in Planner.

This setup improves your productivity, as each new task is automatically logged and tracked, eliminating manual data entry. It helps with prioritization by consolidating tasks in your To Do list, allowing you to visualize and organize tasks more effectively. This enhances your time management and planning.

Before starting to build this flow, make sure that you have created a plan in Microsoft Planner or that you have the right permissions on the plan you want to monitor for tasks assigned to you. To create a plan in Microsoft Planner, follow the instructions in the support documentation (*https://oreil.ly/Ha51d*).

To create a new flow in Power Automate, begin by going to the Power Automate portal (*https://oreil.ly/O-MRf*) and signing in with your Microsoft or organization's account. Next, click on "My flows" in the left navigation bar and select "New flow." Since you want to initiate the flow for tasks assigned to you in Planner, choose the "Automated cloud flow" option. Then, select the trigger in Planner by picking the "When a task is assigned to me" trigger and clicking Create. Finally, configure the trigger parameters, using a recurrence interval of one minute instead of three:

When a task is assigned to me

Parameters   Settings   Code view   About

⌄ How often do you want to check for items?

Recurrence *

Interval *   Frequency *
1   *   Minute   ⌄   *

Time Zone
Select timezone.   ⌄

Start Time
Example: 2017-03-24T15:00:00Z

Now, you need to retrieve task details to get all the underlying subtasks. Search for the Microsoft Planner connector and select the "Get task details" action. Finally, configure the action by setting the Task Id to Id from the dynamic content of the trigger:

Get task details

Parameters   Settings   Code view   Testing   About

Task Id *
Id ×   ×

Add the "Get user profile (V2)" action to retrieve details about the user who created the task. Search for the Office 365 Users connector and select the "Get user profile (V2)" action. You may need to sign in and authenticate your Office 365 user account. Rename the action "Get creator profile," and then configure the action by setting the User (UPN) parameter to Created By User Id input from the trigger:

	Get creator profile (V2)	⋮ ≪

Parameters   Settings   Code view   Testing   About

User (UPN) *

   ▣ Created By User Id ×

Now, add a variable to store all subtasks. Search for "Variable." Choose "Initialize variable" and set the name to "Subtasks," choose Type as String, and keep the Value blank for now. This variable will later collect names of all subtasks:

{x}	Initialize variable	⋮ ≪

Parameters   Settings   Code view   About

Name *

Subtasks

Type *

String   ∨

Value

Enter initial value

Next, add an "Apply to each" action that loops through the checklist (i.e., all subtasks). Search for "Control," and then select the Control actions. From the list of actions, choose "Apply to each." Then configure the "Apply to each" action by setting the Select An Output From Previous Steps parameter by selecting the Checklist from the "Get task details" dynamic content:

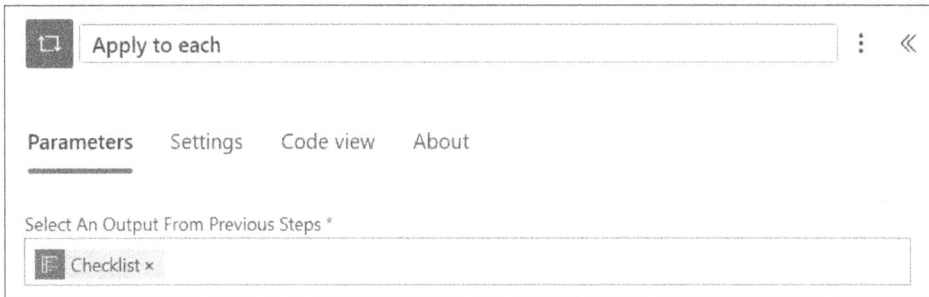

Inside this loop, add the "Append to string variable" action to append each subtask's title to the Subtasks variable you initialized. This will collect the names of all subtasks. Search for "Variable" and choose "Append to string variable." Configure the "Append to string variable" action by selecting Subtasks (the previously initialized variable). Then, customize the value as follows:

```
{Checklist Title} <br/>
```

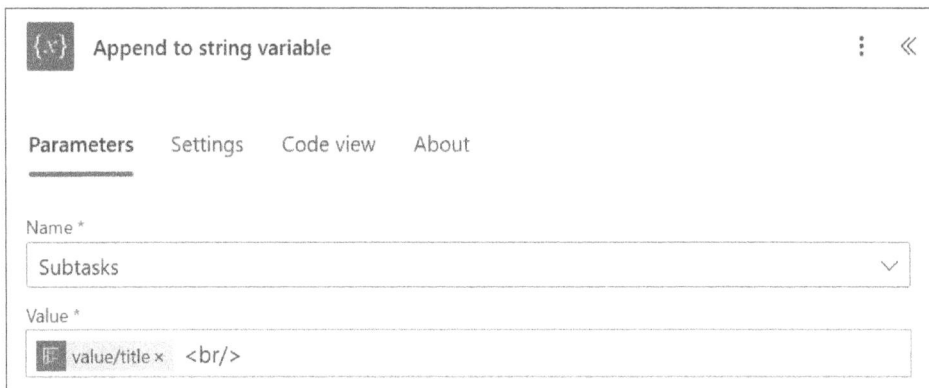

After the loop step, add a compose action and create a link for the corresponding Planner plan in your Microsoft To Do list. Search for the Data Operations actions and select the Compose action. Configure the action by setting the Inputs as follows:

```
<a href="https://planner.cloud.microsoft/webui/plan/{Plan Id}">Plan link</a>
```

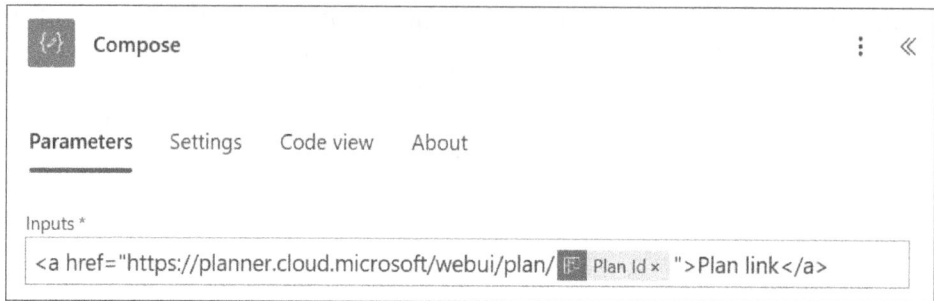

Compose

Parameters   Settings   Code view   About

Inputs *

`<a href="https://planner.cloud.microsoft/webui/plan/` Plan Id × `">Plan link</a>`

The previous action will create an HTML link tag that you'll use in the next and final action to create a task in your Microsoft To Do list. Add a new step to create a task in Microsoft To Do. In the search bar, type `Microsoft To Do`. Then, choose "Add a to-do (V3)."

Fill in the "Add a to-do (V3)" action parameters as follows (the text in braces is dynamic content):

- *To-Do List*: Choose Tasks. Alternatively, you can create your own to-do list under Microsoft To Do.
- *Title*: {`Title`} (from "When a task is assigned to me")
- *Due Date*: {`Due Date Time`} (from "When a task is assigned to me")
- *Body Content*:

```
Plan:
{Outputs}

Description:
{Description}

Subtasks:
{Subtasks}

Created by:
{Display Name}
```

where {`Outputs`} is dynamic content from our Compose action, {`Description`} is from the "Get task details" action, {`Subtasks`} is from our string variable, and {`Display Name`} is from the "Get creator profile" action.

Add a to-do (V3)

Parameters   Settings   Code view   Testing   About

To-Do List *

Tasks

Title *

Title ×

Due Date

Due Date Time ×

Reminder Date-Time

YYYY-MM-DDThh:mm:ss

Importance

Low, normal or high.

Status

notStarted

Body Content

Normal ⌄   Arial   ⌄   15px ⌄   **B**   *I*   U   A   ◇   ⌥   ‹ ›

Plan:
Outputs ×

Description:
Description ×

Subtasks:
Subtasks ×

Created by:
Display Name ×

Give your flow a name, save it, and test it to confirm it behaves as expected.

See Also

- Recipe 11.1, "Sending a Notification on Task Completion"
- Recipe 11.3, "Sending a Summary of Planner Tasks"

11.3 Sending a Summary of Planner Tasks

Problem

You want to send a daily report of Planner tasks categorized by bucket.

Solution

Create a recurring flow that goes through your Planner plan, lists your tasks by bucket, and sends an email of that summary.

Discussion

This flow provides project managers and team members with a quick, organized snapshot of outstanding work, helping to maintain clear visibility on task progress and priorities. By categorizing tasks by bucket, the summary reflects the project structure, making it easier for project managers to see what needs attention in specific areas. This automation reduces the need for manual updates or status meetings, as project managers and team members receive a timely, structured overview directly in their inbox each day. It promotes better alignment across the team by ensuring that everyone is aware of task distributions and immediate priorities.

A daily summary helps identify bottlenecks or overdue tasks, allowing teams to address issues proactively before they escalate. Each team member is regularly reminded of their assignments and deadlines, motivating everyone to keep tasks on track. With tasks neatly organized by bucket in the daily email, team members can plan their day more effectively, prioritize urgent work, and allocate time to tasks that align with project goals, thereby enhancing productivity and team efficiency.

Before starting to build this flow, make sure you have created a plan in Microsoft Planner or that you have the right permissions on the plan you want to generate a summary for. To create a plan in Microsoft Planner, follow the instructions in the support documentation (*https://oreil.ly/Ha51d*).

Start by visiting the Power Automate portal (*https://oreil.ly/O-MRf*). Sign in with your Microsoft account or your organization's account and ensure that you're in the correct Power Automate environment. From the left navigation bar, click on "My flows," and then select "New flow" to begin creating a new flow. Since your goal is to create a daily summary, choose the "Scheduled cloud flow" option. Give your flow a name and input the required parameters to specify when the flow should run. Set the starting date and time (i.e., 8:00 A.M.), and configure the flow to repeat once every day:

Now, add a variable to store the summary of your Planner's plan. Search for "Variable." Choose "Initialize variable," set the name to "Summary," choose Type as String, and keep the Value blank for now. This variable will later collect the summary of all buckets and tasks:

Next, you want to list buckets and then tasks for a specific Planner's plan. Search for the Microsoft Planner connector and select the "List buckets" action. You may need to sign in and authenticate your Microsoft Planner connection. Finally, configure the action by setting the Plan Id to the plan you wish to collect daily summaries for:

List buckets	⋮ ≪

Parameters　　Settings　　Code view　　Testing　　About
──────

Plan Id *

Power Automate Cookbook	∨

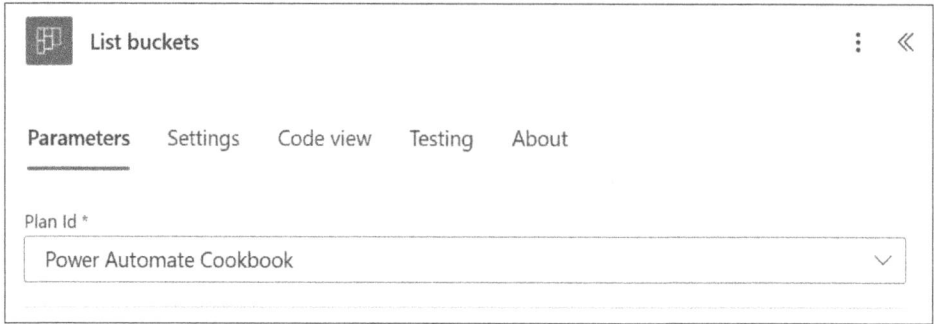

Then add a new action to list tasks. Search for the Microsoft Planner connector and select the "List tasks" action. Configure the action by setting the Plan Id to the plan you wish to collect daily summaries for:

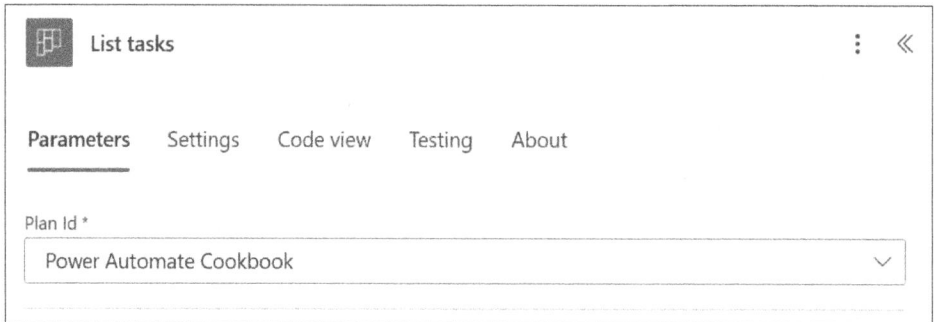

List tasks	⋮ ≪

Parameters　　Settings　　Code view　　Testing　　About
──────

Plan Id *

Power Automate Cookbook	∨

Next, you want to iterate through buckets. Add an "Apply to each" action that loops through the plan buckets. Search for "Control," and then select the Control actions. From the list of actions, choose "Apply to each." Rename the loop action to "Iterate through buckets." Then configure the "Apply to each" action by setting the Select An Output From Previous Steps parameter by selecting the "value" from the "List buckets" dynamic content:

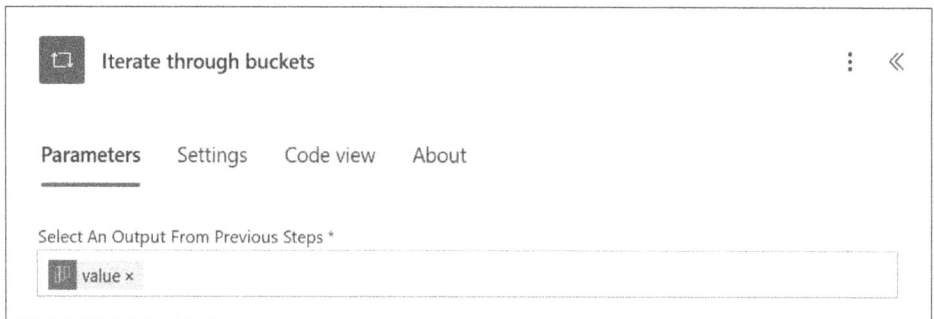

Iterate through buckets	⋮ ≪

Parameters　　Settings　　Code view　　About
──────

Select An Output From Previous Steps *

value ×

Now, you want to collect the name of the bucket(s). Inside this loop, add the "Append to string variable" action to append each bucket's title to the Summary variable you initialized earlier. Search for "Variable" and choose "Append to string variable." Configure the "Append to string variable" action by selecting Summary (the previously initialized variable). Then, customize the Value as follows:

```
<b> Bucket:</b> {expression} <br>
```

where {expression} is:

```
items('Iterate_through_buckets')?['name']
```

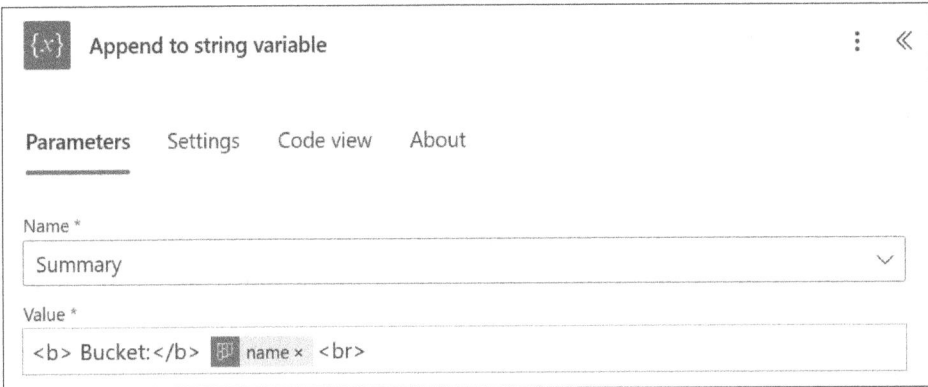

Next you want to filter listed tasks based on the corresponding buckets. Search for the Data Operations actions and select the "Filter array" action. Configure the action by setting the From to "value" from the dynamic content of the "List tasks" action. Then, in Filter Query, set the lefthand side to "value Bucket Id," make sure that the operator is set to "is equal to," and set the righthand side to the following expression:

```
items('Iterate_through_buckets')?['id']
```

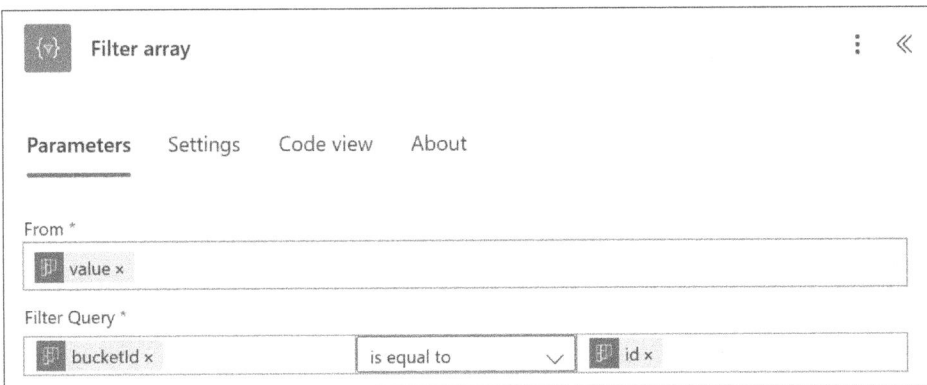

Next, you want to iterate through the filtered tasks to collect them in the summary variable. Add an "Apply to each" action that loops through the filtered tasks. Search for "Control," and then select the Control actions. From the list of actions, choose "Apply to each." Rename the loop action to "Iterate through tasks." Then configure the "Iterate through tasks" action by setting the Select An Output From Previous Steps parameter by selecting the "value" from the "Filter array" dynamic content:

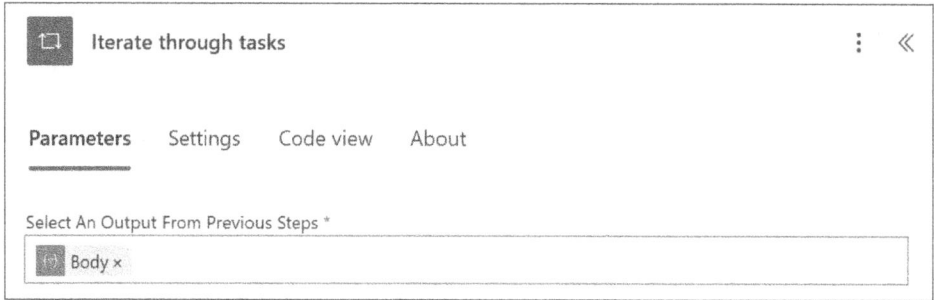

🔲 Iterate through tasks	⋮ «

Parameters   Settings   Code view   About

Select An Output From Previous Steps *

`{·} Body ×`

Inside the loop, you want to collect the title and the due date of the tasks. Search for "Variable" and choose "Append to string variable." Rename the action to "Append tasks to string variable." Then, configure the "Append tasks to string variable" action by selecting Summary (the previously initialized variable). Then, customize the value as follows:

    {title} ({expression})

where {expression} is:

    formatDateTime(item()?['dueDateTime'], 'dd-MM-yyyy')

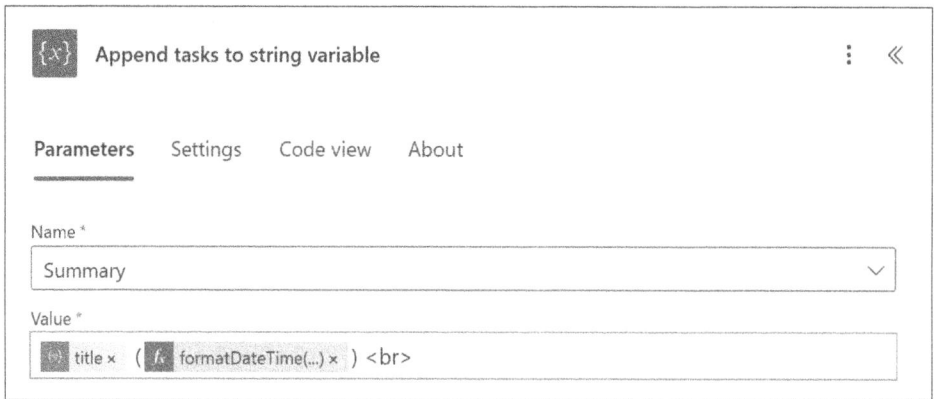

{x} Append tasks to string variable	⋮ «

Parameters   Settings   Code view   About

Name *

Summary ⌄

Value *

`{·} title ×  ( ƒ formatDateTime(...) ×  ) <br>`

After this loop and inside the first loop, you want to enter a space between each bucket and their corresponding tasks. Search for "Variable" and choose "Append to string variable." Rename the action to "Append an extra line." Then, configure the "Append an extra line" action by selecting Summary (the previously initialized variable). Next, customize the Value to <br>:

{x} Append an extra line	⋮ ≪
Parameters Settings Code view About	
Name *	
Summary	⌄
Value *	

Finally, after the first loop, send an email to yourself, project manager, or team members with the collected summary. Search for the "Office 365 Outlook" connector and select the "Send an email (V2)" action.

Fill the "Send an email (V2)" action parameters as follows (the text in braces is dynamic content from our variable):

- *To*: Your email, your project manager's email, and/or your team members' emails
- *Subject*: Planner Task Summary by Bucket
- *Body*:

  Hi,

  This is a summary of Planner tasks by bucket:

  {Summary}

  Have a nice day!

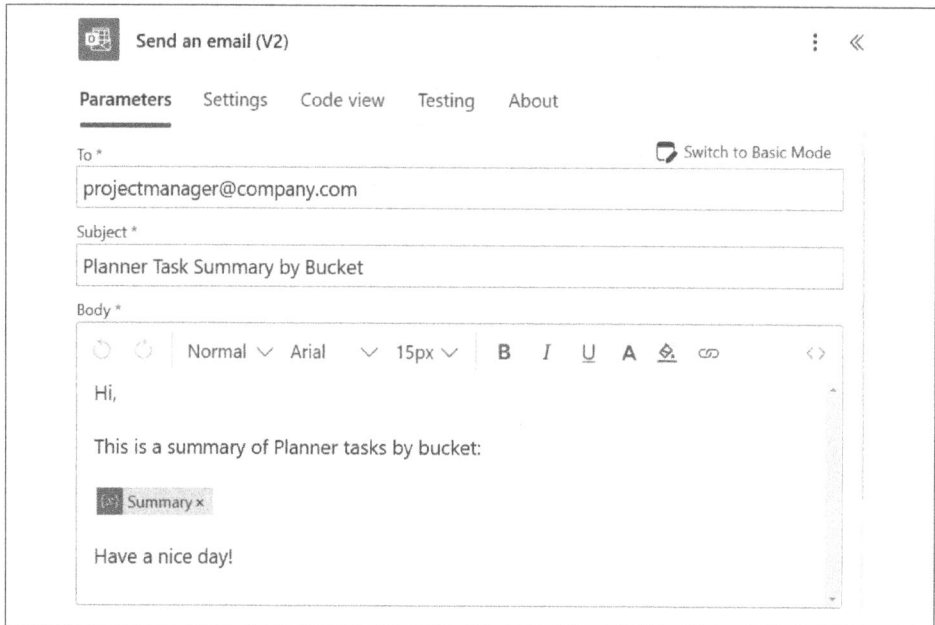

Save and test the flow to confirm it behaves as expected.

See Also

- Recipe 11.1, "Sending a Notification on Task Completion"
- Recipe 11.2, "Creating a Microsoft To Do Task from a Microsoft Planner Task"

Conclusion

Power Automate and Microsoft Planner create a robust combination for simplifying task management and improving team collaboration. Through this integration, users can automate routine tasks such as task assignment, status tracking, and notification management, reducing manual efforts and keeping teams synchronized. Beyond basic automation, Power Automate with Planner can drive more advanced scenarios, particularly in project coordination.

Businesses can set up flows to handle complex project stages, automatically update task progress across teams, and create dynamic notifications that ensure team members stay informed. This integration allows users to tailor workflows to specific project needs, automate cross-department interactions, and maintain clear visibility over task distribution. As teams grow and project demands become more intricate, the ability to customize and scale these automations in Planner becomes increasingly valuable, ensuring teams remain organized and aligned in achieving project goals.

CHAPTER 12

Power Automate and AI Builder

In this chapter, I'll briefly explain AI in layman's terms. Then, I will lay out an understanding of what AI Builder is and how it simplifies tasks such as text recognition, sentiment analysis, and data prediction through prebuilt models and intuitive interfaces, empowering users to save time and reduce errors. Integrated with Power Automate, AI Builder enhances everyday operations, enabling businesses to automate processes, improve productivity, and focus on impactful work with minimal resources. Finally, I'll go through common use cases where AI Builder and Power Automate work together effortlessly, demonstrating their ability to drive productivity and optimize task management.

A Brief Introduction to AI

AI is a way of teaching computers to mimic how humans think and solve problems (human cognitive functions). Instead of giving a computer strict instruction for every task, AI allows it to learn patterns and make decisions based on the data it's exposed to.

AI heavily relies on data, as this is the "fuel" that drives its learning. The more data AI systems have, and the better the quality of that data, the smarter and more accurate they become. Imagine trying to teach a self-driving car to recognize stop signs—it needs thousands of pictures of stop signs in various shapes, colors, and conditions to learn what they look like in different scenarios. If the data is incomplete or incorrect, the AI might struggle to perform its tasks accurately, potentially leading to mistakes.

Behind the scenes, AI uses algorithms, which are like detailed recipes, to process data and learn from it. Some of the most common algorithms include decision trees, which simulate a series of if-then questions to make choices; neural networks, which are inspired by how the human brain works; and clustering, which helps group similar items together. For example, when online streaming services recommend movies that you might like, they use algorithms to analyze your viewing habits and compare them to those of others with similar tastes.

Early attempts to make AI accessible to everyone included tools such as Microsoft's AI Builder. It allows people without deep technical knowledge to use prebuilt AI models or extend AI models by providing simple interfaces to handle things like prediction, text recognition, or sentiment analysis. For instance, a small business might use AI Builder to scan customer feedback and automatically categorize it as positive, negative, or neutral, saving hours of manual sorting.

AI is already all around us, often in ways we don't notice. It powers facial recognition on smartphones, suggests routes in navigation apps, and even helps farmers monitor their crops with precision. By understanding the role of data and algorithms and making AI easier for everyone to use, tools like AI Builder are opening up opportunities for businesses and individuals to benefit from AI in practical and impactful ways.

Understanding AI Builder: Simplifying AI for Everyone

AI Builder is a tool from Microsoft that makes it easier for people to use AI in their everyday work, with minimal technical or programming skills. It was first introduced in 2019 as part of Microsoft's Power Platform. The idea behind AI Builder was to give businesses a way to add smart capabilities to their workflows and applications without needing to build complex AI models from scratch.

Over the years, AI Builder has grown significantly. Initially, it focused on basic features such as recognizing text from images or categorizing information. Now, it includes more advanced capabilities, such as detecting objects in photos, analyzing customer sentiment, and predicting future outcomes based on historical data. For example, you could use AI Builder to automatically process invoices by extracting key information like due dates and amounts from scanned documents, saving hours of manual work.

One of the biggest advantages of AI Builder is how user-friendly it is. Instead of requiring deep technical knowledge, it offers simple interfaces where you can use prebuilt (pretrained) models or even train AI models by providing examples. This allows businesses to take advantage of AI without needing dedicated data sciences. It's also tightly integrated with Power Automate, which means you can easily use AI Builder in automated workflows. For example, you could create a flow where incoming emails are scanned and specific actions are triggered based on the text or attachments —like forwarding an email if it mentions a critical issue or filing it in a specific folder.

Having tools like AI Builder in Power Automate is vital because it allows businesses to unlock the power of AI in practical ways. Instead of using AI for large, specialized projects, teams can incorporate it into their daily processes to save time, reduce errors, and focus on more meaningful tasks. By combining automation with AI, organizations can work smarter and achieve more without needing large budgets or advanced technical expertise.

12.1 Extracting Identity Document Details

Problem

You want to extract identity document details when a document is uploaded to a SharePoint document library.

Solution

Create a flow that triggers when a document is uploaded/created, extracts identity document details, then updates the corresponding item properties with the extracted information.

Discussion

This flow significantly reduces manual effort and errors in data entry. Extracting key details such as name, identity document number, nationality, and expiration date automatically ensures that critical information is accurately captured without relying on time-consuming manual input. This increases efficiency, especially in processes that handle large volumes of documents, such as HR onboarding, visa processing, or Know-Your-Customer (KYC) scenarios (in banks).

Furthermore, this flow makes the extracted information instantly usable. For example, the flow can store the details in a structured format within the same SharePoint library or database, enabling quick searches, filtering, and reporting. This ensures the data is organized and ready for further processing, such as notifying you about upcoming passport expirations or integrating the data into other business systems.

Before building this flow, ensure that you have created a SharePoint library, such as Identity Documents, then create the following columns from the library settings:

- First Name (single line of text)
- Last Name (single line of text)
- Date of Birth (date and time)

- Identity Document Expiration Date (date and time)

- Identity Document Number (single line of text)

- Nationality (single line of text)

Start by visiting the Power Automate portal (*https://oreil.ly/O-MRf*). Sign in with your Microsoft account or your organization's account and ensure that you're in the correct Power Automate environment. From the left navigation bar, click on "My flows," and then select "New flow" to begin creating a new flow. Because your goal is to trigger the flow on newly uploaded/created images, choose the "Automated cloud flow" option. Then, select the trigger in SharePoint by picking the "When a file is created (properties only)" trigger and clicking Create. You may need to sign in and authenticate your SharePoint account. Configure the Site Address (the relevant site URL where the library you want to monitor resides) and Library Name (the SharePoint library to be monitored for uploaded files) trigger parameters:

⑤ When a file is created (properties only)	⋮ ≪

Parameters   Settings   Code view   About

Site Address *

https:// ███████████████████ /sites/ContosoBank	✕

Library Name *

Identity Documents - KYC	∨

Add an action to get the file content (binaries) from the document library. Search for the SharePoint connector and select the "Get file content" action. Configure the action parameters, including Site Address (the relevant site URL where the documents library resides), File Identifier (the Identifier dynamic content from the trigger), and Infer Content Type (set to Yes):

Now, add an action to extract identity information details from the uploaded file content. Search for the AI Builder connector and select the "Extract information from identity documents" action. Configure the Identity Document File action parameter (the document binary content)—in this case, the File Content from the output of the "Get file content" action:

The "Extract information from identity documents" action leverages AI Builder to analyze and extract data from identity documents, such as passports, driver's licenses, or ID cards. It automatically identifies and retrieves information such as the following:

- First name
- Last name
- Date of birth
- Document type
- Document number
- Expiration date
- Nationality
- Other relevant fields, depending on the document type and format

Finally, update the file item columns with the corresponding information extracted from the AI Builder action. Search for the SharePoint connector and select the "Update file properties" action. Configure the trigger parameters, including Site Address (the relevant site URL where the library you want to monitor resides), Library Name (the SharePoint library to be monitored for uploaded files), and Id (the file ID, the ID dynamic content from the trigger):

Now, from the "Advanced parameters" drop-down, select all the columns you want to update with the corresponding information extracted in the previous action:

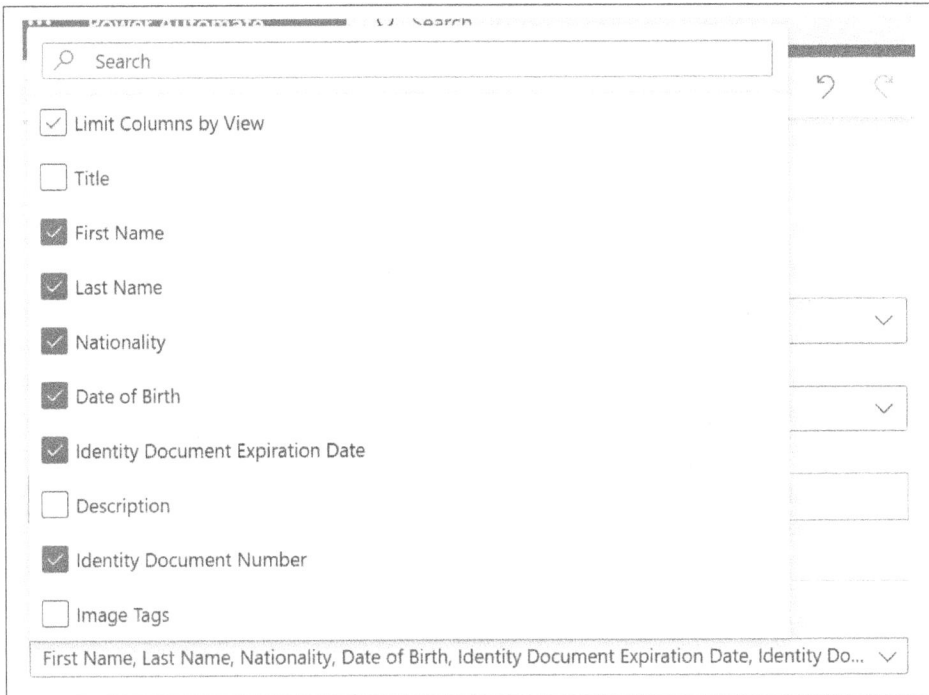

Finally, map the extracted information with their respective columns in the Share-Point Library. The Date of Birth and Expiration Date values are extracted as strings. Therefore, you need to parse them to DateTime before assigning them to their respective columns. Use the following `parseDateTime()` expressions to do so:

```
parseDateTime(outputs('Extract_information_from_identity_documents')
?['body/responsev2/predictionOutput/result/fields/dateOfBirth/value'])

parseDateTime(outputs('Extract_information_from_identity_documents')
?['body/responsev2/predictionOutput/result/fields/dateOfExpiration/value'])
```

First Name

First name ×   ✕

Last Name

Last name ×   ✕

Nationality

Nationality ×   ✕

Date of Birth

parseDateTime(...) ×   ✕

Identity Document Expiration Date

parseDateTime(...) ×   ✕

Identity Document Number

Identity documen... ×   ✕

Give your flow a name, save it, and test it to confirm it behaves as expected.

See Also

- Recipe 12.2, "Analyzing Feedback Sentiment"
- Recipe 12.3, "Extracting Images or PDFs as Text"
- Recipe 12.4, "Suggesting Email Replies"

12.2 Analyzing Feedback Sentiment

Problem

You want to collect feedback, analyze the feedback's sentiment, and save the feedback and analysis.

Solution

Create a flow that triggers when a Microsoft Form is submitted, analyzes the feedback sentiment, and saves the feedback and analysis result to a SharePoint list.

Discussion

This flow brings valuable insights to the feedback process. It eliminates manual intervention, ensuring every submission is processed consistently and stored securely. Using sentiment analysis provides immediate insights into whether the feedback is positive, neutral, or negative, giving a high-level view of overall sentiment without having to read through each response individually. This is particularly useful for tracking trends or identifying areas requiring attention.

Furthermore, storing the feedback and sentiment analysis in a SharePoint list makes organizing, searching, and sharing data with relevant users easy. Teams can use this centralized repository to collaborate, create reports, or even trigger further actions, such as sending follow-up surveys or addressing concerns.

Before building this flow, create a Microsoft Forms survey (Feedback form). Then add the following fields:

- What is this about? (required text field)
- Description (required long text field)

Feedback form

...

* Required

1. What is this about? *

Enter your answer

2. Description *

Enter your answer

Submit

Furthermore, make sure you have created a SharePoint list with the following fields:

- Title (default, single line of text)
- Feedback (multiple lines of text)
- Sentiment (choice):
  — positive
  — neutral
  — negative

> I deliberately formatted the choice values here in all lowercase letters, as the sentiment returned from the AI Builder action is also lowercase.

To create a new flow in Power Automate, visit the Power Automate portal (*https://oreil.ly/O-MRf*) and sign in with your Microsoft or organization's account. Ensure that you're in the correct Power Automate environment, then click on "My flows" in the left navigation bar and select "New flow" to begin. Since you want the flow to start when feedback is submitted, choose the "Automated cloud flow" option. On the pop-up, choose "When a new response is submitted" (Microsoft Forms), then click Create. You may need to sign in and authenticate your Microsoft Forms account. Finally, configure the trigger's parameter, selecting the Form Id of the Microsoft form from which you want to collect feedback:

When a new response is submitted	⋮ ≪

Parameters   Settings   Code view   About

Form Id *

Feedback form   ∨

Add a new action to get response details. Search for "Microsoft Forms" and choose "Get response details" to collect the data from the submitted response. Then configure the action's parameters, including Form Id (the relevant Microsoft form from which you want to collect feedback) and Response Id (the corresponding response ID from the trigger's dynamic content):

FO Get response details		⋮	≪

Parameters   Settings   Code view   Testing   About

Form Id *

Feedback form	⌄

Response Id *

AI Response Id ×

Now, add an action to analyze feedback sentiment from the feedback description. Search for the AI Builder connector and select the "Analyze positive or negative sentiment in text" action. Configure the Language (English, the language the feedback is written in) and Text (the feedback text, or text to analyze) action parameters. Notice, we are passing the Description from the feedback form:

⬡	Analyze positive or negative sentiment in text	⋮	≪

Parameters   Settings   Code view   Testing   About

Language *

English	⌄

Text *

AI Description ×

Finally, create an item in the SharePoint list using the feedback form details and the analyzed feedback text. Search for the SharePoint connector and select the "Create item" action. Configure the Site Address (the relevant site URL where the library you want to monitor resides) and List Name (the SharePoint to create the item in) trigger parameters:

Now, from the "Advanced parameters" drop-down, select the following:

- Title
- Feedback
- Sentiment Value

Finally, map the information gathered in the feedback form and the result of the analyzed text:

Give your flow a name, save it, and test it to confirm it behaves as expected.

See Also

- Recipe 6.1, "Saving Microsoft Forms Responses to SharePoint"
- Recipe 12.1, "Extracting Identity Document Details"
- Recipe 12.3, "Extracting Images or PDFs as Text"
- Recipe 12.4, "Suggesting Email Replies"

12.3 Extracting Images or PDFs as Text

Problem

You want to extract text from an image or a PDF document and save the extracted text.

Solution

Create a flow that triggers when a file (image or PDF) is uploaded, extracts text, then updates the corresponding item column with the extracted text.

Discussion

This flow can save a lot of time and effort. Usually, someone would have to open the file, read the content, and manually enter it into SharePoint, which is slow and prone to mistakes. With this flow, the process becomes automatic. As soon as a file is uploaded, the flow uses AI to read the text inside and update the relevant column, making the data ready almost instantly.

This automation is especially helpful for businesses with many documents, contracts, or reports. It ensures consistency, reduces errors, and speeds up workflows by keeping information well-organized and easy to find. For example, if you upload a contract in PDF, the flow could automatically extract the terms and conditions and then save them where they are needed.

Before building this flow, ensure that you have created a SharePoint library, such as "Extracted Images and PDFs," then create an "Extracted text" (multiple lines of text) column from the library settings.

Start by visiting the Power Automate portal (*https://oreil.ly/O-MRf*). Sign in with your Microsoft account or your organization's account and ensure that you're in the correct Power Automate environment. From the left navigation bar, click on "My flows," and then select "New flow" to begin creating a new flow. Since your goal is to trigger the flow on newly uploaded images or PDFs, choose the "Automated cloud flow" option. Then, select the trigger in SharePoint by picking the "When a file is created (properties only)" trigger and clicking Create. You may need to sign in and authenticate your SharePoint account. Configure the Site Address (the relevant site URL where the library you want to monitor resides) and Library Name (the SharePoint library to be monitored for uploaded files) trigger parameters:

Add an action to get the file content (binaries) from the document library. Search for the SharePoint connector and select the "Get file content" action. Configure the action parameters, including Site Address (the relevant site URL where the documents library resides), File Identifier (the Identifier dynamic content from the trigger), and Infer Content Type (set to Yes):

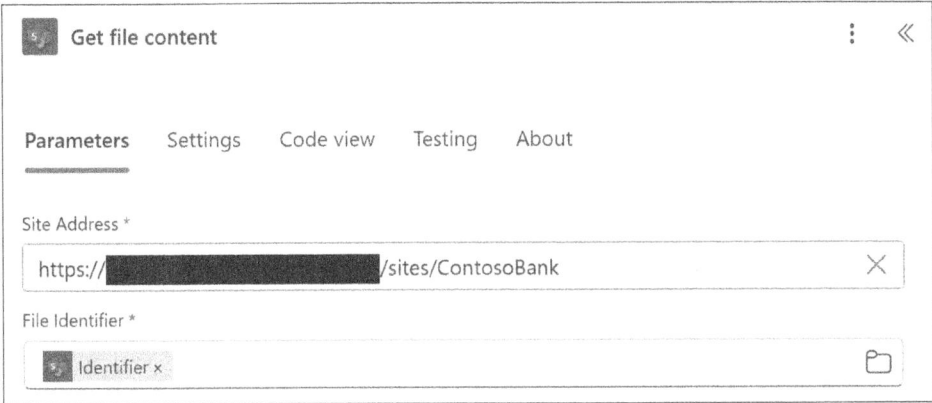

Get file content	⋮	≪

Parameters   Settings   Code view   Testing   About

Site Address *

https://█████████████/sites/ContosoBank   ✕

File Identifier *

📁 Identifier ✕

Now, add an action to extract text from the uploaded file content. Search for the AI Builder connector and select the "Recognize text in an image or a PDF document" action. Configure the Image action parameter (the file binary content)—in this case, the File Content from the "Get file content" action:

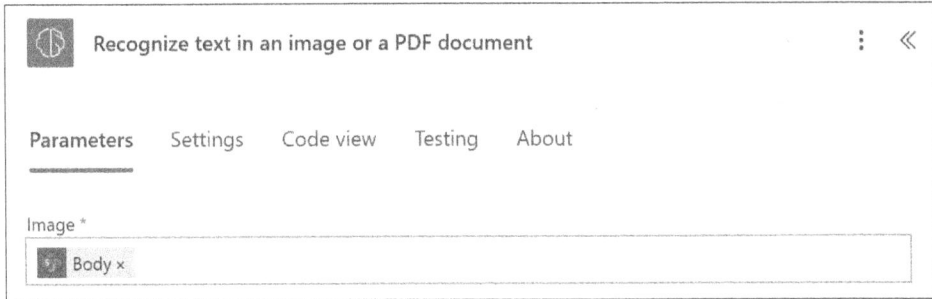

Recognize text in an image or a PDF document	⋮	≪

Parameters   Settings   Code view   Testing   About

Image *

Body ✕

Finally, update the file item columns with the corresponding extracted text from the AI Builder action. Search for the SharePoint connector and select the "Update file properties" action. Configure the trigger parameters, including Site Address (the relevant site URL where the library you want to monitor resides), Library Name (the SharePoint library to be monitored for uploaded files), and Id (the file ID, the ID dynamic content from the trigger):

Now, from the "Advanced parameters" drop-down, select "Extracted text":

Finally, assign "Full text of the document" property from the "Recognize text in an image or a PDF document" action:

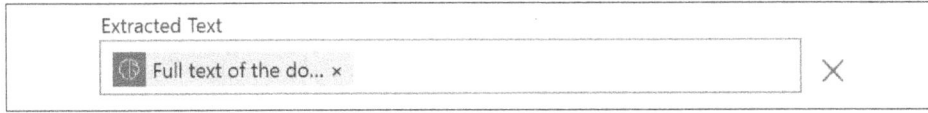

Extracted Text

```
⟨⊕⟩ Full text of the do... ×                                              ✕
```

Give your flow a name, save it, and test it to confirm it behaves as expected.

See Also

- Recipe 12.1, "Extracting Identity Document Details"
- Recipe 12.2, "Analyzing Feedback Sentiment"
- Recipe 12.4, "Suggesting Email Replies"

12.4 Suggesting Email Replies

Problem

You want to have suggested email replies to emails from certain senders.

Solution

Create a flow that triggers when an email from a specific sender is received. Then, the email content is processed by AI Builder to generate a suggested reply, which is then sent back to you for review.

Discussion

Creating this flow saves you time by automating the process of drafting email replies. Instead of spending time thinking about and typing a response, the flow uses AI Builder to suggest a reply based on the email's content. This can be especially helpful if you receive similar emails regularly, as the AI can draft a response quickly. You still get the final say, as the draft is sent back to you for review, ensuring you stay in control!

In this scenario, the AI can handle the heavy lifting, especially when you often reply to inquiries with standard information. Having this flow allows you to focus on more important tasks. By automating this part of your workflow, you work more efficiently and handle emails faster.

Start by visiting the Power Automate portal (*https://oreil.ly/O-MRf*). Sign in with your Microsoft account or your organization's account and ensure that you're in the correct Power Automate environment. From the left navigation bar, click on "My flows," and then select "New flow" to begin creating a new flow. Since your goal is to trigger the flow on newly received emails, choose the "Automated cloud flow" option. Search for the Office 365 Outlook connector. You want the trigger to be related to when an email has been received, so choose the "When a new email arrives (V3)" trigger. You may need to sign in and authenticate your Office 365 Outlook account. Configure the From (the sender's email, or user account) and Folder (the email folder to be monitored for arriving emails) trigger parameters:

Now, add an action to get the email body content with HTML tags. Search for the Content Conversion connector and select the "Html to text" action. Configure the Content action parameter (the content you want to clean the HTML tags from). In this case, you want to pass in the Body from the dynamic content of the trigger:

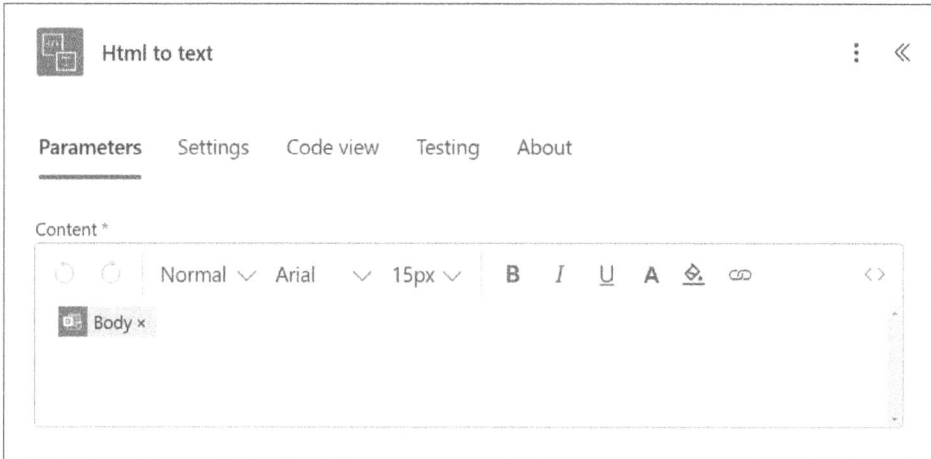

Then, you want to generate AI-driven text (email reply) directly in the flow. Search for the AI Builder connector and select the "Create text with GPT using a prompt" action. Configure the Prompt action parameter (the AI model to be used to get the AI-driven text). In our case, the best fit is AI Reply. I believe that this parameter should have been called AI Model instead of Prompt.

Next, set the Input Text as follows:

```
Please respond to the email below. Only include the body of the reply;
do not include the email subject in the generated response.

{The plain text content.}
```

where {The plain text content.} is dynamic content from our "Html to text" action.

In the world of AI, the preceding text is called an *AI prompt*.

An AI prompt is simply the input or question you give to an AI model (like ChatGPT) to get a response or result. Think of it as starting a conversation with the AI—you tell it what you want, and it tries to give you the best answer based on what you asked. For example, if you're using AI to find a recipe, a prompt might be:

```
prompt = "What is the recipe for pumpkin pie?"
```

The AI will take that prompt and generate a recipe for you.

The clearer and more specific your prompt is, the better the AI can understand what you're asking for and provide a useful response. If the prompt is vague, the AI might give you something less helpful because it doesn't know exactly what you want. In short, a prompt is how you guide the AI to do what you need.

⊕ Create text with GPT using a prompt   ⋮ ≪

Parameters   Settings   Code view   Testing   About

Prompt *

| AI Reply   ⌄ |

🧪 Test prompt

Input Text *

Please respond to the email below. Only include the body of the reply; do not include the email subject in the generated response.

🔲 The plain text con... ✕

Finally, send an email to yourself, with the AI-generated text. Search for the Office 365 Outlook connector and select the "Send an email (V2)" action.

Fill the "Send an email (V2)" action parameters as follows (the text in braces is dynamic content from the trigger and previous actions):

- *To*: {To} (from "When a new email arrives (V3)")

- *Subject*: Suggested reply to email from {From} :: {Subject} (from "When a new email arrives (V3)")

- *Body*:

  Hi,

  Here is a suggested reply to the email you got from {From}:

  Suggested reply:

  {Text}

  Received email:

  {Body}

where {From} is dynamic content from the "When a new email arrives (V3)" trigger, {Text} is from the "Create text with GPT using a prompt" action, and
{Body} is from the "Html to text" action.

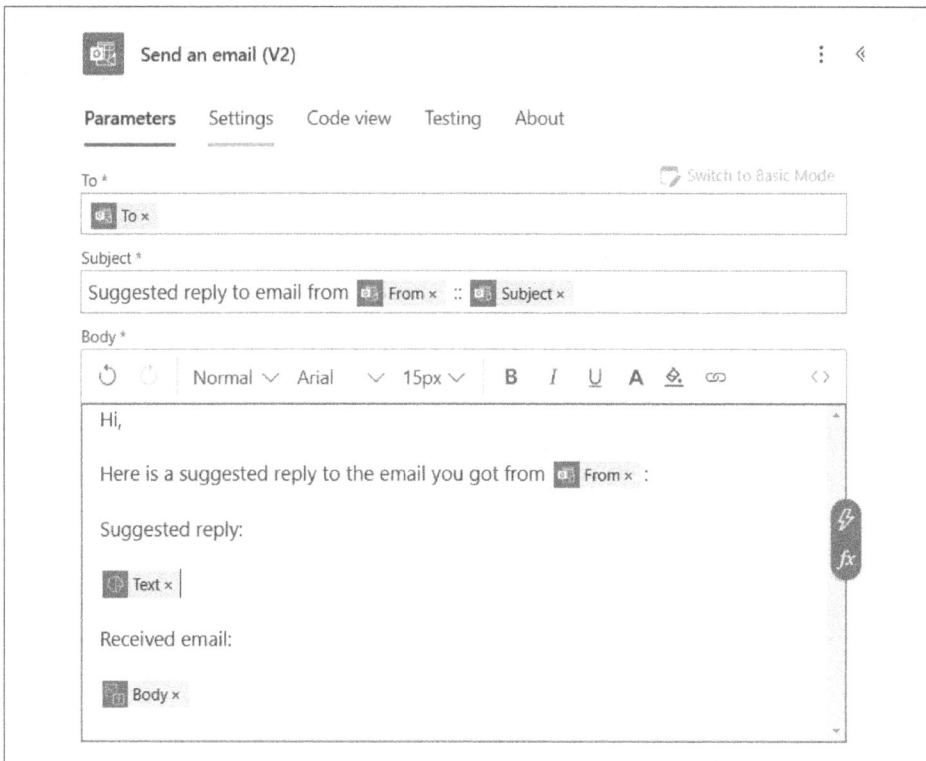

Name, save, and test the flow to confirm it behaves as expected.

See Also

- Recipe 12.1, "Extracting Identity Document Details"
- Recipe 12.2, "Analyzing Feedback Sentiment"
- Recipe 12.3, "Extracting Images or PDFs as Text"

Conclusion

Power Automate and AI Builder create a powerful duo for democratizing AI and empowering business users to solve their everyday challenges with ease. Nontechnical users can incorporate AI capabilities such as text recognition, sentiment analysis, or prediction into their workflows, all without needing deep programming skills. This enables organizations to harness the power of AI in practical, accessible ways, bridging the gap between complex technology and real-world business needs.

The democratization of AI through tools like AI Builder is crucial, especially as the demand for AI solutions continues to grow faster than the availability of technical expertise. With AI Builder, businesses can design tailored solutions that meet specific requirements, such as processing invoices, analyzing feedback, or generating insights. As businesses scale and AI becomes central to operations, tools such as Power Automate and AI Builder ensure that AI capabilities are within reach for everyone, helping organizations stay competitive in a rapidly evolving digital landscape!

Appendix

This appendix provides supplementary information on two key technical components developed during the book. The first section outlines creating a registration app using Microsoft Power Apps, detailing the steps involved in designing a basic user-friendly interface and integrating it with a Power Automate flow. The second section focuses on creating a custom table in Microsoft Dataverse, explaining how to structure columns to support the flow's functionality.

Creating a Registration App (Power Apps)

Power Apps is a low-code application development platform within Microsoft's Power Platform that enables users to build custom business applications without requiring extensive coding knowledge. It allows you to enhance productivity by creating apps that integrate seamlessly with Microsoft 365, Dataverse, SharePoint, and various third-party services. By providing a drag-and-drop interface, prebuilt templates, and connectors, Power Apps empowers both citizen developers and professional developers to build tailored solutions quickly and efficiently.

Among the different types of apps that can be built with Power Apps, canvas apps stand out for their flexibility and customization. With canvas apps, users can design the UI freely (WYSIWYG), similar to working on a blank canvas, placing controls, images, and data sources exactly where they need them. These apps are particularly useful for task-specific applications, such as data entry forms, mobile-friendly apps, and process automation tools. By connecting to Dataverse, SharePoint, SQL, or external APIs, canvas apps allow organizations to create highly tailored solutions without being confined to a predefined structure.

Create a New Canvas App

Open Power Apps (*https://oreil.ly/V1r2r*) and click Create:

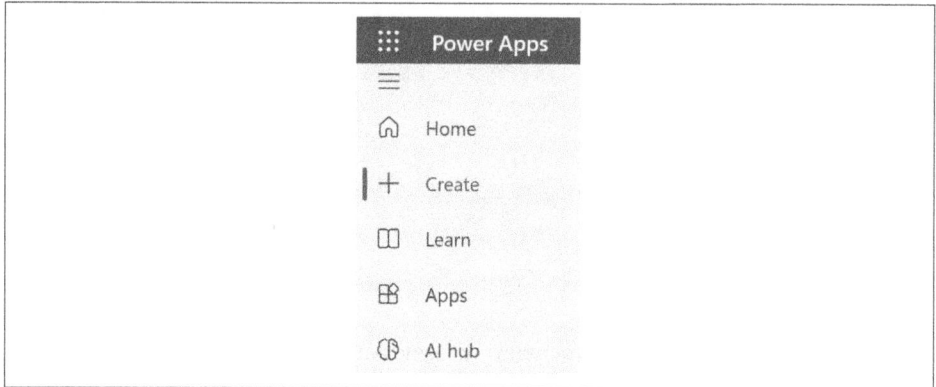

Choose the option to start with a blank canvas:

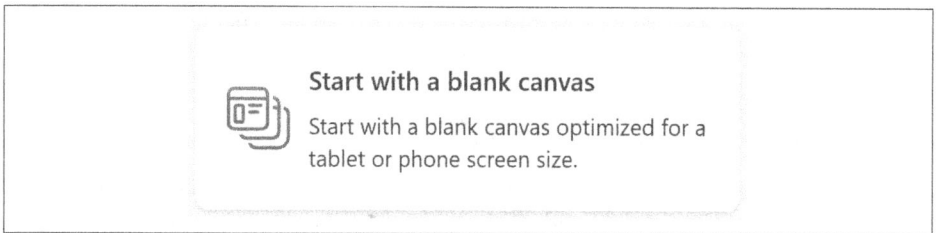

Start with a blank canvas

Start with a blank canvas optimized for a tablet or phone screen size.

Selecting the Tablet layout from the pop-up menu will open the Power Apps editor:

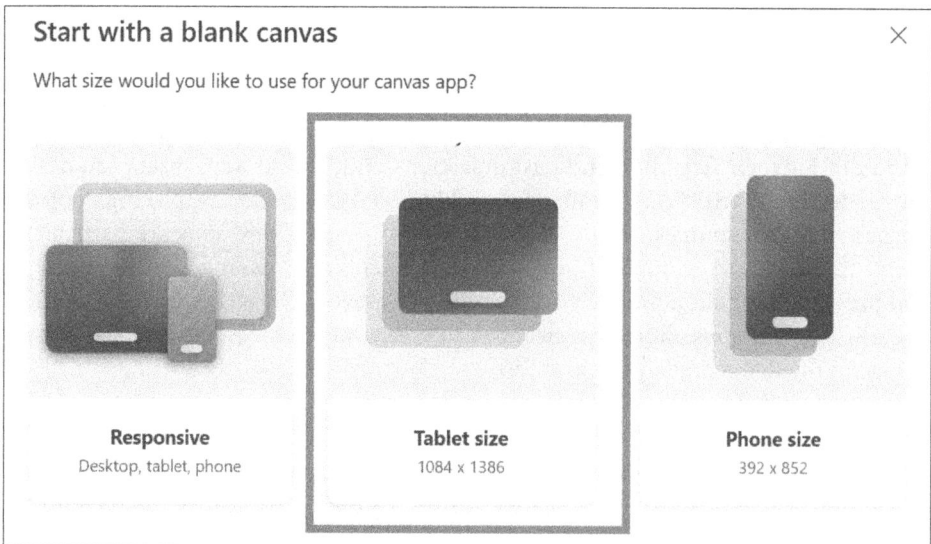

Start with a blank canvas   ✕

What size would you like to use for your canvas app?

Responsive
Desktop, tablet, phone

Tablet size
1084 x 1386

Phone size
392 x 852

Add a Screen Header

From the left toolbar, select Insert, then choose "Text label" and drag the label to the top of the screen:

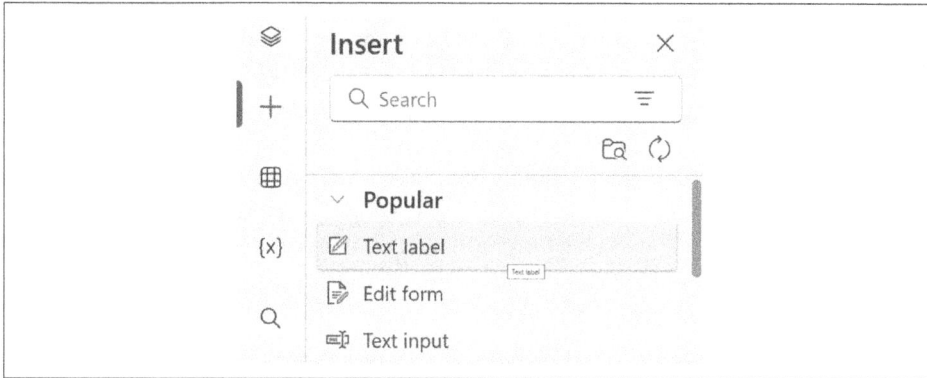

Set the label's Text property to "Guest Registration":

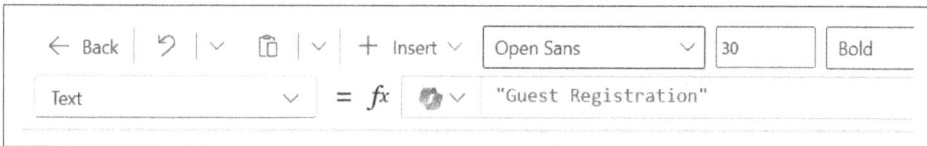

Customize its font size, color, and alignment using the properties pane on the right to ensure it is prominent and visually appealing:

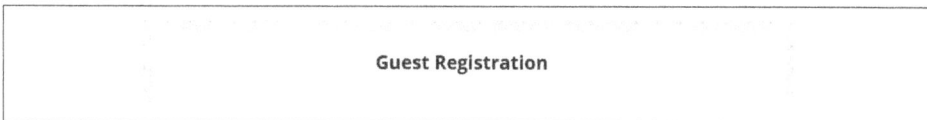

Add Input Fields

Start with the guest name field by inserting a Text Input from the Insert menu and placing it below the header. Set the HintText property to "Guest name" and add a Label above it with the Text property set to "Guest Name". Rename the Text Input control to FullNameInput. Next, add the mobile number field by inserting another Text Input below the full name field. Set its HintText property to "Enter mobile number", change the Format property to "Number", and add a label above it with the Text property set to "Mobile". Rename this input control to "MobileNumberInput." For the Visitee (Microsoft 365 user) combo box, insert a Combo Box below the mobile number field. Add a label above it with the Text property set to "Visitee", and rename the combo box to "UserComboBox." Set the combo box's SelectMultiple property to "False" and the SearchFields property to ["DisplayName"]. Next, set the combo box's Items property to the following:

```
Office365Users.SearchUser({searchTerm: cbVisitee.SearchText})
```

Set its DisplayFields property to ["DisplayName","JobTitle"] to display usernames and job titles:

Guest name	
Mobile	
Visitee	Find a visitee ⌄

Add a Submit Button

Insert a button from the Insert menu and place it below the combo box (to the right). Set its Text property to "Submit" and rename it to "SubmitButton." This button will trigger the Power Automate flow to process the form data:

Submit

Wire the Submit Button to a Power Automate Flow

First, create the flow in Power Automate (Recipe 9.5). In Power Apps, you need to add the flow you created to the app. From the left toolbar menu, click the ellipsis (…) and then select Power Automate:

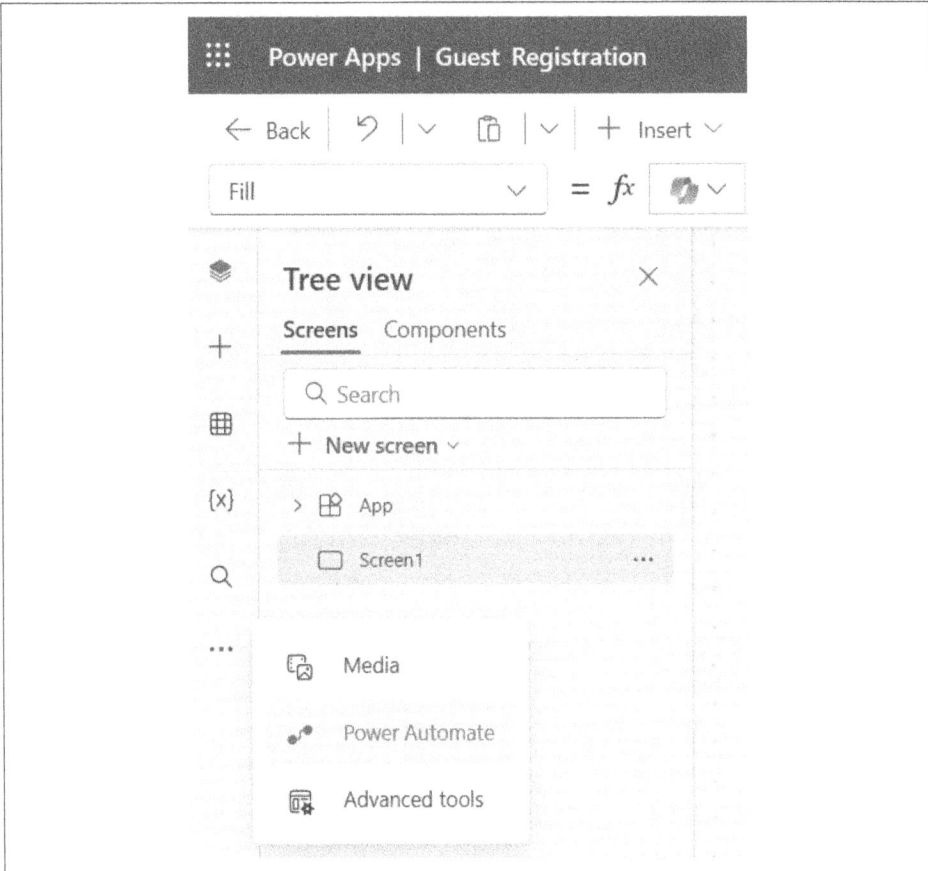

Then, look for your flow and click it to add it to the app:

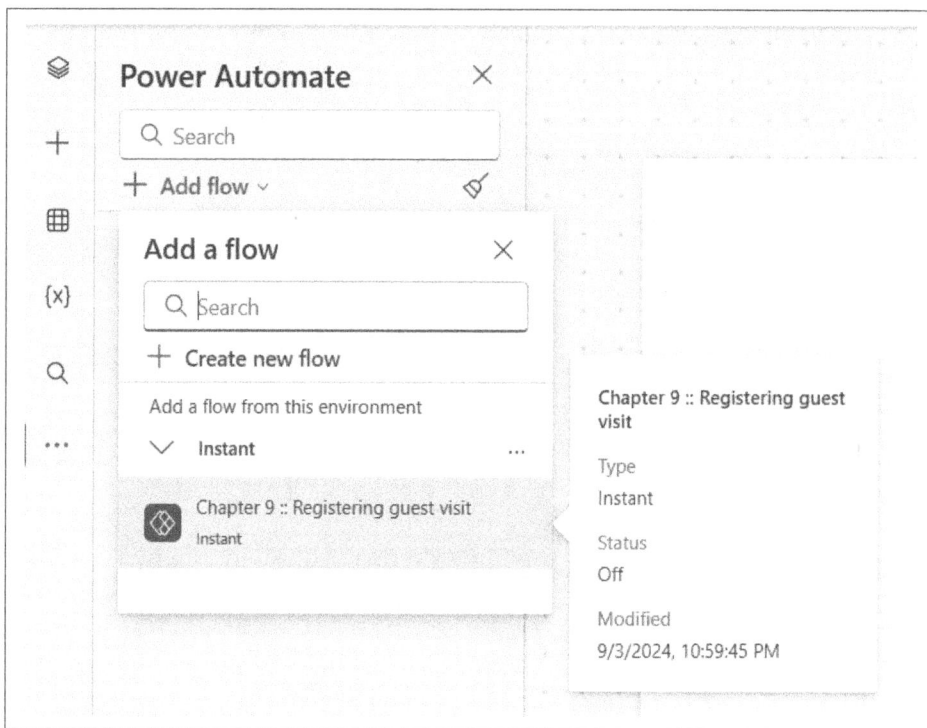

Finally, select the SubmitButton, and in its OnSelect property, call the flow and pass the form values using the following code:

```
'YourFlowName'.Run(FullNameInput.Text, MobileNumberInput.Text,
UserComboBox.Selected.Id).
```

Save, Test, and Publish the App

To save the app, click on the floppy disk icon at the top-right. Name your app "Guest Registration" (or the name of your preference), then click Save. Next, click the Preview button (the Play icon in the top-right corner) to test your app. Enter required information, then click Submit to verify the values are sent to the Power Automate flow. Once tested, publish the app:

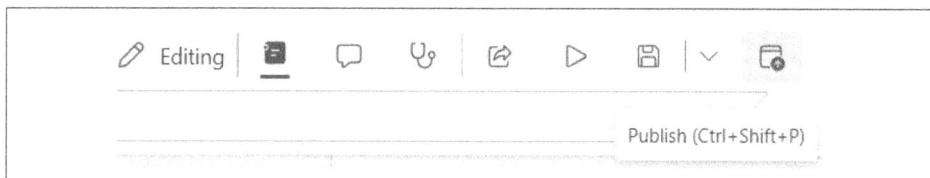

Creating a Custom Table in Dataverse

Creating a custom table in Dataverse is all about defining your app's unique data structure in a secure and scalable cloud environment. Microsoft Dataverse, integral to the Power Platform, lets you build custom tables that are tailored to your specific business needs, without requiring in-depth coding expertise. By abstracting away the complexities of traditional database management, it empowers both citizen developers and experienced IT professionals to model and manage data efficiently. This approach ensures that key information is stored in an organized format, laying a solid foundation for building integrated solutions that work seamlessly with Microsoft 365, Dynamics 365, and a host of third-party applications.

Access the Environment

Open Power Apps (*https://oreil.ly/V1r2r*). Ensure that you're in the correct environment by selecting it from the Environment drop-down in the top-right corner of the Power Apps portal:

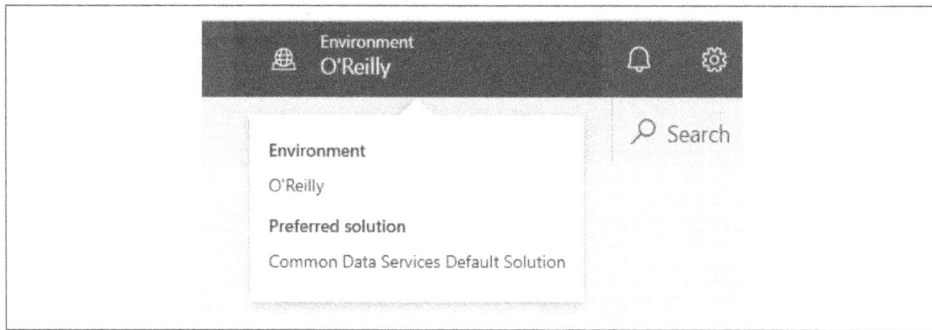

Navigate to Tables

In the lefthand navigation pane, click Tables. If Table is not visible in the lefthand navigation, click on More to select Table. Pin Tables for easy navigation the next time:

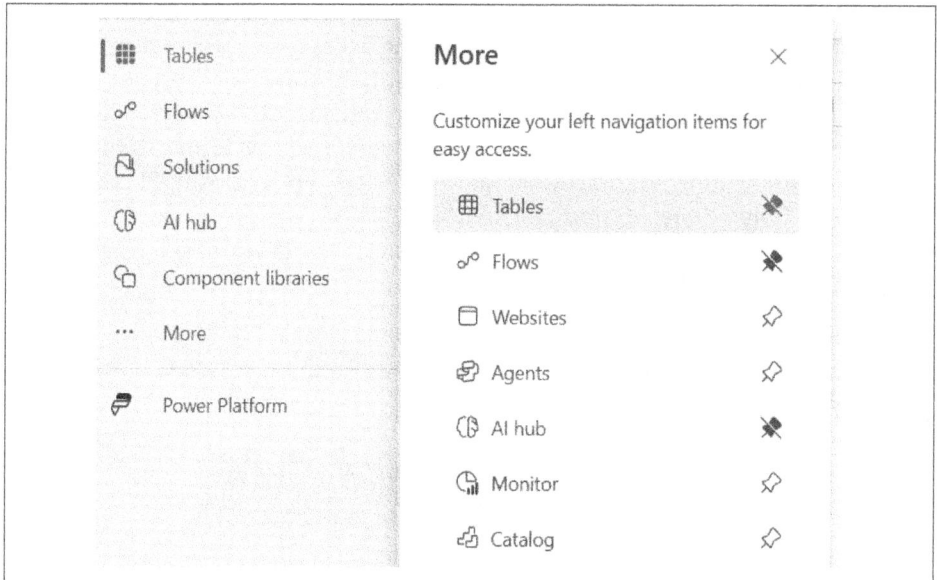

Tables			More	✕
Flows				
Solutions			Customize your left navigation items for easy access.	
AI hub			⊞ Tables	📌
Component libraries			Flows	📌
⋯ More			Websites	📌
			Agents	📌
Power Platform			AI hub	📌
			Monitor	📌
			Catalog	📌

Clicking on Tables will open the table management screen, where you can view existing tables and create new ones:

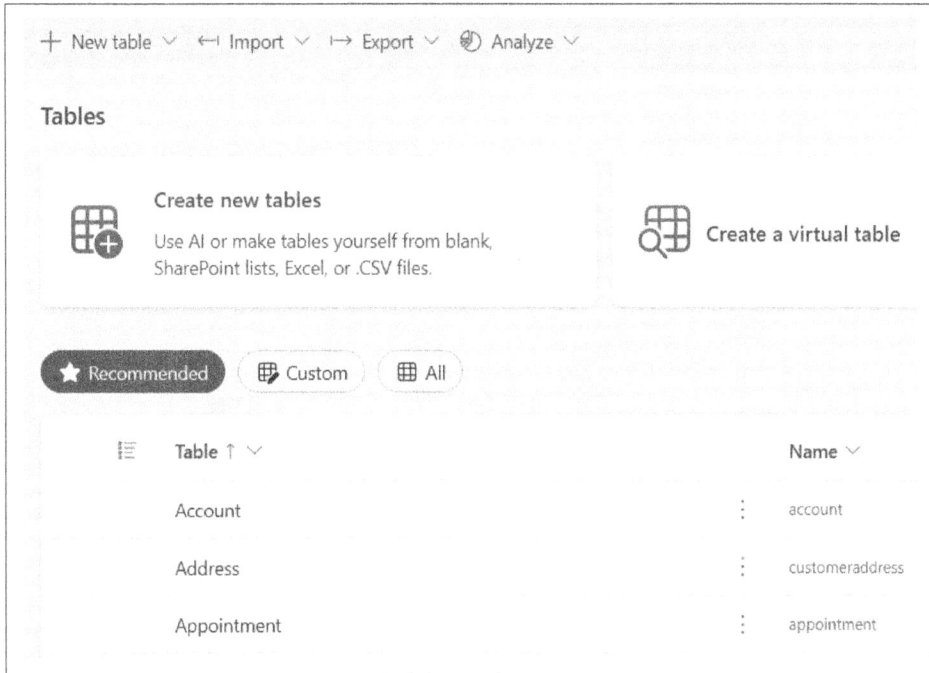

Create a New Table

Click the "+ New table" button at the top of the page, then choose Table (advanced properties). In the New table righthand pane, provide the following details:

- *Display name*: Enter the name for your table (e.g., "Guest Registration").
- *Plural name*: This is automatically populated but can be adjusted if needed (e.g., "Guest Registrations").
- *Description*: Add a brief description of the table's purpose (optional but recommended).

- *Table name (optional)*: The system-generated unique name is based on the display name. You can edit this if necessary under Advanced options:

New table

Use tables to hold and organize your data. Previously called entities
Learn more

Properties   Primary column

Display name *

Guest Registration

Plural name *

Guest Registrations

Description

[ ] Enable attachments (including notes and files) [1]

Advanced options ∧

Schema name *

cr304_   GuestRegistration

Type *

Standard   ∨

Record ownership *

User or team   ∨

Choose table image

None   ∨   ✎

+ New image web resource

Color

Enter color code

- *Primary column*: This is the default column for the table (e.g., "Name"). Rename it to suit your table's primary data field:

Properties	Primary column

Display name *

FullName

Description

Advanced options ∧

Schema name *

cr304_ FullName

Column requirement *

Business required   ∨

Maximum character count *

850

Add Columns to the Table

Click Save to create the table. Once the table is created, you'll be directed to the table management screen:

Click Columns (under Schema) to manage your table columns:

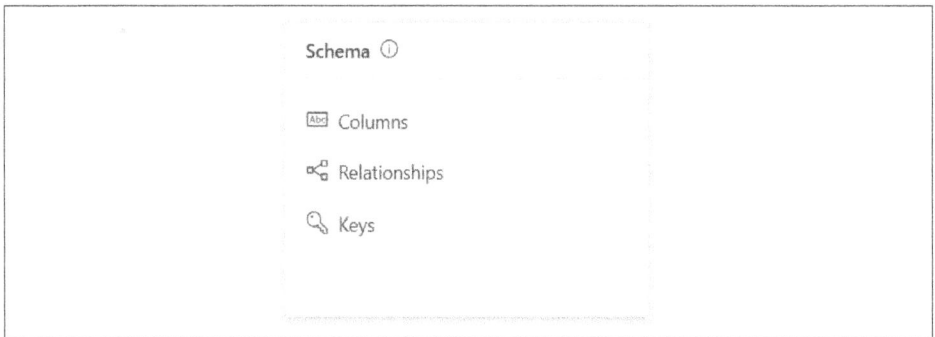

Click "+ New column" (on the top) to define custom fields for your table. For each column, provide the following:

- *Display name*: The user-friendly name (e.g., "Mobile Number").
- *Data type*: Choose the type of data the column will store (e.g., Text, Number, Date, Lookup).
- *Format*: Formatting for the data type, such as URL, phone number, etc.

- *Required*: Define whether the column is optional, recommended, or required.
- *Searchable*: Specify whether the column should be searchable in Dataverse.

Index

About the Author

Ahmad Najjar is a seasoned solution architect with over two decades of experience designing and delivering complex solutions across Microsoft's cloud ecosystem. As a Microsoft MVP, MCT, and FastTrack Recognized Solution Architect, he has established himself as a trusted expert in Power Platform, Azure, Microsoft 365, and Dynamics 365. Ahmad has led large-scale transformation projects across industries, specializing in automation, integration, and AI-driven solutions. He is also an influential speaker at global conferences and an active contributor to tech communities worldwide.

Ahmad is a tech book author and reviewer, and a strong advocate for AI ethics and scalable solution design. He has written comprehensive guides on solutions using Microsoft's low-code platform, along with innovating coding patterns for .NET and SharePoint, in his early beginnings. As a tech reviewer, he has helped professionals navigate the evolving landscape of business applications and AI, providing practical insights for both new and experienced developers.

Beyond architecture, Ahmad is a firm believer in community and responsible innovation. He has co-organized major tech events, empowering professionals worldwide through workshops, mentoring, and thought leadership. He is committed to fostering ethical tech practices and open knowledge sharing, as well as helping organizations make confident, strategic decisions in a rapidly evolving digital world. His mission is to bridge technology and people, transforming ideas into sustainable, future-ready solutions.

Colophon

The animal on the cover of *Microsoft Power Automate Cookbook* is the blue mackerel (*Scomber australasicus*), also known as the Japanese or Pacific mackerel.

Blue mackerel inhabit tropical and subtropical waters of the Pacific Ocean, ranging from Japan to Australia and New Zealand, as well as some parts of the eastern Pacific, such as around Hawaii. They're also found in the Red Sea, the Persian Gulf, the Gulf of Oman, and the Gulf of Aden.

Blue mackerel are members of the *Scombridae* family, which counts tuna among its members. Like tuna, mackerel are open-ocean predators of notable speed, due to their streamlined bodies and retractable fins. Their diet typically consists of plankton and small crustaceans, as well as fish and squids.

Blue mackerel are commercially fished throughout much of their range and are often consumed by humans smoked or grilled. They are also frequently used as game bait and as a protein source in cat food.

Blue mackerel have been categorized by the International Union for Conservation of Nature as being of least concern, from a conservation standpoint. Many of the animals on O'Reilly covers are endangered; all of them are important to the world.

The cover illustration is by José Marzan Jr., based on an antique line engraving from *Meyers Kleines Lexicon*. The series design is by Edie Freedman, Ellie Volckhausen, and Karen Montgomery. The cover fonts are Gilroy Semibold and Guardian Sans. The text font is Adobe Minion Pro; the heading font is Adobe Myriad Condensed; and the code font is Dalton Maag's Ubuntu Mono.

O'REILLY®

Learn from experts.
Become one yourself.

60,000+ titles | Live events with experts | Role-based courses
Interactive learning | Certification preparation

**Try the O'Reilly learning platform
free for 10 days.**